The Complete Mandolinist Volume 3

The Creative Impulse

by Marilynn Mair

Audio Contents

Études en couleurs *for solo mandolin*

1. Étude grise
2. Étude orange
3. Étude verte
4. Étude d'ombre
5. Étude de crépuscule
6. Étude d'ambre
7. Étude noire
8. Étude blanche
9. Étude bleue
10. Étude violette

Fantasia in dialogue *for two mandolins*

11. Fantasia: floating
12. Fantasia: planting gardens
13. Fantasia: peaches
14. Fantasia: in the dark
15. Fantasia: dragon dream
16. Fantasia: holding fast
17. Fantasia: by the sea
18. Fantasia: old folks
19. Fantasia: in the groove

Tracks 1–19, *Marilynn Mair, mandolin*

Marilynn plays with friends on all tracks except 33 & 34.

Nocturnes for Vincent *for mandolin & guitar*

20. Sometimes when I am wearied suddenly
21. Oh, oh, you will be sorry for that word!
22. I shall go back again to the bleak shore
23. Only until this cigarette is ended
24. Mindful of you the sodden earth in spring
25. The light comes back with Columbine
26. Women have loved before as I love now
27. Tranquility at length, when autumn comes

Tracks 20–27, *with Robert N. Martel, guitar*

28. Siga em Frente *(with Vinicius Dorin, sax; Arismar do Espirito Santo, guitar; Rogerio Boccato, percussion*
29. Isso *(with Luiz Simas, piano)*
30. Madrugada *(with Luiz Simas, piano)*
31. Um Quinto do Ludwig *(with Luiz Simas, piano)*
32. Uma Coisa Feliz *(with Choro das 3)*
33. Estação Carioca *(Paulo Sa, bandolim; Marcus Ferrer, guitar)*
34. Buscando Baden *(Marcilio Lopes, bandolim;; Lucas Porto, guitar)*
35. Saudades do Rio *(with Paul Dressel, guitar)*
36. Enrolado *(with Enigmatica)*

3-4-3 (3/4) *(with Alex Wohlhueter, bass)*

37. maruque
38. birthday waltz
39. wedding hoedown

All tracks recorded by Joe Auger, QORQ Productions, except for Track 33, recorded by Paulo Sá & Marcus Ferrer in Rio; Track 34, recorded by Felipe Larrosa Moura in Rio; Track 36, recorded by Charles Moser; Tracks 37–39, recorded by Jason Keeler in Minneapolis.

Online Audio

www.melbay.com/31043MEB

Exclusive Sales Agent: Mel Bay Publications, Inc.
WWW.MELBAY.COM

Acknowledgements

The author would like to thank:
Jacque Russom, for impeccably editing the manuscript for this book, as always.
Holly Peppe, Literary Executor, The Millay Society, for permission to include the two sonnets still under copyright.
Robert N. Martel, for editing the Nocturne guitar parts, and recording them with me.
Paul Dressel, for playing every mandolin–guitar duet with me, suggesting changes, and for recording "Saudades do Rio" with me. Playing Choro daily with Paul was an oasis during the pandemic.
Marcílio Lopes, for suggesting edits to the chords in nearly all of my Choro, and for recording "Buscando Baden" in Rio for me.
Paulo Sá, for our many musical collaborations in Brazil and the USA, and for recording "Estação Carioca" in Rio for me.
Mitch Nelin, for inspiring my quartet version of "East of Here" with his, and for suggesting chords for its leadsheet.
Enigmatica, for playing all my ensemble pieces with exuberance, and for their patience when I changed my mind and sent new parts.
Joe Auger, for recording, mixing, and mastering the download tracks for this book.
My friends and family, for getting me through the pandemic with zoom holiday gatherings, outdoor socially distanced meet-ups, video-call Pokemon games, WhatsApp cocktail hours, and other ingenious methods of keeping pessimism at bay.

About the Author

Marilynn Mair has shown the world what the mandolin can achieve in the hands of a skillful artist. Internationally praised for her concerts and recordings, she helped establish classical mandolin in chamber music circles worldwide, and is often called, "First Lady of the American Mandolin." Marilynn has performed at prestigious venues in the USA, such as Carnegie Hall, the White House, Lincoln Center, the Brooklyn Academy of Music, Merkin Concert Hall, the Newport Music Festival, Birdland, and NPR, and has given concerts throughout Europe, and in Japan, China, Canada, and Brazil. She has represented the USA at international music festivals in Canada, Brazil, Japan, Spain, Italy, Germany, Sweden, France, and England. She has released two dozen solo and ensemble CDs, including: *Mandolin in the 18th century, Leave Something Unexplained. Meu Bandolim, Madrugada,* and her most recent, *Silver Lining of a Quiet Year.*

Marilynn has previously published 4 books with Mel Bay Publications: her 224-page method book, *The Complete Mandolinist*, in 2008; her bilingual *Choro* method book for bandolim, *Brazilian Choro – A Method for Mandolin,* written with Rio-based bandolimist and professor Paulo Sá, in 2010; *The 100 – Techniques and Exercises for Mandolinists*, in 2017, a book that chronicles Marilynn's journey on mandolin with a series of original exercises and ideas to improve practice technique and performance; and *The Complete Mandolinist, Volume Two – Music in Context*, in 2021, a 288-page resource for mandolinists, filled with repertoire presented within its musical and historical context, ranging from the Renaissance to the present day, along with suggestions for further music exploration. Besides Mel Bay, Marilynn's arrangements and editions have also been published by Barenreiter, Berben, Zimmermann, and Plucked Strings.

Marilynn is a Professor Emeritus at Roger Williams University, where she created and taught courses in music and cultural history for over 30 years, specializing in music of the Americas. Her love for Brazilian *Choro* frequently takes her to Rio de Janeiro, where she continues to perform *Choro* music in concerts and *rodas* throughout the city. Marilynn is the Founding Director of The American Mandolin & Guitar Summer School, which she has run since 1986. She also founded and directs Enigmatica – a plucked-string chamber ensemble that has released several recordings.

More information on Marilynn, articles on mandolin technique and Brazilian music, and information on upcoming events can be found on her webpage: MarilynnMair.com. She keeps in touch with mandolin friends and colleagues worldwide through her Facebook page.

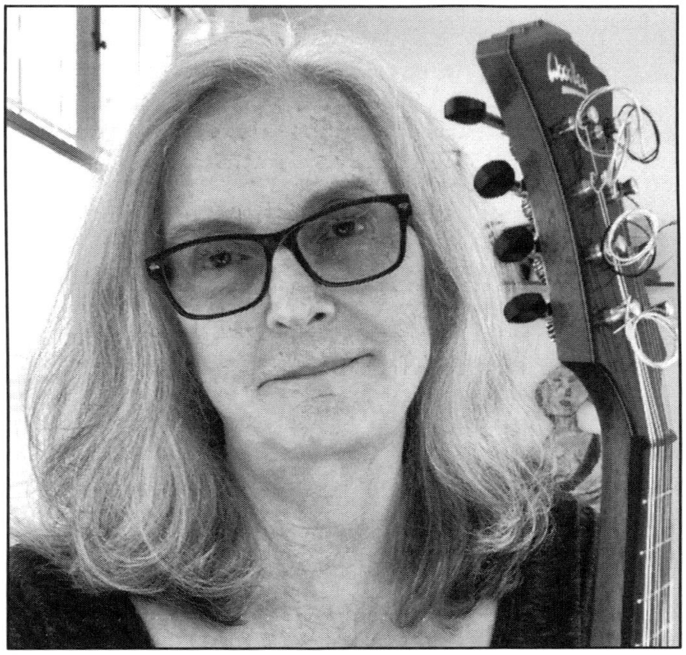

This is my 5th book for Mel Bay. In many ways it's the culmination of the series. I started out 15 years ago with a big fat method book[1.], focused on opening a path to good mandolin technique. I followed that with a book of exercises and ideas to help clean up your playing, to move securely from home to public performance[2.]. Most recently I added a book of repertoire selected with an eye to music history, including essays on how an understanding of context, historical and stylistic, can improve your playing[3.]. In the middle I took a detour to introduce Brazilian Choro[4.], an amazing style of music I added to my classical career a couple of decades ago, studying and playing for years in Rio to learn the nuances of its musical roots and context in person.

In all of these books I've dropped breadcrumbs, walking ahead of you, sharing my path to improving your mandolin musicianship. This book is different. Here, I turn around with my arms full of music, dozens of my own compositions, pieces you may never have seen or heard before. In this book I am adding my own personality to mandolin repertoire, staking out an additional spot in mandolin history through composing.

When you first decide to play the mandolin, you pick a path through. For most, the goal is playing with others. For some, it's playing for audiences. Others go on to recording, playing for posterity, for those you will never meet. For some that necessitates finding new sources for music, a path that can lead to research and arranging, or commissioning revered composers to write for you. And for a few, the final step is deciding it's time to go for it, to add your own compositions for mandolin to the available repertoire.

I've explored all those options and have shared my discoveries with you in previous books. This book gives you a glimpse into how I've negotiated the final step, writing original music for mandolin. I hope you will enjoy playing the many and varied results in: *The Complete Mandolinist Volume 3 – The Creative Impulse.*

---

1. The Complete Mandolinist *(2007)*
2. The 100 – Techniques and Exercises for Mandolinists *(2017)*
3. The Complete Mandolinist Volume 2 – Music in Context *(2020)*
4. Brazilian Choro - A Method for Mandolin and Bandolim *(2015)*

Table of Contents

Credits 2
Introduction 3
Table of Contents 4
The Creative Impulse 6

Études en couleurs (solo mandolin) 7
About my Études 8
grise [grey] 9
orange [orange] 10
verte [green] 11
d'ombre [shadow] 12
de crépuscule [twilight] 13
d'ambre [amber] 14
noire [black] 15
blanche [white] 16
bleue [blue] 17
violette [violet] 18

Fantasia in dialogue (mandolin duet) 19
About my Fantasia 20
floating 21
planting gardens 22
peaches 24
in the dark 26
dragon dream 27
trouble in mind 28
holding fast 30
by the sea 31
old folks 32
in the groove 34

Nocturnes for Vincent (mandolin & guitar) 35
About my Nocturnes 36
Sonnets for Nocturnes 1 & 2 37
Sometimes when I am wearied suddenly 38
Oh, oh, you will be sorry for that word! 40
I shall go back again to the bleak shore 42
Only until this cigarette is ended 44
Mindful of you the sodden earth in spring 46
The light comes back with Columbine 48
Women have loved before as I love now 50
Tranquility at length, when autumn comes 52

Choro–The Roots of Brazilian Music 54

Choro do Brasil (leadsheets) 55
About my Choro 56
Garoa [Drizzling] 57
Siga em Frente [Go Straight Ahead] 58
Por que não? [Why Not?] 60
Isso [That's It] 62
Madrugada [Daybreak] 64
Farrapinho [A Little Rag] 66
Sonatinha [Sonatina] 68
Um Quinto do Ludwig [A Fifth of Ludwig] 70
Balbuciando [Mumbling] 72
Outro Verão [Another Summer] 74
Uma Coisa Feliz [A Happy Thing] 76
Enrolado [Spaceshot] 78
Terças no Trapiche [Tuesdays at Trapiche] 80
Nadando em Luz [Swimming in Light] 82
Faça a Pergunta [Ask the Question] 84
Se Não Agora [If Not Now] 86
É Bom Saber [Good to Know] 88
Estação Carioca [Carioca Station] 90
Buscando Baden [Chasing Baden] 92
Saudade do Rio [Missing Rio] 94

Ensembles 95
About my Ensembles 96
Ayton's Farewell *score* 97
parts 102
Badi no Rio [Badi in Rio] *score* 108
parts 112
Enrolado *score* 118
parts 124
Nadando em Luz *score* 131
parts 134
Goodin's Gigue *score* 140
parts 142
East of Here *score* 143
parts 147
The Jabberwock *score* 153
parts 158

Table of Contents

Selected Early Works 167

About Early Works 168

East of Here *solo* 169

East of Here *leadsheet* 170

3–4–3 (3/4) *duet* 171

And She Has Flown *solo* 178

Margery *duet* 180

Champagne *leadsheet* 182

Diablo *leadsheet* 183

Champagne *duet* 184

Diablo *duet* 186

The Brinsley Waltz 188

Valse Isabel 190

3 Directions 191

When Everything's Been Done 194

Final Thoughts 195

Compositions on my CDs 196

The Creative Impulse

Composing isn't limited to those with degrees in composition, for whom the big symphonic canvases call. Composing can simply be a desire to let the melody in your head out. To write successfully, however, takes an understanding of how music works best. It takes a lot of listening and playing, storing up a vocabulary, figuring out what sounds good, what bends constraints without breaking them, and what resonates authentically as your own take on a genre.

I think of myself as a composer in the tradition of the 19th century "Yankee Tunesmiths" who wrote music for their friends and neighbors. Not complicated, sometimes not even "correct," but strongly original, and embraced by performers at the time and even today. Theirs was an intuitive approach, based on having a feel for music rather than knowing all the rules. The first piece I remember "composing" came as a young piano student, under-practiced and uninspired by the tune my teacher had given me to perform in the agony-inducing spring recital. At my lesson I launched instead into "Dance of the Gypsies," my own improvised creation. To my delight, my teacher asked me to play that at the recital instead. I came to realize the benefits of creativity.

As my classical mandolin career advanced, I began to arrange pieces I liked better than the available mandolin repertoire, and arranging became a back door into composition. Later, I was inspired by the cool beauty of Brazilian Choro repertoire, most pieces written by the players themselves. I began to write Choro 15 years ago, running my pieces by Brazilian friends who helped nudge me toward a more Brazilian sound. When I gushed my thanks for their help, they encouraged me to continue, saying "I don't know anyone who thinks like you," and "I wasn't expecting you to be so original." I found I nearly always wrote music during my stays in Rio, where my life was less full of distraction, and my repertoire of original Choro gradually grew.

When the Covid pandemic hit, pushing nearly all performing, teaching, and travel out of my life, the surprising silver lining was that in the empty space, I began to write music for mandolin. I had friends and students in mind as I wrote, creating pieces to pass on my unique perspective on what makes classical mandolin cool. I decided I should collect my pieces in a book, so others would have access, and so the manuscripts wouldn't just disappear when I do. Mel Bay graciously agreed to continue our collaboration, adding this as the 3rd book to my *Complete Mandolinist* series.

I begin the book with my three brand-new series, Études, Fantasias, and Nocturnes, composed during the pandemic. Then I proceed to my many Choro, add some ensemble pieces, mostly written for my chamber group, Enigmatica, and end with some early works I am still fond of. Are my pieces worthy? Do they add something of interest to 21st-century music for mandolin? That is not for me to decide. I know they reflect my personality, are quirky, fun, possibly intriguing, and playable by many mandolinists. My work here is done. Yours, if you wish, begins as you turn the page.

Études
en couleurs

grise
orange
verte
d'ombre
de crépuscule
d'ambre
noire
blanche
bleue
violette

summer 2020

Études en couleurs

I wrote "Études en couleurss" (Studies in color) during the first summer of the Covid pandemic. It was a time without my touchstones of music—no rehearsals or concerts with my ensemble Enigmatica, the cancellation of my two summer schools, AMGuSS (The American Mandolin & Guitar Summer School) and Mandolin Week at SummerKeys. It was also a time without travel, without family, and without an understanding of how the future would unfold. I had just finished up a big project for Mel Bay Publications, the manuscript of my book *The Complete Mandolinist 2 – Music in Context.* I was still playing Choro with my partner Paul, as we had quarantined together. But, quite suddenly and somewhat unexpectedly, my noodling on mandolin began to take on form and structure. I decided to write some of them down, and this series began to take shape.

Does adversity trigger creativity? It has often been true throughout history. For me, though, I think it was a direct result of the open space in my brain created by the loss of music events to prepare for or to organize. I had no other mandolinists to play with so I played alone. The usual pathways for my creative impulse were stymied, and this led me to a new outlet.

I have long been distressed by the lack of cool solo repertoire for dedicated amateurs, advanced students, and professionals not drawn to the existing virtuoso Romantic-style Italian solos. I am one of the latter, and although I have performed many works of Calace, Munier, and others, they are not pieces that I love. So most of my solo performance has been works for other instruments that I have arranged. I have always admired personalized solo pieces, like the lovely miniature études of Chopin, and the "Estudios Sencillos" of Leo Brouwer—short spiky pieces for guitar that rock the performances of classical guitarists of all levels.

This series of 10 Études embodies my musical sense of the 21st-century mandolinist. All finish quickly and leave a distinct impression. Why are they études? Because it is a form that made the transition from student works to the concert stage in the 19th century. A "concert étude" became an artistic work based around a technique, without a set form. Mine are based more on impressions, but the idea of a study remains.

Why are they French? I don't really know. Perhaps missing my son and his wife who live in France. Why are they colors? It's partly because I visualized a color for each piece as I wrote. I am fascinated by the phenomenon of synesthesia, where stimulating one sense triggers another. Oliver Messiaen, the most famous composer to recognize and utilize synesthesia wrote, "When I hear or read music, I always see colour complexes in my mind that go with the sound complexes." It's also partly because they are French, so I linked them with Impressionism, and memories of paintings titled "Study in Blue," and other colors.

If you perform them, I suggest you list them on the program as they are on my title page: *Études en couleurs*, with the ones you choose to play listed as movements. If you just perform one, you can list it as it is titled on the music itself. But most of all—have fun playing them, as that was my intention in writing them.

"When I compose, I find out who I am. I compose my identity, through my life and my work." - Linda Catlin Smith, composer

Étude grise

Study in grey

Marilynn Mair

summer 2020

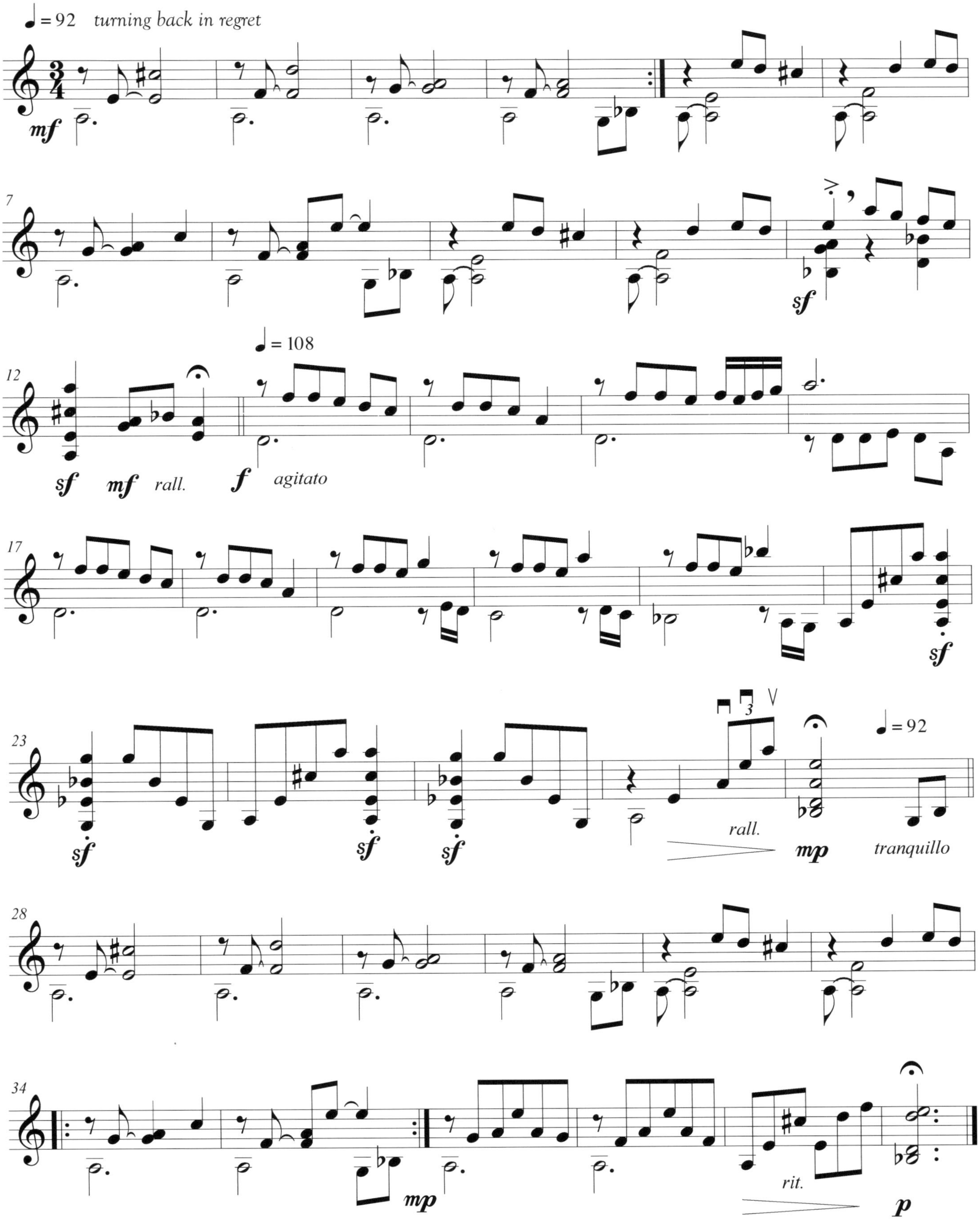

Étude orange

Study in orange

Marilynn Mair
summer 2020

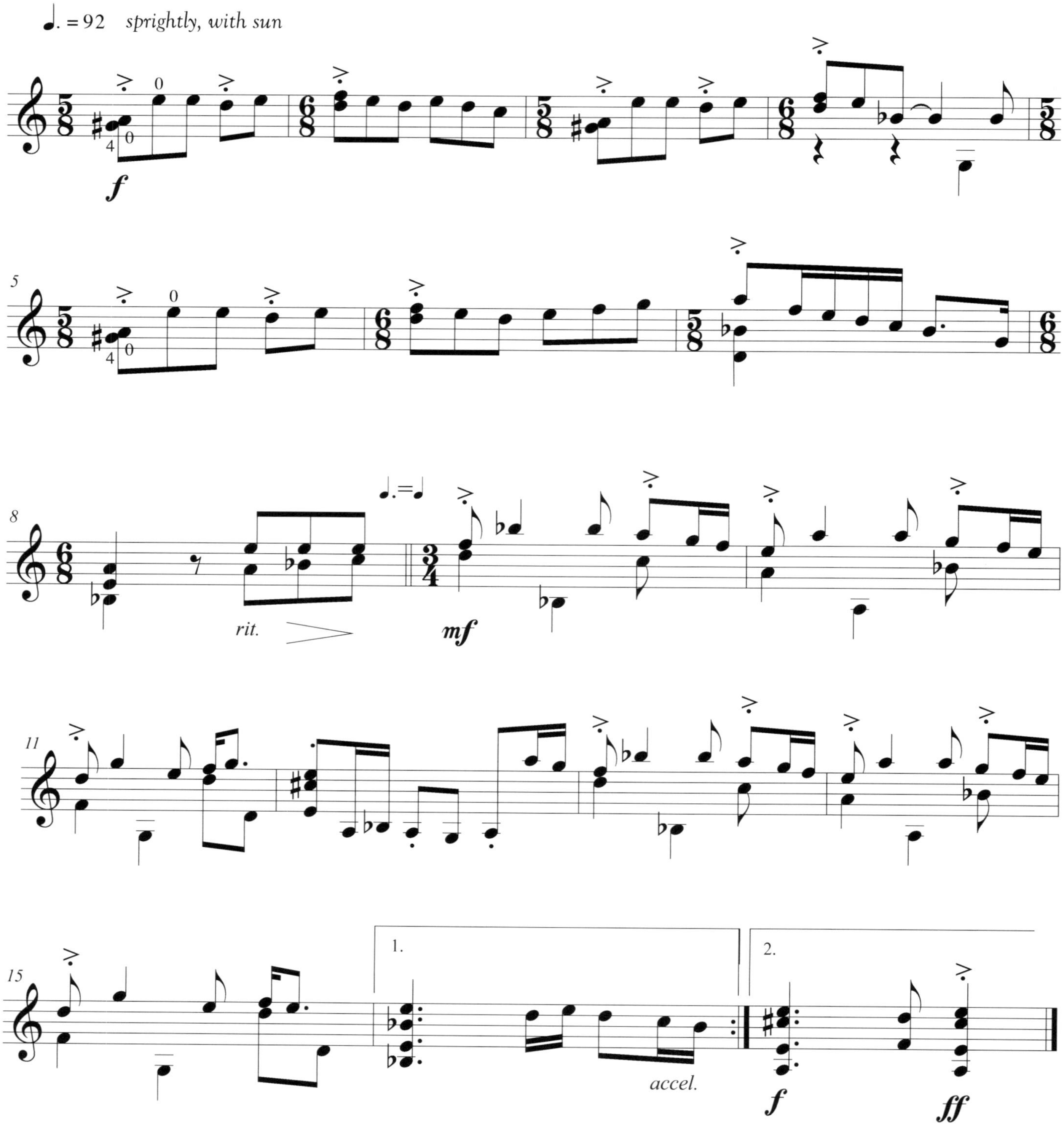

Étude verte

Study in green

Marilynn Mair
summer 2020

♩ = 80 *with cautious optimism*

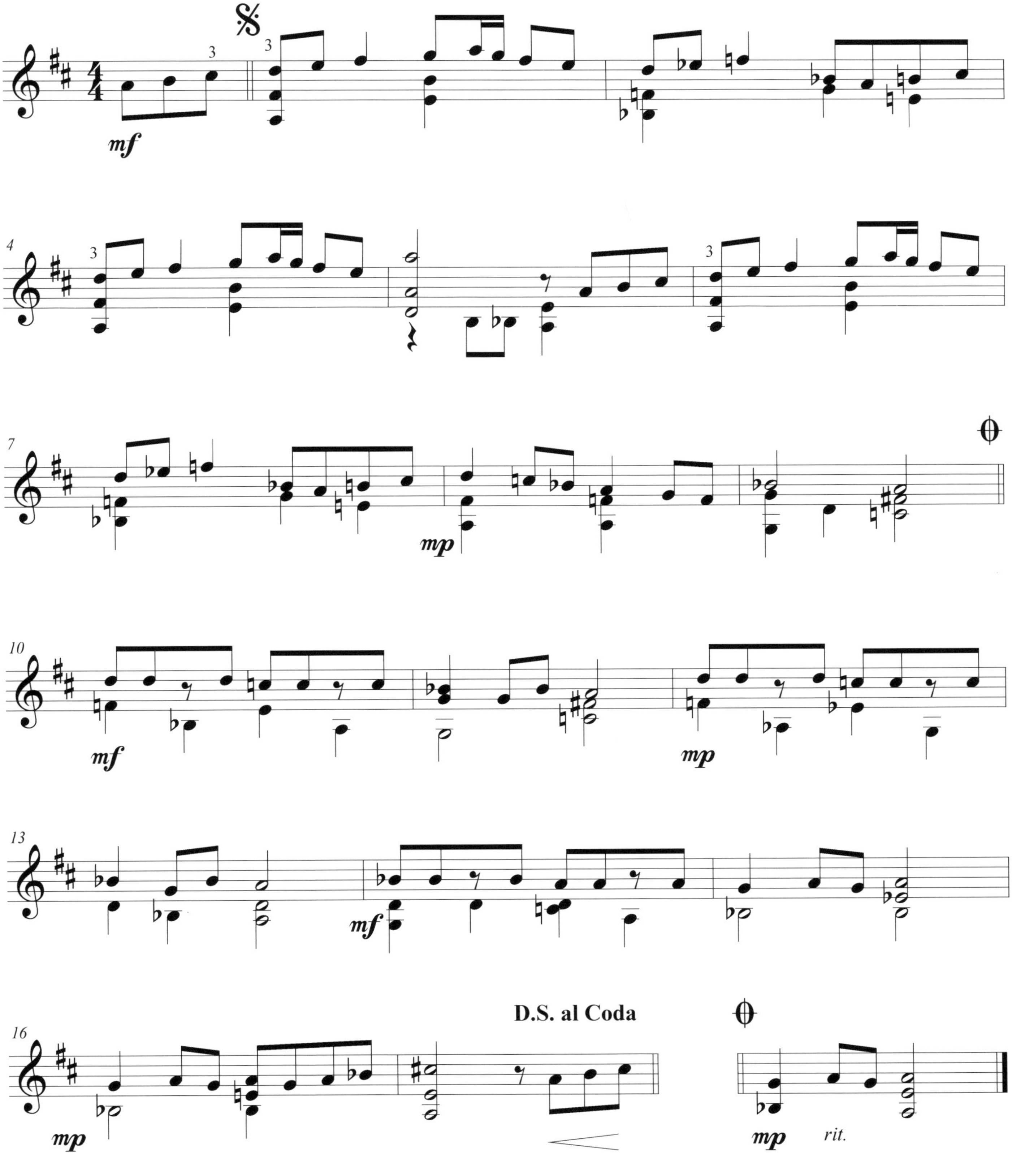

Étude d'ombre

Study in shadow

Marilynn Mair
summer 2020

♩ = 104 *running on uneven ground*

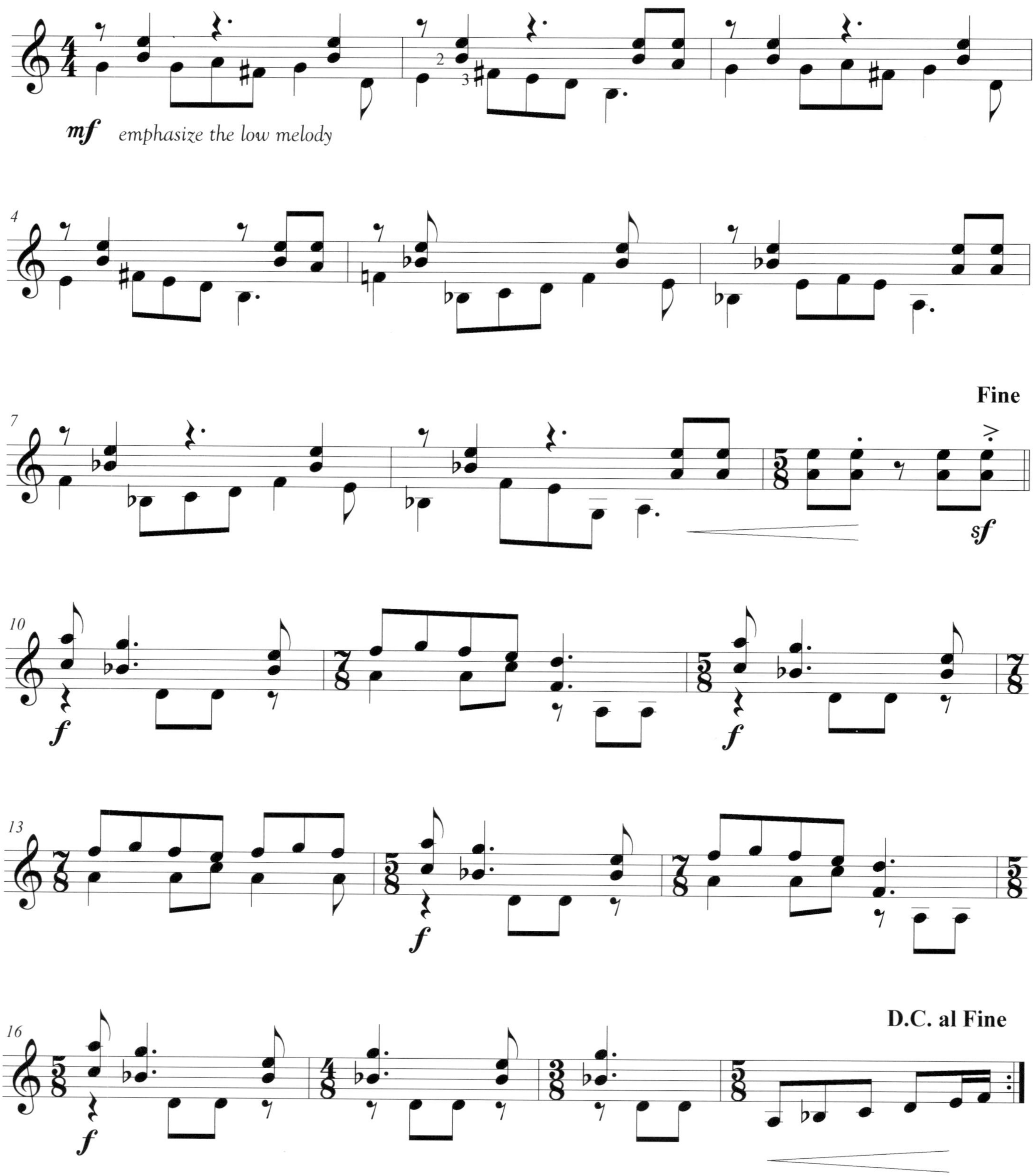

Étude de crépuscule

Study in twilight

Marilynn Mair

summer 2020

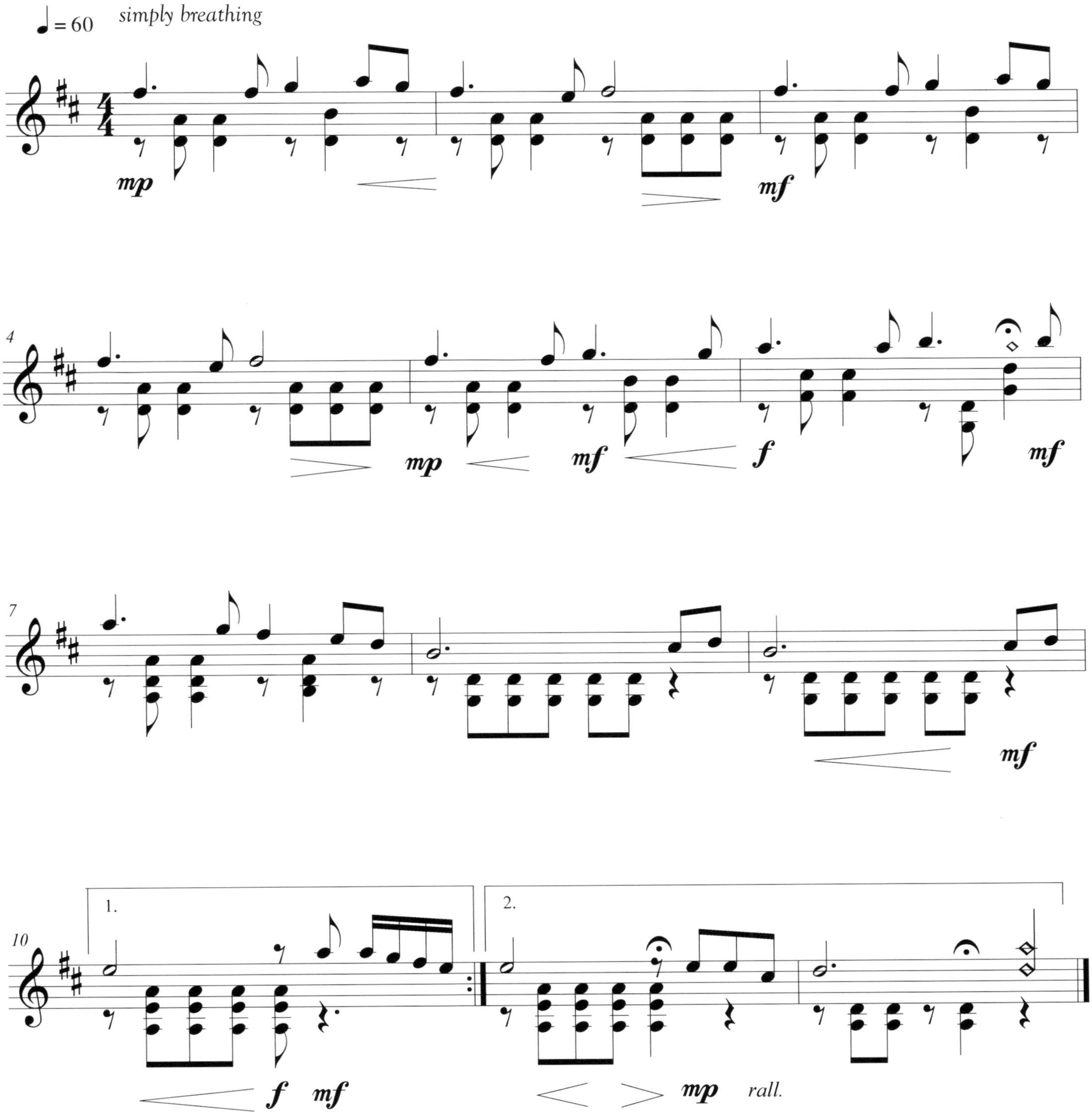

Étude d'ambre

Study in amber

Marilynn Mair

summer 2020

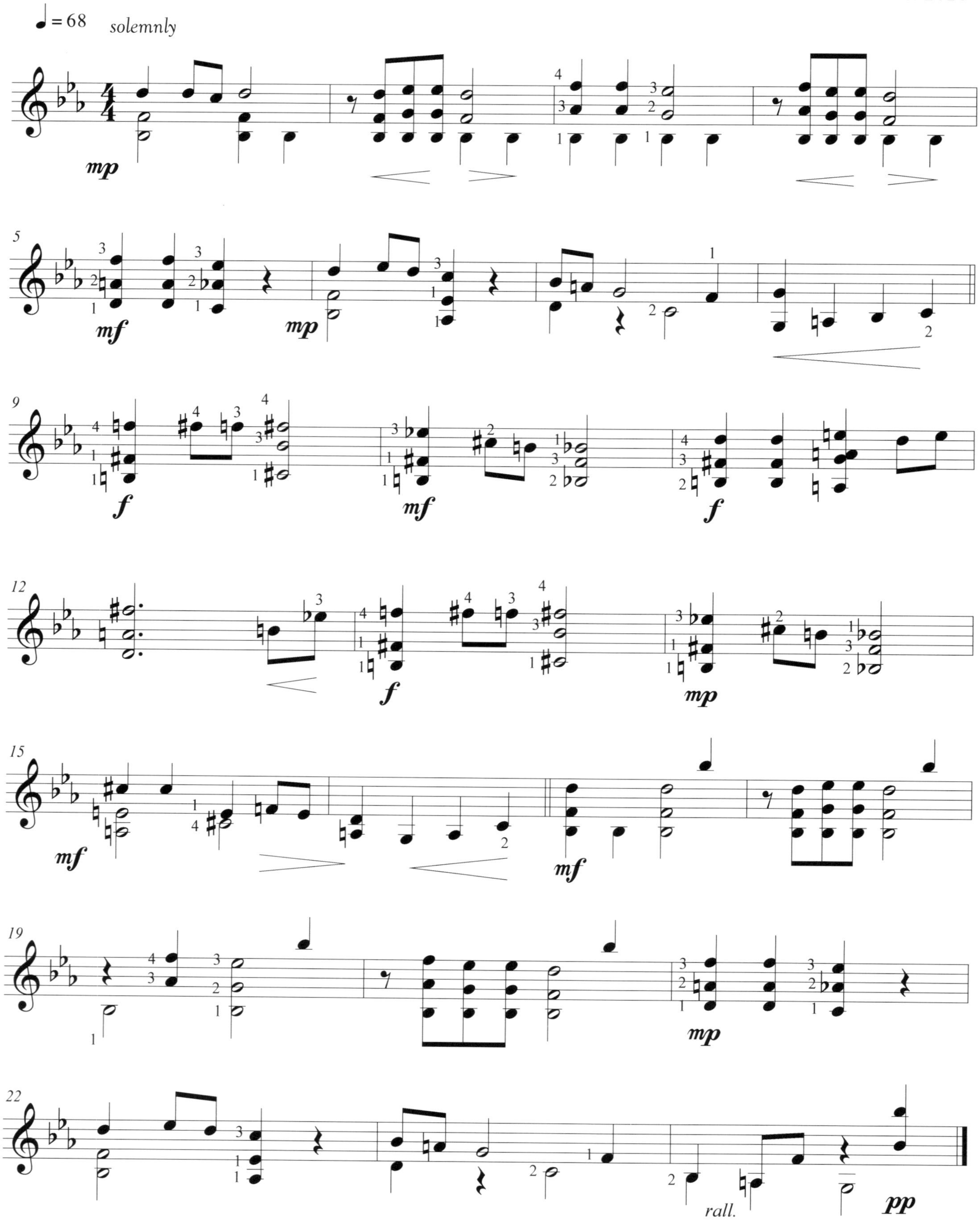

Étude noire

Study in black

Marilynn Mair
summer 2020

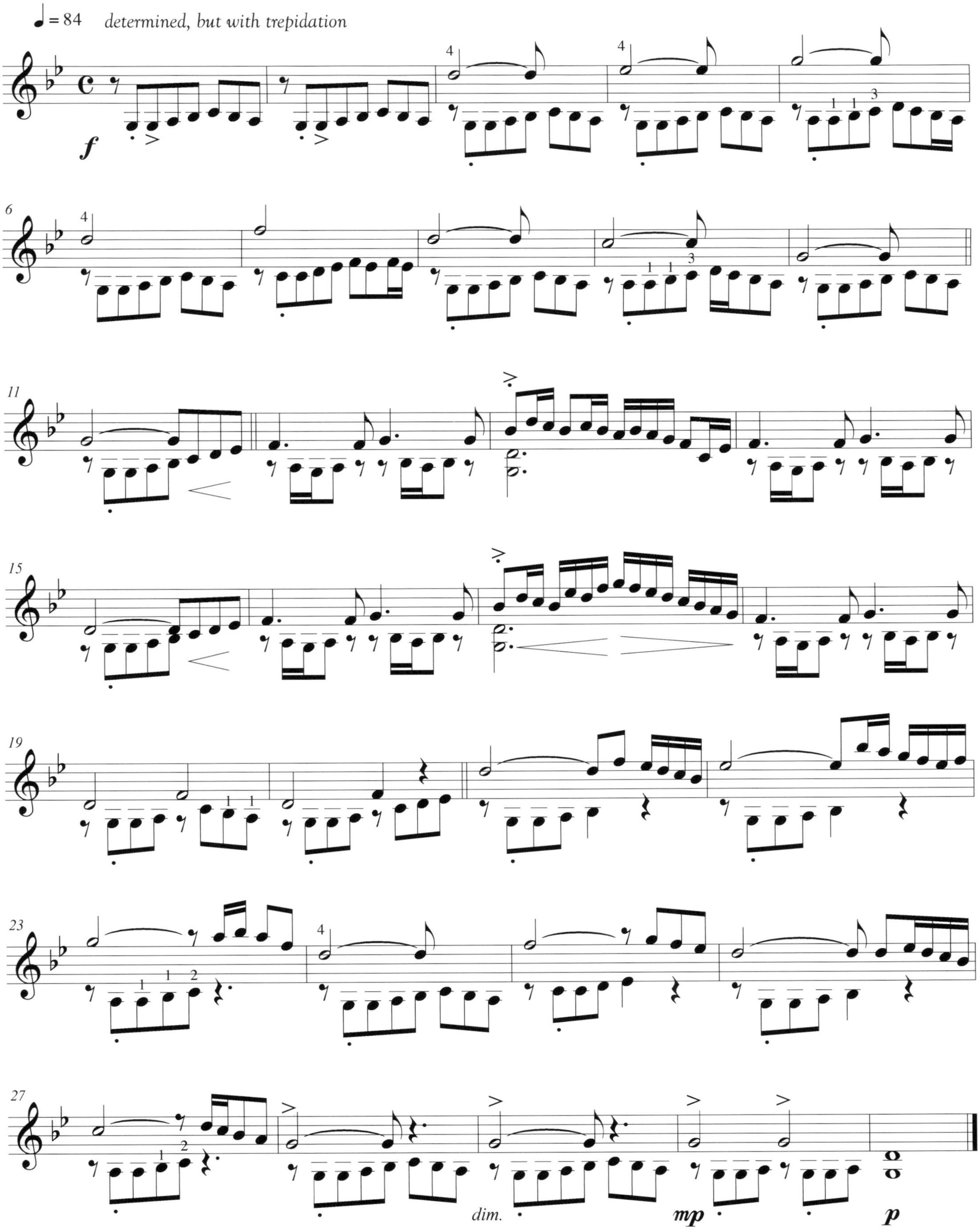

Étude blanche

Study in white

Marilynn Mair

summer 2020

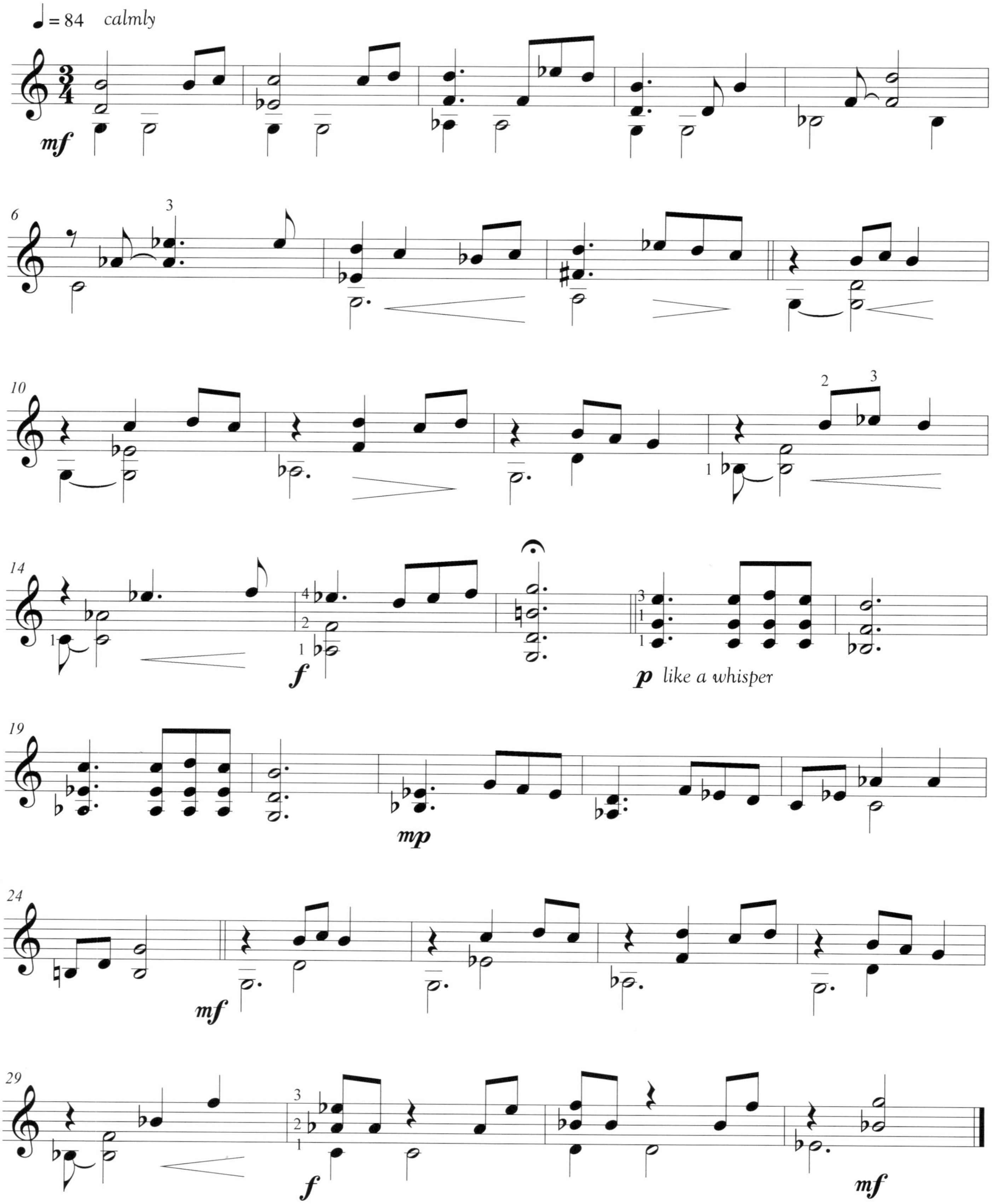

Étude bleue

Study in blue

Marilynn Mair
summer 2020

♩ = 64 *daydream, with sky*

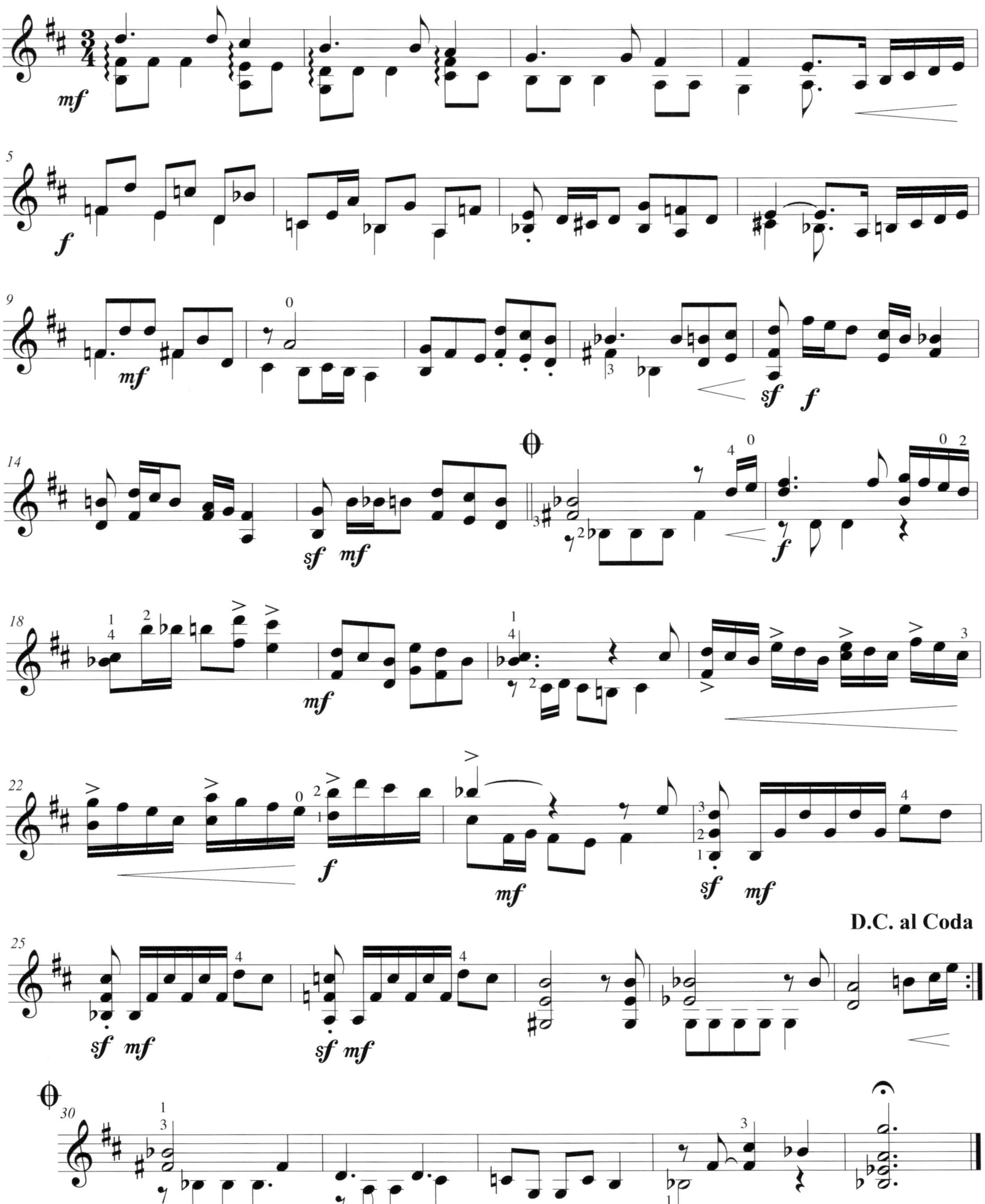

Étude violette

Study in violet

Marilynn Mair
summer 2020

♩ = 68 *peacefully, in evening's light*

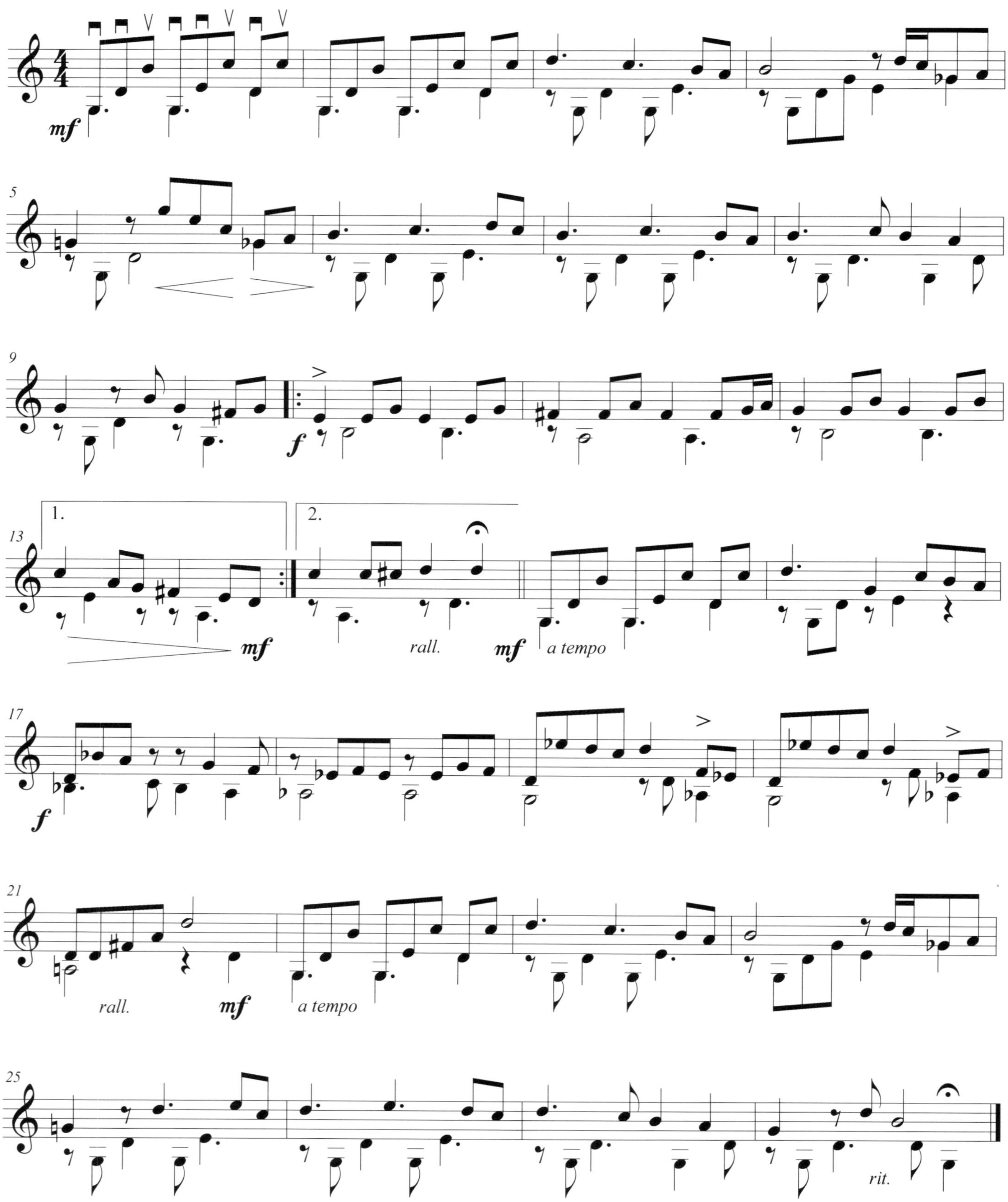

Fantasia
in dialogue

floating
planting gardens
peaches
in the dark
dragon dream
trouble in mind
holding fast
by the sea
old folks
in the groove

summer, autumn & winter 2020

Fantasia in dialogue

After writing my 10 *Études en couleurs* for solo mandolin, I decided to move ahead to create a series of mandolin duets. I chose to call these *fantasia*, as the term is historically used for a type of composition with an improvisatory feel that doesn't follow a strict set of rules. A theme is set out at the beginning and the rest of the piece is spun out freely from that, sometimes using counterpoint and imitation between the voices. Often fantasia are based on a theme from an earlier composer. My inspirations were the 2-part Renaissance fantasia written by Thomas Morley (1557–1602), and the contemporary fantasia written by Will Ayton, a wonderful composer and longtime friend, who frequently bases his work on themes from the Renaissance.

I think of my fantasia as conversations between two musicians, each piece on a different topic. Some are based on my own original themes, and some explore themes written by other composers. So the dialogues are between the two players, and also often between me and an earlier composer. When I borrow a theme, I have chosen well-known pieces, so the sources will be readily apparent to players and listeners. These duets are short, fun, sometimes funny, and most lie within the playing ability of good amateurs.

Floating, In the Dark, Dragon Dream, and *Holding Fast* are composed from my own themes. *In the Dark* is perhaps my most traditional use of the fantasia form as it begins as a fugue.

Planting Gardens and *By the Sea* are based on themes from well-loved classical pieces, with the former keeping more strictly to the theme. *Old Folks* is based on a few themes by Stephen Foster.

Peaches, Trouble in Mind, and *In the Groove* are inspired by rock and blues.

Before you begin, read the title, the dedication, and the playing instructions, smile, and set forth. I hope you will enjoy exploring these non-verbal dialogues I've written. As with my Études, if you are playing a single Fantasia, simply use the title as written on the music page. If you are playing a series of several, list them as they are on the previous page.

In a time period when my music-making options were significantly limited due to pandemic isolation, these fantasia allowed me to open a world of imagination and create duets I could envision playing with friends, students, and colleagues. They were a welcome escape. Special thanks to Laura Gulley, violin, and Charlie Moser and Fran Rivkin, mandolins, who were the first people who actually performed some of these with me.

"Art is the only way to run away without leaving home."
– Twyla Tharp, choreographer

Fantasia: floating

Marilynn Mair
summer 2020

♩ = 104 *like a bird*

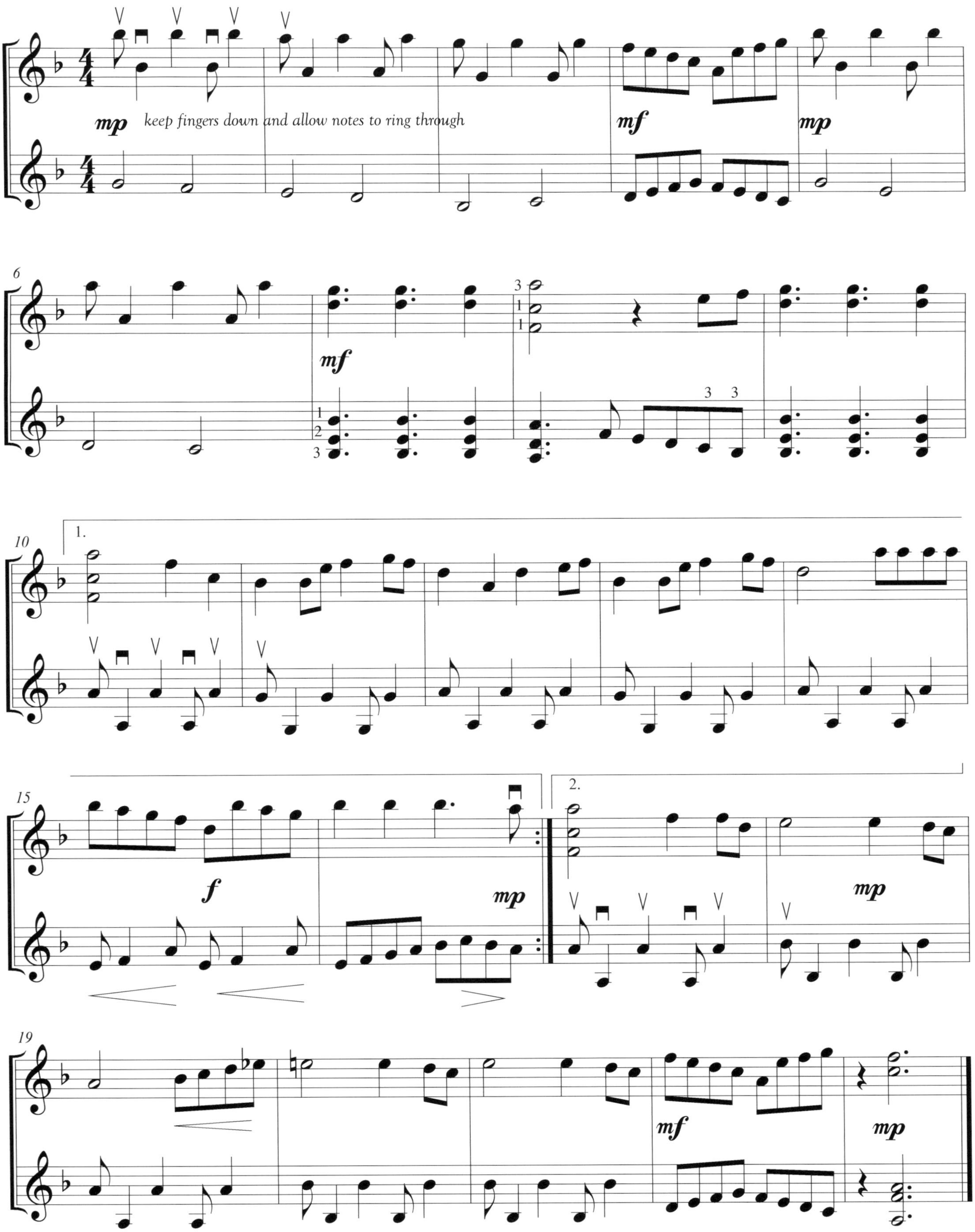

12

Fantasia: planting gardens

on an ancient Morris dance

Marilynn Mair
autumn 2020

♩ = 112 *playfully, as a game of tag*

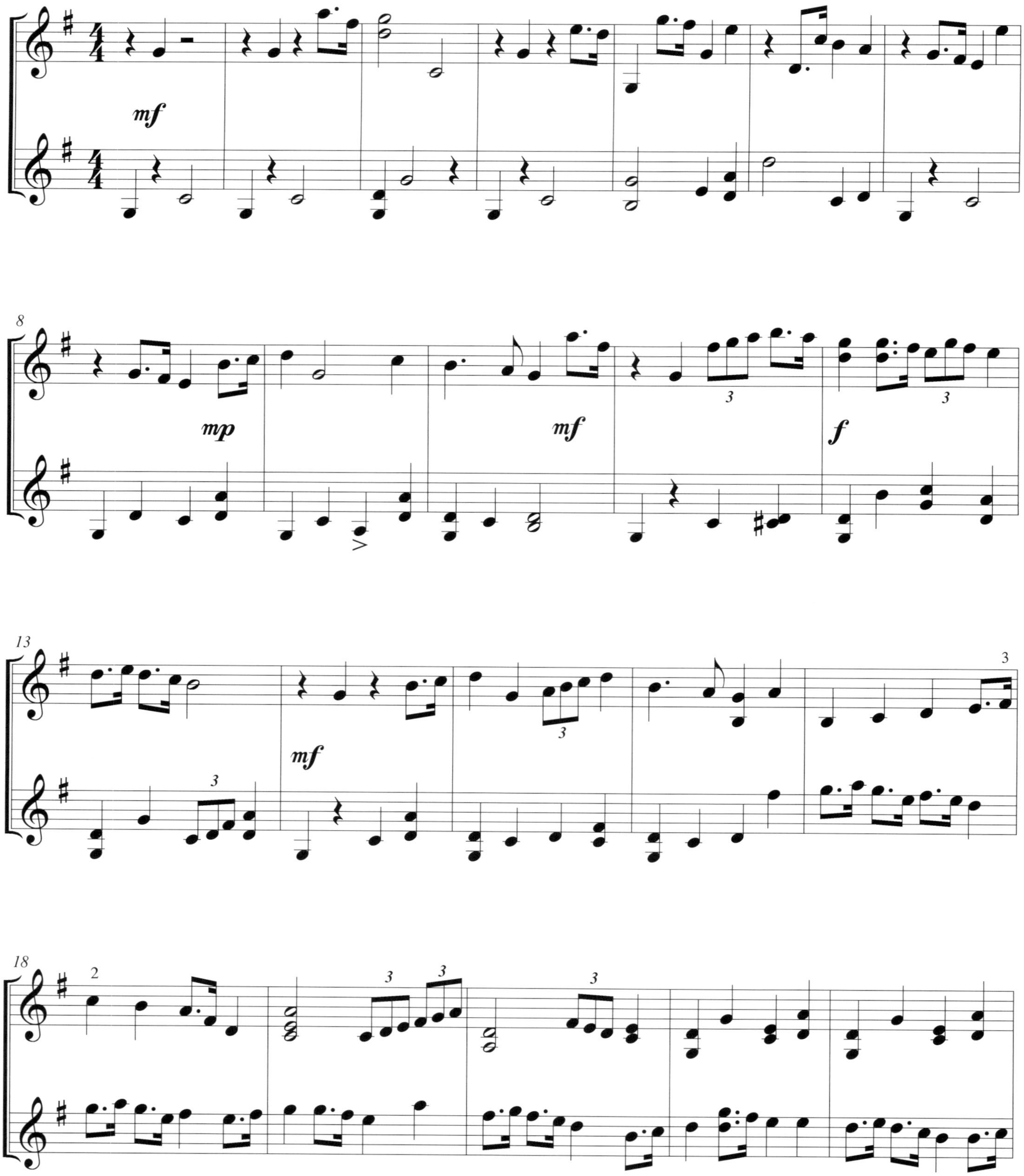

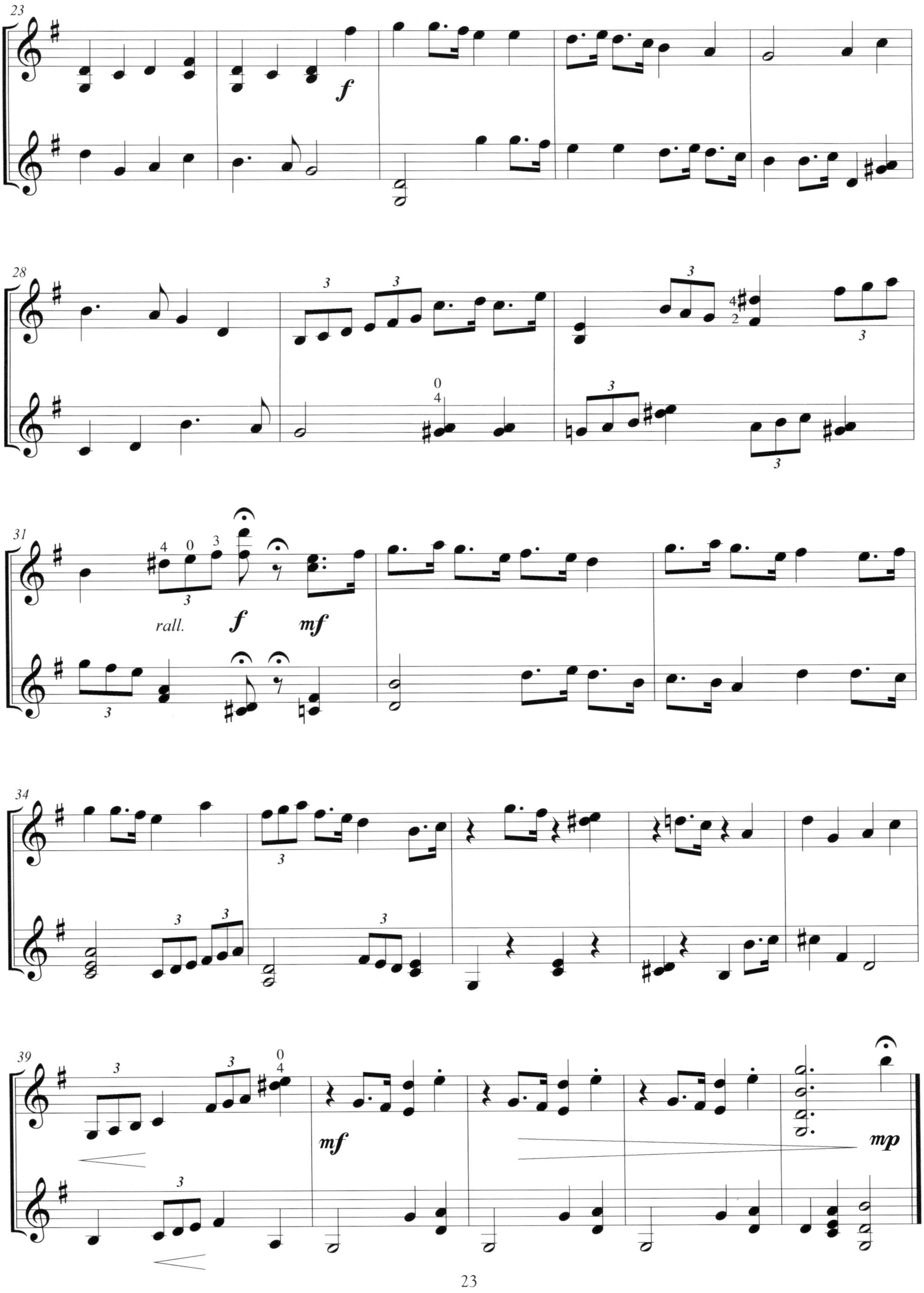
23
f
28
31
rall.
f
mf
34
39
mf
mp

13

Fantasia: peaches

inspired by Frank Zappa

Marilynn Mair
autumn 2020

♩ = 84 *strutting to the fruit stand*

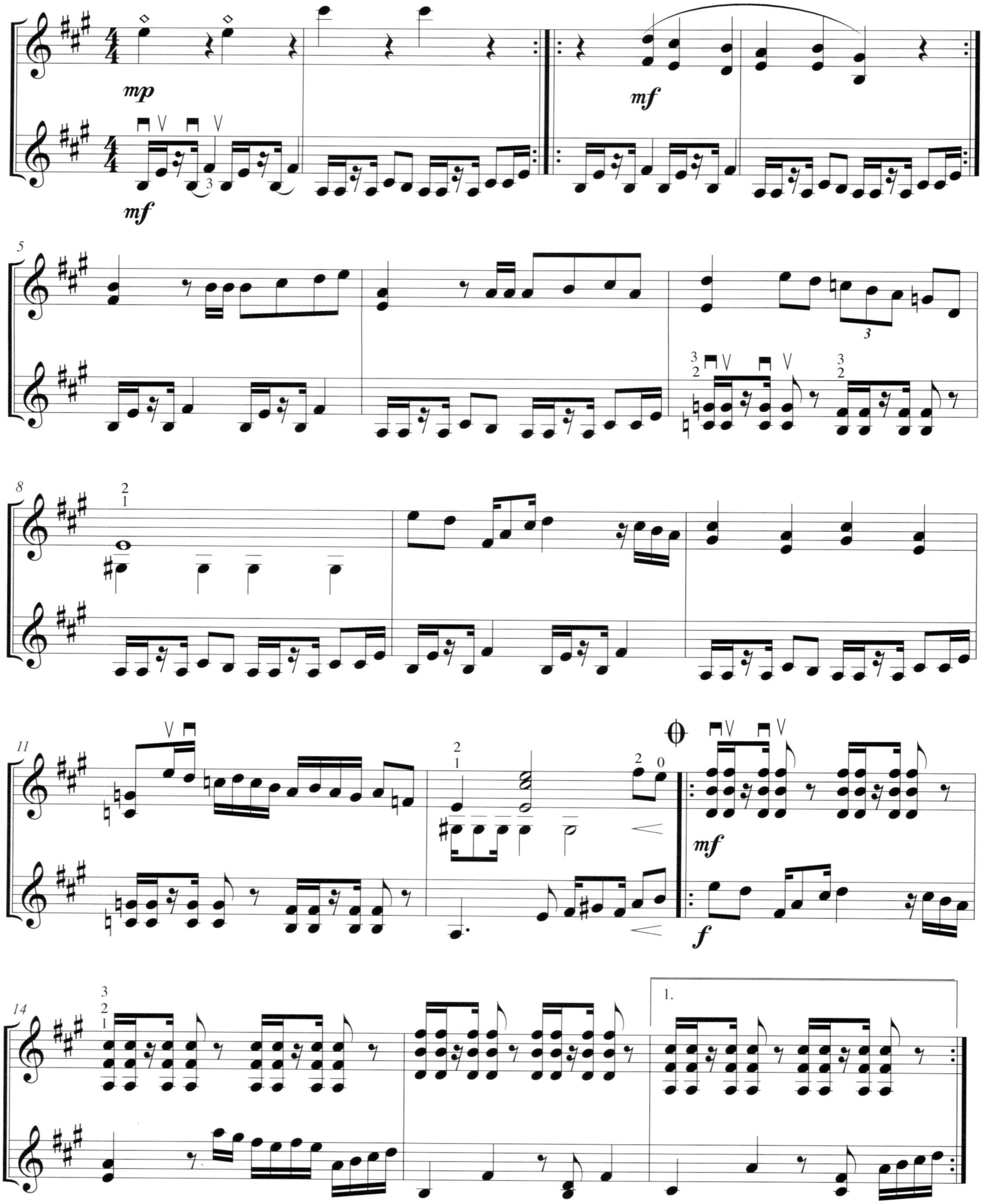

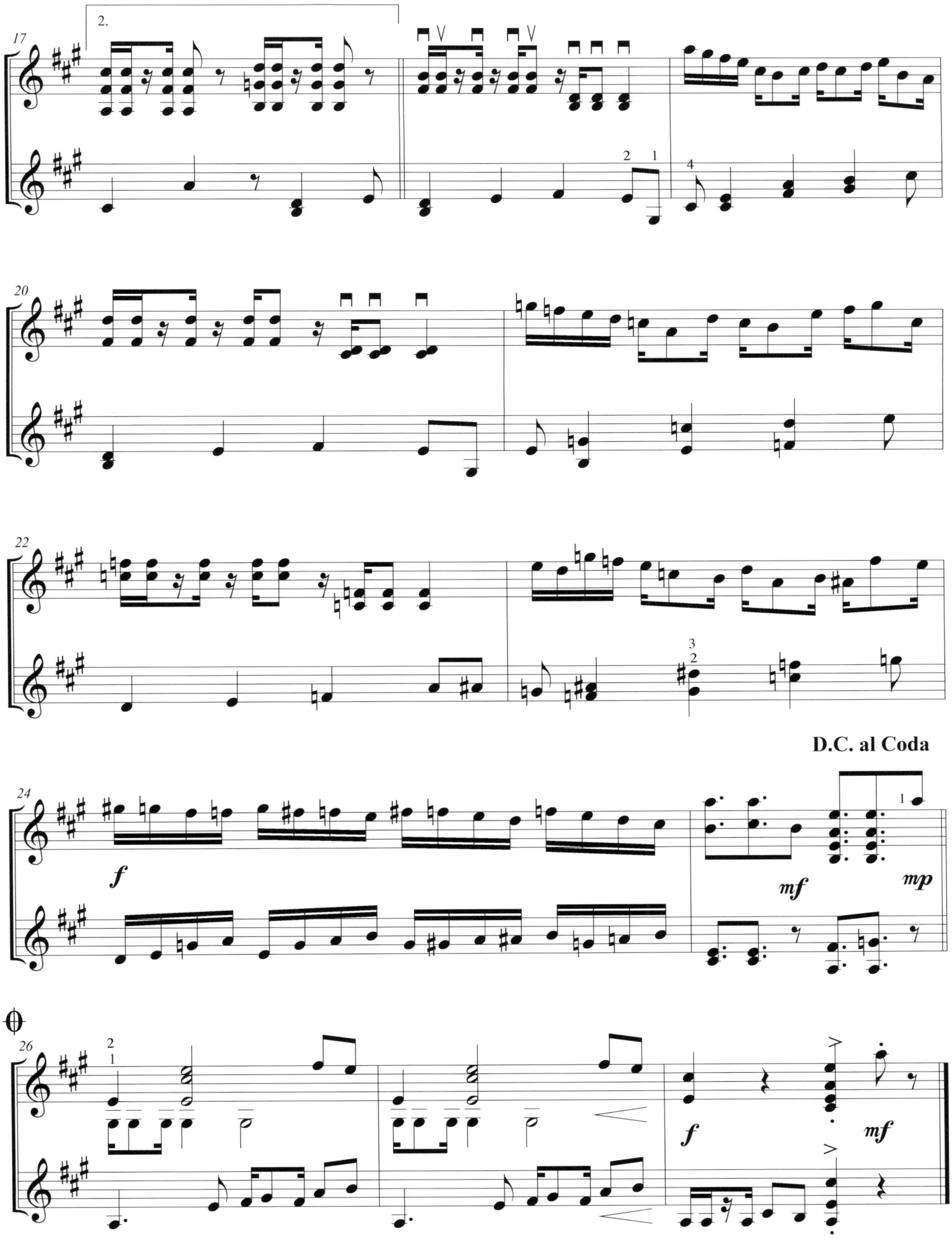
2.
D.C. al Coda
f
mf
mp
f
mf

14

Fantasia: in the dark

Marilynn Mair
summer 2020

♩ = 108 *restless, stalking*

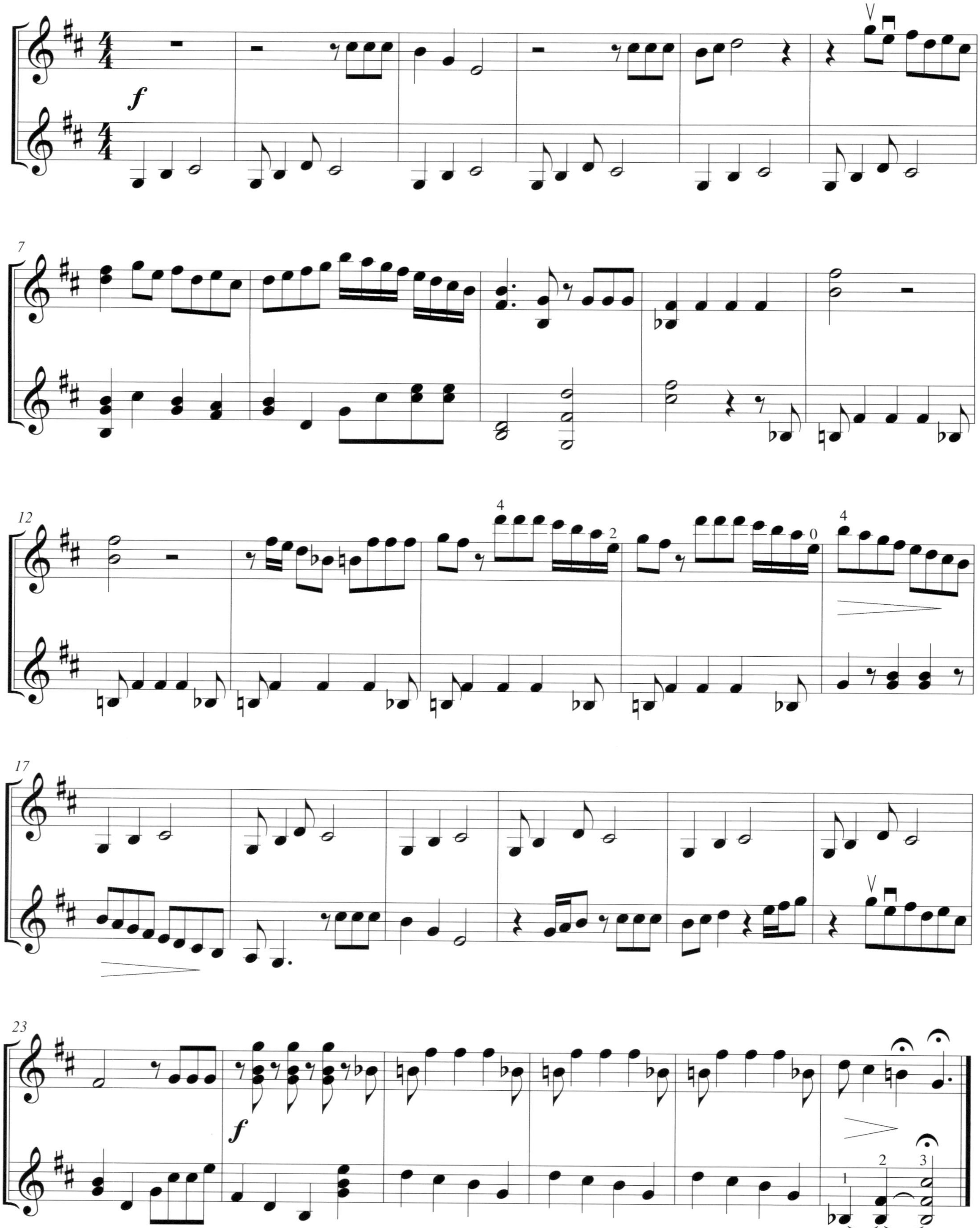

15

Fantasia: dragon dream

Marilynn Mair

winter 2020

♩ = 100 *fiercely*

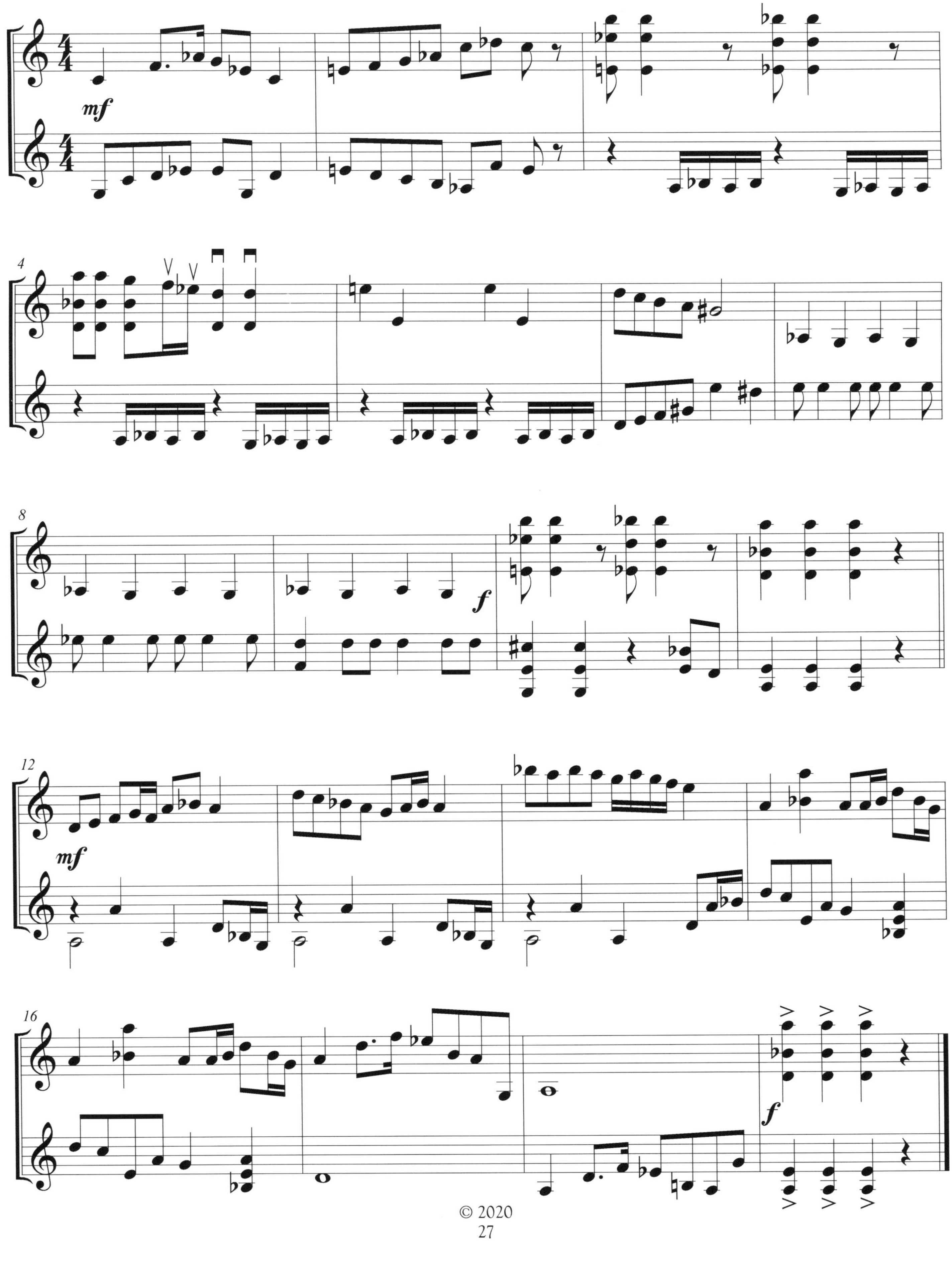

Fantasia: trouble in mind

Marilynn Mair

winter 2020

♩ = 104 *heading for the happy ending*

swing the 8th notes

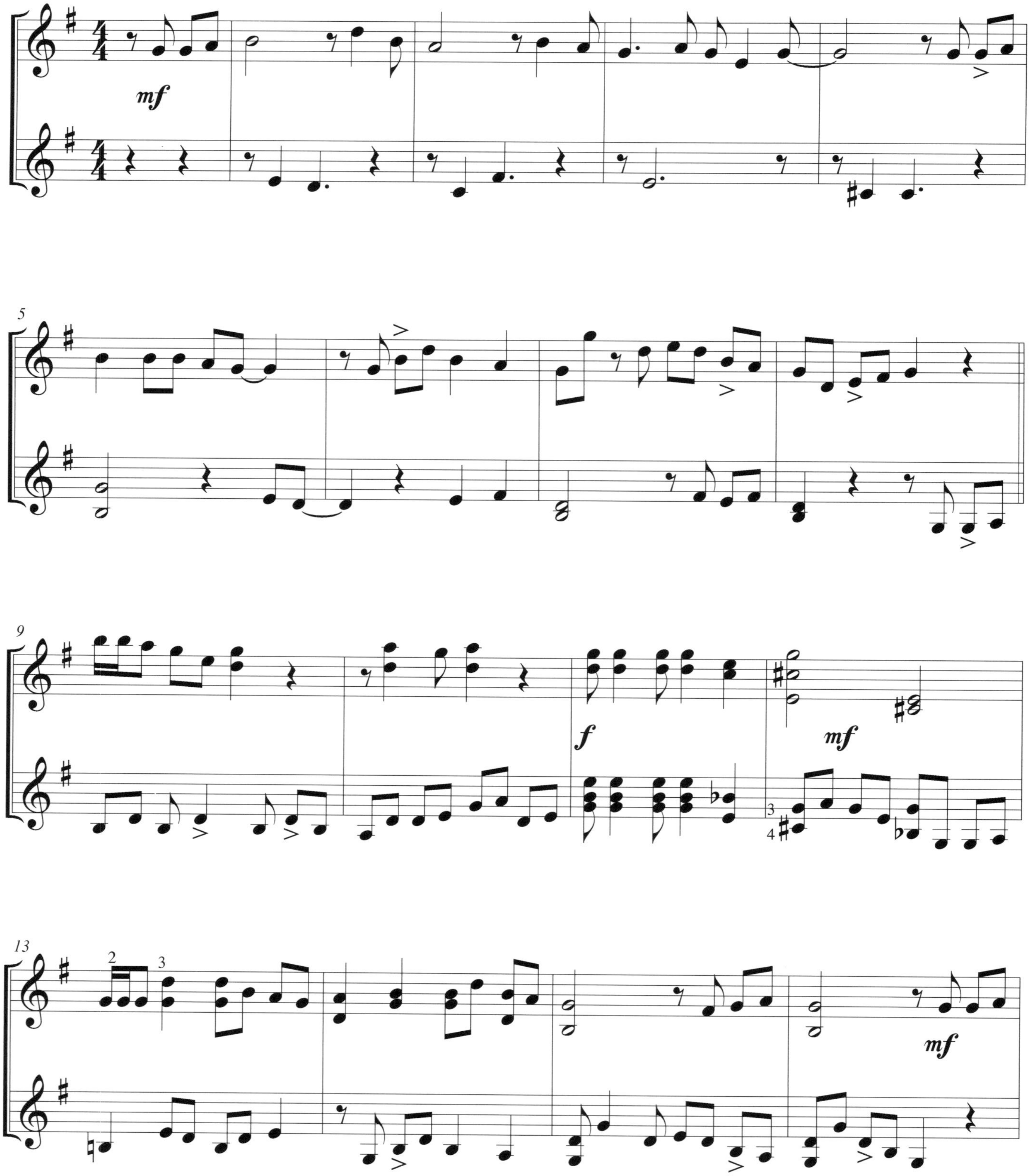

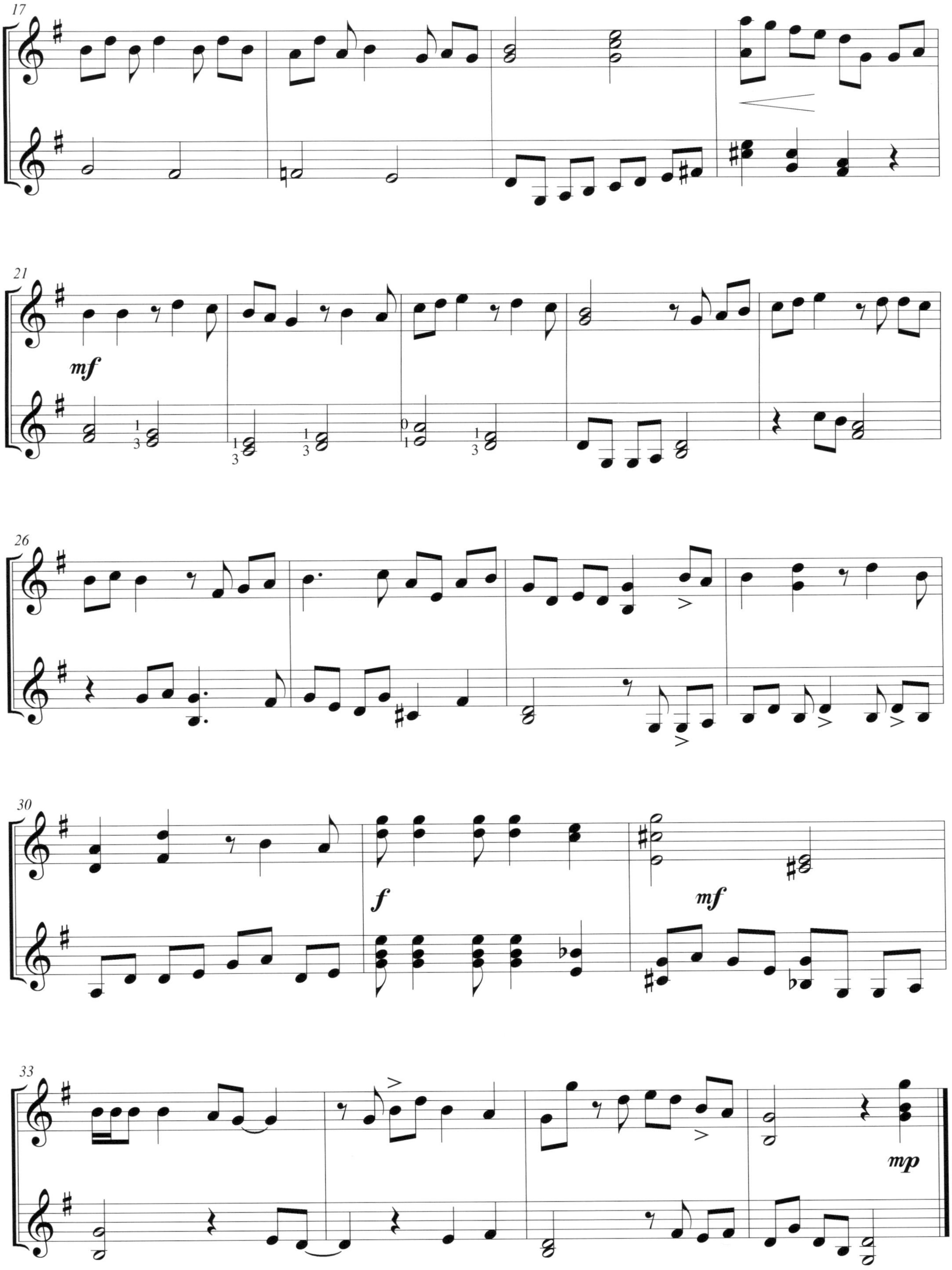
17
21
mf
26
30
f
mf
33
mp

16

Fantasia: holding fast

Marilynn Mair

summer 2020

♩ = 120 *stubbornly*

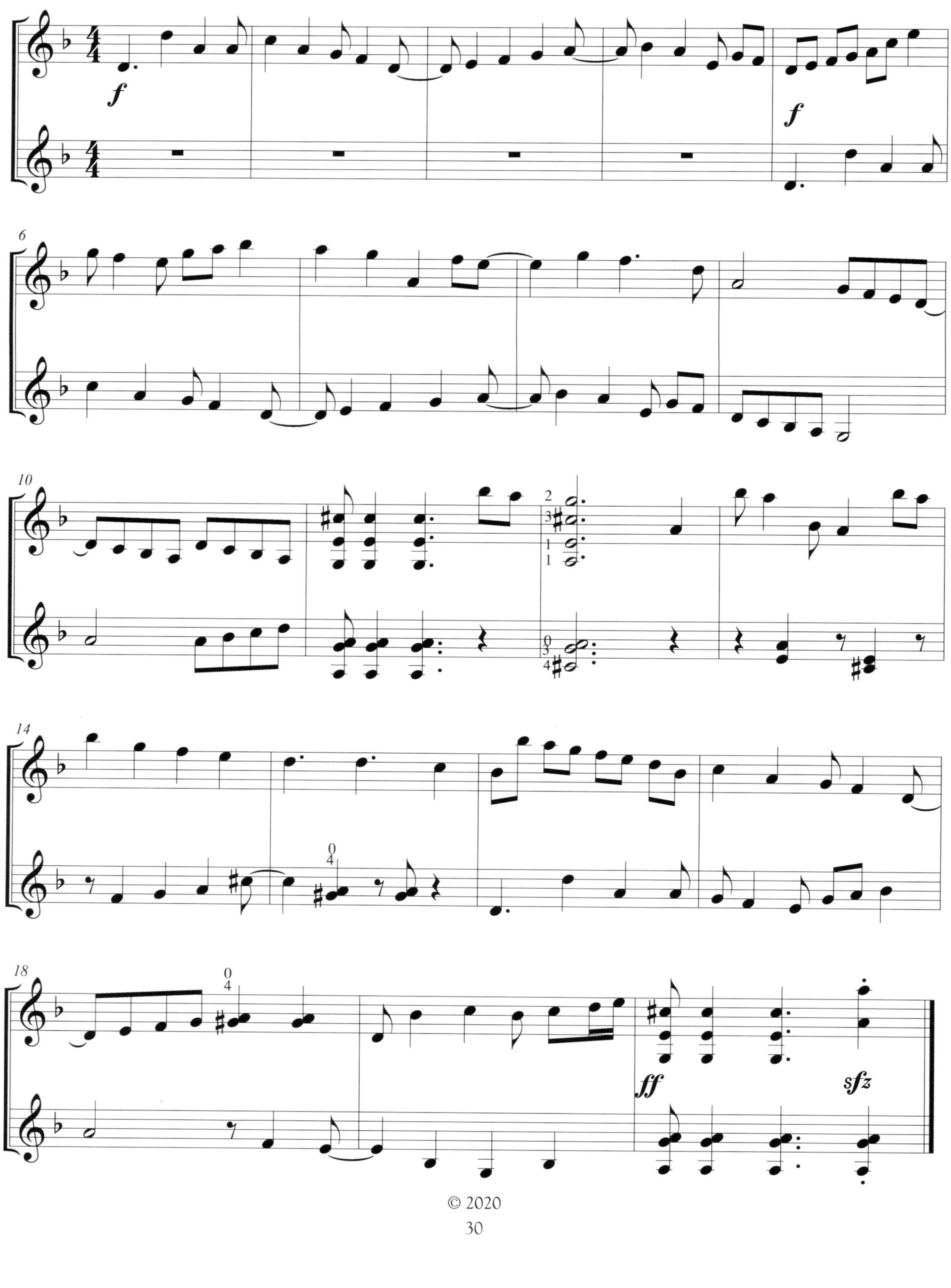

17

Fantasia: by the sea

on a theme by Eric Satie

Marilynn Mair
summer 2020

♩ = 104 *peacefully*

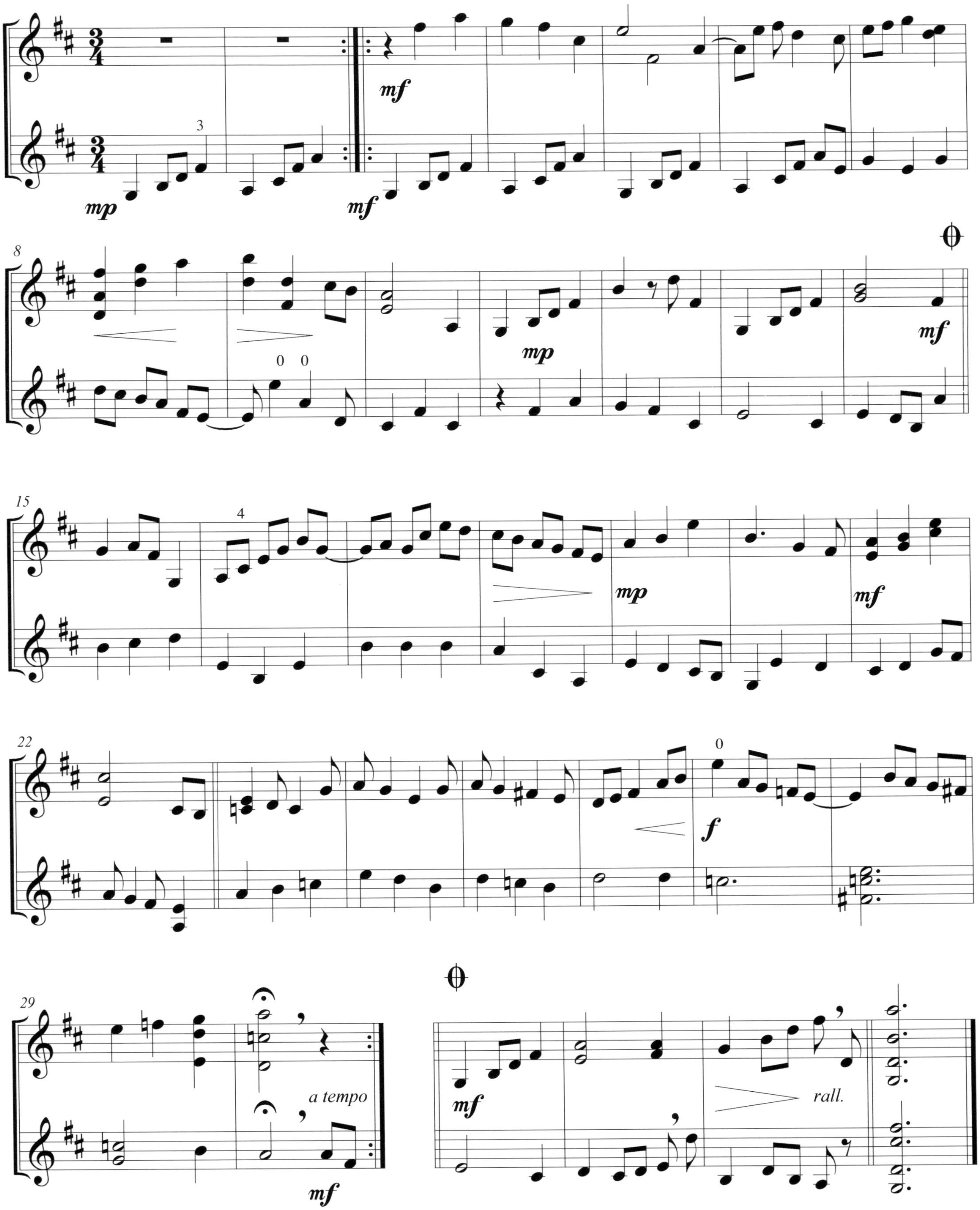

18

Fantasia: old folks

on themes by Stephen Foster

Marilynn Mair

autumn 2020

♩ = 84 *happily occupied at home*

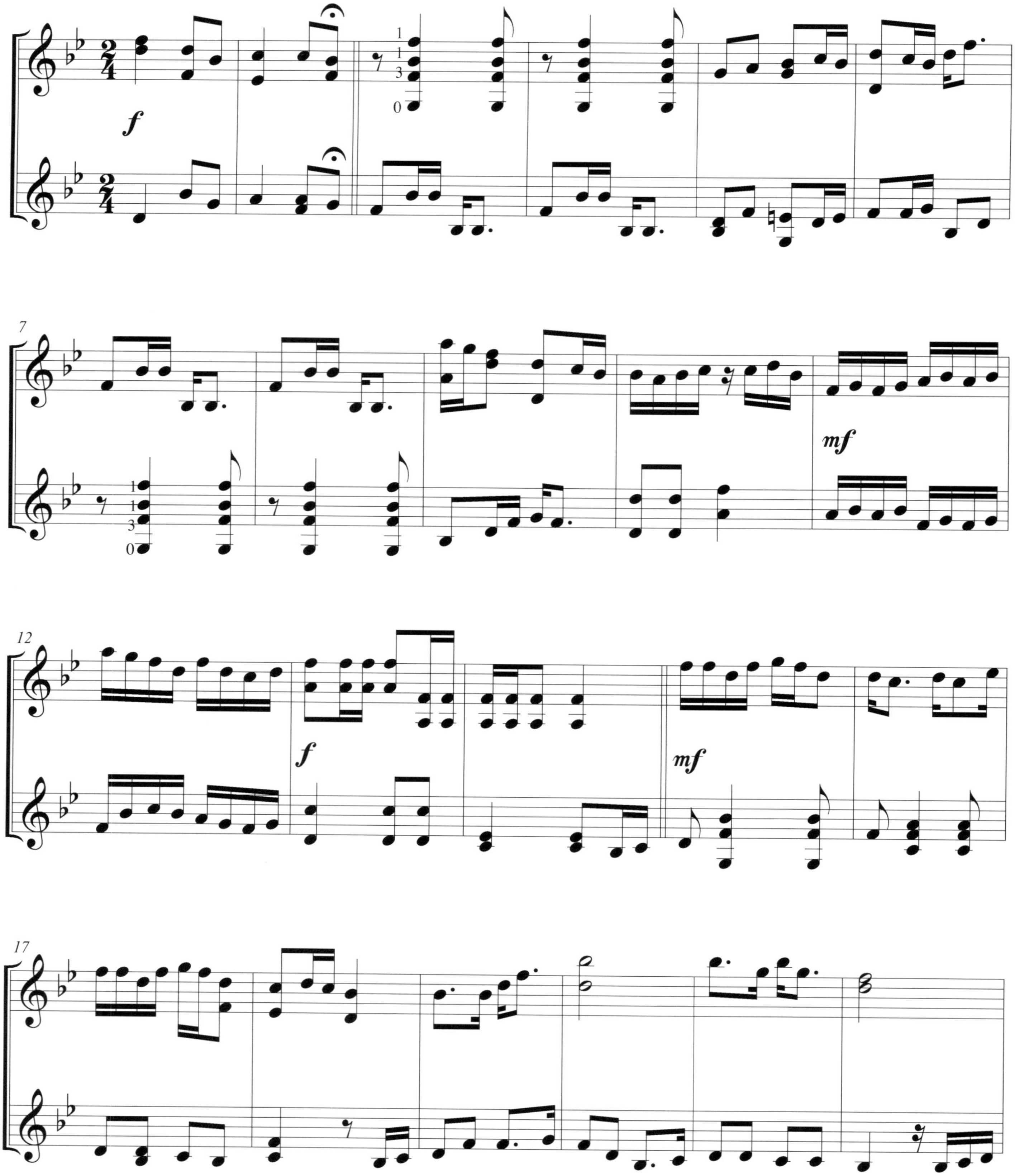

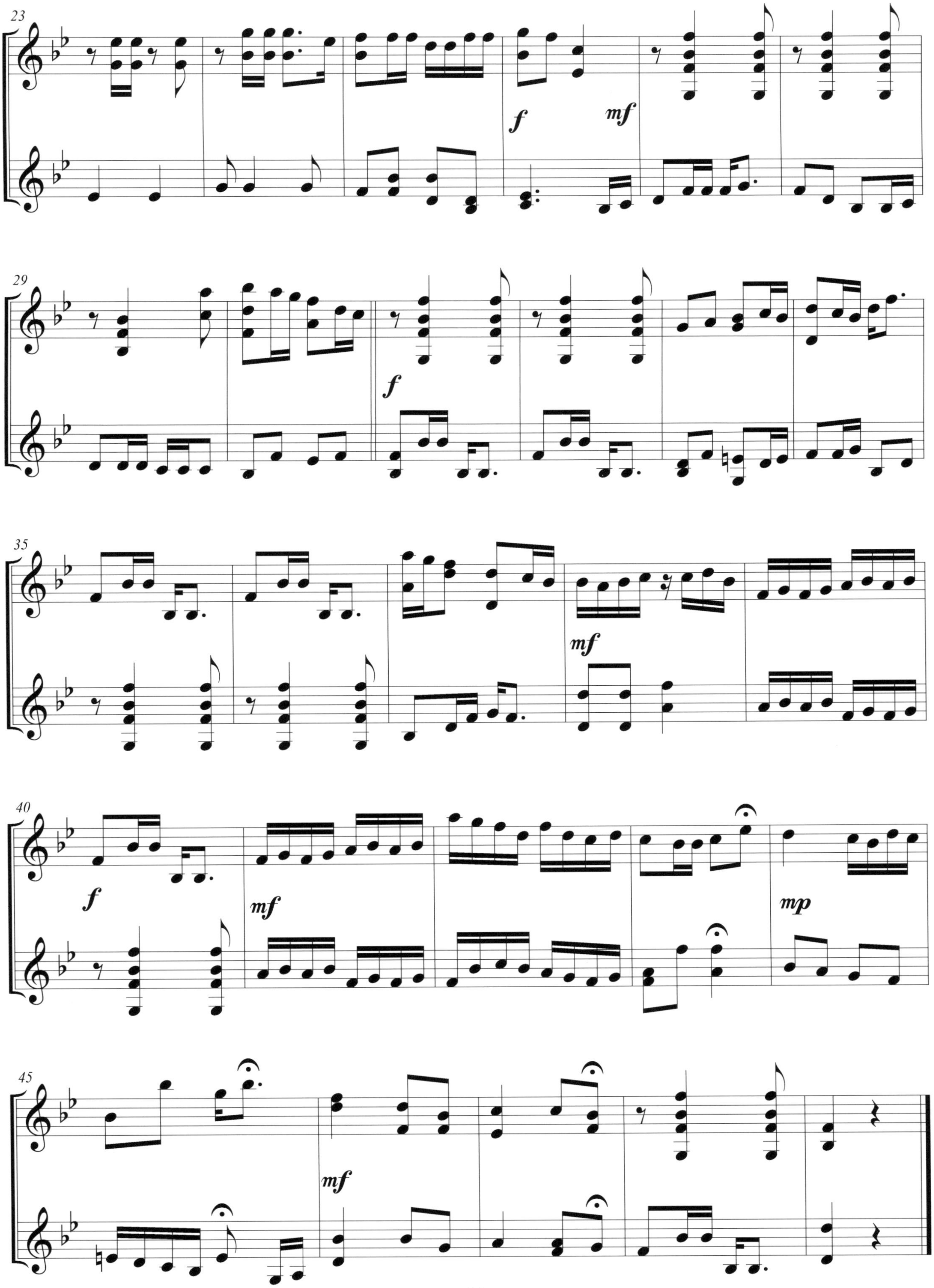

19

Fantasia: in the groove

Marilynn Mair
autumn 2020

♩= 116 *a conversation with attitude*

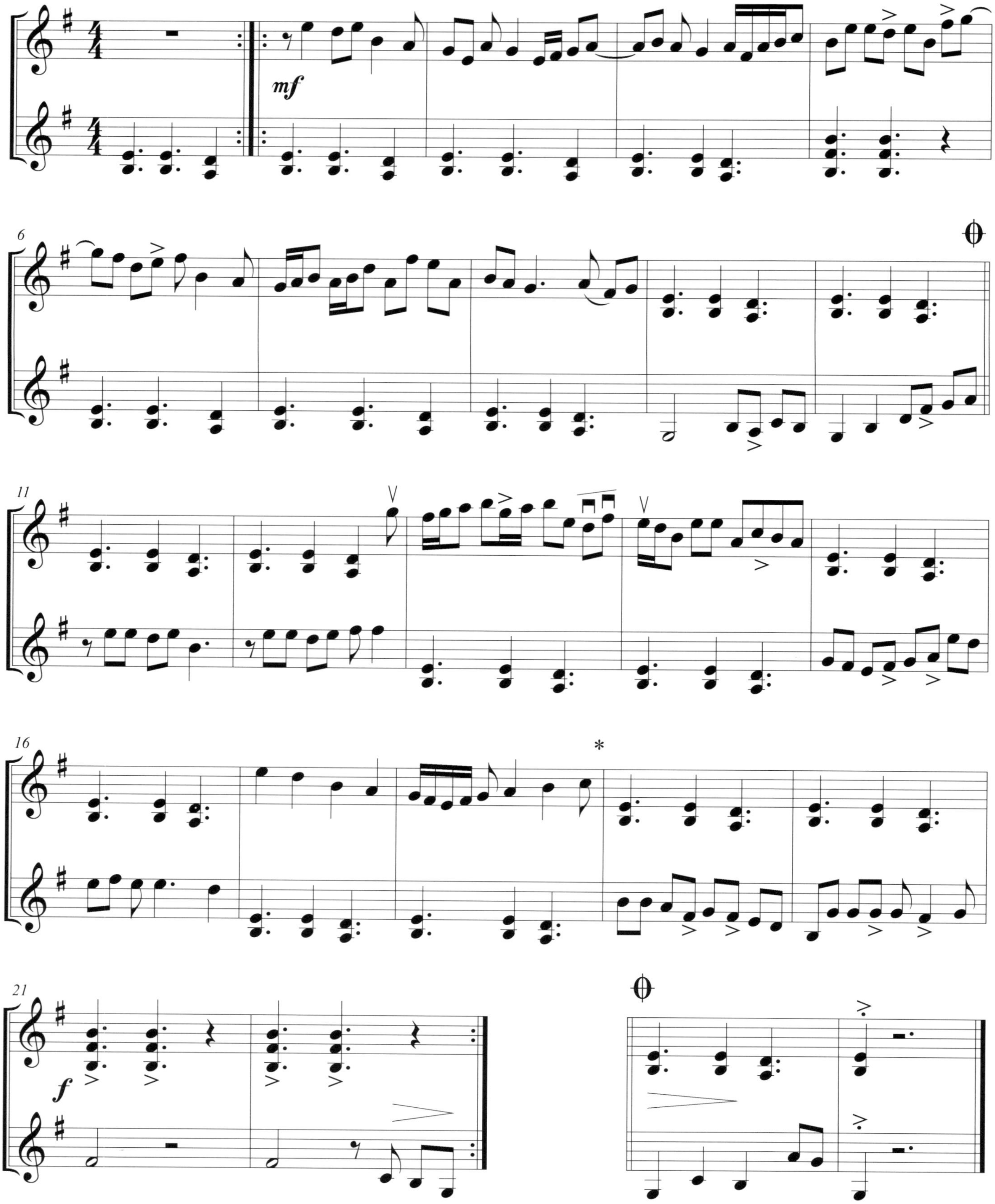

* *Performers may add a 4- or 8-bar section of their own between measures 18 and 19, trading 2-bar riffs over the groove.*

8 Nocturnes for Vincent

Sometimes when I am wearied suddenly
Oh, oh, you will be sorry for that word!
I shall go back again to the bleak shore
Only until this cigarette is ended
Mindful of you the sodden earth in spring
The light comes back with Columbine
Women have loved before as I love now
Tranquility at length, when autumn comes

written in spring & autumn 2021

8 Nocturnes for Vincent

A *nocturne* simply denotes a composition evocative of the night. The form originated in the Romantic Era, when music became less about structure and more about emotional expression. Some of the loveliest and most well-known nocturnes were written by Frédéric Chopin for solo piano. After completing my series of solo Études and the Fantasia duets for mandolin, I thought to undertake writing for mandolin and guitar, and chose the designation Nocturne, to evoke a feeling of darkness and mystery.

I have always loved playing duets with guitar or piano. The complexity of larger ensembles has its appeal, but the intimate interchange of notes and expression that is possible between two performers who bring different palettes of sound and texture to the process can, with the right partner, be transcendently beautiful. I have been lucky to have several amazing duo partners in my career, and when I decided to write a set of mandolin-guitar duets, I called on two for their help.

Robert N. Martel is a fantastic composer and guitarist, and for years we have performed our compositions and arrangements together. Although we were distanced by pandemic isolation, Bob gallantly read through and commented on my guitar parts via email, suggesting notational and voicing changes that would make the parts more idiomatic. Paul Dressel, my love, and live-in guitarist for the pandemic, cheerfully added these pieces to our usual Choro repertoire, and patiently suggested substitute chords when I was unhappy with my original choice. I owe them both a debt of gratitude.

The final inspiration for this series was the sonnets of Edna St. Vincent Millay. I have always loved her quirky takes on poetry, love, and emotion, and reread most of her work as a solace during our pandemic isolation. I chose poems that resonated with me at this time in history, and this time in my life. Many thanks to Holly Peppe, the Literary Executor for Edna St. Vincent Millay (www.Millay.org), for her support of my project, and permission to include the two sonnets that are still under copyright.

As with my Études and Fantasias, if you perform just one, please list it by the title on the music page; if you play more than one, you may list them as they are on the previous page.

"Being creative is not so much the desire to do something as the listening to that which wants to be done: the dictation of the materials."
– Anni Albers, textile designer and pioneer of 20th-century modernism

Edna St. Vincent Millay (1892-1950) was an American poet, and is a longtime hero of mine. Her spirited feminism, her independence, and her modern approach to traditional sonnet form all speak to me. I have written sonnets since I was a teenager, love the form, and since 2008 have posted a couple of hundred on my blog, "Celebrating a Year." I find writing and reading sonnets contemplative, and enjoy contrasting their formal structure with a modern subject. Millay and e. e. cummings are two poets who do this well. St. Vincent was the hospital where Millay was born, and "Vincent" is what her family and friends called her. I've chosen 8 of her sonnets as inspiration for my *Nocturnes*. Here are the full texts of the first two:

Nocturne 1:

Sometimes when I am wearied suddenly
Of all the things that are the outward you,
And my gaze wanders ere your tale is through
To webs of my own weaving, or I see
Abstractedly your hands about your knee
And wonder why I love you as I do,
Then I recall, "Yet *Sorrow* thus he drew;"
Then I consider, "*Pride* thus painted he."
Oh, friend, forget not, when you fain would note
In me a beauty that was never mine,
How first you knew me in a book I wrote,
How first you loved me for a written line:
So are we bound till broken is the throat
Of Song, and Art no more leads out the Nine.

Edna St. Vincent Millay, 1923
The Nine are the Muses; painting and sculpture are first and second, music is fourth, literature is eighth.

Nocturne 2:

Oh, oh, you will be sorry for that word!
Give back my book and take my kiss instead.
Was it my enemy or my friend I heard,
"What a big book for such a little head!"
Come, I will show you now my newest hat,
And you may watch me purse my mouth and prink!
Oh, I shall love you still, and all of that.
I never again shall tell you what I think.
I shall be sweet and crafty, soft and sly;
You will not catch me reading any more:
I shall be called a wife to pattern by;
And some day when you knock and push the door,
Some sane day, not too bright and not too stormy,
I shall be gone, and you may whistle for me.

Edna St. Vincent Millay, 1922

Nocturne 1

Sometimes when I am wearied suddenly

Marilynn Mair

spring 2021

♩ = 80 *hold guitar notes under slurs to form chords where possible, and let all open strings ring*

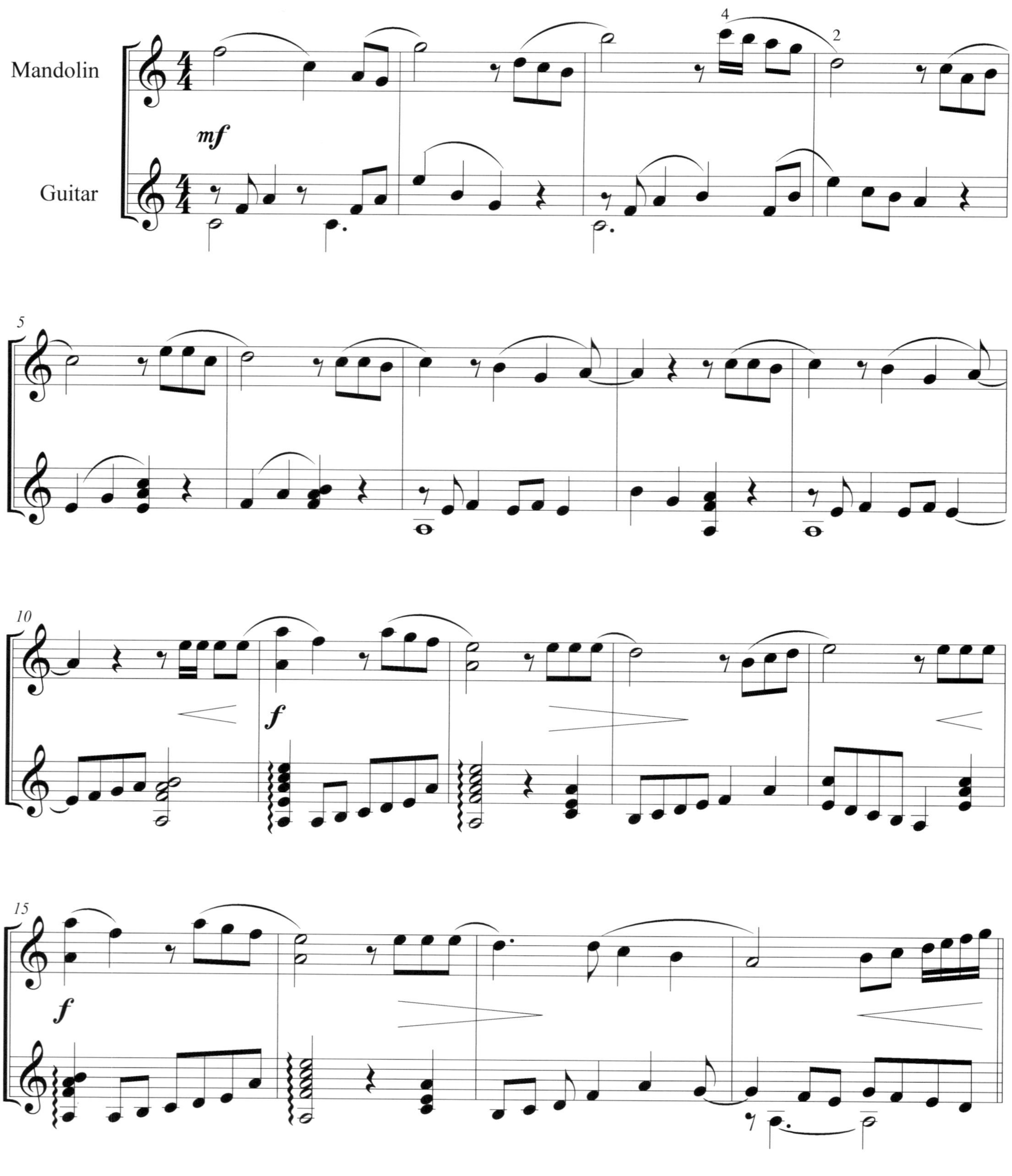

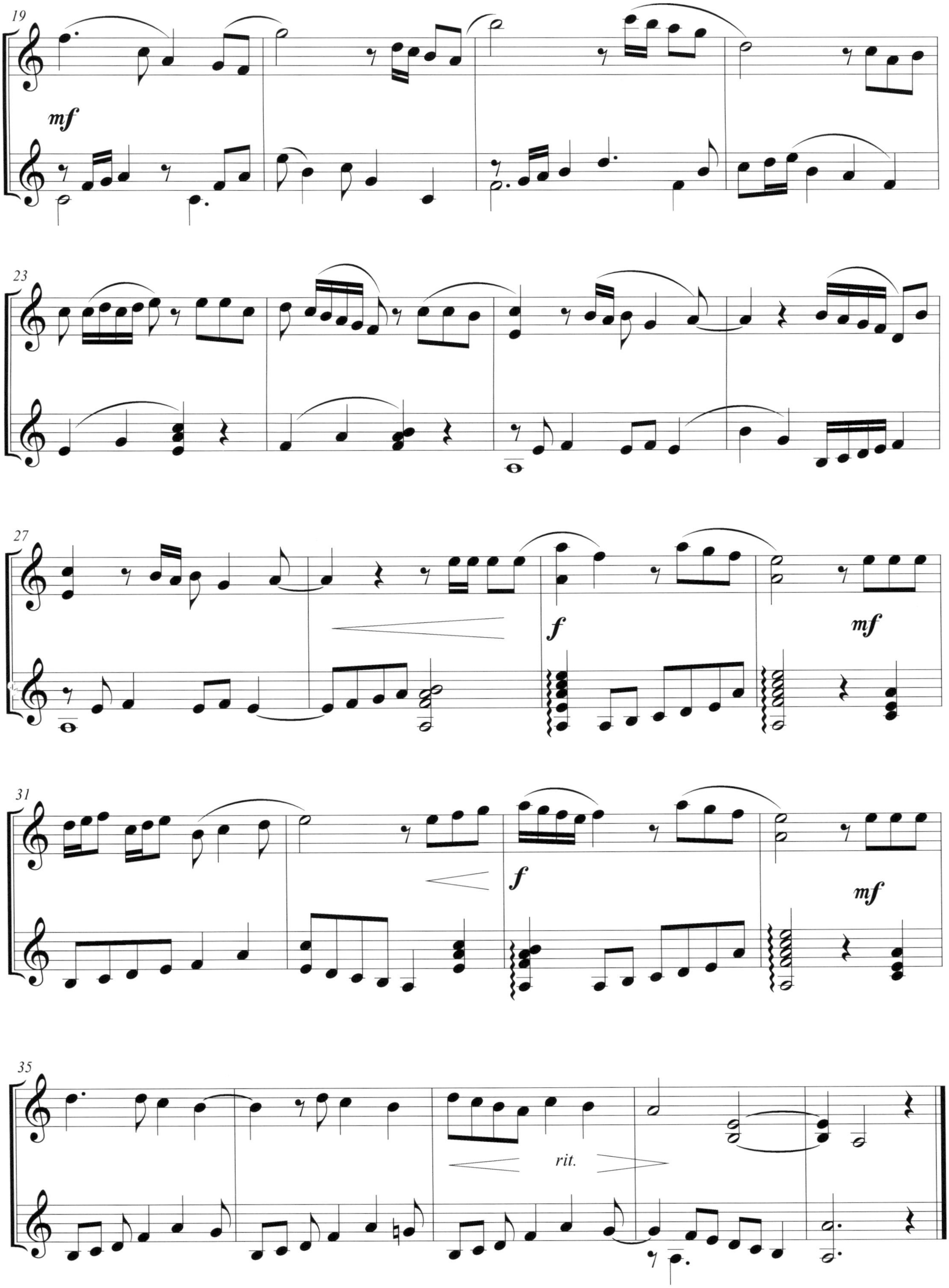
19
mf
23
27
f
mf
31
f
mf
35
rit.

21

Nocturne 2

Oh, oh, you will be sorry for that word!

Marilynn Mair

spring 2021

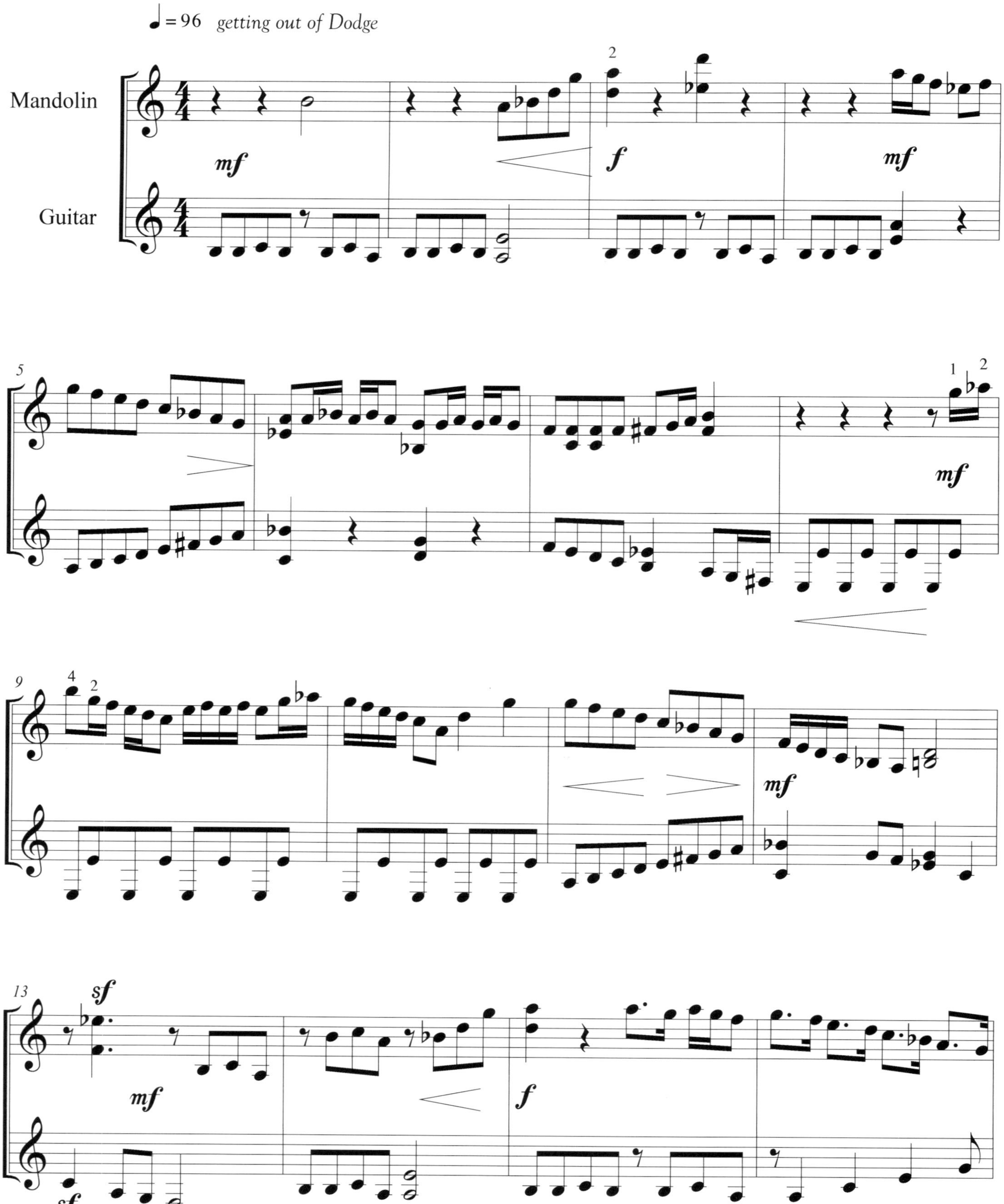

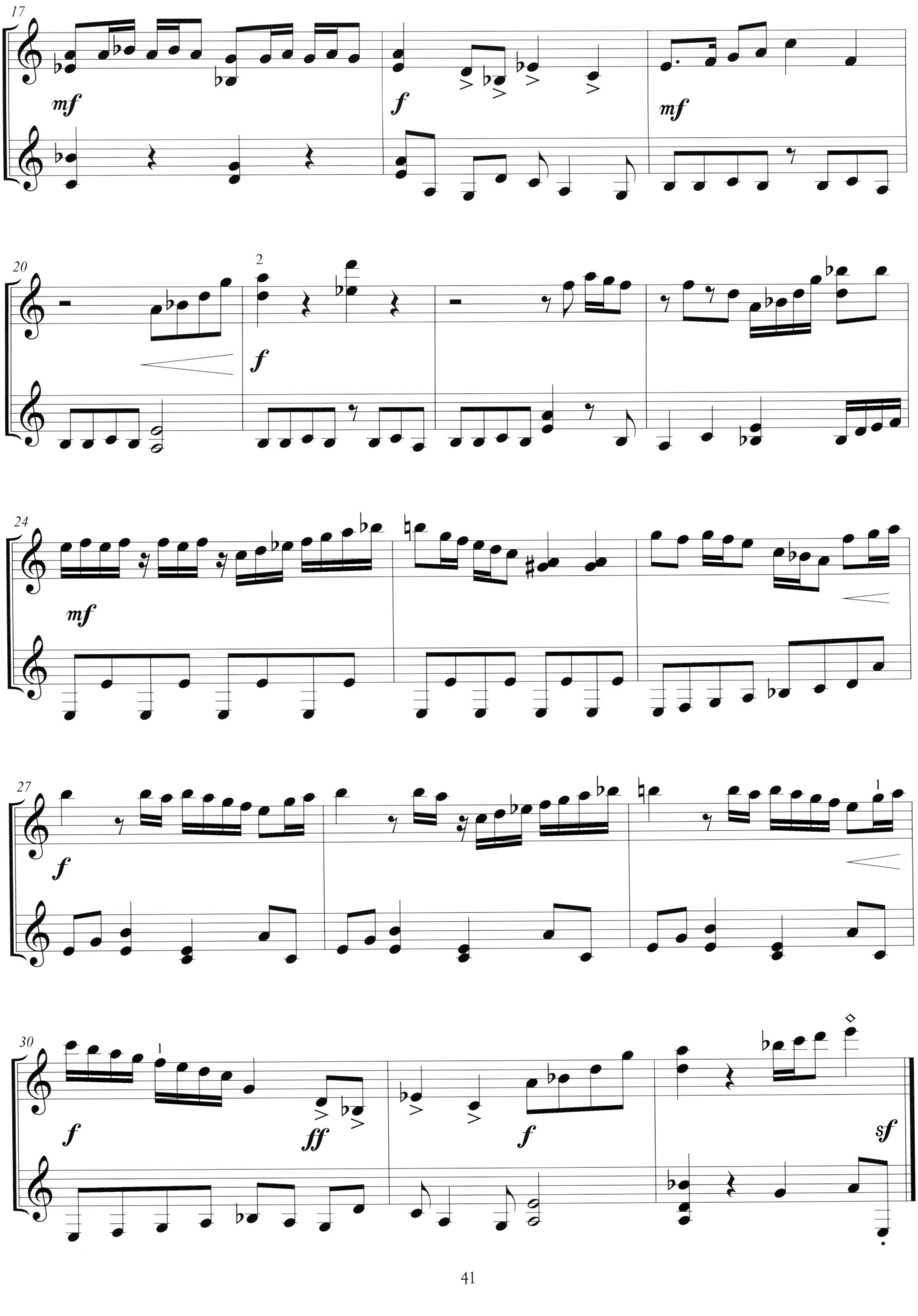
17
mf
f
mf
20
f
24
mf
27
f
30
f
ff
f
sf

22

Nocturne 3

I shall go back again to the bleak shore

Marilynn Mair
spring 2021

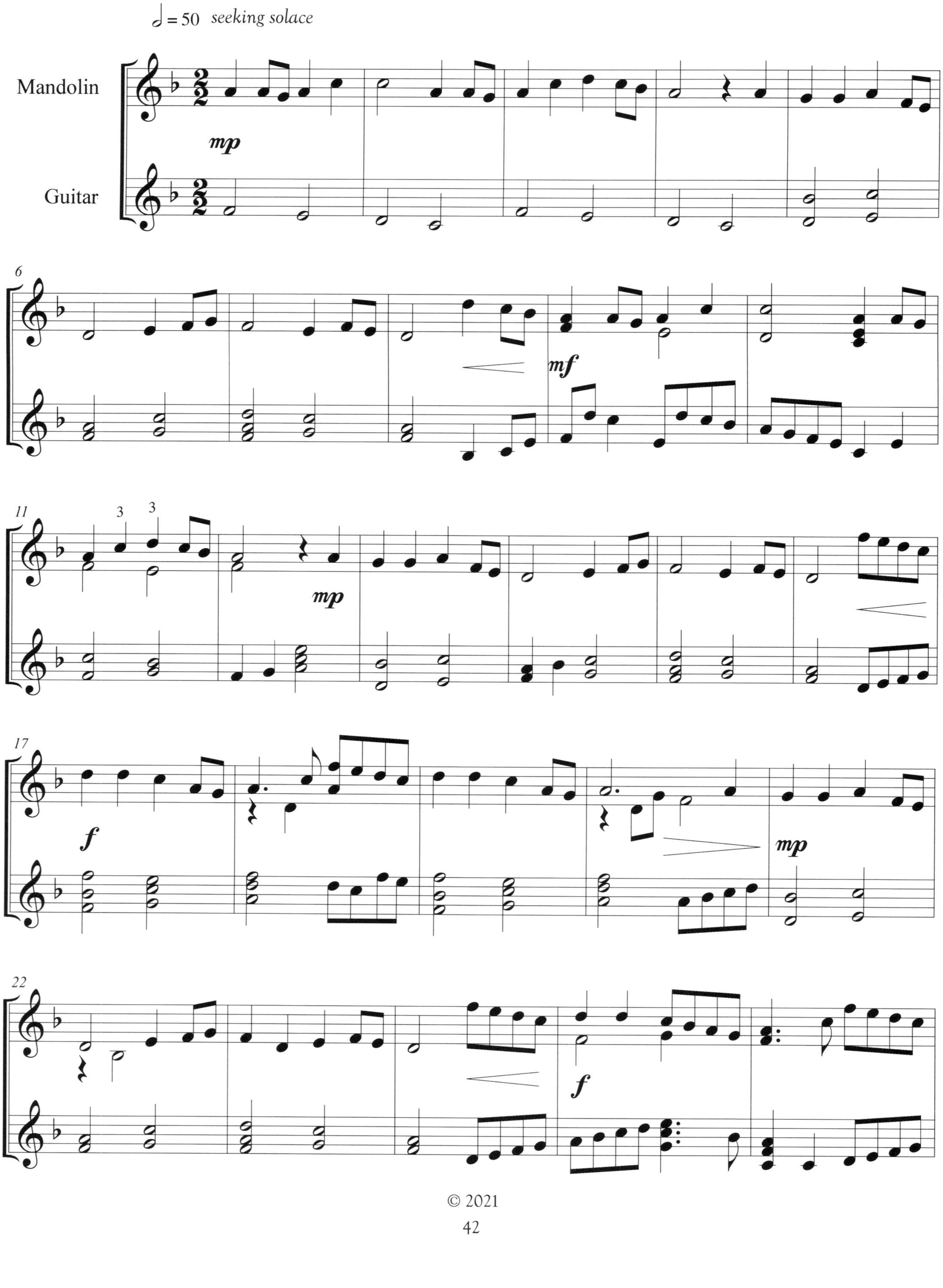

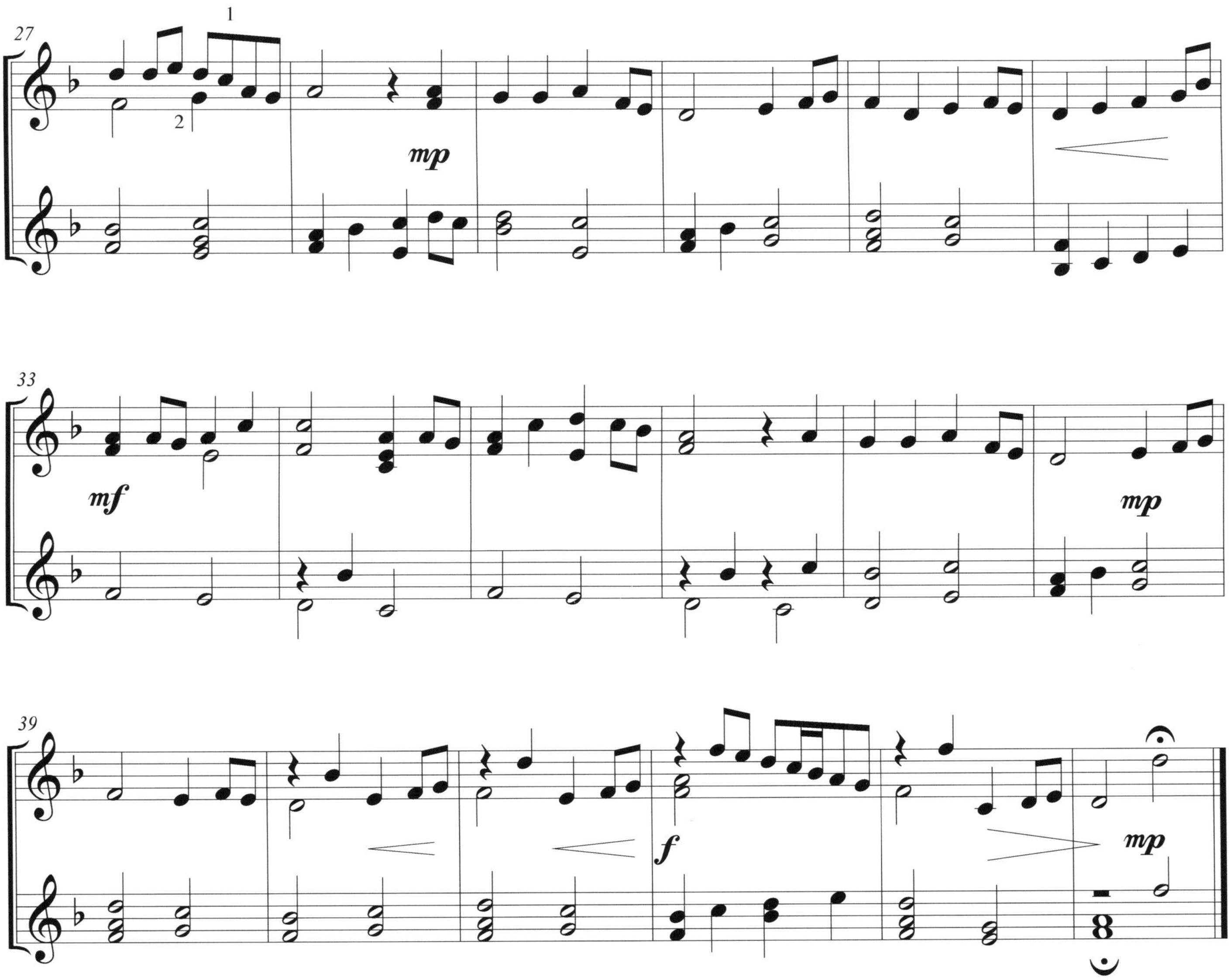

I shall go back again to the bleak shore
And build a little shanty on the sand,
In such a way that the extremest band
Of brittle seaweed will escape my door
But by a yard or two; and nevermore
Shall I return to take you by the hand;
I shall be gone to what I understand,
And happier than I ever was before.
The love that stood a moment in your eyes,
The words that lay a moment on your tongue,
Are one with all that in a moment dies,
A little under-said and over-sung.
But I shall find the sullen rocks and skies
Unchanged from what they were when I was young.

Edna St. Vincent Millay, 1923

23

Nocturne 4

Only until this cigarette is ended

Marilynn Mair
spring 2021

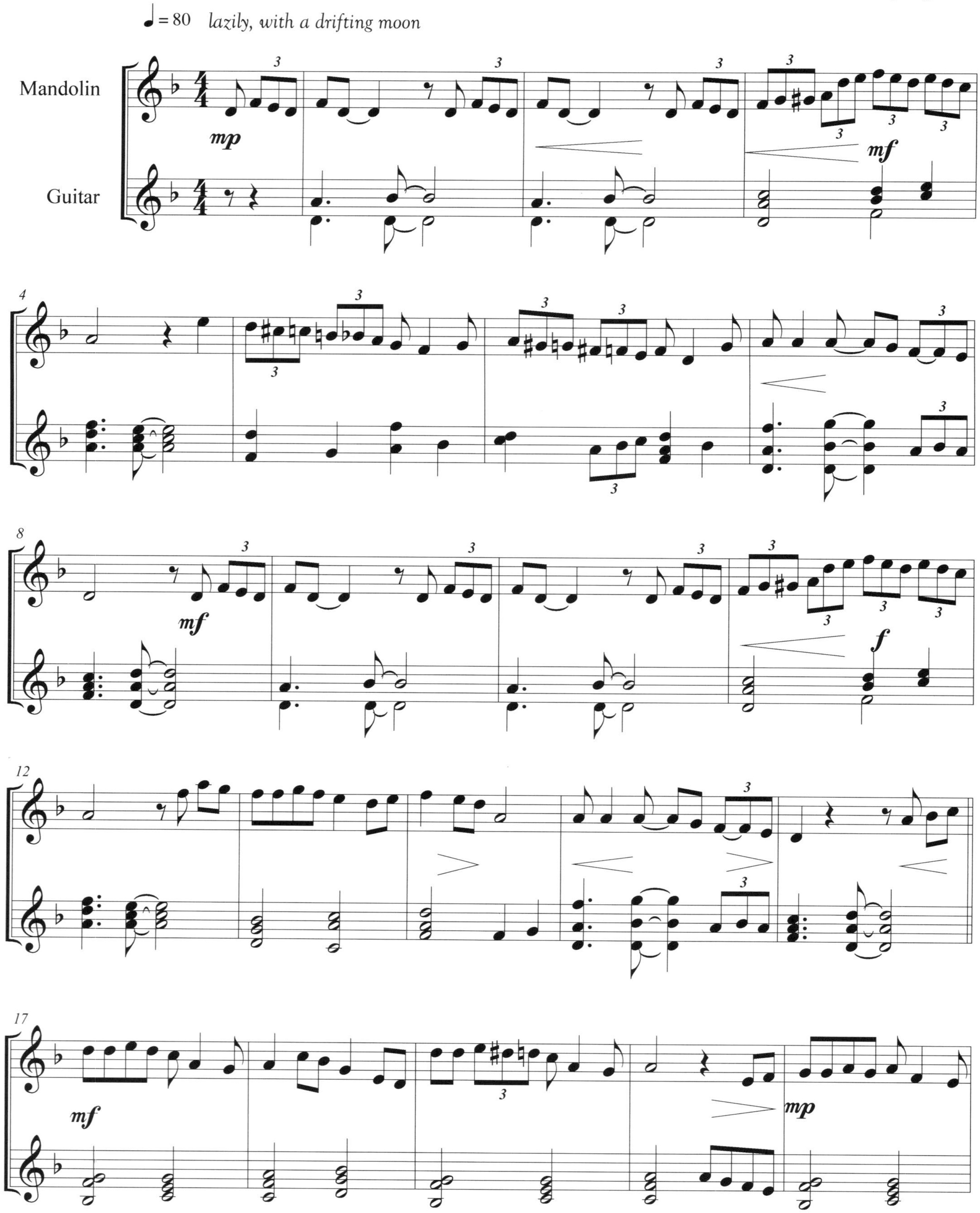

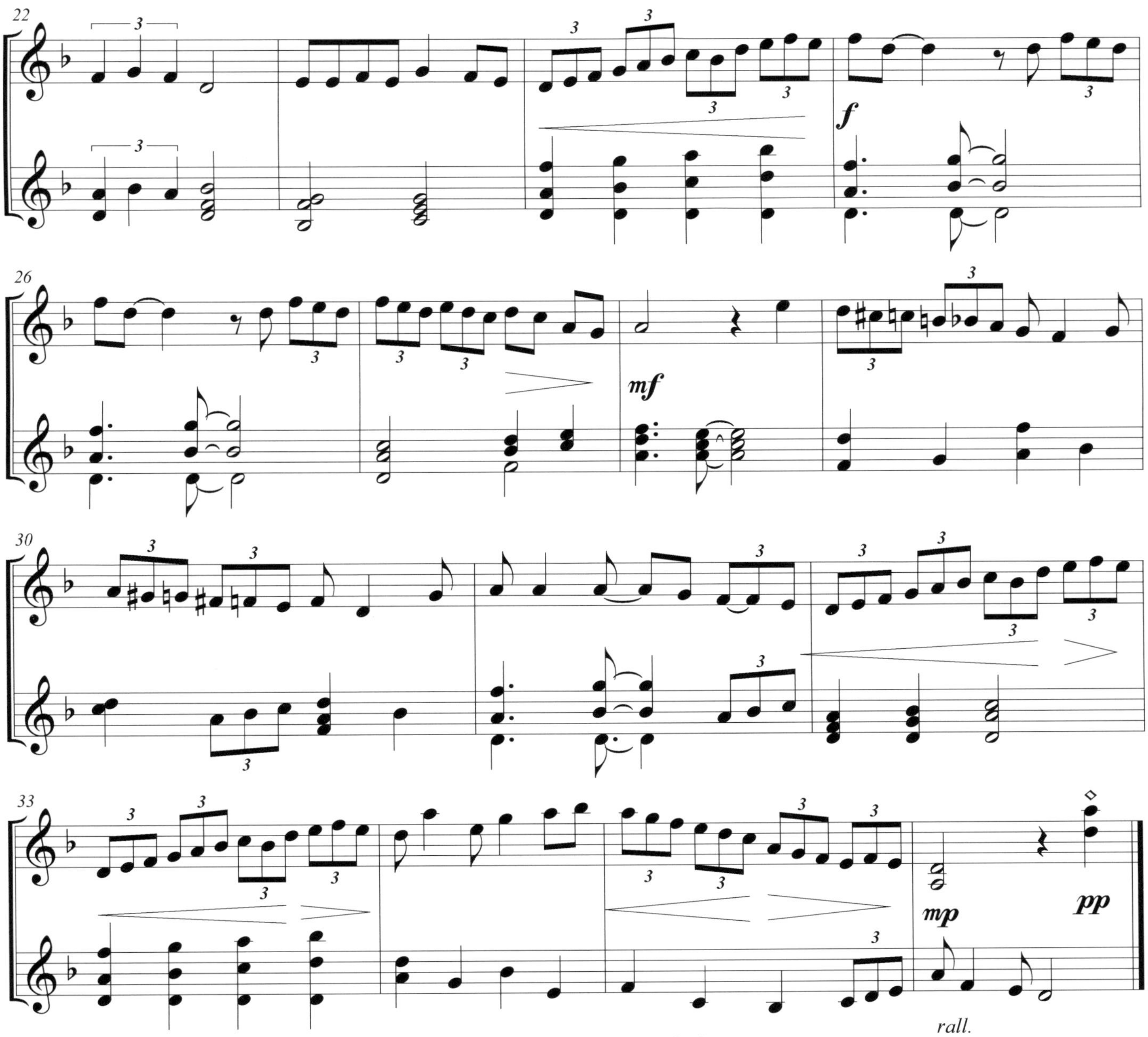

Only until this cigarette is ended
A little moment at the end of all
While on the floor the quiet ashes fall
And in the firelight to a lance extended
Bizarrely with the jazzing music blended
The broken shadow dances on the wall
I will permit my memory to recall
The vision of you, by all my dreams attended
And then adieu,—farewell!—the dream is done
Yours is a face of which I can forget
The color and the features, every one
The words not ever, and the smiles not yet;
But in your day this moment is the sun
Upon a hill, after the sun has set

Edna St. Vincent Millay, 1921

24

Nocturne 5

Mindful of you the sodden earth in spring

Marilynn Mair
spring 2021

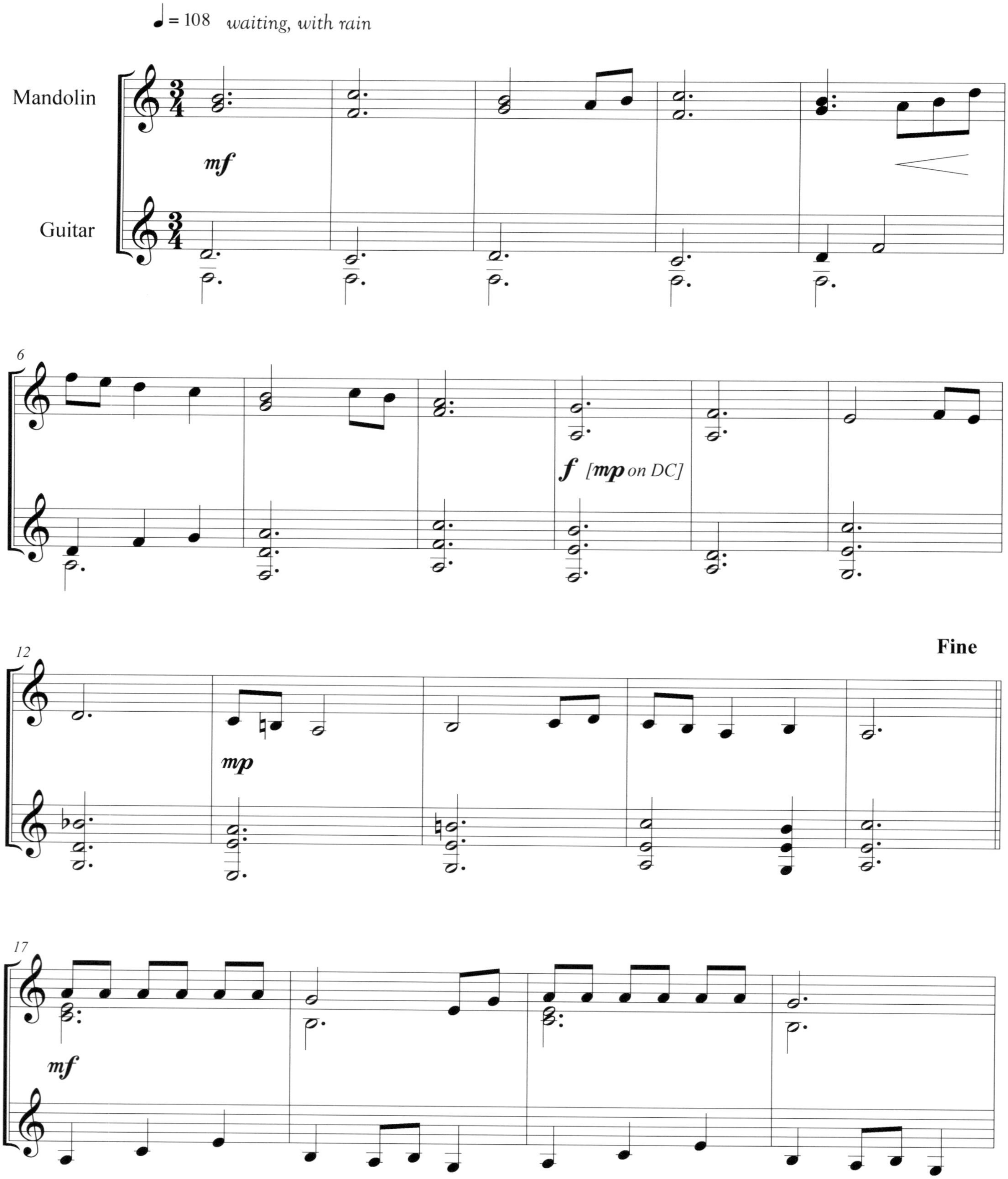

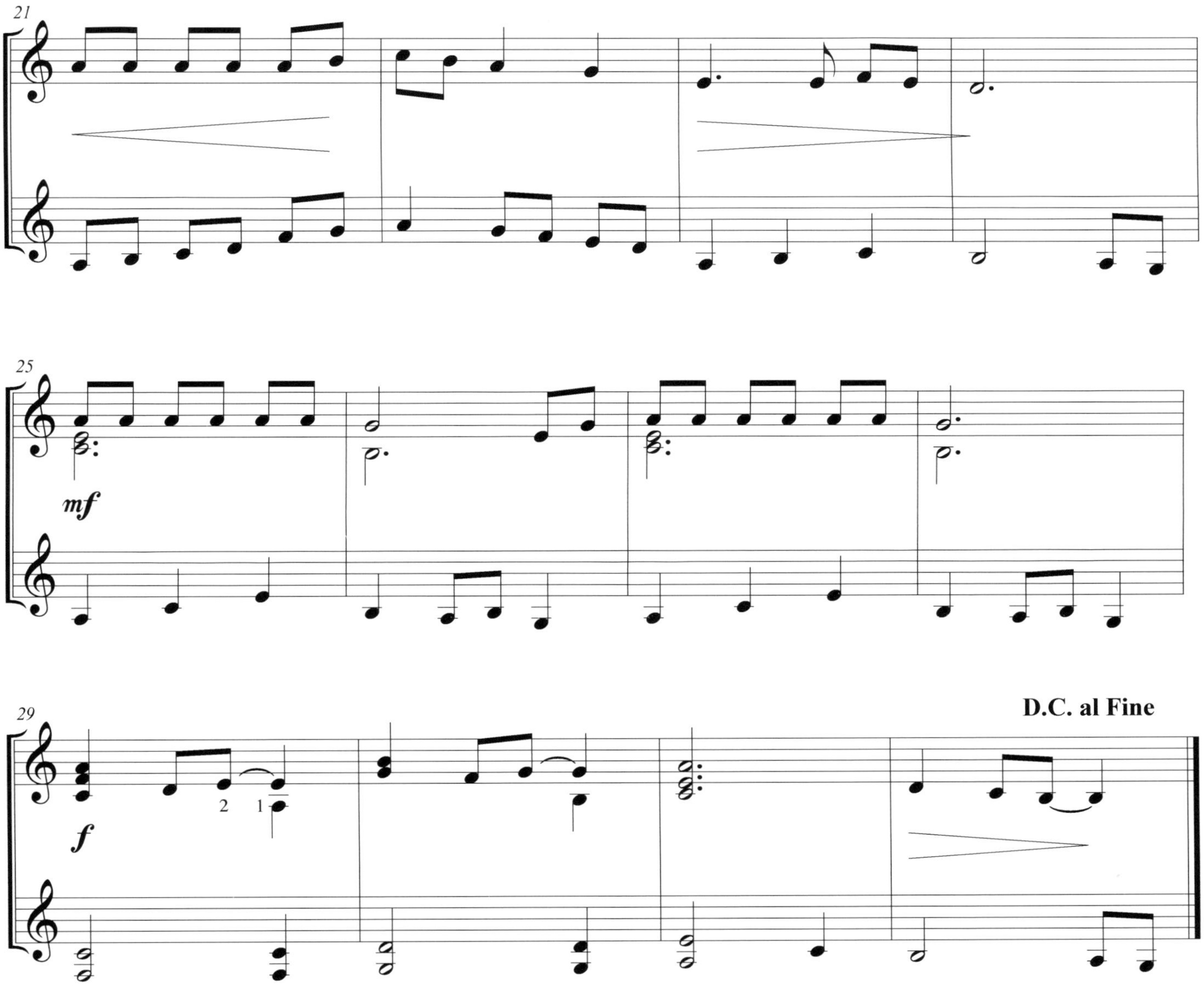

Mindful of you the sodden earth in spring,
And all the flowers that in the springtime grow,
And dusty roads, and thistles, and the slow
Rising of the round moon, all throats that sing
The summer through, and each departing wing,
And all the nests that the bared branches show,
And all winds that in any weather blow,
And all the storms that the four seasons bring.
You go no more on your exultant feet
Up paths that only mist and morning knew,
Or watch the wind, or listen to the beat
Of a bird's wings too high in air to view,—
But you were something more than young and sweet
And fair,—and the long year remembers you.

~ Edna St. Vincent Millay, 1917

25

Nocturne 6

The light comes back with Columbine

Marilynn Mair
autumn 2021

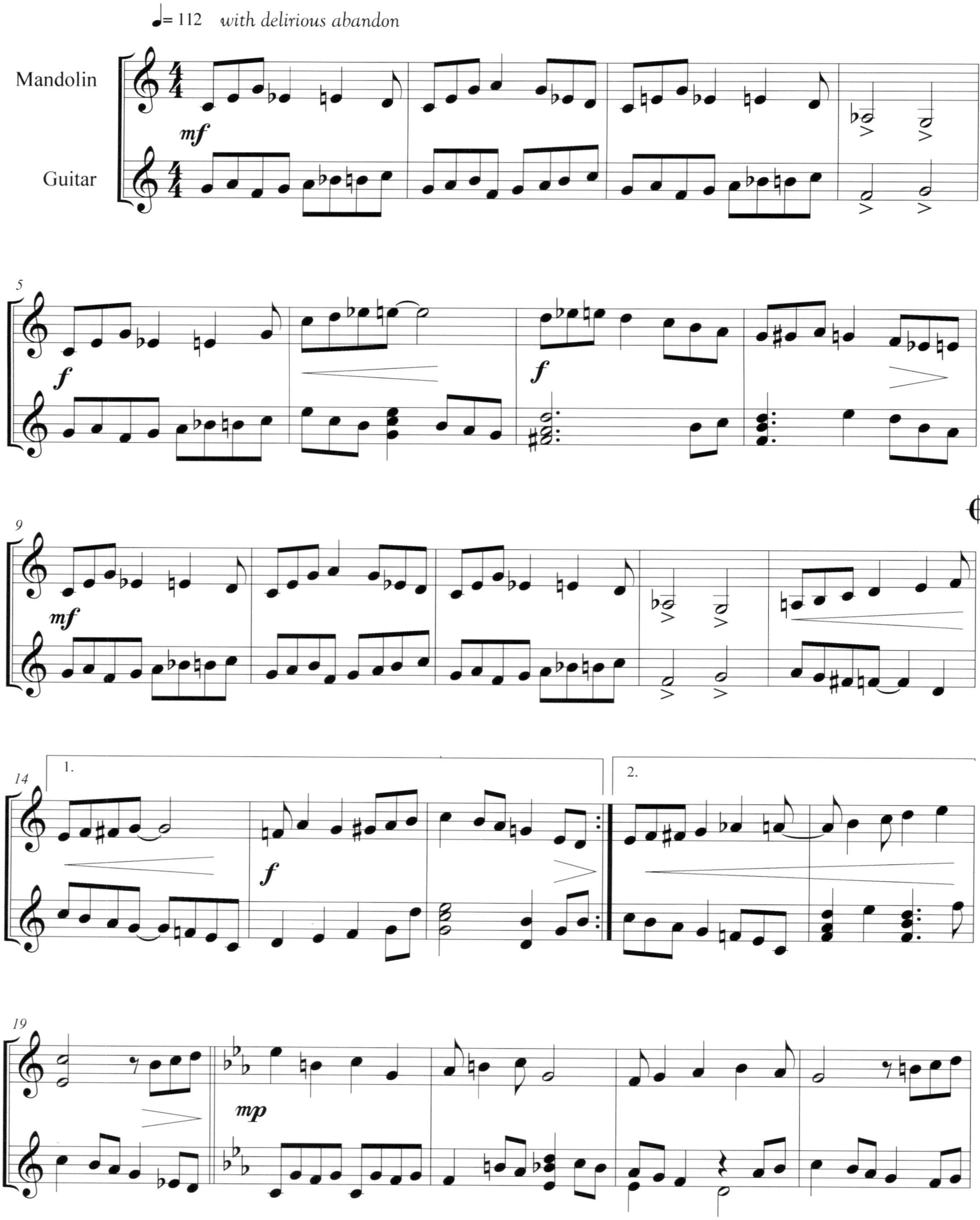

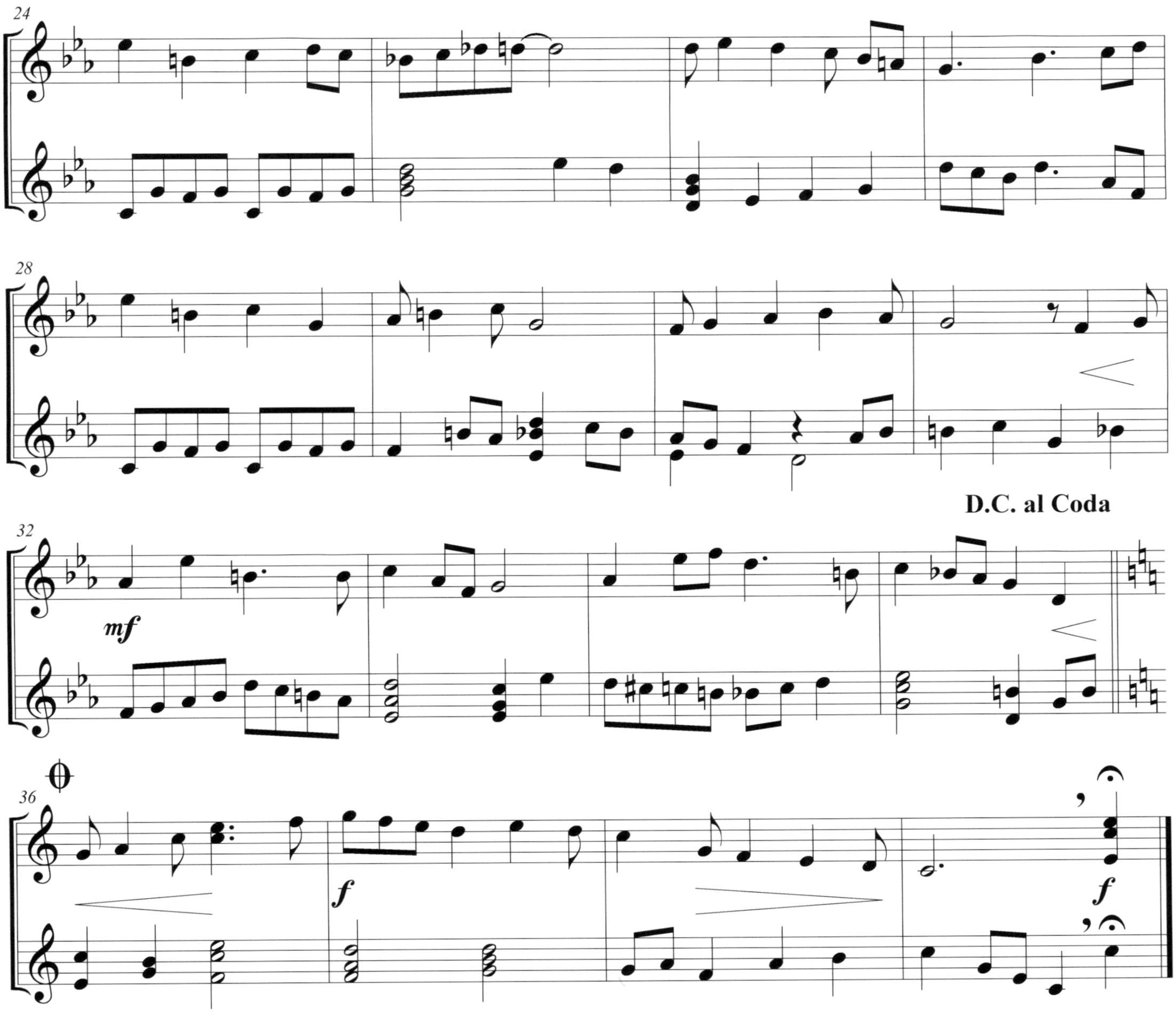

The light comes back with Columbine; she brings
A touch of this, a little touch of that,
Coloured confetti, and a favour hat,
Patches, and powder, dolls that work by strings
And moons that work by switches, all the things
That please a sick man's fancy, and a flat
Spry convalescent kiss, and a small pat
Upon the pillow,—paper offerings.
The light goes out with her; the shadows sprawl.
Where she has left her fragrance like a shawl
I lie alone and pluck the counterpane,
Or on a dizzy elbow rise and hark—
And down like dominoes along the dark
Her little silly laughter spills again!

Edna St. Vincent Millay, 1918

26

Nocturne 7

Women have loved before as I love now

Marilynn Mair
spring 2021

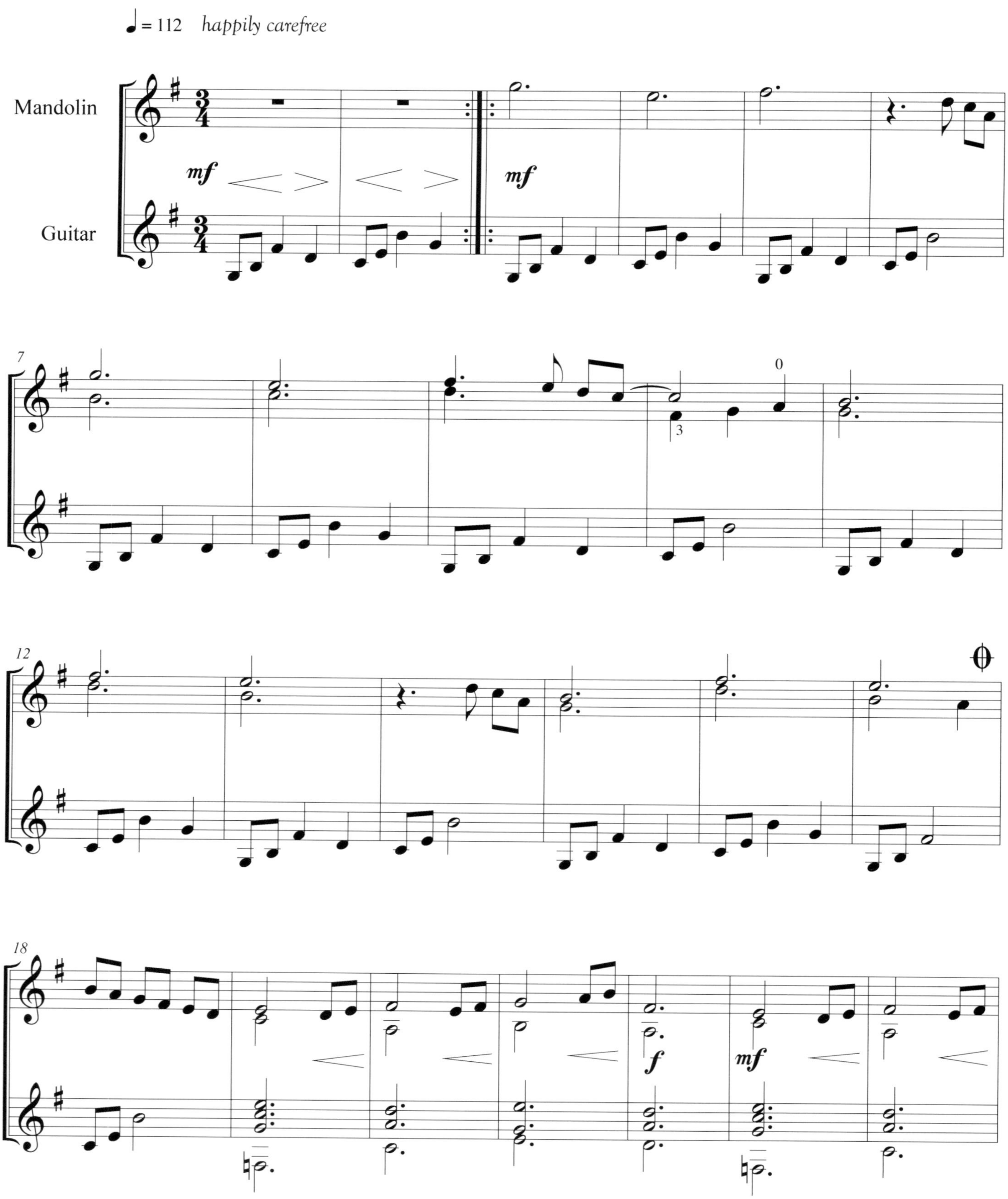

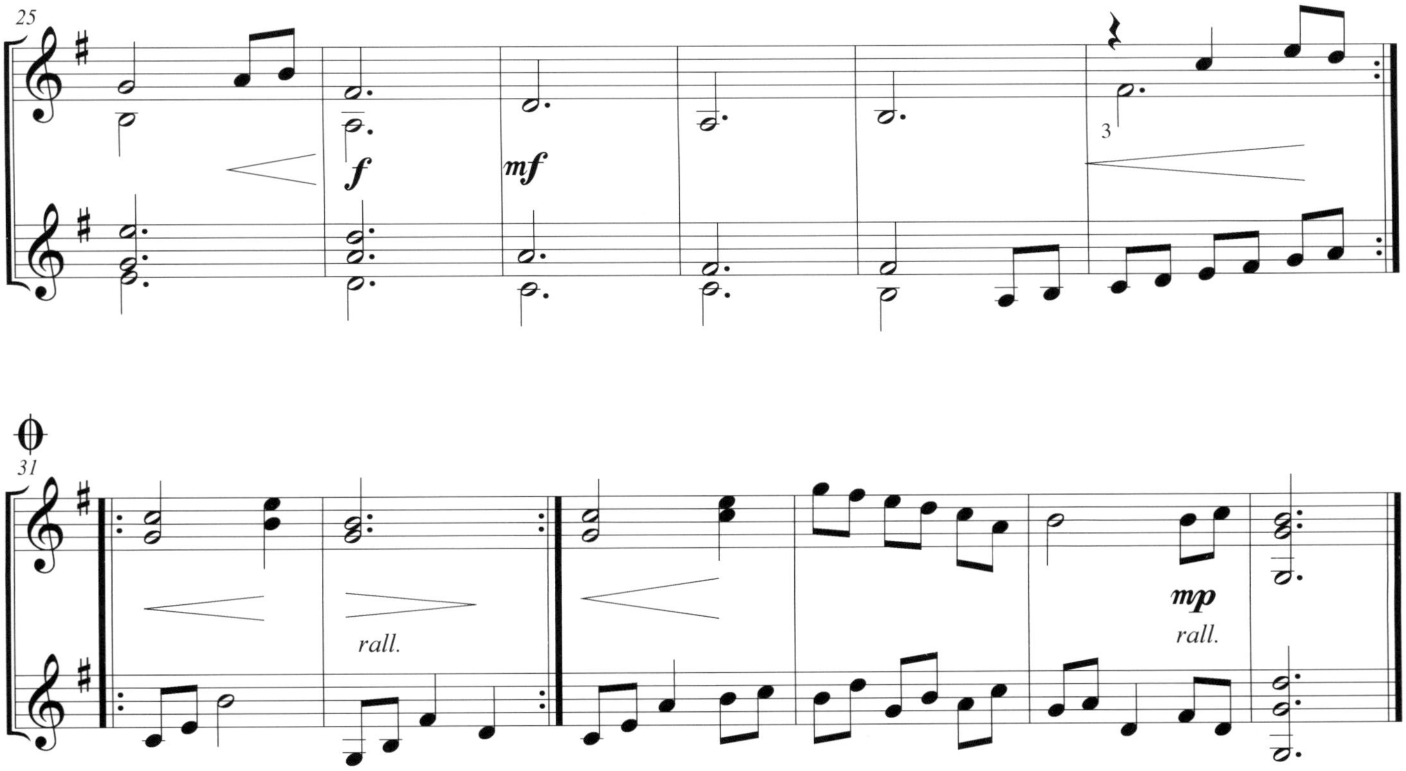

Women have loved before as I love now;
At least, in lively chronicles of the past—
Of Irish waters by a Cornish prow
Or Trojan waters by a Spartan mast
Much to their cost invaded—here and there,
Hunting the amorous line, skimming the rest,
I find some woman bearing as I bear
Love like a burning city in the breast.
I think however that of all alive
I only in such utter, ancient way
Do suffer love; in me alone survive
The unregenerate passions of a day
When treacherous queens, with death upon the tread,
Heedless and willful, took their knights to bed.

Edna St. Vincent Millay, 1931

27

Nocturne 8

Tranquility at length, when autumn comes

Marilynn Mair
autumn 2021

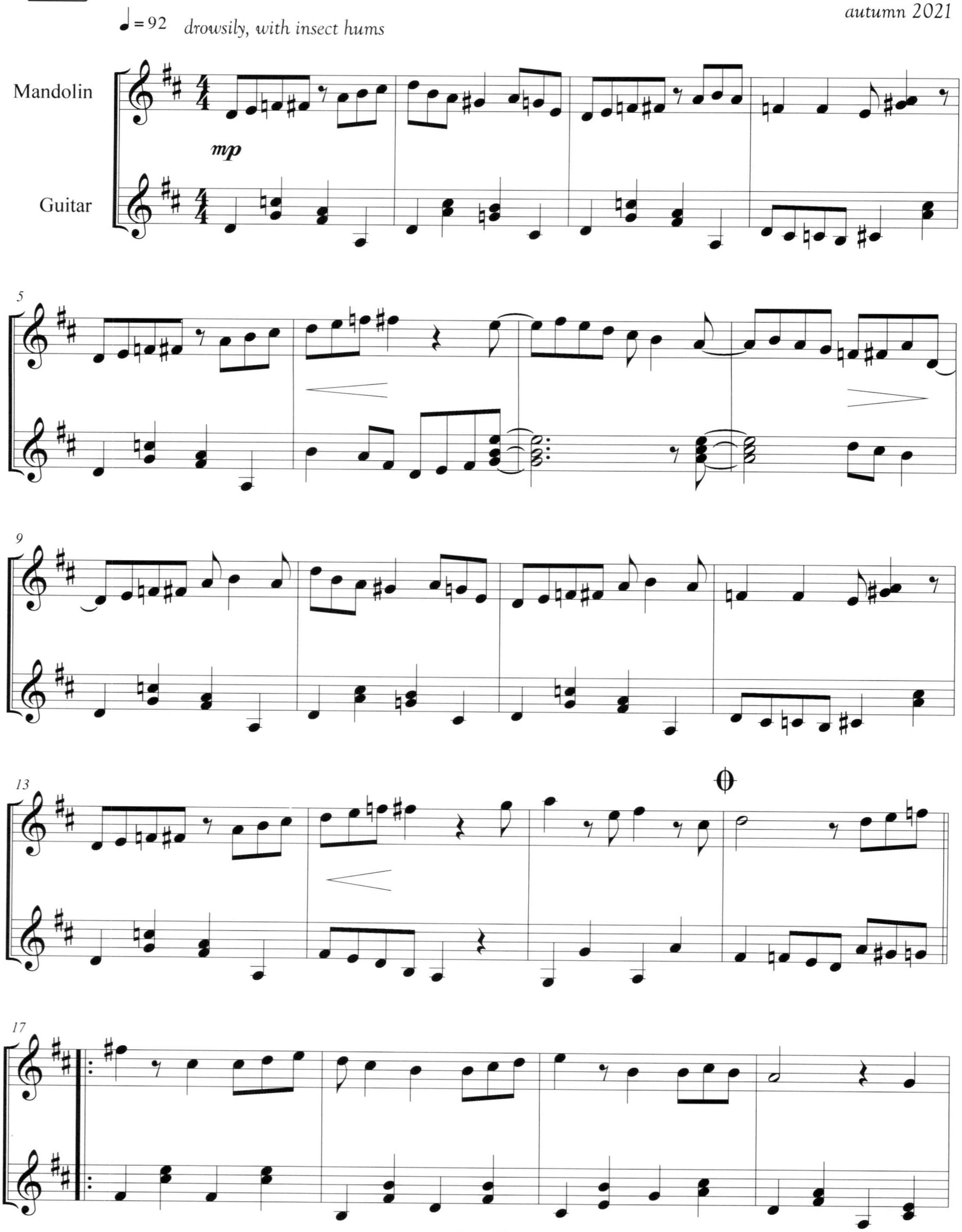

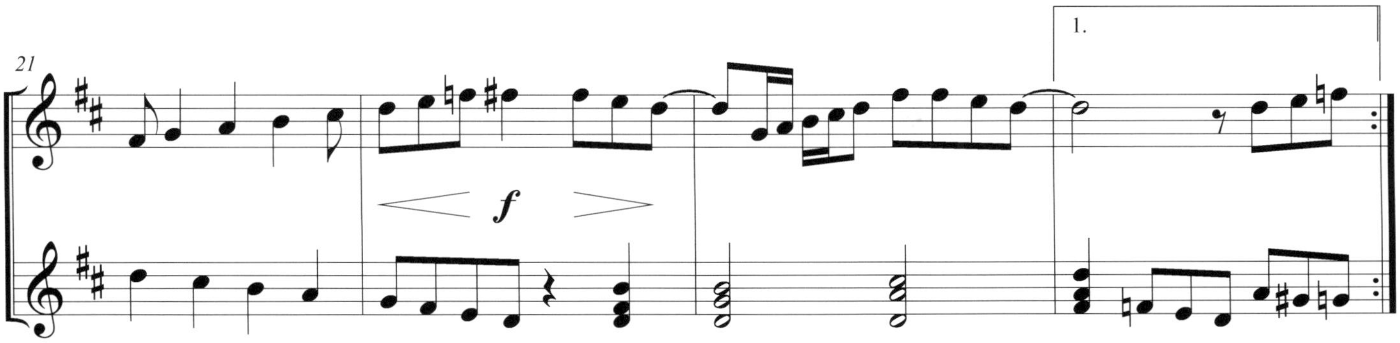

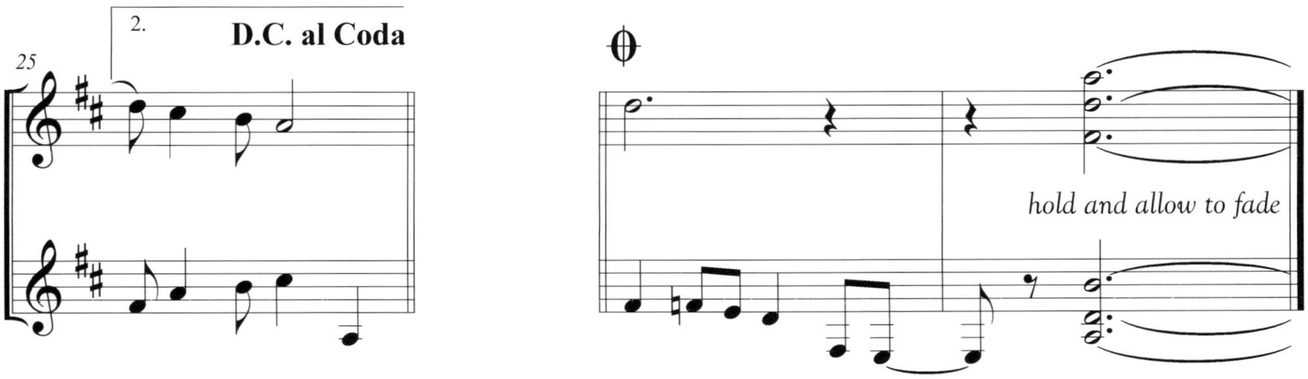

Tranquility at length, when autumn comes,
Will lie upon the spirit like that haze
Touching far islands on fine autumn days
With tenderest blue, like bloom on purple plums;
Harvest will ring, but not as summer hums,
With noisy enterprise — to broaden, raise,
Proceed, proclaim, establish: autumn stays
The marching year one moment; stills the drums.
Then sits the insistent cricket in the grass;
But on the gravel crawls the chilly bee;
And all is over that could come to pass
Last year; excepting this: the mind is free
One moment, to compute, refute, amass,
Catalogue, question, contemplate, and see.

Edna St. Vincent Millay, 1954

Choro—The Roots of Brazilian Music

Choro is one of the earliest music styles to originate in the Americas. It began in the mid-19th century, a time period that also saw the development of North American blues and ragtime, styles that led to jazz. These styles combine influences from European and African music, a hybridization characteristic of and unique to music of the Americas. But beyond similarities in roots and development, Choro music sounds very different from its North American counterparts. I have written an entire book for Mel Bay on Choro if you'd like to know more, but I'll briefly outline the parameters of the style for you here.

Choro is a syncopated music, written in 2/4 meter, usually in a form similar to the European rondo form: AA-BB-A-CC-A, sometimes with a Coda at the end. A 2-part form, AA-BB-A, is a modern variation. Choro is usually notated in leadsheet form, with a written melody and chord symbols. The biggest difference between Choro and jazz is in performance style, as the written Choro melody is never "swung." Unwritten rhythmic alterations are indeed part of Choro's performance style, but these mainly occur by 16th-note anticipation or delay, in sync with the typical accompaniment rhythm of | 𝅘𝅥𝅯♪𝅘𝅥𝅯_♪♪ |.

Tempos are mainly quick and melodies are virtuosic, although Choro *canção* are slower. *Valses* (waltzes) are also part of the repertoire, and their performance usually involves rubato. Choro melodies are complex and chromatic, yet clearly show their European roots. The standard Choro ensemble includes a *cucina* (kitchen *aka* rhythm section) consisting of 6- and 7-string guitars that play chords and basslines, a *cavaquinho* (a small ukulele-like instrument) and a *pandeiro* (a tambourine-like hand drum) that together play 16th-note rhythms. One or more soloists play the melody, but only one at a time, as soloists are expected to personalize their performance, adding ornaments or rhythmic alterations. If there are 2 or 3 soloists in a group, they take turns playing sections of the tune. When not playing melody, a soloist can improvise a counter melody, or join "the kitchen" and play chords. The only time all the soloists play together is on the final A section and Coda.

Few early Choro composers had music degrees or even formal lessons on their instruments. What they did have was a deep immersion in the style through regular and often competitive *rodas* (Choro jam sessions). As with any style of popular music written in leadsheet form, nuances of performance practice are largely absent from the written page. You need to hear the music played in its authentic context to understand those.

Early on in my love affair with Choro I realized I had to go to Rio de Janeiro to play with Brazilians, to figure out the stylistic parameters of Choro for myself. There, my trajectory as a performer and composer was shaped by the Rio *rodas* I played in, my weekly lessons with bandolim master Joel Nascimento, *Escola Portátil de Música* (the Saturday Choro school), and my Brazilian bandolim friends—especially Paolo Sá and Marcilio Lopes. It's been an enlightening and intoxicating journey. One of my favorite memories, following a particularly good *roda* session in Rio, was when a musician who didn't know me expressed surprise that I was from the USA, pronouncing my playing, "*bem brasileiro*," truly Brazilian. It was a dream come true.

"First you dream and then you lace up your boots."
– Portia White, early 20th-century musician

Choro
do Brasil

Garoa [Drizzling]
Siga em Frente [Go Straight Ahead]
Por Que Não? [Why Not?]
Isso [That's It]
Madrugada [Daybreak]
Farrapinho [A Little Rag]
Sonatinha [Sonatina]
Um Quinto do Ludwig [A Fifth of Ludwig]
Balbuciando [Mumbling]
Outro Verão [Another Summer]
Uma Coisa Feliz [A Happy Thing]
Enrolado [Spaceshot]
Terças no Trapiche [Tuesdays at Trapiche]
Nadando em Luz [Swimming in Light]
Faça a Pergunta [Ask the Question]
Se Não Agora [If Not Now]
É Bom Saber [Good to Know]
Estação Carioca [Carioca Station]
Buscando Baden [Chasing Baden]
Saudade do Rio [Missing Rio]

written from 2007 through 2021

About My Choro

I began writing Choro as playing it became second nature, and the melodies popping up in my head begged to be explored. I had some help early on, moving harmonies away from my default classical setting, along with welcome encouragement to continue writing, from Brazilian friends who enjoyed the originality of my work. I've included most of my Choro in the next section of the book. Unlike the previous pieces, born out of pandemic isolation during the past two years, my Choro span 15 years, and most were written in Rio, where the flow of language and music inspires me. Writing Choro, for me, was a compositional breakthrough. I went from composing for events, usually writing for a specific group or occasion, to creating and recording a series of original works in a particular style.

As is the custom when writing Choro, many of my pieces have dedications to players and friends. The titles are quirky, and I have written them in Portuguese with an English translation. As a composer who comes to Choro from a classical background, with a lifelong immersion in rock and jazz, I have many varied sources of inspiration to draw upon when composing. As a result, although some of my Choro are completely original, inspired by my adventures in Rio, others I call "hybrid," as they weave classical or popular themes into a Choro context. This "hybrid" idea of music is one that I particularly enjoy, you saw it in my Fantasias for two mandolins, as it suits my eclectic musical background.

My Choro leadsheets are mostly written in the traditional 3-part form, with an AA-BB-A-CC-A-Coda roadmap. You will always find a Coda symbol in the A section of my Choro. On the 3rd time through A, this indicates you jump to the C section. On the 4th time through, it marks a jump to the Coda, if there is one. As is traditional, the sections are not labeled, but they are easy to recognize, and they frequently change key signature. Tempo markings are also absent, as these are not traditionally notated either. Most of my Choro are meant to be played at a lively tempo. Besides leadsheets, Choro are also written or arranged for ensembles, with a score and set of parts. I've arranged many Choro to play with my octet Enigmatica, and written a couple of my own for the group, which you will find in the "Ensemble" section of this book.

I have included a few CD recordings of my Choro with this book, and I list the CDs where you can hear others in the Appendix. I did write two Choro during the pandemic, dedicating them to bandolimist friends from Rio who I was missing, Marcílio Lopes and Paulo Sá. Happily for us all, at my request, they each recorded theirs and sent the recordings so I could include them in this book. *Muito obrigada, meus amigos do música!*

My Choro have been influenced by many Brazilians, some of whom I've played with, others who are merely ghosts whose music has whispered enticingly in my ear. All are imbued with the glories of Rio as I have found them. Your travel adventure awaits ahead—enjoy!

"To create one's own world takes courage." – Georgia O'Keeffe, painter

Garoa

Drizzling

ao Choro das 3: Corina, Lia, Elisa, e Dudu

Marilynn Mair

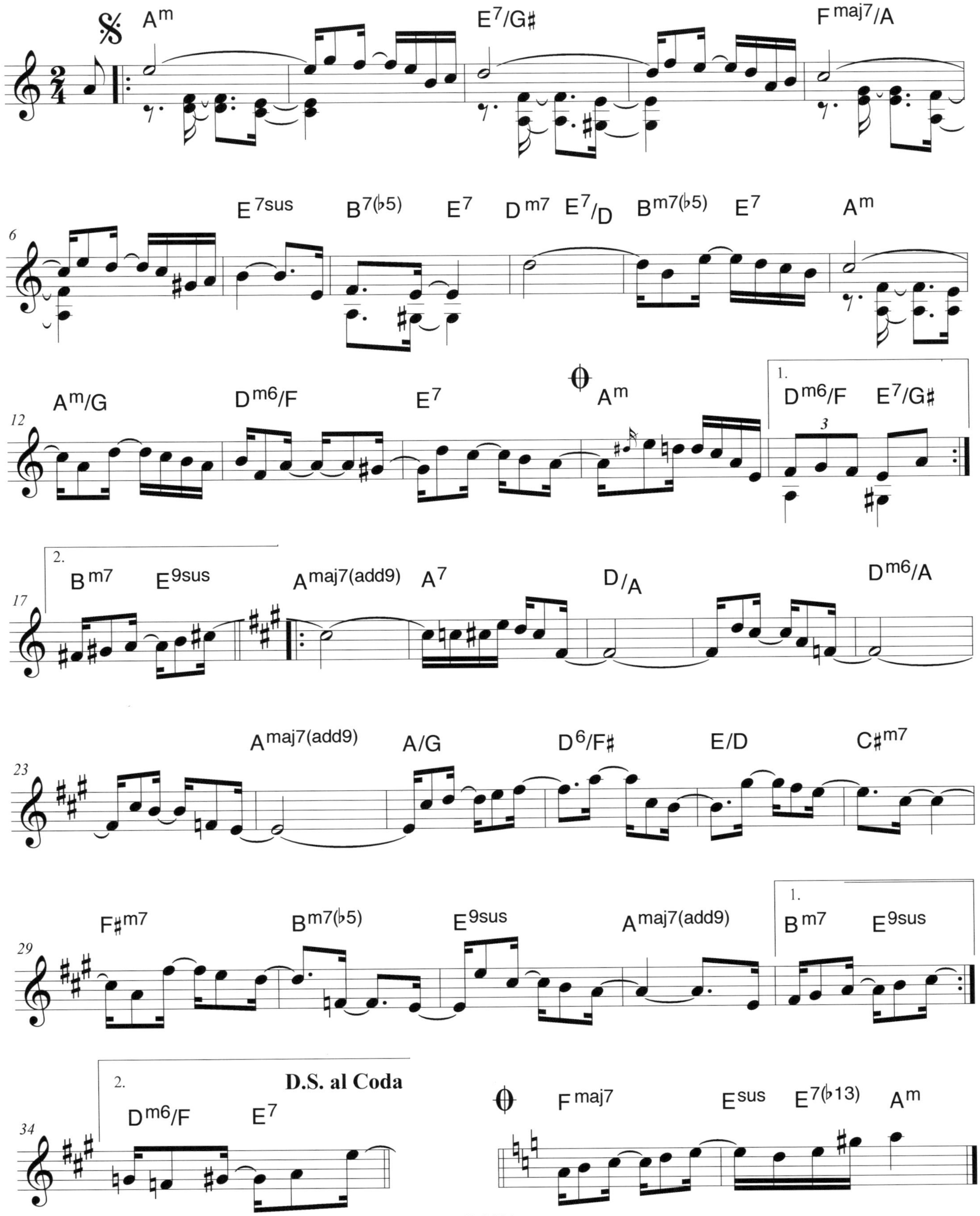

28

Siga em Frente

Go Straight Ahead

ao Paulo, o meu amigo do taxi

Marilynn Mair

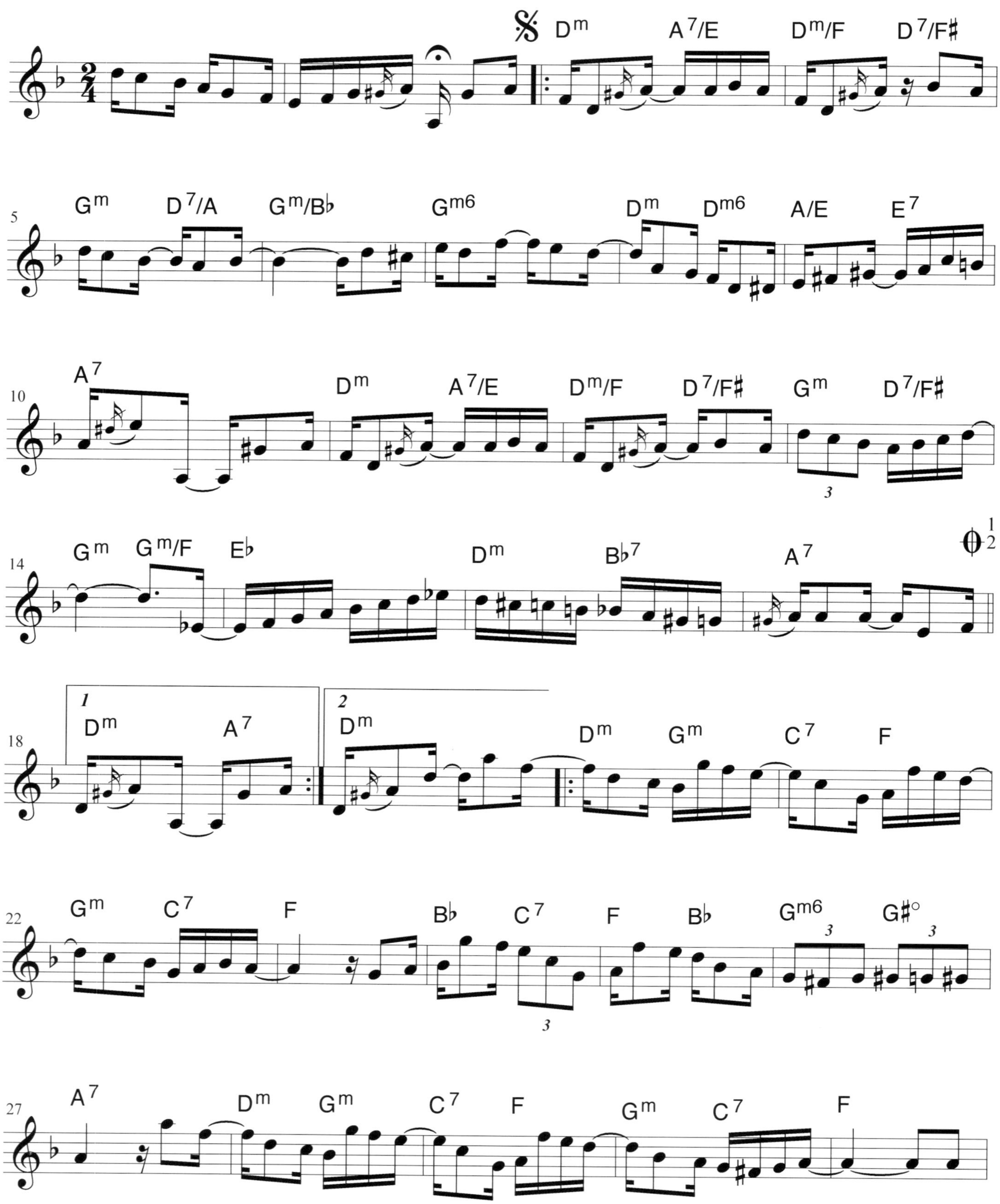

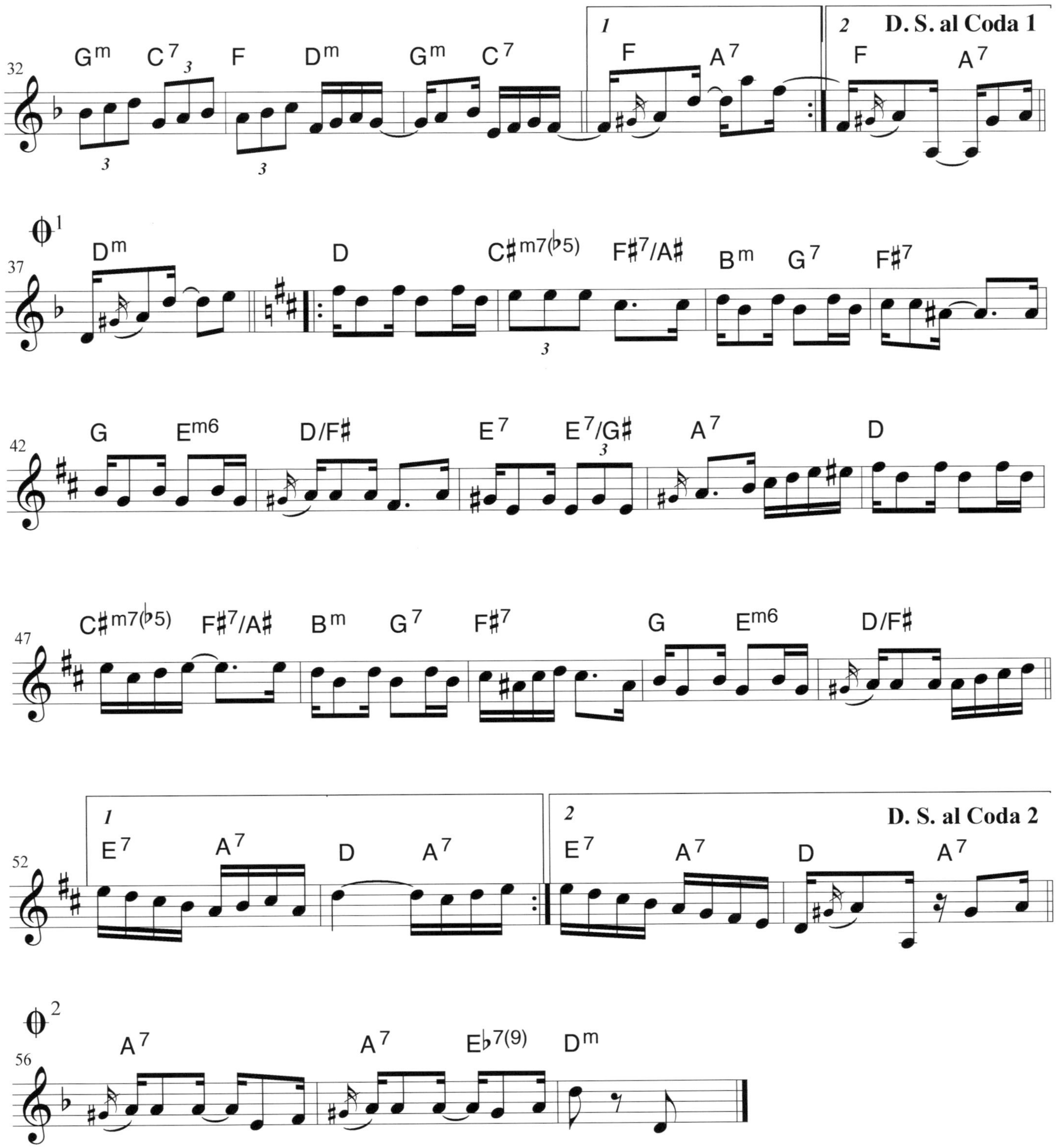

This is the first Choro I wrote after my stay in Rio in 2007. “Siga em frente” is an instruction I often gave on my taxi rides home. I dedicated this piece to my regular taxi driver, who got me safely to and from many bandolim lessons, concerts, and rodas. This is a lively Choro, meant to express the often nail-biting frenzy of a car ride through Rio, a city where I will never attempt to drive.

Por que não?

Why Not?

ao meu regional, Água no Feijão

Marilynn Mair

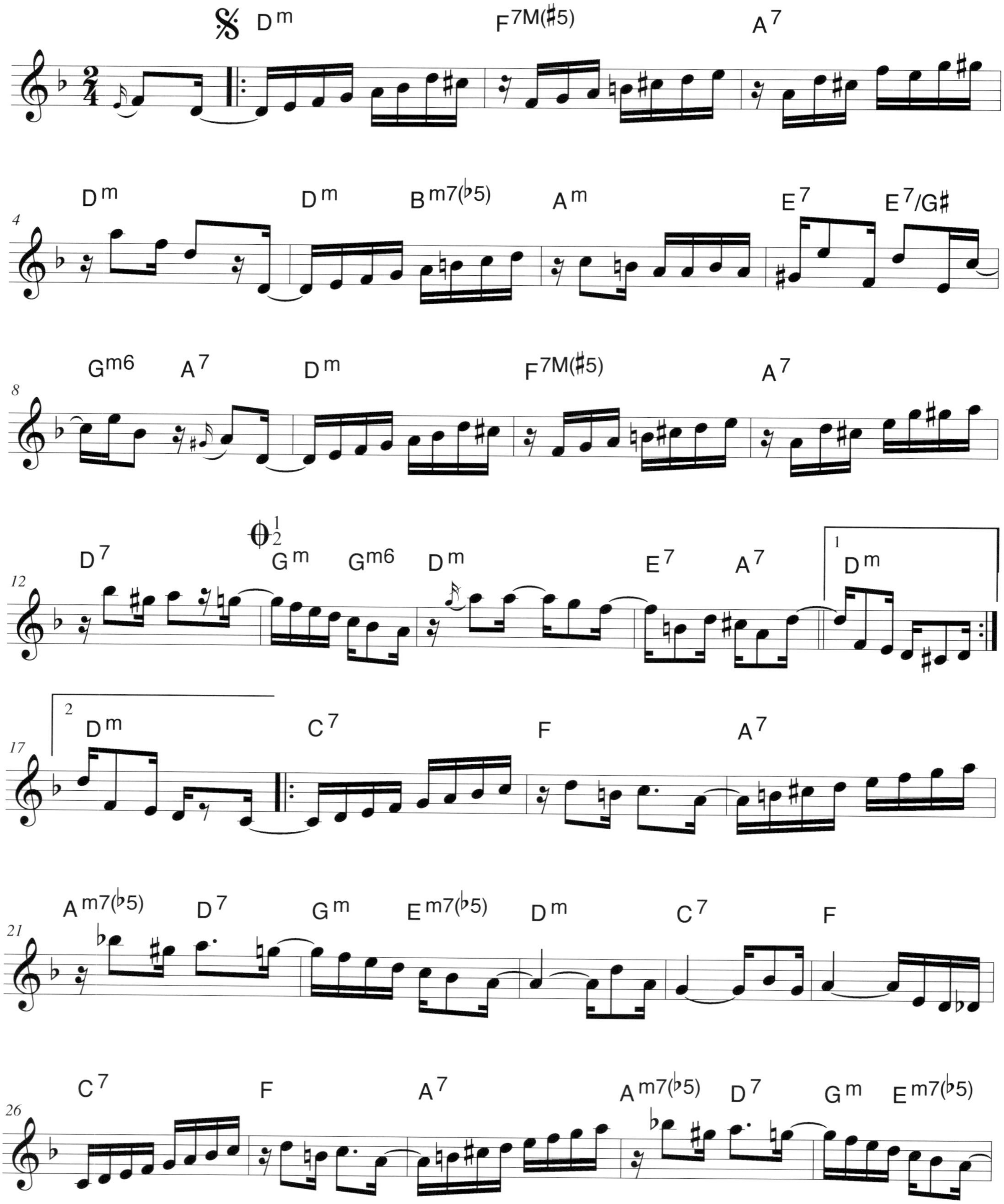

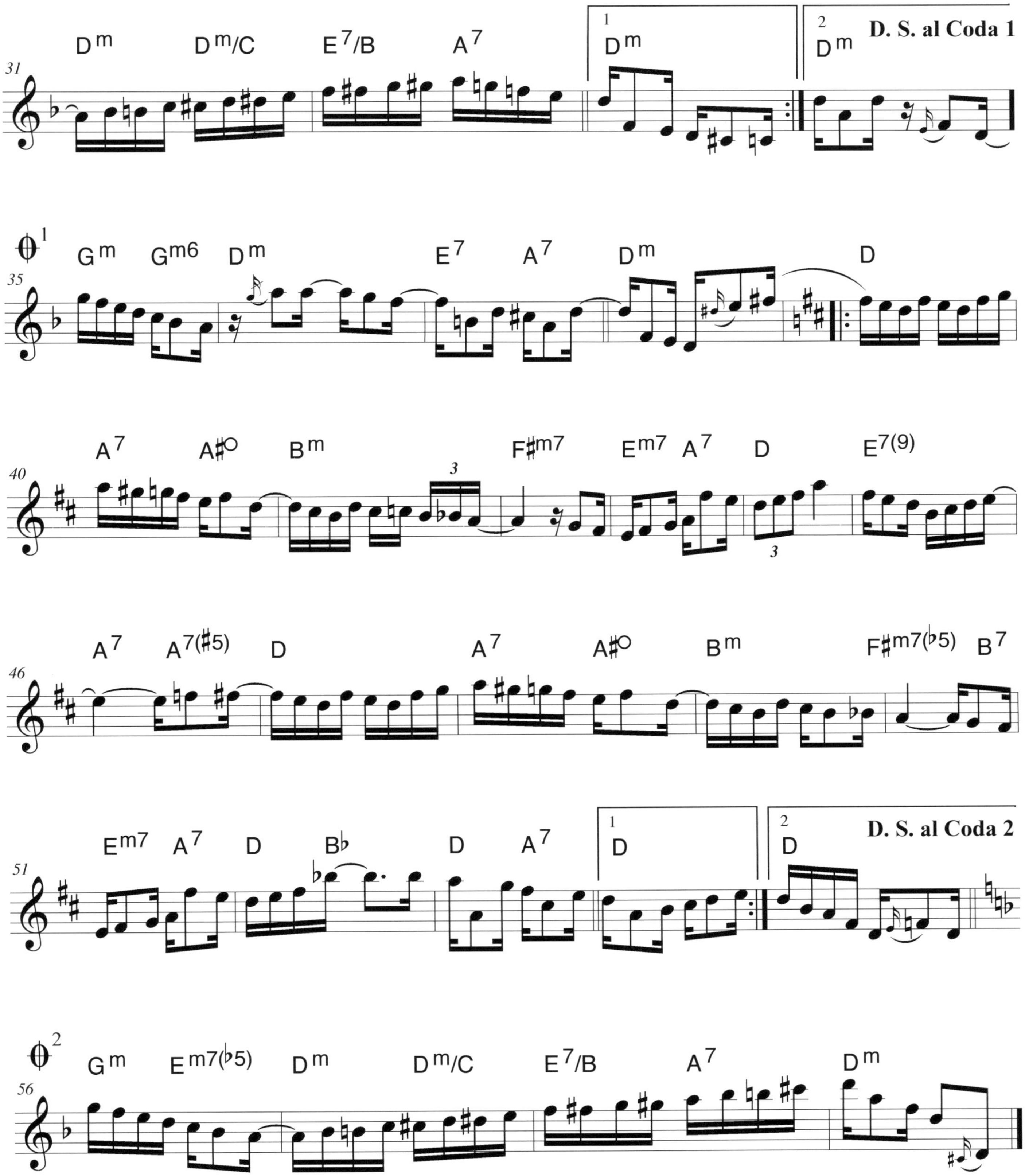

I wrote this Choro for my Rio band, *Água no Feijão*. We met and began playing during my first stay in Rio, in 2007, when I didn't know very much Portuguese. Often one of them would rattle off a long question and look to me for an answer or opinion. Whether I understood everything or not, my reply was usually, "Por que não?" This is a lively Choro with an off-balance sense of expectation. The grace notes are to be played as a slide into or simultaneously with the main note.

29

Isso

That's It

ao Joel Nascimento

Marilynn Mair

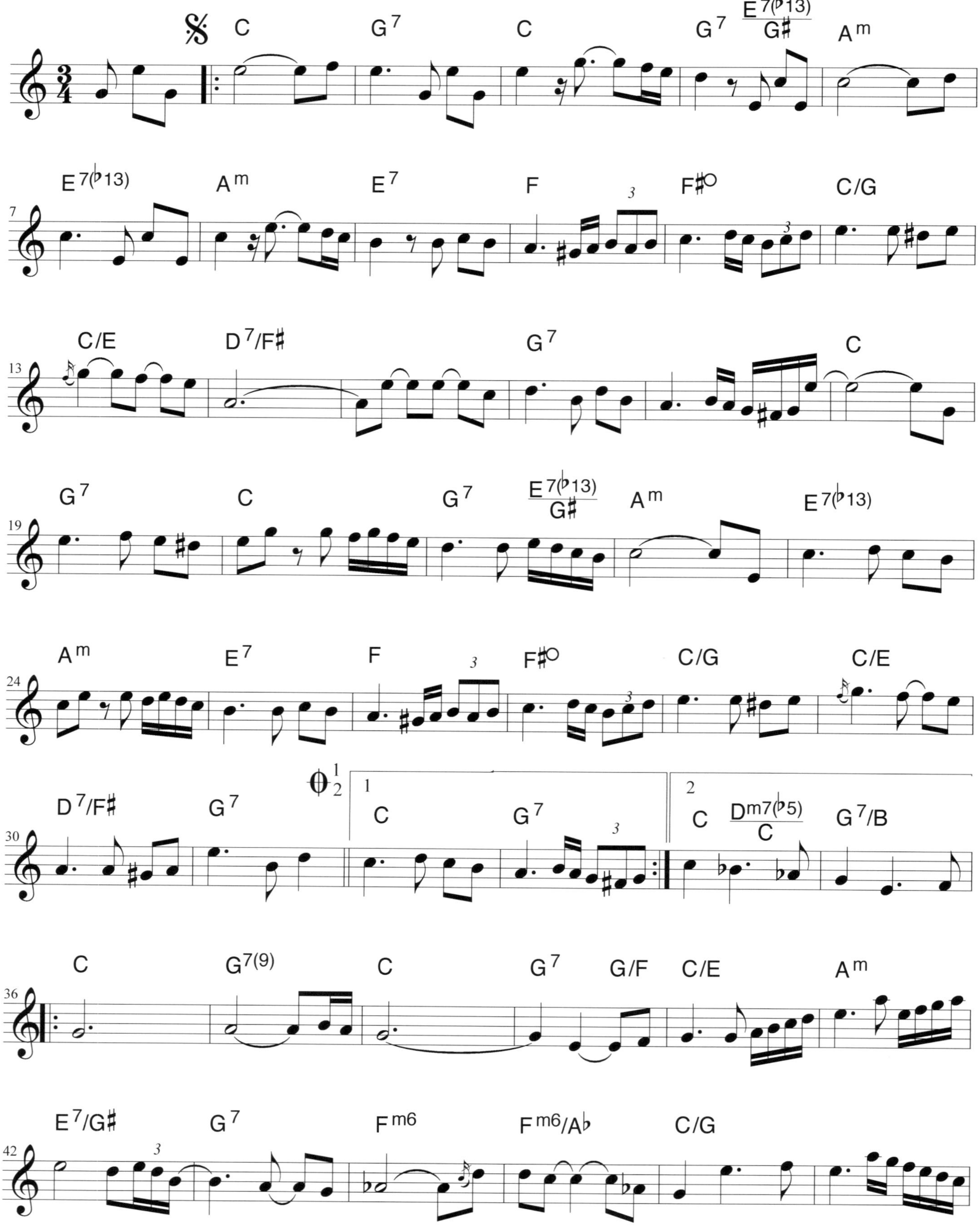

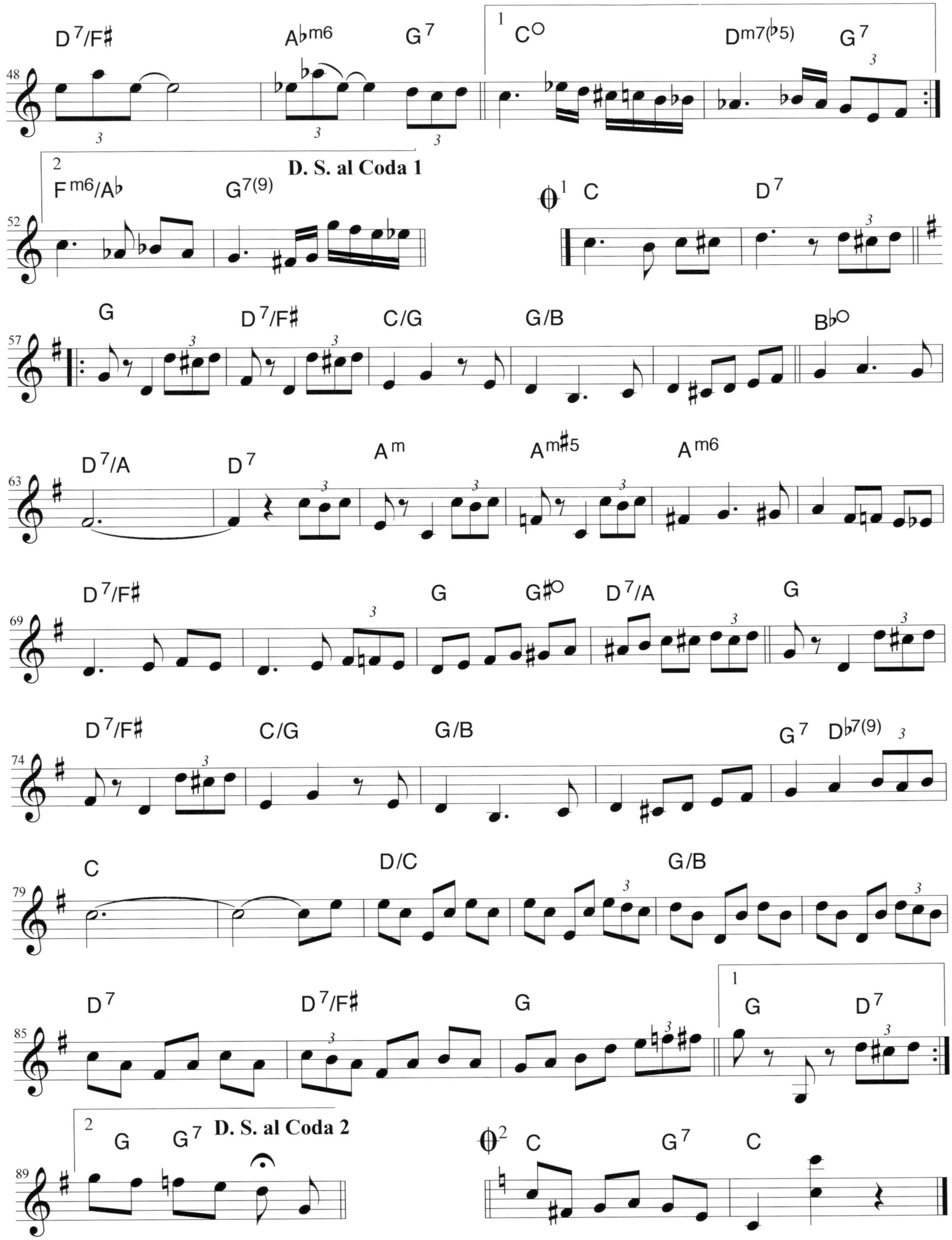

I wrote this *valse* for my bandolim teacher, the brilliant Joel Nascimento. "Isso" means "that's it," and it was a rare compliment from him that I treasured. Joel is known for his waltz style, incorporating lots of rubato.

30

Madrugada

Daybreak

Marilynn Mair

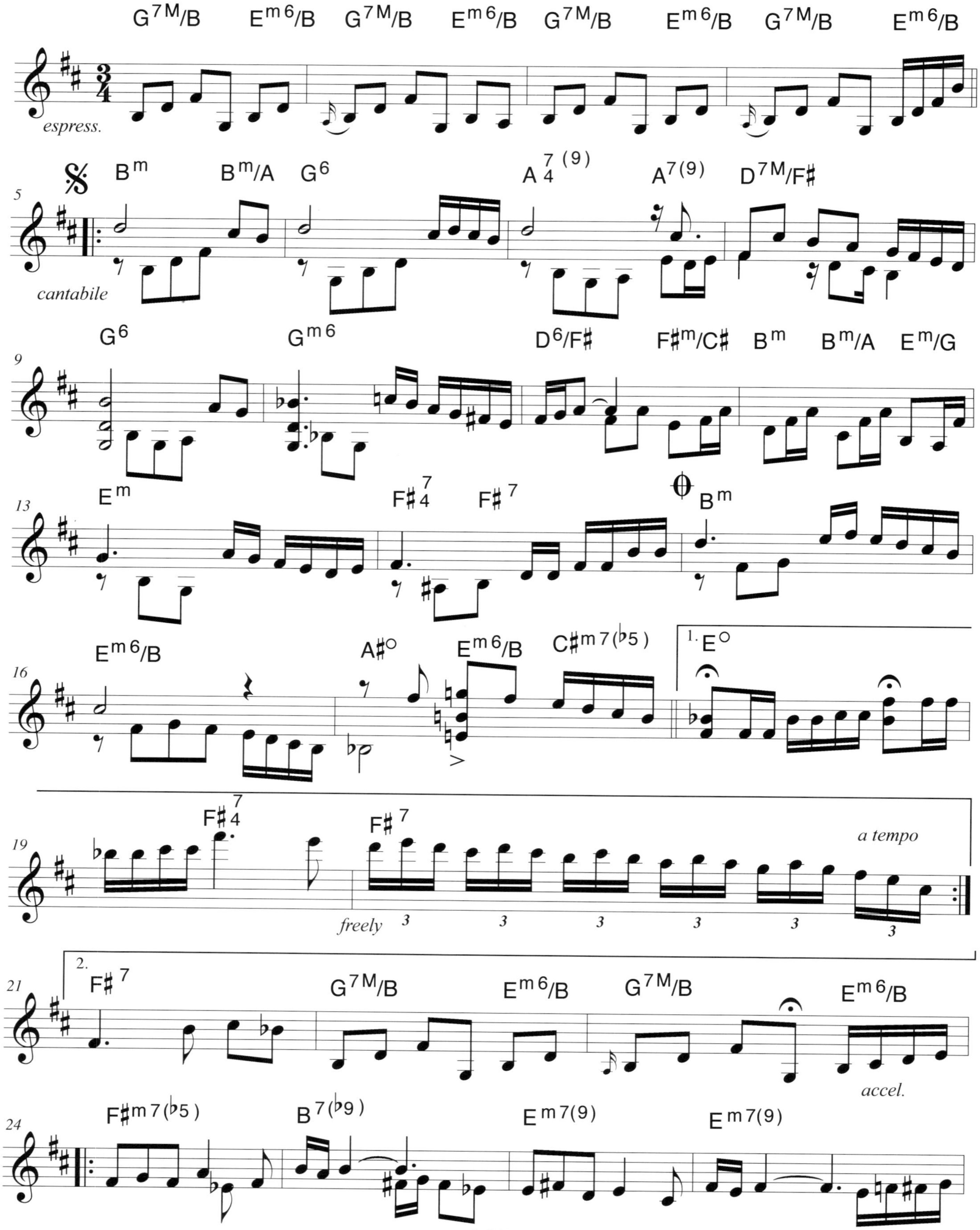

lively, to be played like a jazz waltz in 3/8

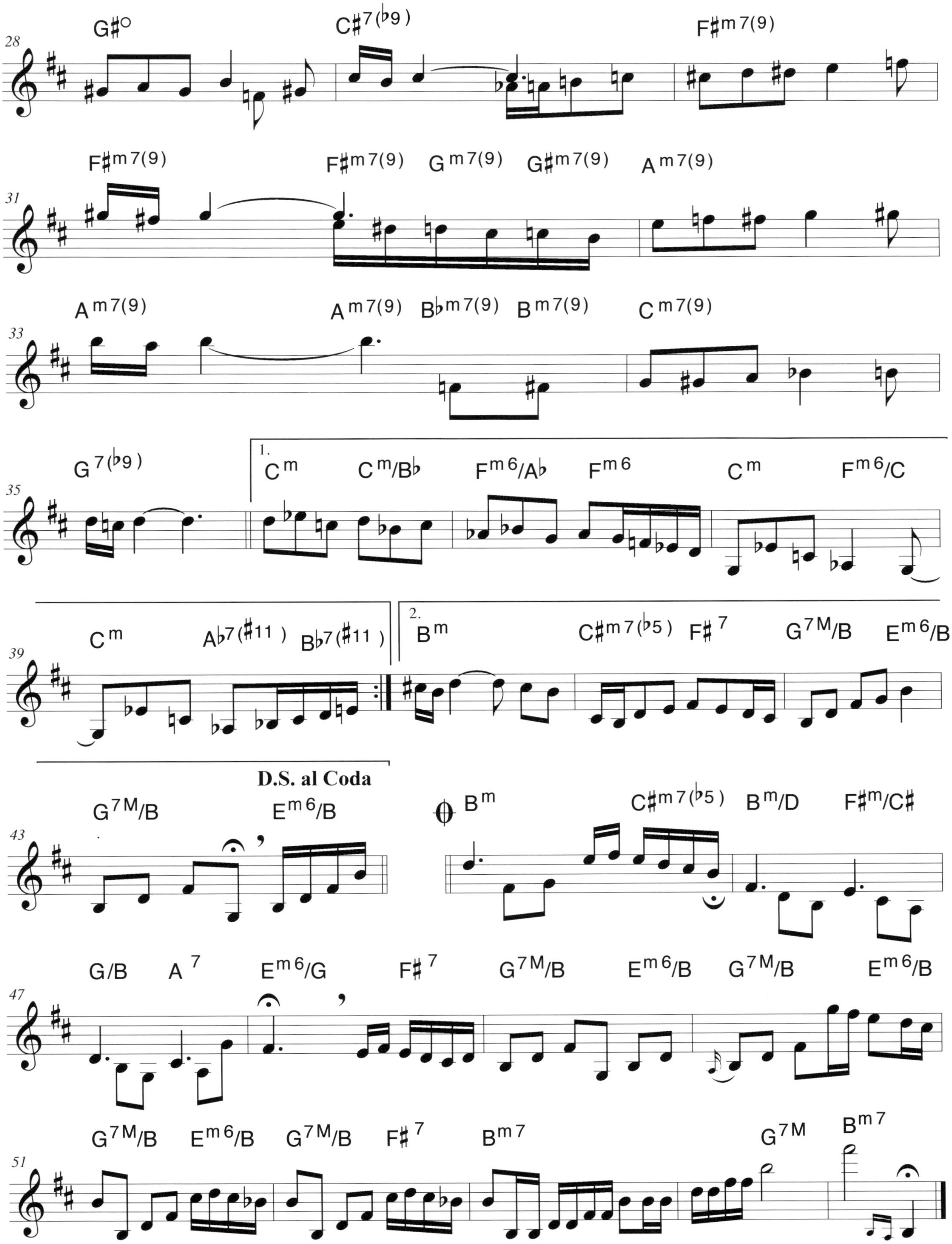

This piece is one of my series of hybrid Choro, combining influences from the different musical areas of my life. It was inspired by Astor Piazzolla's tangos, and a dawn walk home in Buenos Aires on New Year's Day.

Farrapinho

A Little Rag

for Dylan & Spencer

Marilynn Mair

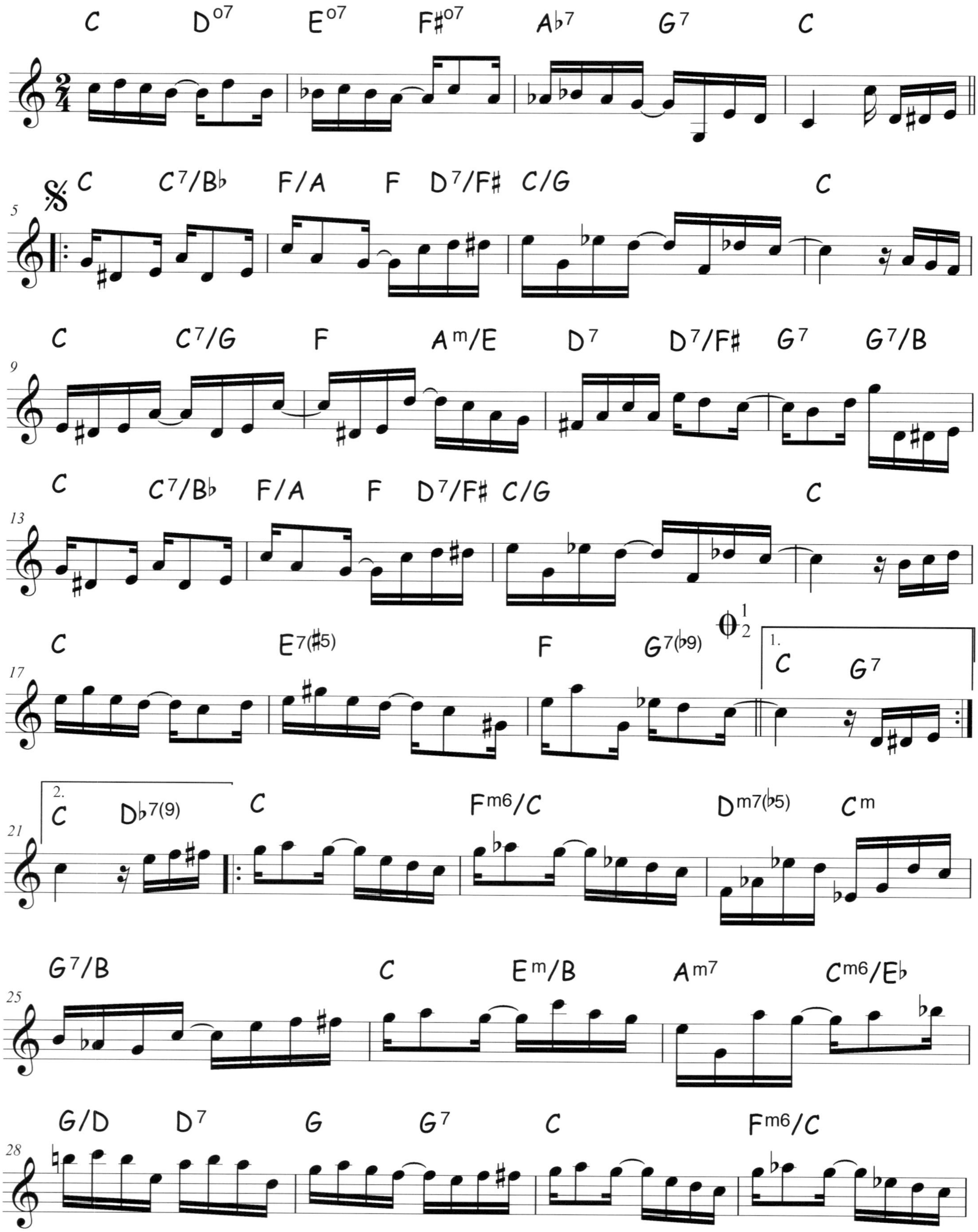

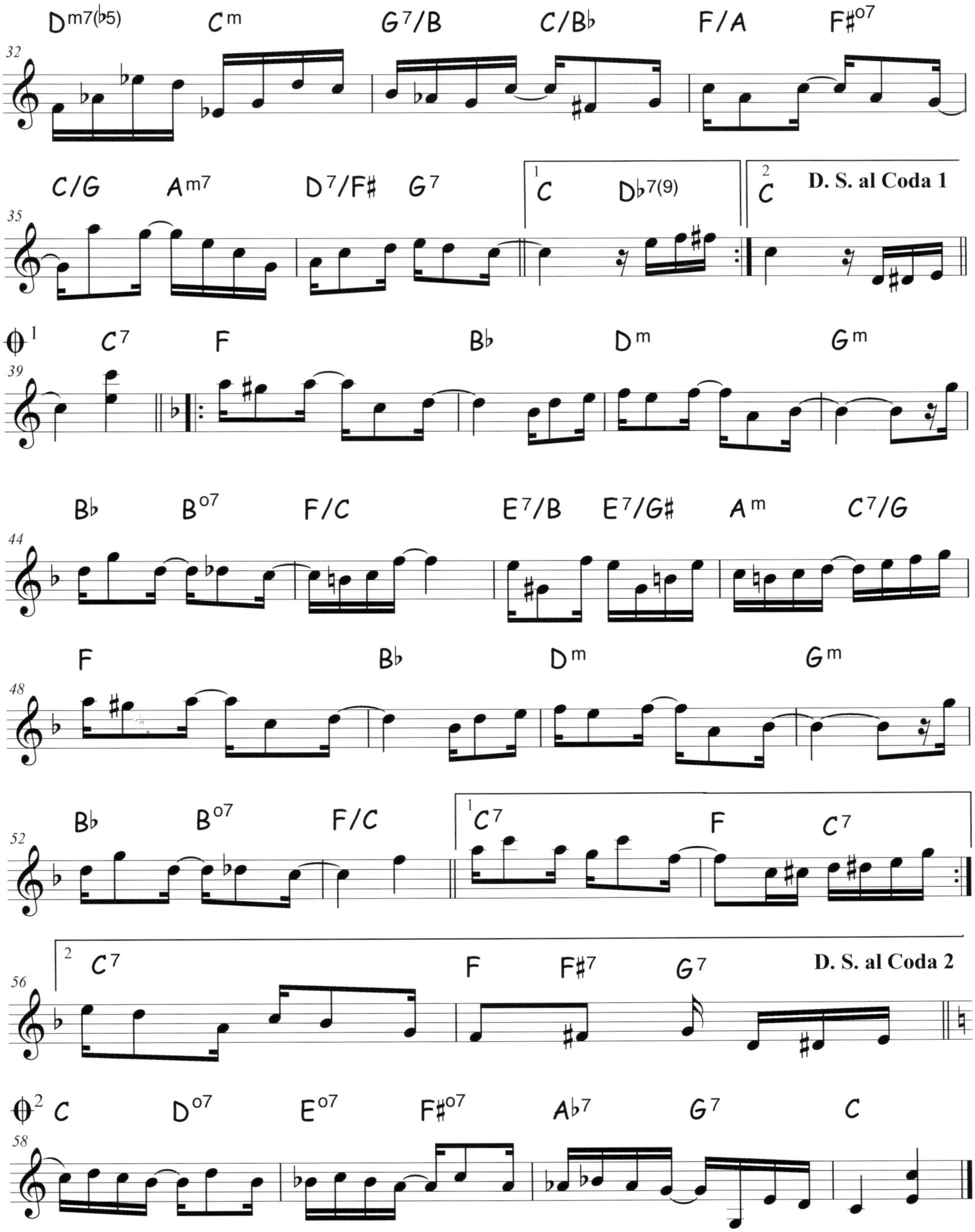

A piece from my hybrid Choro series, this one inspired by a famous ragtime composition written by Scott Joplin. The name is a pun of sorts as a *farrapo* is a rag and a *farrapinho* is its diminutive. I dedicated it to my delightful grandboys who love to dance. Play it languidly, and not too fast, as befits a ragtime piece.

Sonatinha

after Beethoven's Sonatina for Mandolin

ao Fernando Duarte

Marilynn Mair

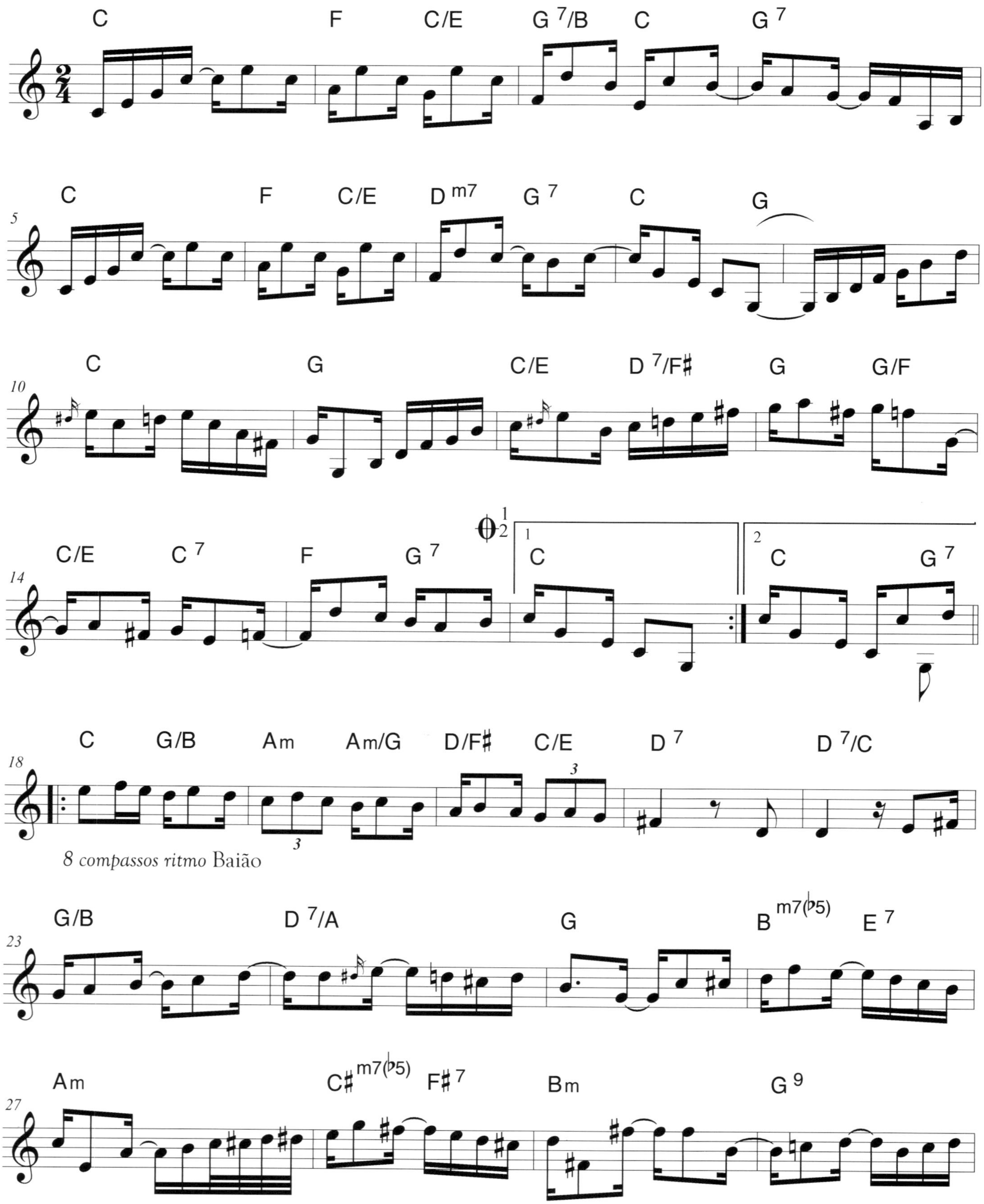

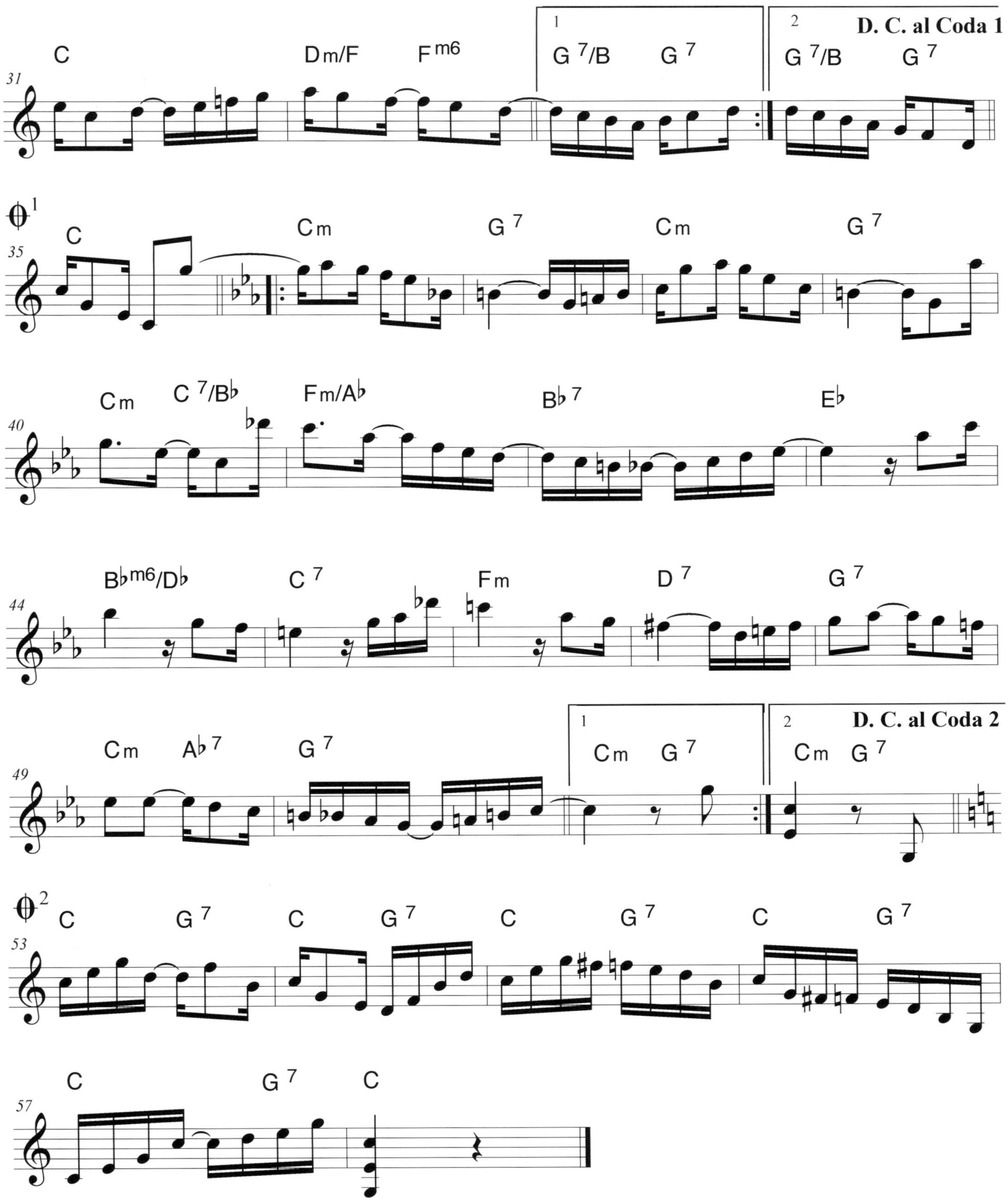

One of the first pieces I thought of for my group of hybrid Choro was Beethoven's C minor *Sonatina*. It's a lively, cheerful piece in rondo form, so it already has 3 sections plus a Coda, as many Choro do. Fernando was one of my first bandolim friends, and shares my love for classical mandolin music as well. "8 compassos ritmo Baião" indicates that for 8 measures the accompaniment changes from Choro rhythm (𝅘𝅥𝅯𝅘𝅥𝅮𝅘𝅥𝅯) to Baião (𝅘𝅥𝅮.𝅘𝅥𝅮.𝅘𝅥𝅮).

31

Um Quinto do Ludwig

A 5th of Ludwig

Marilynn Mair

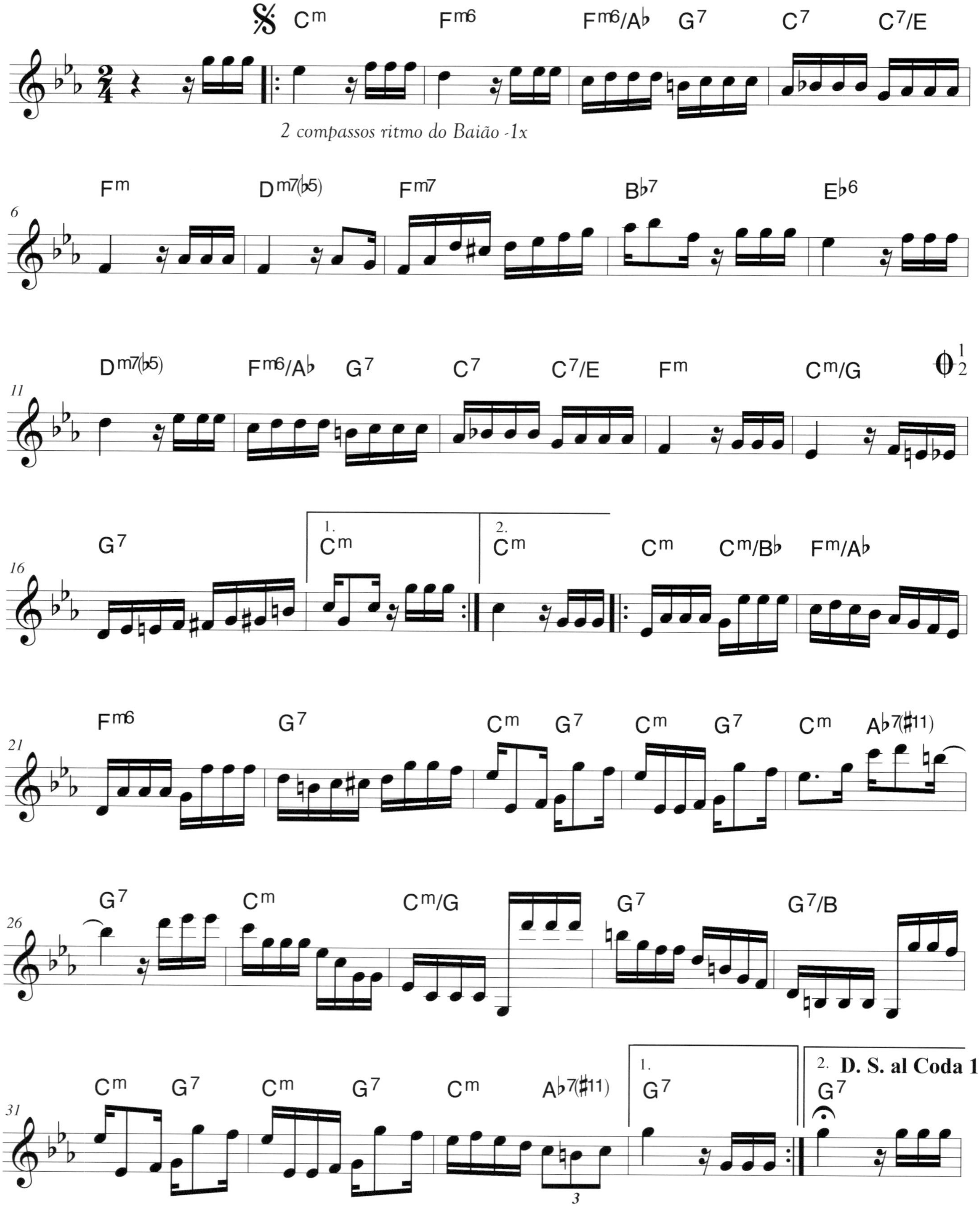

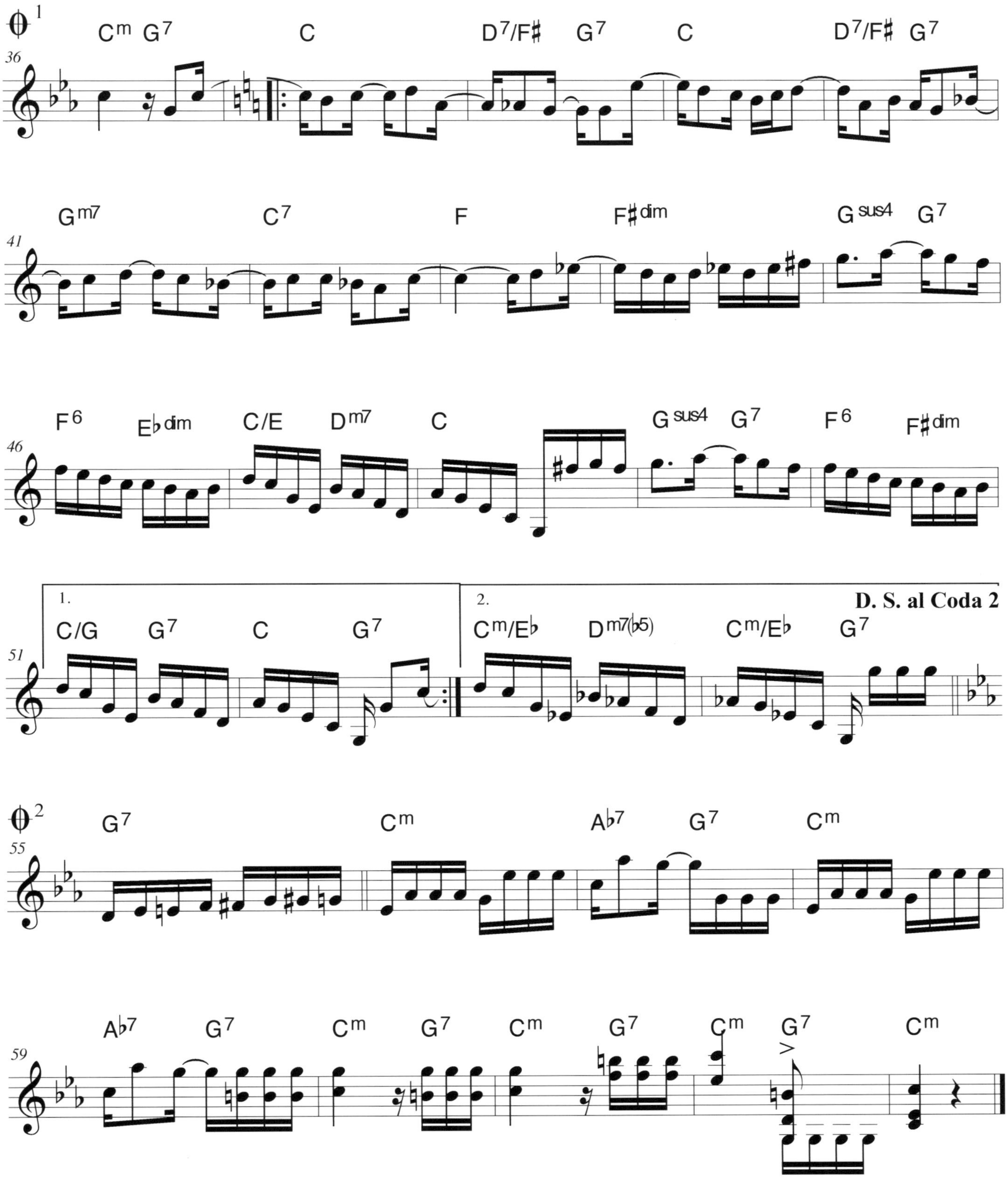

I wrote this thinking that it would be pretty cool to meld Choro with the most famous of all symphonies, Beethoven's Fifth. It was fun to write and is always a hit with audiences. I created my melody out of phrases from the original and added syncopation and chromaticism. The direction "2 compassos ritmo do Baião - 1x" indicates that the chords in the first 2 measures should be ♪. ♪. followed by an 8th-note rest the first time.

Balbuciando

Mumbling

aos músicos do Chorinho no Forte

Marilynn Mair

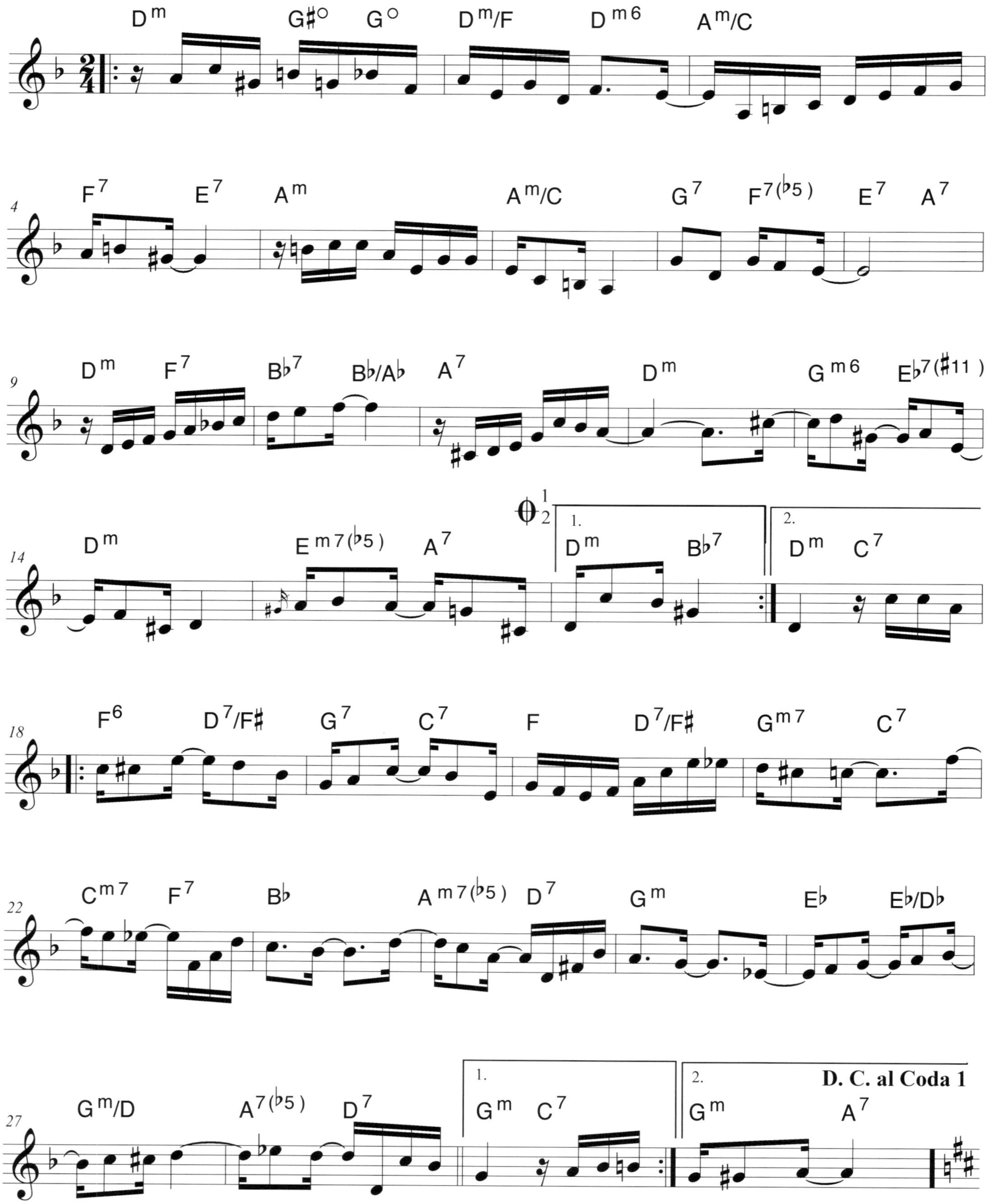

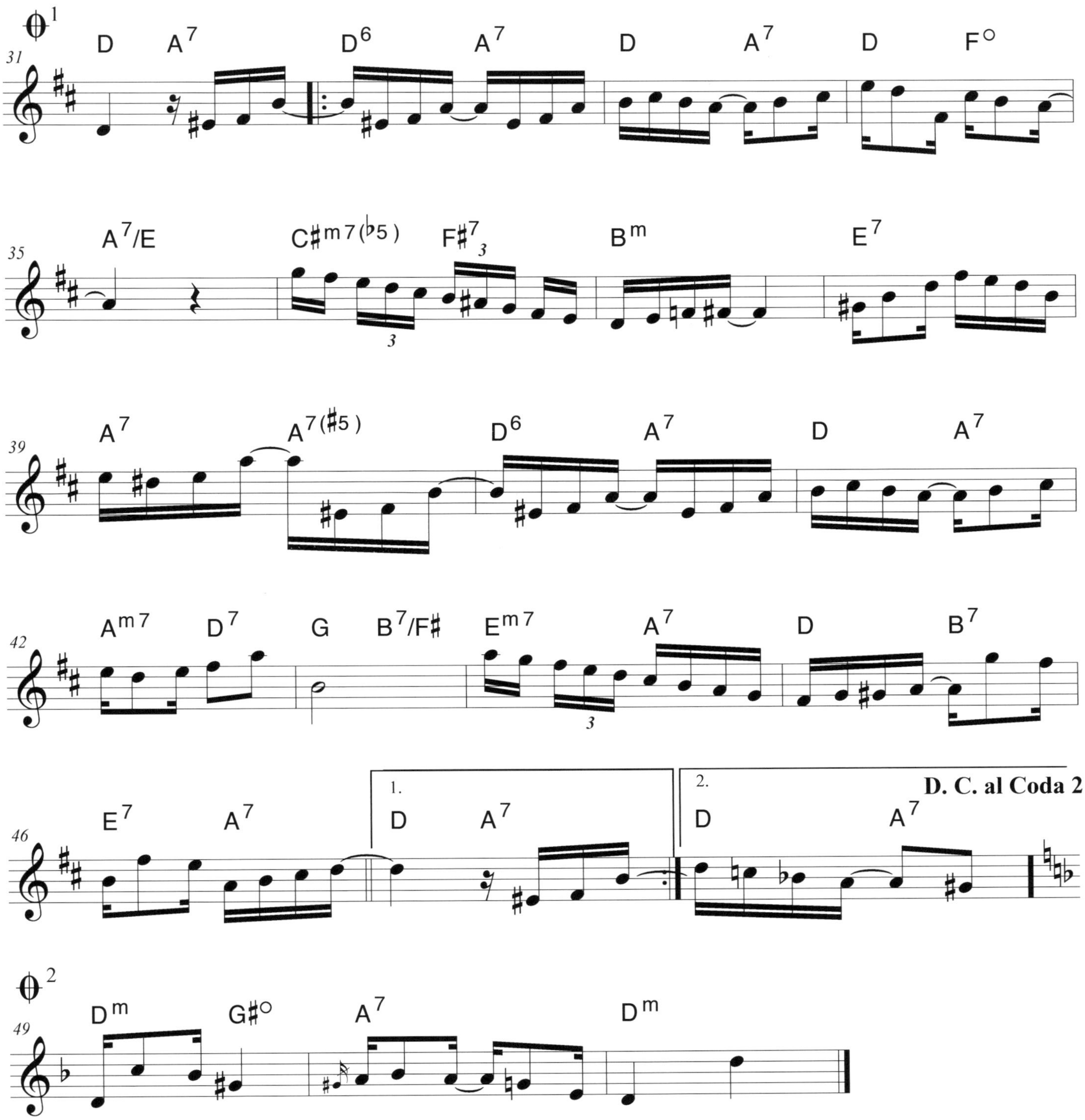

This Choro was inspired by Pixinguinha's *Cochichando (Whispering)*, and each section begins with one measure from the original before moving on to my new ideas. I dedicated it to the musicians at one of my favorite Rio rodas, held at the *Forte Copacabana*, a historic site and museum overlooking the beach. I got the idea for writing this while waiting with friendly impatience for my Rio band, *Água no Feijão*, to stop chatting and move on to *Cochichando* by repeatedly playing and extending *its* opening riff. A cheerful piece, this should be played quickly.

Outro Verão

Another Summer

ao Luiz Simas

Marilynn Mair

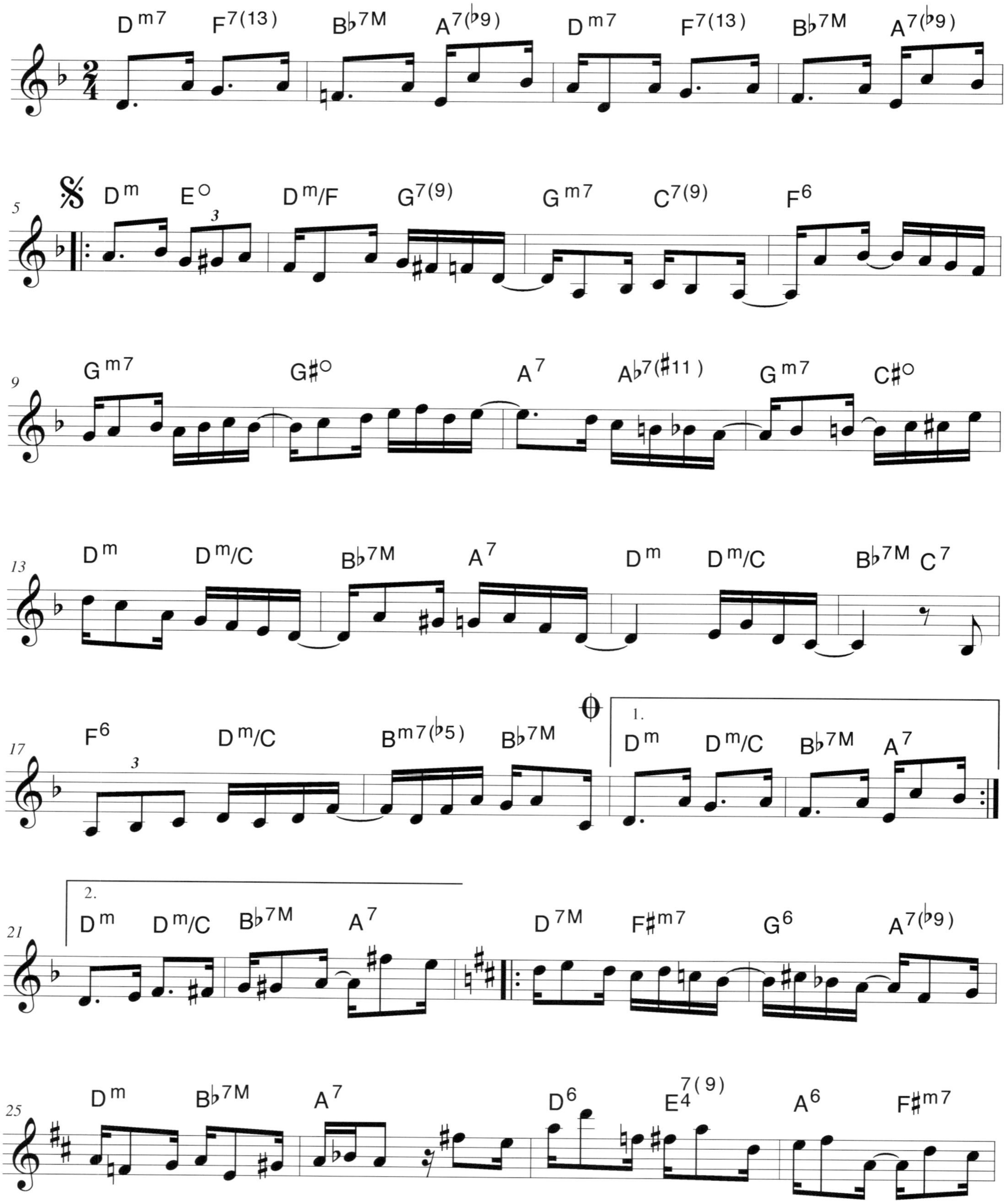

© 2014

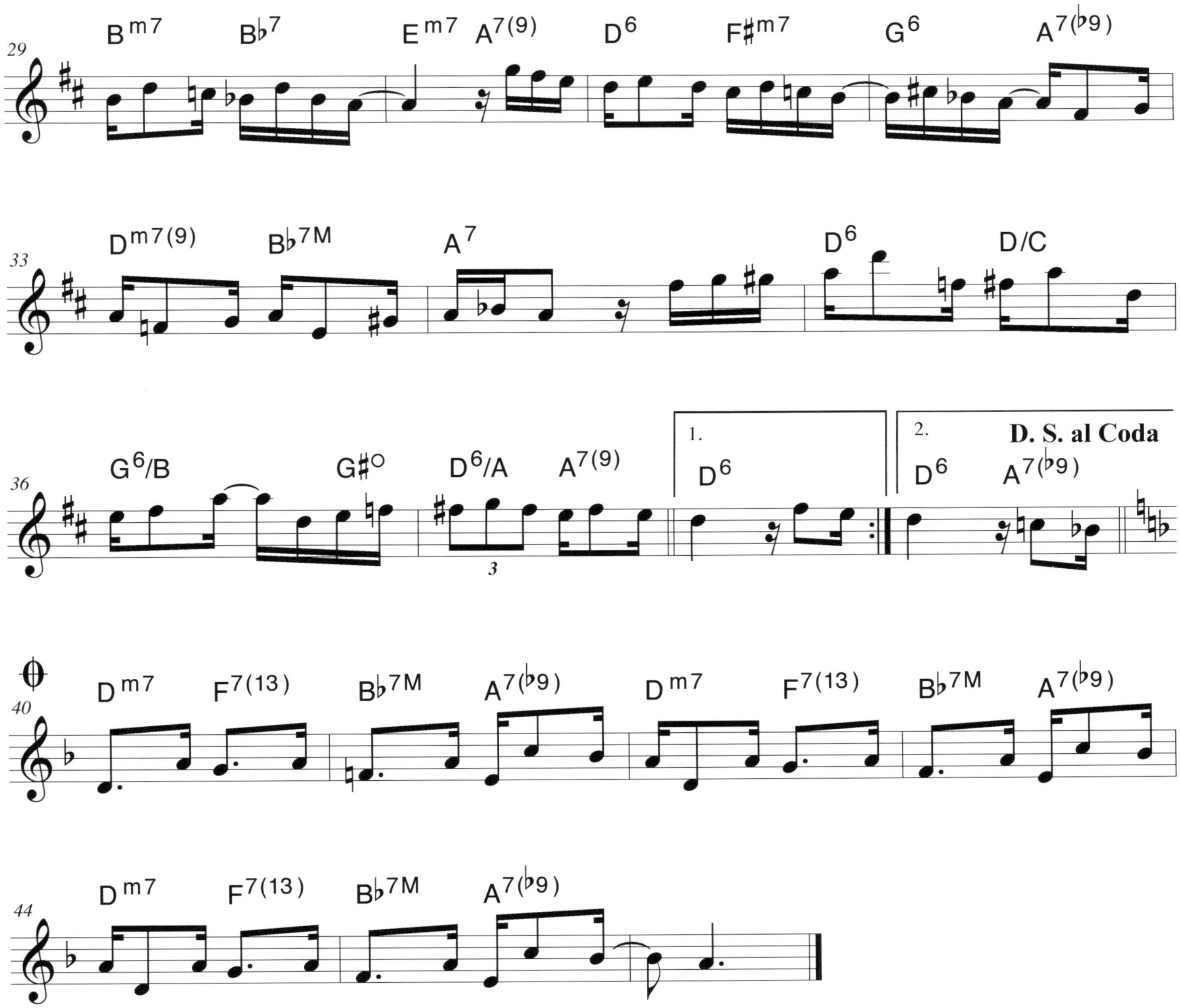

I wrote the first part of this Choro with George Gershwin's "Summertime" in mind, but I was on my own for the second section, as Gershwin's masterpiece is brilliant but short. I dedicated it to composer/pianist Luiz Simas, and recorded it with him. This is a *Choro canção*, and should be played slowly, but with momentum. The second part has a more optimistic feel to contrast with the languid melancholy of the first section.

32

Uma Coisa Feliz

A Happy Thing

for Paul Dressel

Marilynn Mair

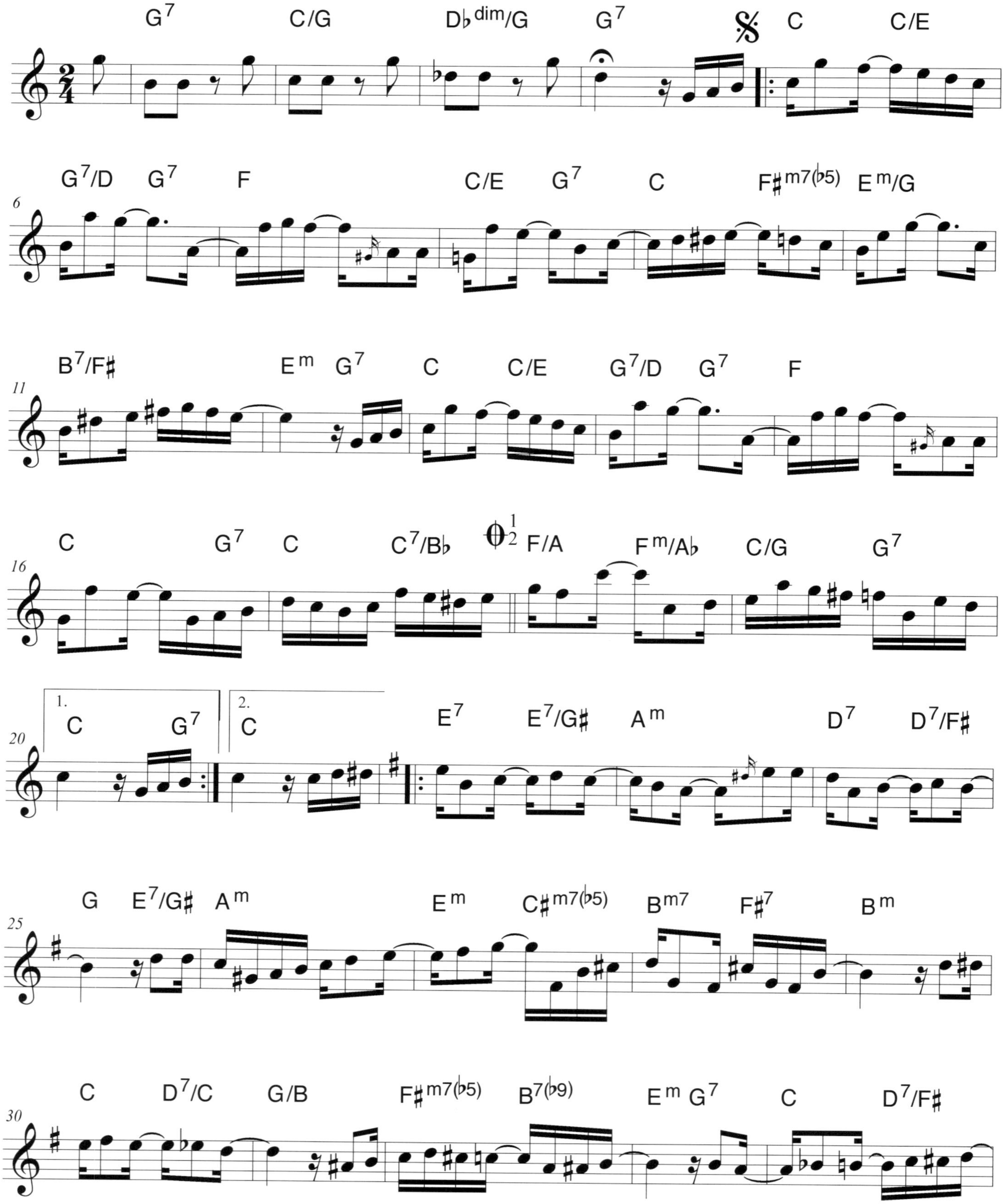

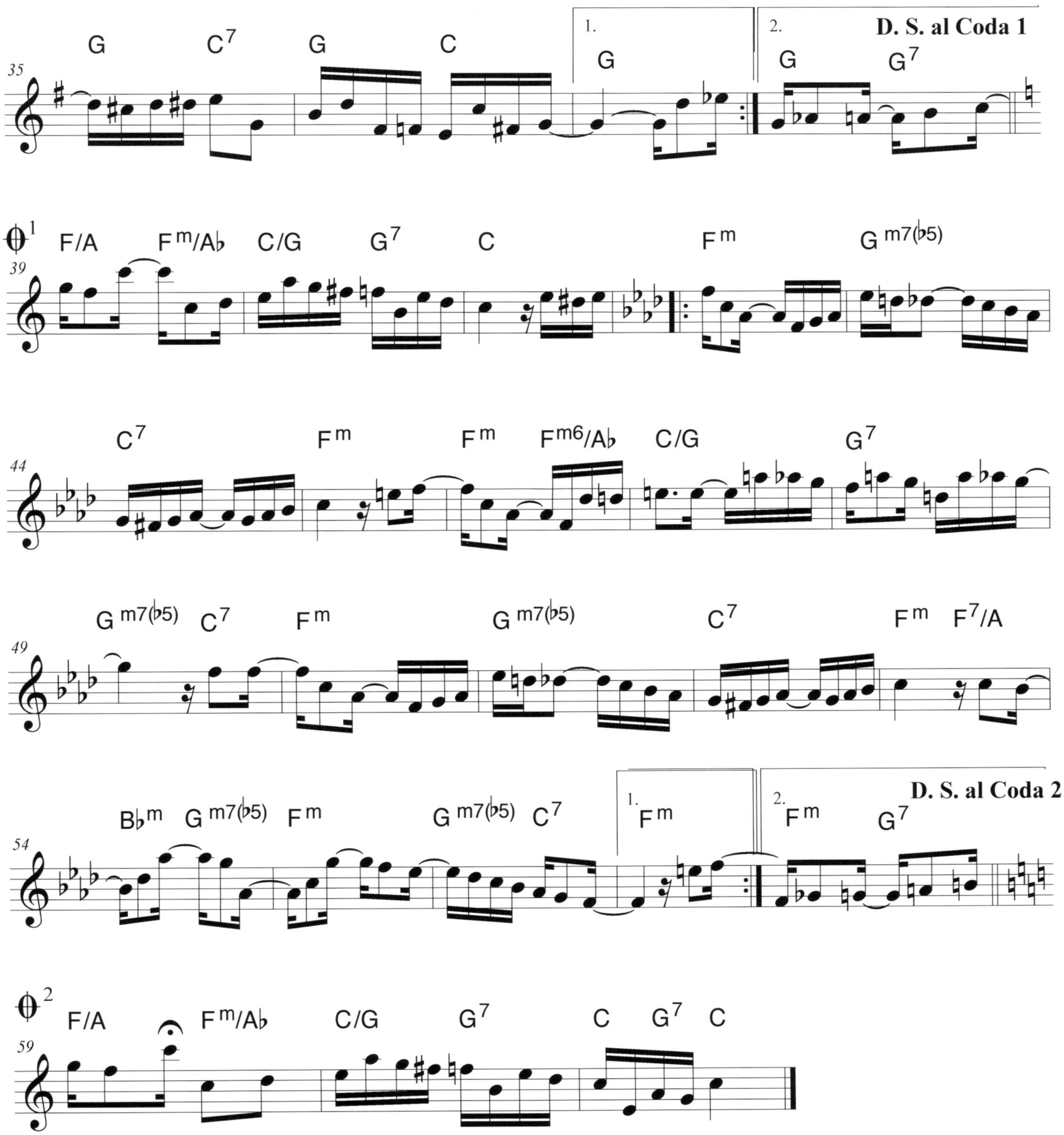

I wrote this Choro in Rio, missing my love who was back home in the USA. The melody has a sprightly feel, and I gave it a short introduction that is meant to be playful, with a pause before launching into the tune.

Enrolado

Spaceshot

for Enigmatica

Marilynn Mair

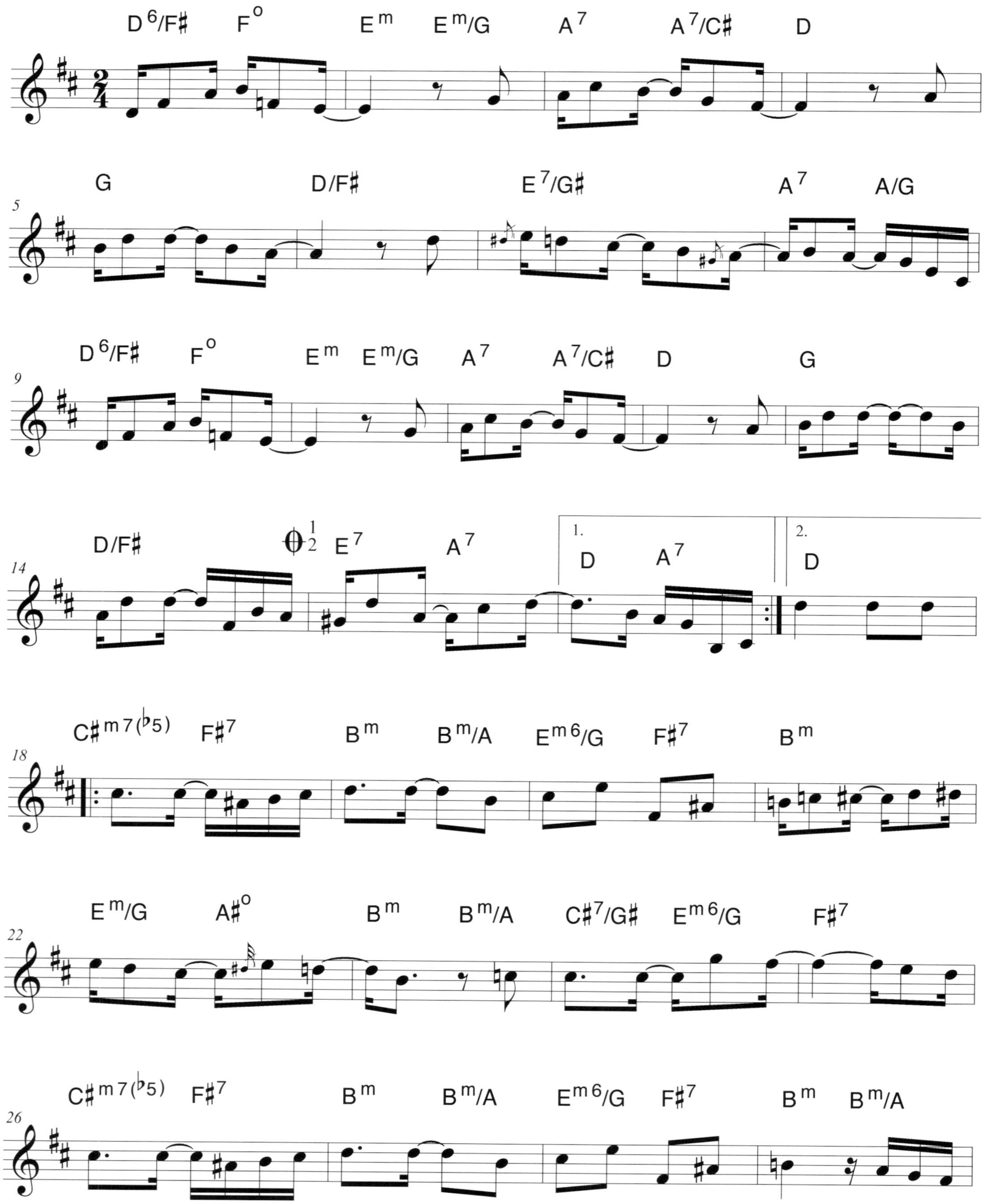

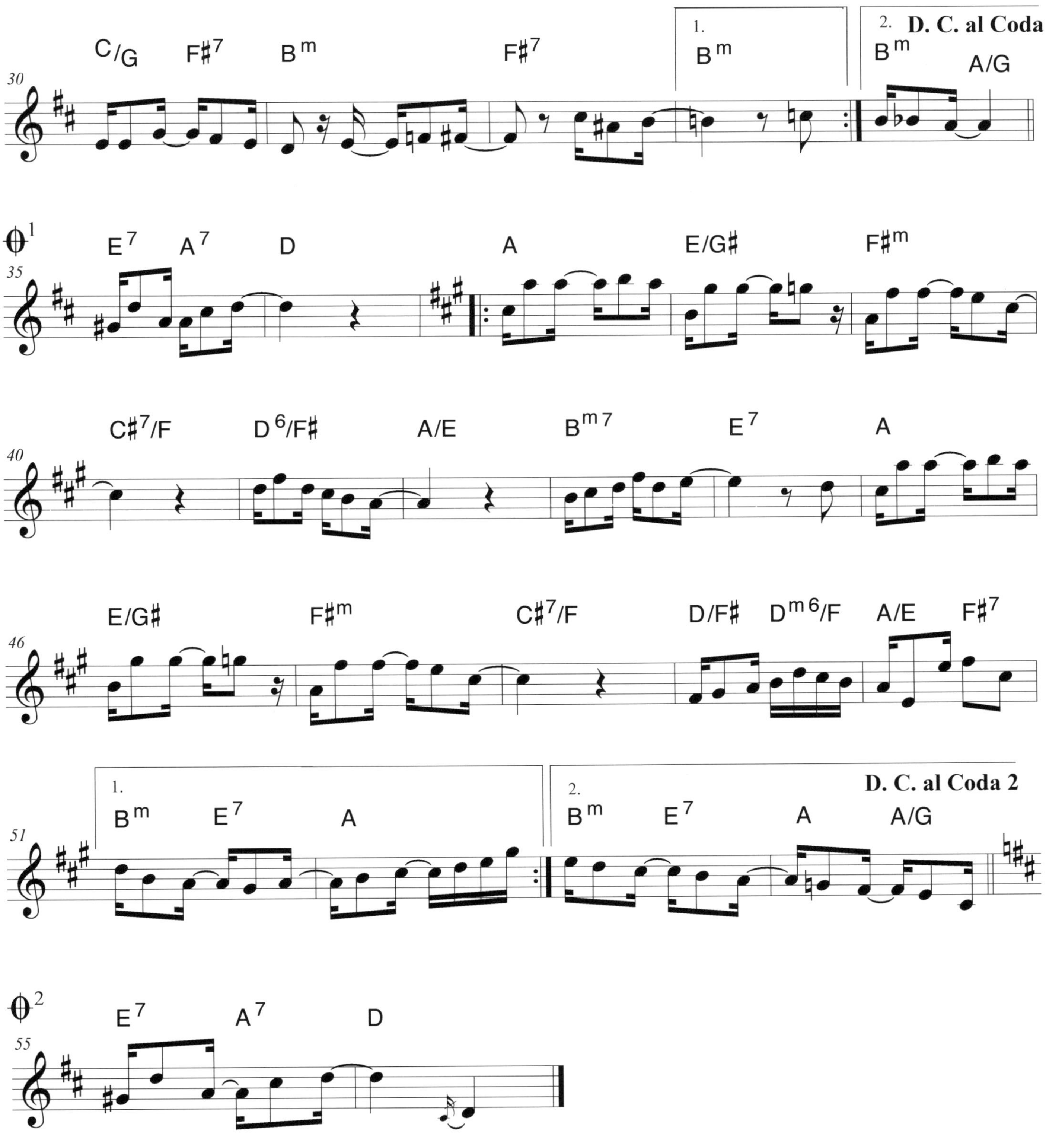

Although the dictionary definition of *Enrolado* is "curled," its slang meaning implies a person is a "spaceshot." I wrote this piece for my ensemble Enigmatica, so there are 2 versions– this leadsheet and a 4-part version in the Ensembles section of the book. Note that, in Choro, a grace note on the 6th fret attached to an open-string note, is played simultaneously with the main note, giving a characteristic bandolim zing to the melody. This is a lively carefree piece, and should be played with a jaunty flair.

Terças no Trapiche

Tuesdays at Trapiche

ao Rômulo Aguiar

Marilynn Mair

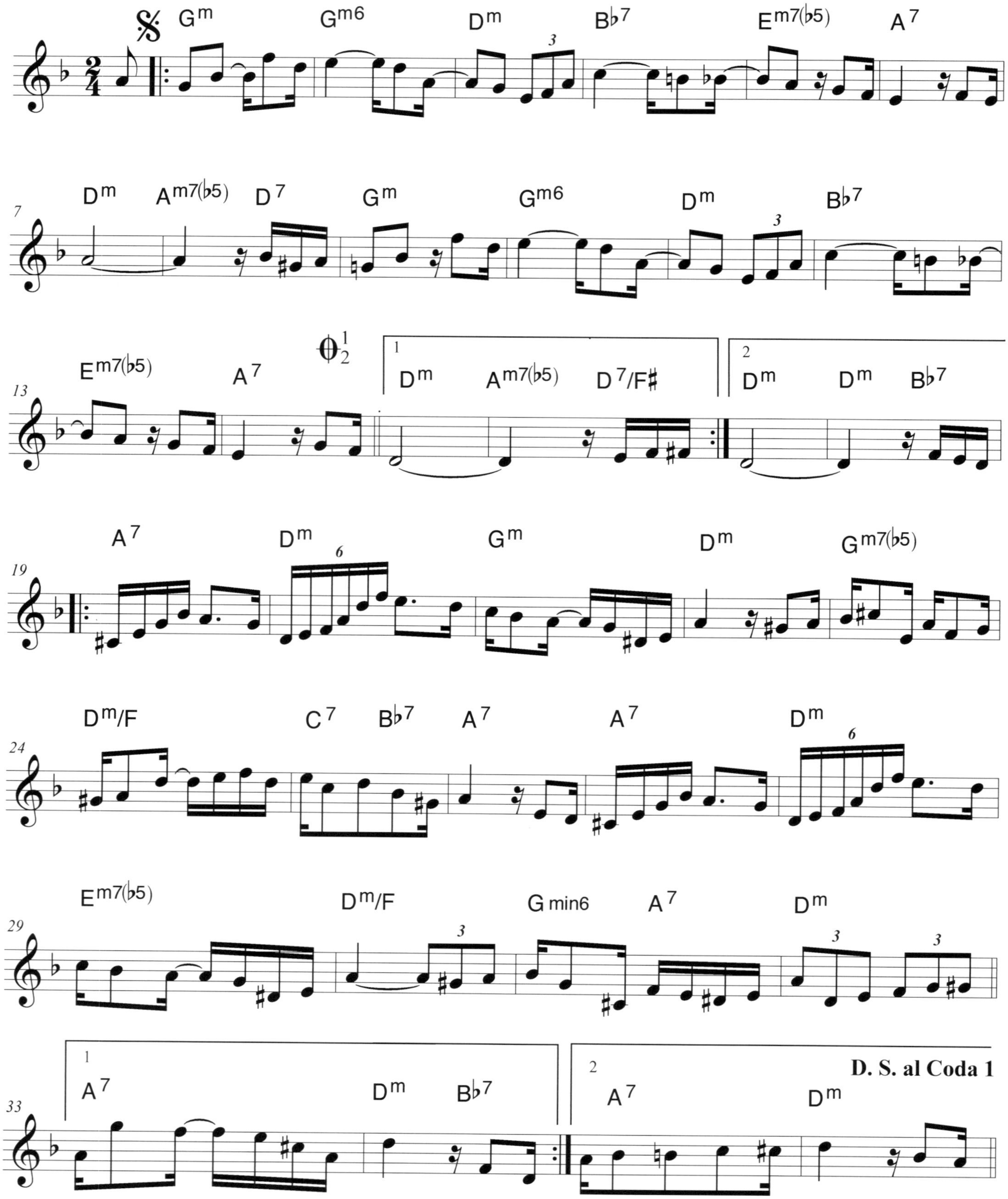

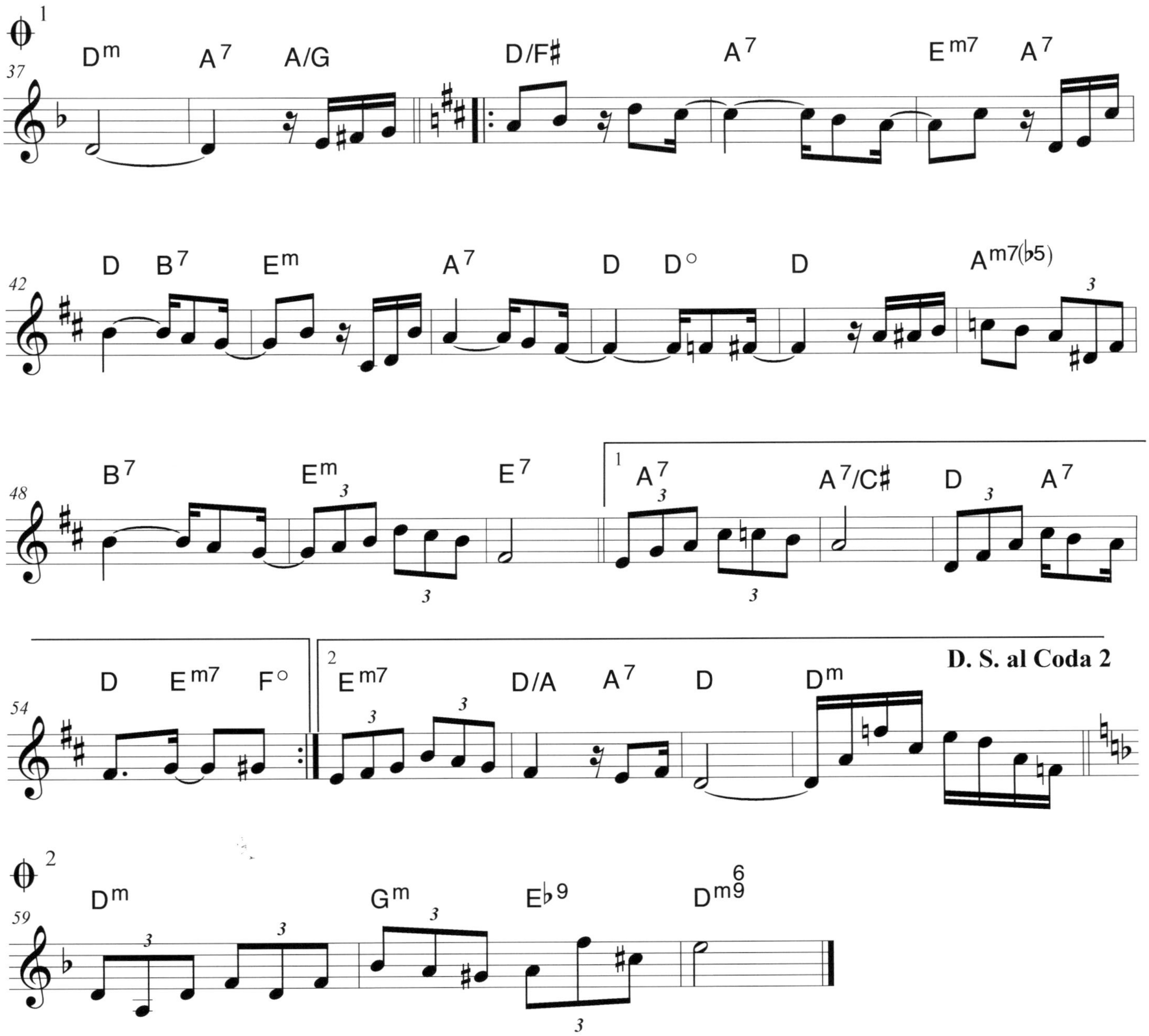

In the first months of 2007, Tuesday nights would usually find me at the Rio bar *Trapiche Gamboa*, hanging with Rômulo, the saxophonist in our band *Água no Feijão*, listening to a *roda* featuring some of the best players in the city. Back in the USA that spring, missing the music and my friends, I wrote this tune. It's wistful, embodying the Brazilian feeling of *saudade*, missing people and times gone by, and should be played at a moderate tempo. I recorded it with Rômulo and the rest of our band for my CD, *Meu Bandolim*.

Nadando em Luz

Swimming in Light

Marilynn Mair

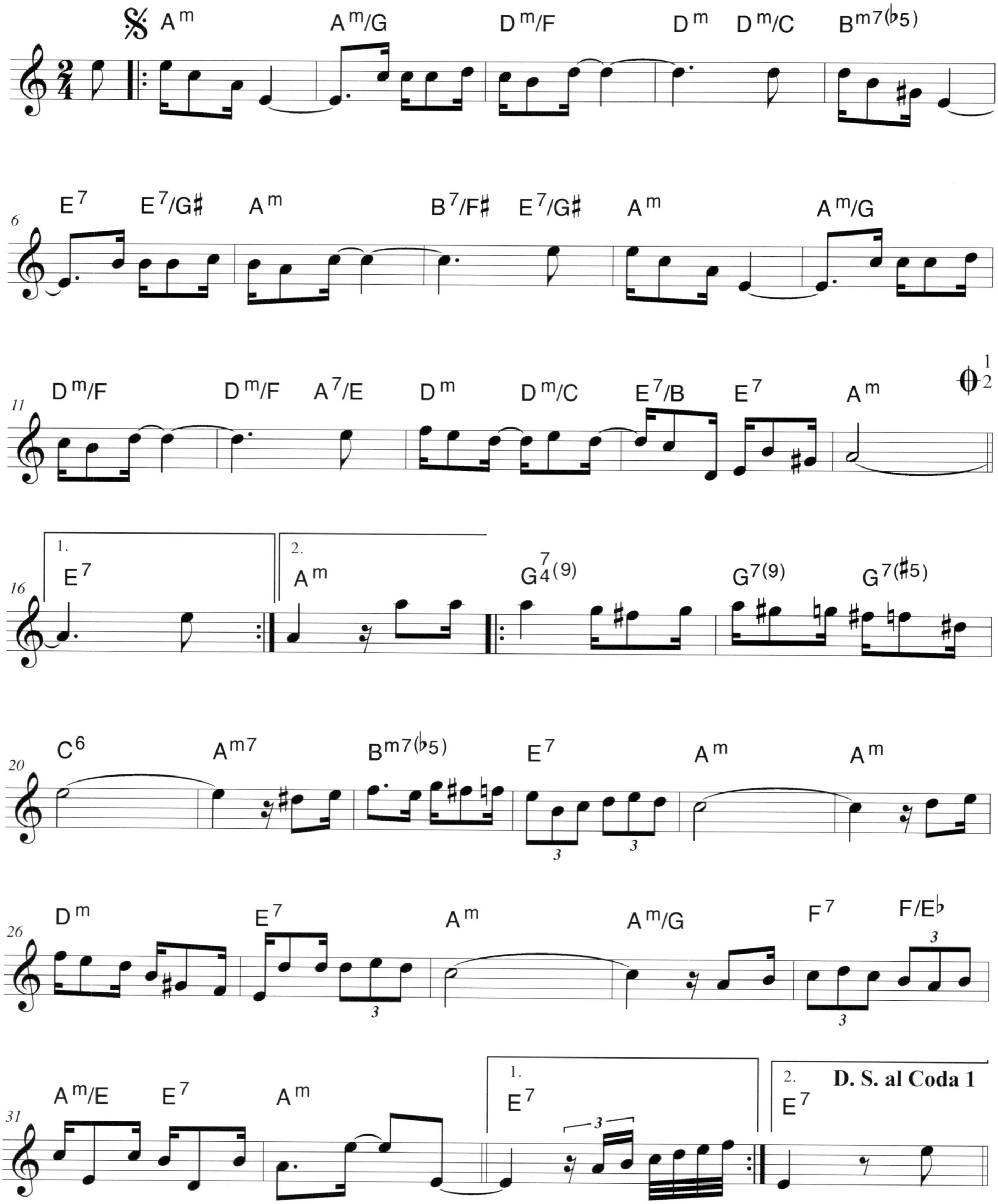

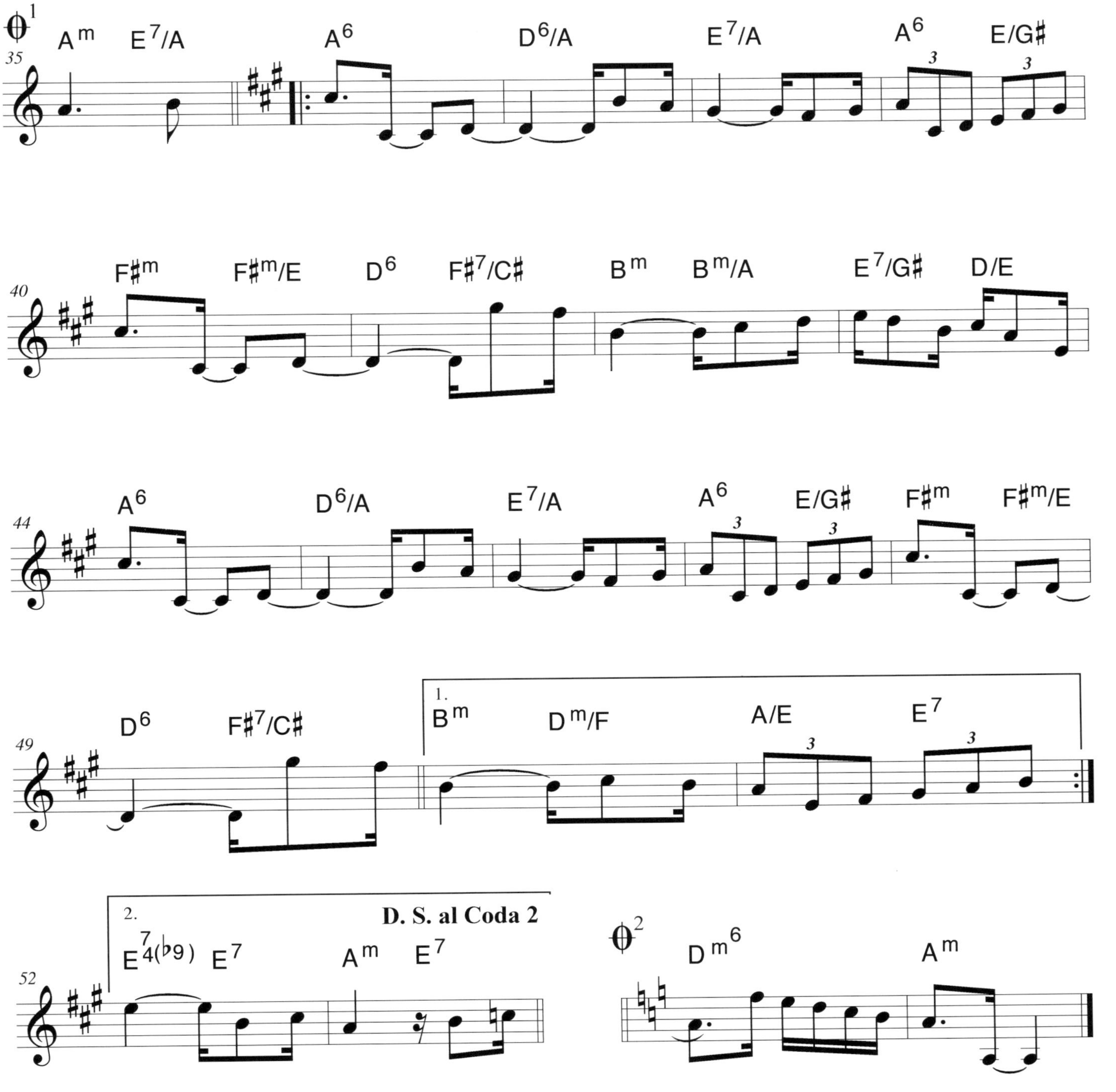

I wrote *Nadando* in 2000, as I was finishing my sabbatical research into the history and style of Choro, and years before I would go to Brazil. I did my research on a dial-up internet connection to the archives of the *Biblioteca Nacional* in Rio. At the time, libraries in the USA had few resources, but I visited most of them. Choro CDs had to be ordered online and took months to arrive. But I persisted, with the same intensity I had used earlier to research classical mandolin music. I recorded this tune for my 2001 CD of the same name, and later arranged it for my octet, Enigmatica. You'll find that arrangement in the Ensembles section of the book. It's a lively tune, inspired by the rhythm of swimming laps, in and out of reflections of light on the water.

Faça a Pergunta

Ask the Question

Marilynn Mair

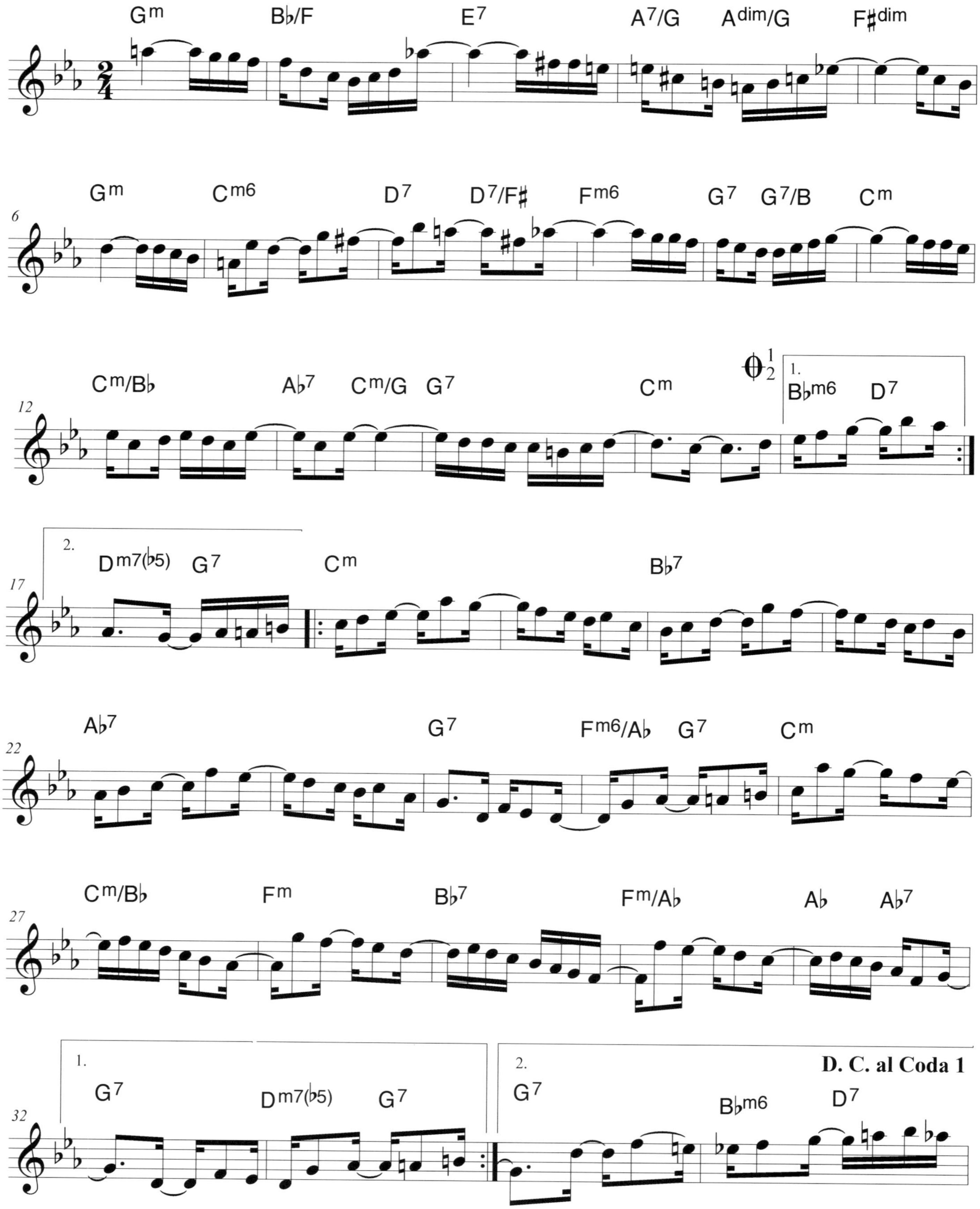

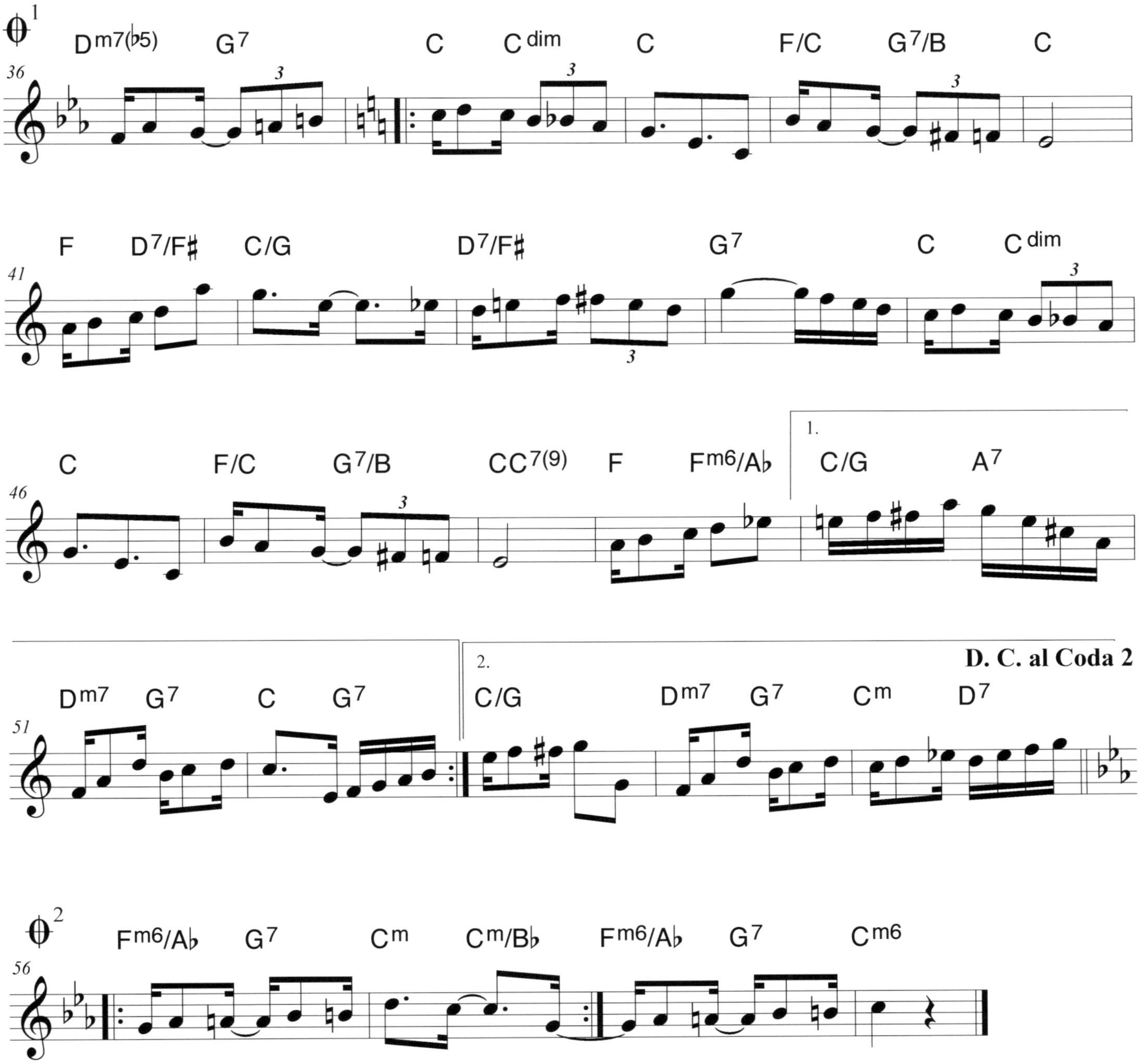

This is one of 3 Choro I wrote for the concert to celebrate my retirement as a Professor of Music at Roger Williams University, in the spring of 2017. I had been weighing the pros and cons of the decision to leave, and there were benefits both ways, but in the end when I asked the question, my personal connection with music won out. Play this piece languidly, at a moderate tempo. This is one of the few Choro I have written that I haven't recorded. I leave it to you to answer the question the music asks.

Se Não Agora

If not now

Marilynn Mair

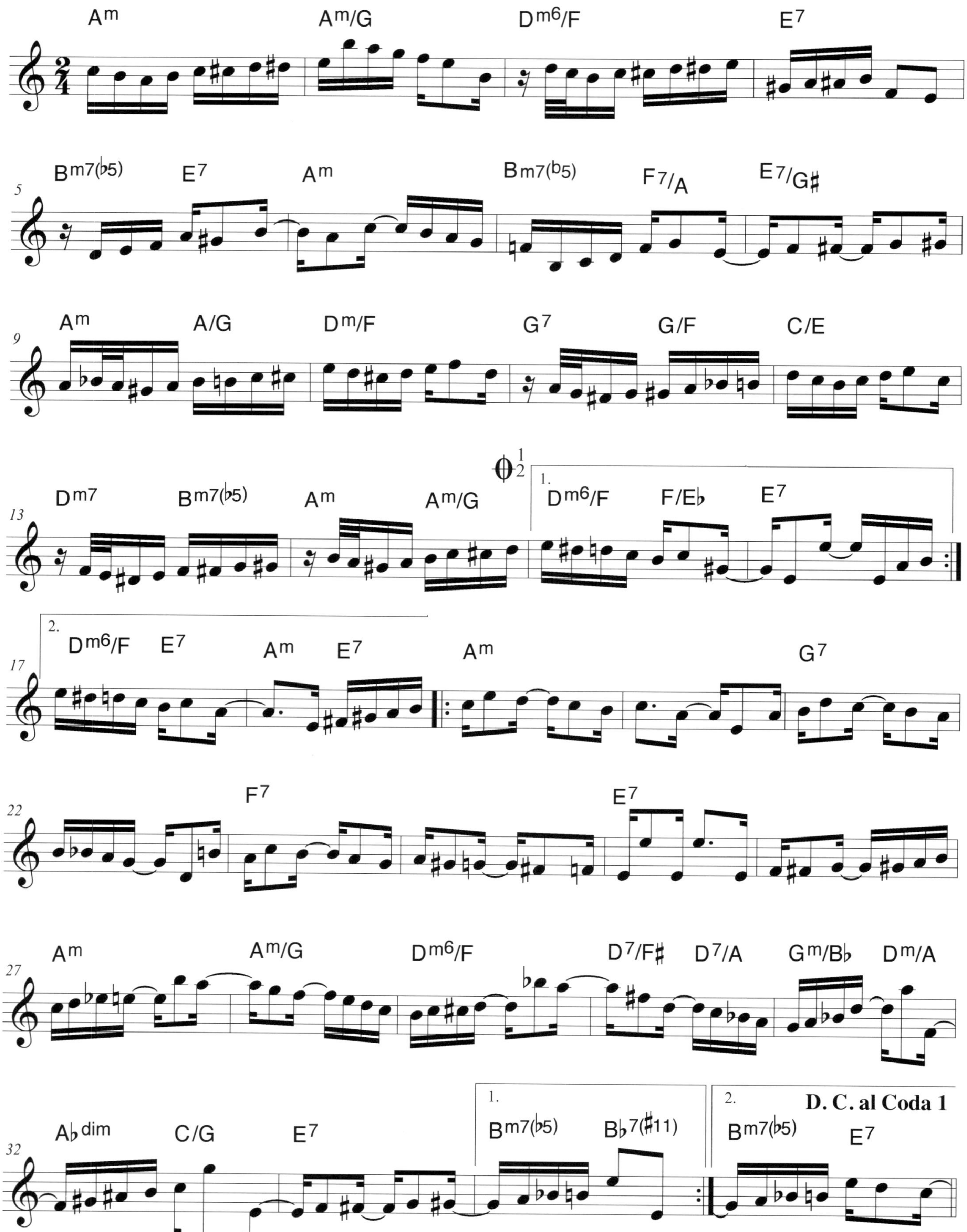

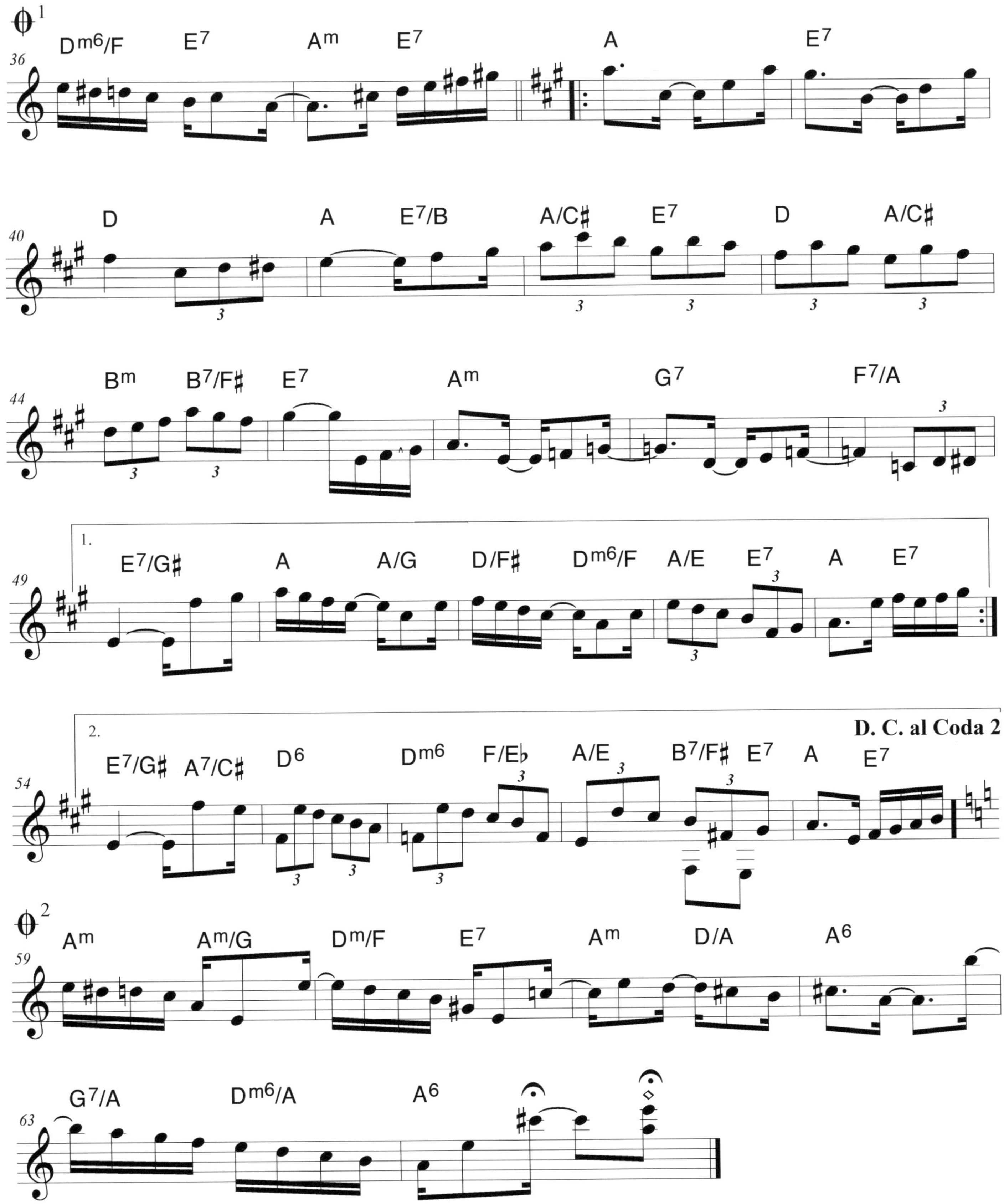

The second of my retirement Choro, the title again acknowledges my hesitation about retiring. The first section reflects the often hectic pace of my life at that time, the second asks the title's question, and the third section and Coda reflect the calm I envisioned ahead.

É Bom Saber

Good to Know

Marilynn Mair

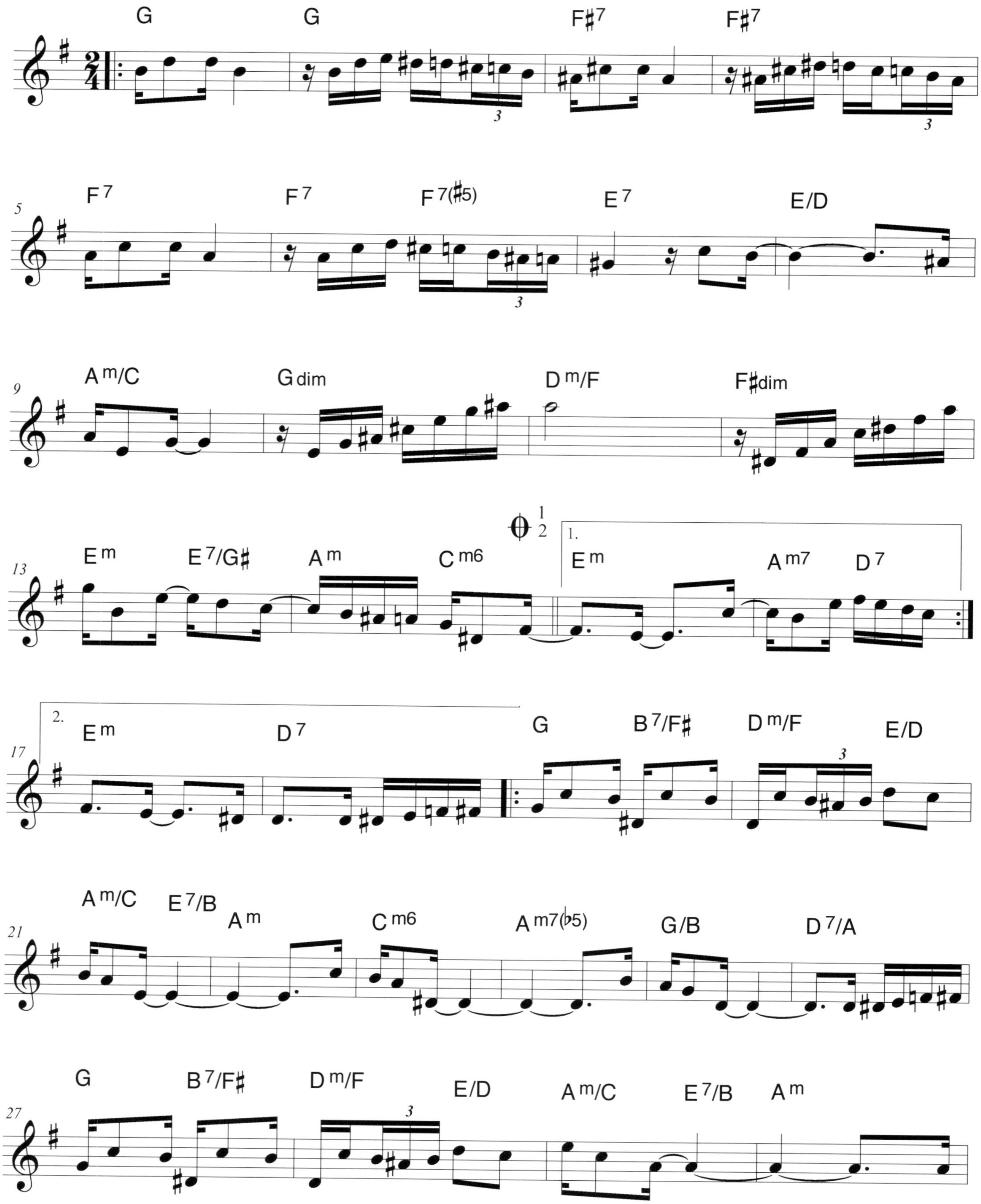

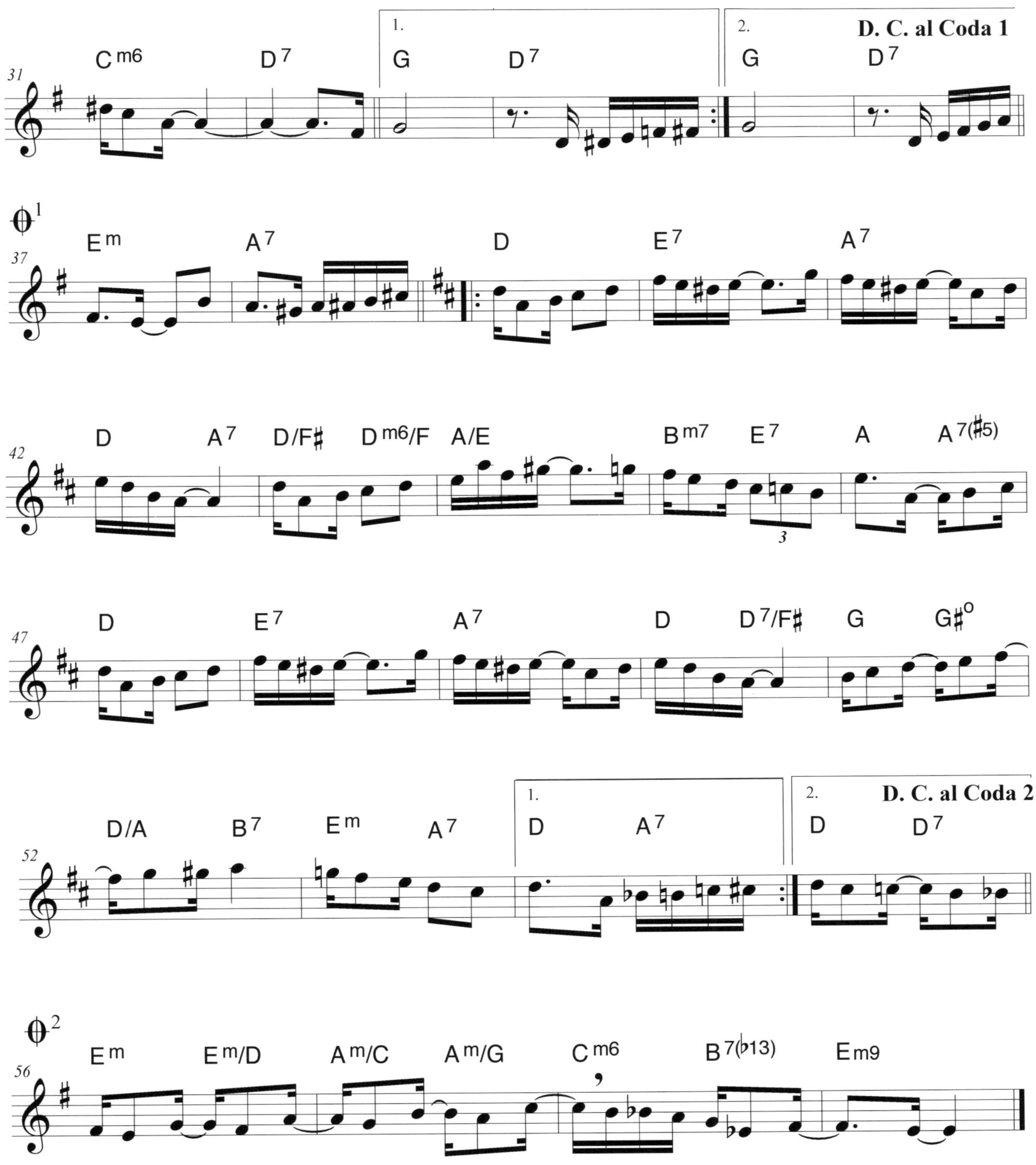

The third of my retirement Choro, decision made, leaving nostalgia behind, progressing cheerfully.

33

Estação Carioca

Carioca Station

ao Paulo Sá

Marilynn Mair

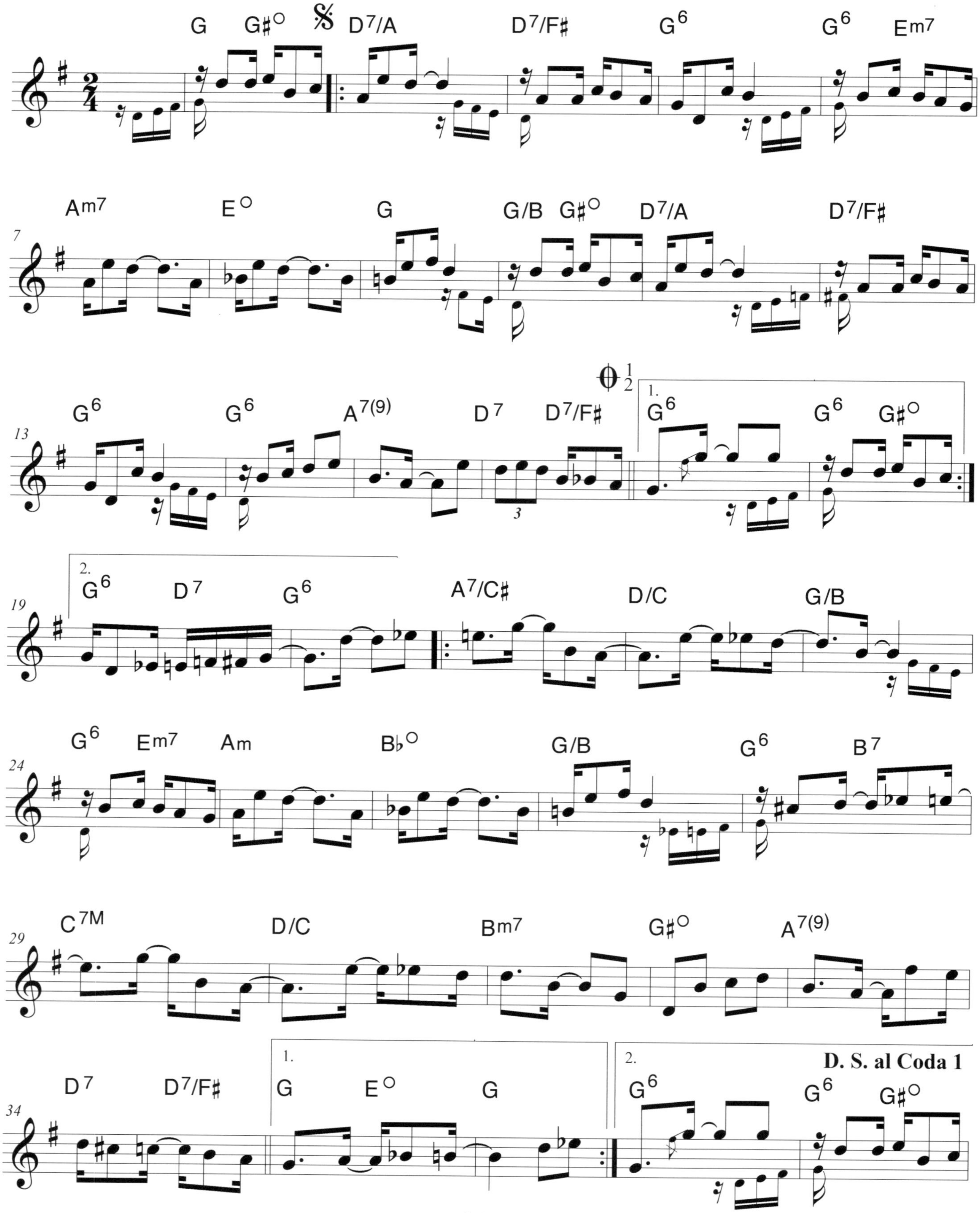

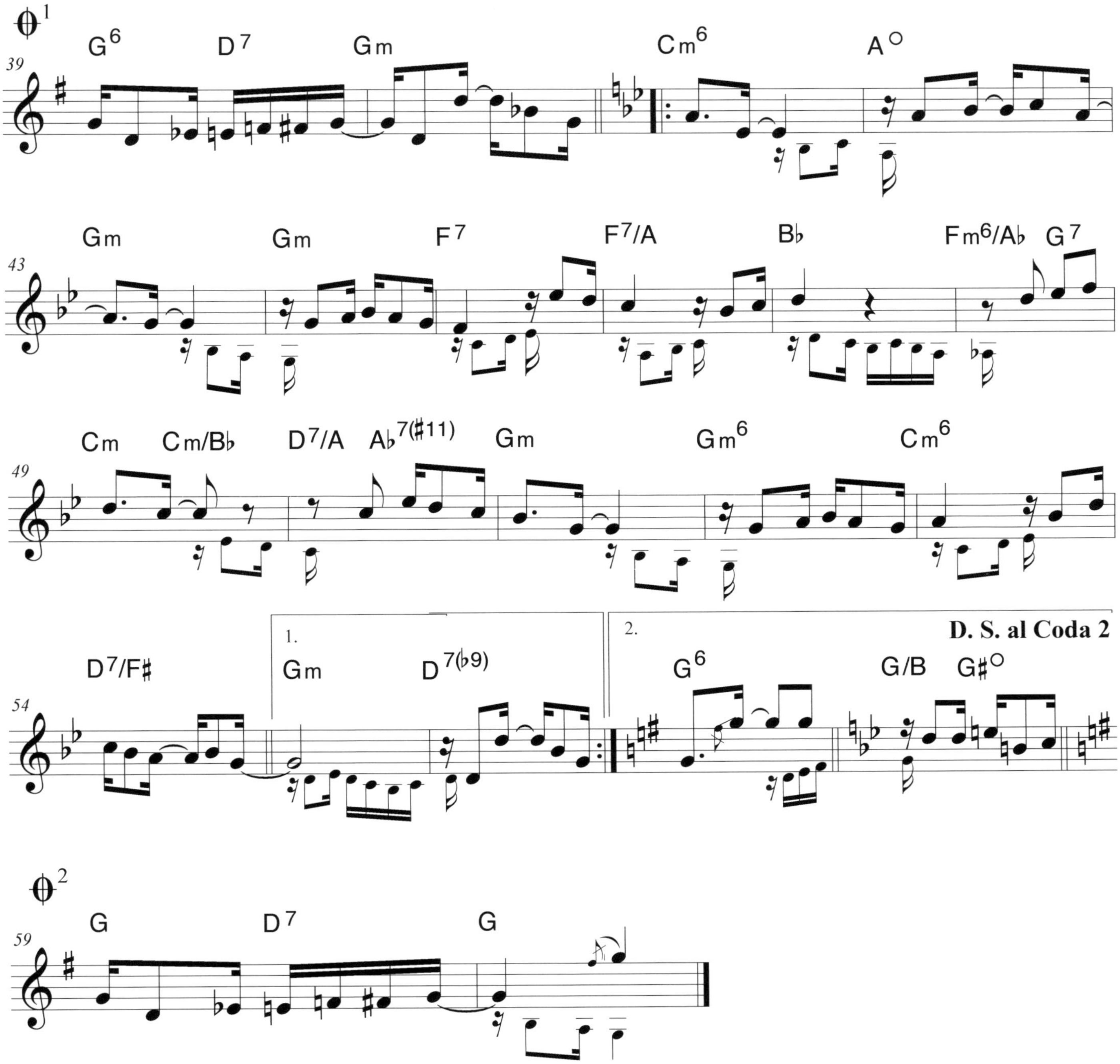

Carioca Station is a metro stop in the center of Rio. When I first went to Brazil, it was the place I would meet bandolimist, Paulo Sá, my longtime friend and collaborator on many projects, when he would have a break from teaching. We'd grab coffee or lunch and he'd walk me to a good music store or back to his university. In time, it became a place I would head to on my own for many reasons and adventures. Paulo suggested I write a Choro to commemorate our meeting point, so I gathered my ideas and finally, during the pandemic, completed it for this book. When I asked, Paulo agreed to record it for the book download files. It's a cheerful piece and should be played at a lively tempo. The small notes with the stems down are suggestions for the guitar to play, along with the chords, for the Choro "conversation."

34

Buscando Baden

Chasing Baden

ao Marcílio Lopes

Marilynn Mair

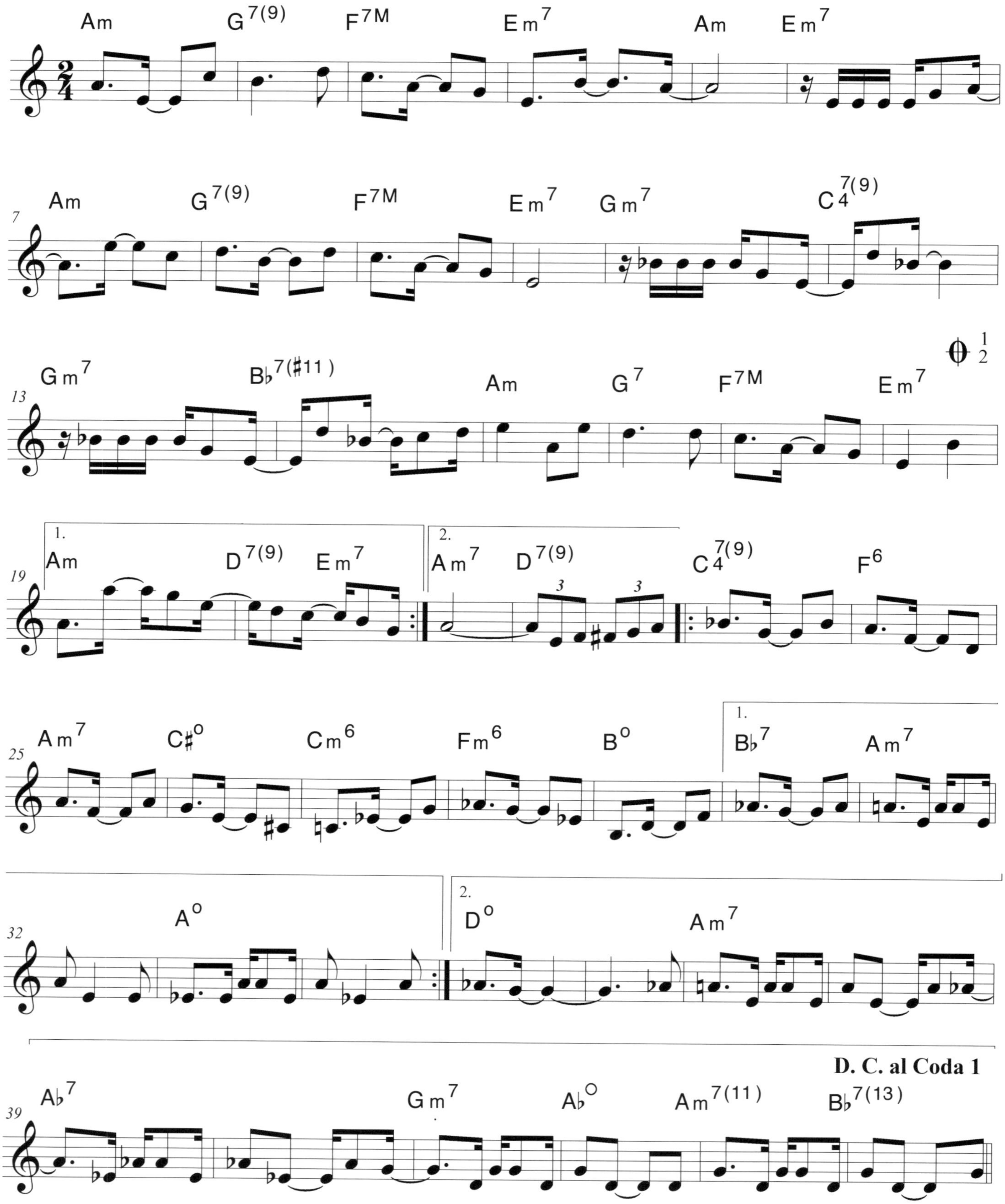

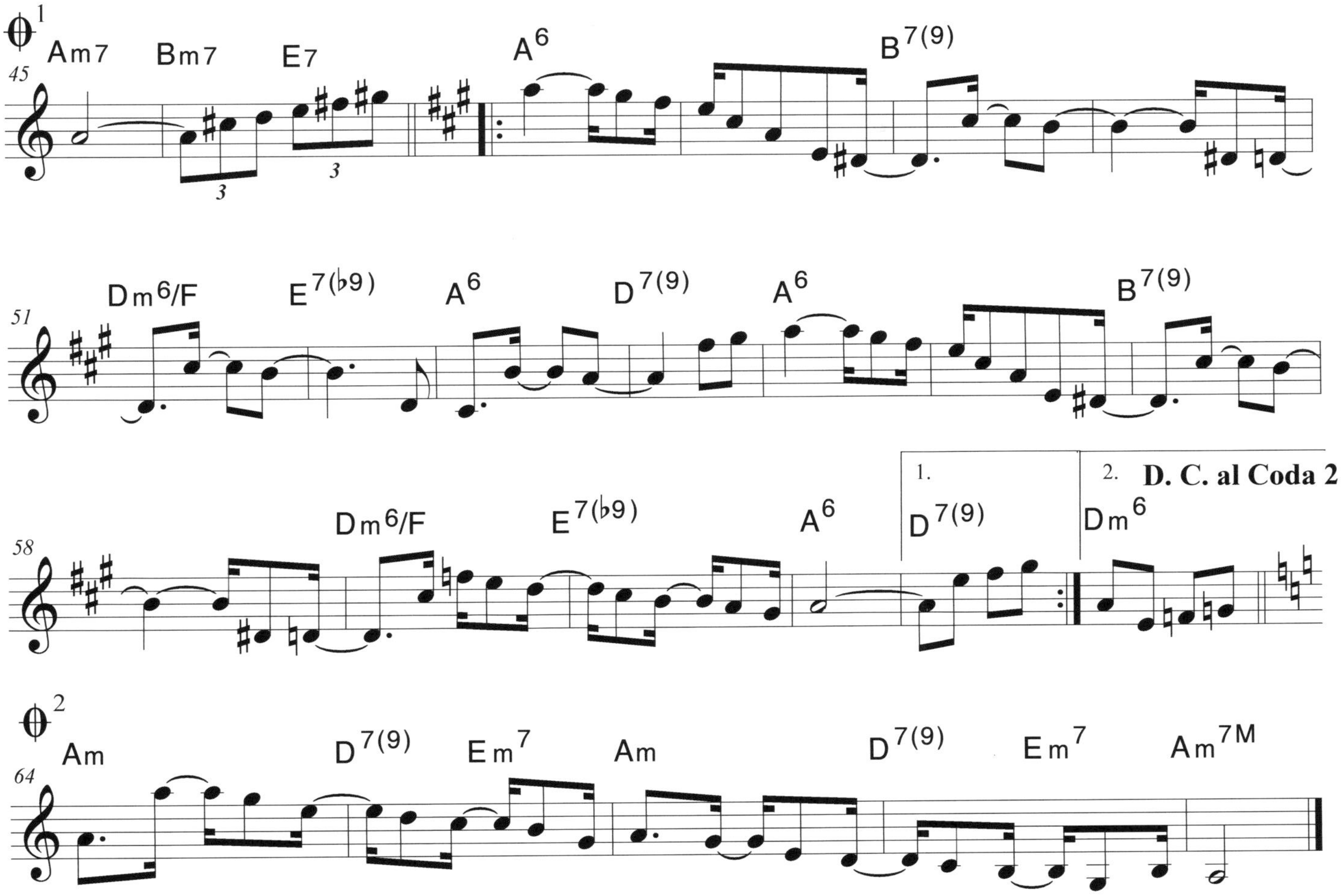

Baden Powell (1937–2000) was a brilliant composer and guitarist whose music combines influences from samba, Choro, bossa nova, and Afro-Brazilian styles. I fell in love with his album, *Os Afro Sambas*, when I first heard it, and later discovered his innovative solo guitar works. I've drawn on elements of Baden's style in this samba-choro that I dedicate to Marcílio Lopes, fantastic bandolimist, composer, and arranger, who has mentored me in Brazilian harmony since we first met at *Escola Portátil de Música* in Rio, where he was teaching theory. Marcílio also recorded this tune for me for the book download files. I suggest you check out his recordings with the amazing group, *Água de Moringa!*

Saudade do Rio

Missing Rio

ao Luiz e Valle e sua roda de terça-feira

Marilynn Mair

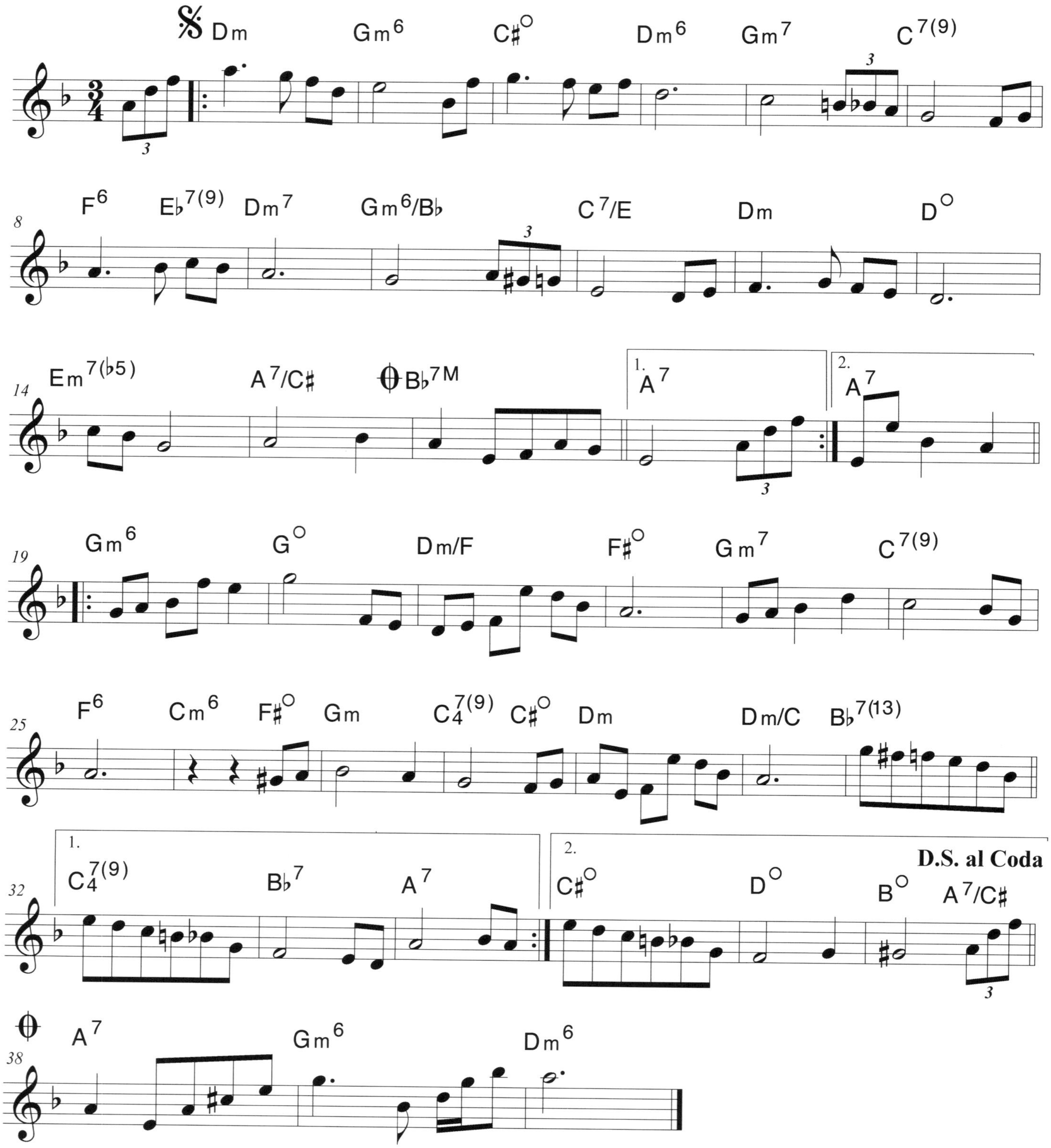

"Saudade" is a Brazilian sentiment, not easily translatable, that combines missing and remembering, with some sadness, times and people from the past. Because of pandemic interruptions to travel, I have been missing Rio, the *rodas* I played in, and the musicians I played with. I dedicate this *valsa* to one *roda* in particular, hoping I will soon be able to return. Sadly, as I was working on this manuscript, Valle passed away. *Saudade do Valle também.*

Ensembles

Ayton's Farewell
Badi no Rio
Enrolado
Nadando em Luz
Goodin's Gigue
East of Here
The Jabberwock

About My Ensembles

I've written most of my ensemble pieces for Enigmatica, my mandolin group, which has performed and recorded them, including four for a CD to be released in 2023. Although I thought about including several earlier ensemble pieces, written for a variety of ensembles, only one made the cut. The scores are written for the original instrumentations, with additional parts to make them more easily playable by other ensembles.

Ayton's Farewell was written to celebrate the retirement of Will Ayton, composer, performer on viola da gamba, a frequent duo partner, and my colleague at Roger Williams University. Will often composes fantasia based on themes from Renaissance composers. Here, I have written a fantasia on a theme that Will plucked from a dream and sent to me, but never used himself. It was included on the CD *Engimatica 3*.

Badi no Rio [Badi in Rio] was written for Enigmatica to perform at the wonderful Bach–to–the–Future marathon, hosted by Community MusicWorks at Brown University, where music written or inspired by Bach is performed by a variety of groups from 7:00 PM to 7:00 AM the next morning. For one of our performances I reimagined Bach's famous *Badinerie* as a Choro. Enigmatica will include this on their upcoming 2023 CD.

Enrolado [Spaceshot] was written for Enigmatica for our CD, *Enigmatica 3*. The ensemble version came first, and the leadsheet was derived from that.

Nadando em Luz [Swimming in Light] was first written as a leadsheet in 2000, recorded then, and later arranged for Enigmatica. Enigmatica will include this on their upcoming CD.

Goodin's Gigue was written as an homage in memory of John Goodin, mandolinist and composer, soon after his death. Enigmatica will include this on their upcoming CD.

East of Here, as an ensemble, comes from my solo of the same name, to be found in the section, "Early Works." Mitch Nelin arranged the solo for our jazz mandolin quartet, The New England Mandolin Ensemble, that also included Jim Dalton and August Watters. We recorded it for our CD, *Sip a Little New*, and Mitch's version inspired me to write this arrangement. Enigmatica will include it on their upcoming CD.

The Jabberwock is the early piece, written for one manifestation of the Contemporary Social Orchestra, a group of musical friends who put on a series of eclectic concerts in the 1980s and '90s. These featured such gems as a whole–tone version of "O Bla Di," arrangements of Eric Satie's "Sports et Divertissements," works from Stephen Foster's dance tunes for social orchestra, and a concert as Halley's Stardust Orchestra, to commemorate the passing of Halley's comet in 1986 with music written for its passing in 1910.

"When the songs are coming out, it's usually because they're songs I would like to hear myself. It's like I need a paint color I've never seen, so I mix it myself." – Eddie Vedder, Pearl Jam

Ayton's Farewell

Fantasia on a theme by Will Ayton

for Enigmatica

Marilynn Mair

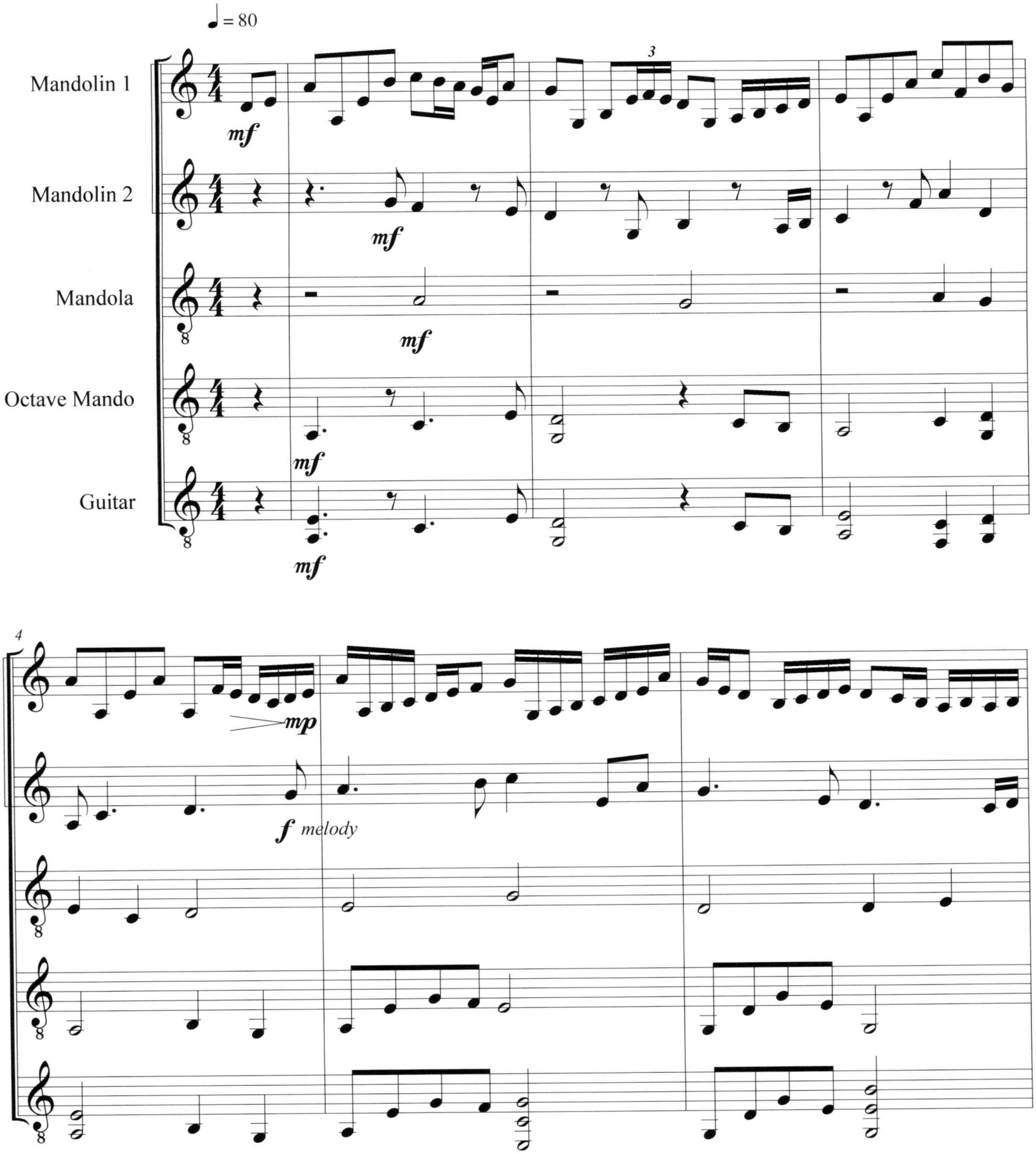

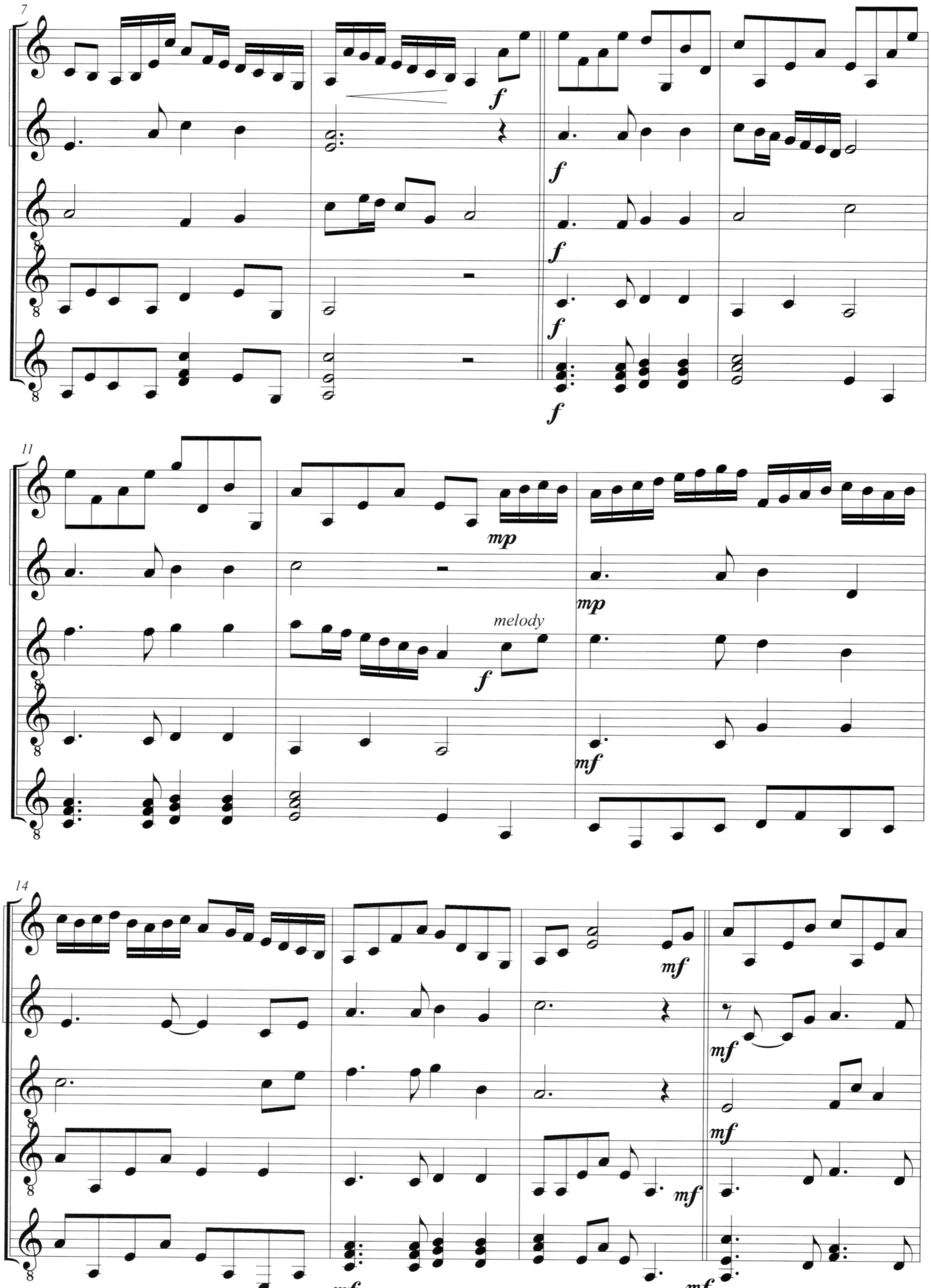
7
11
melody
14

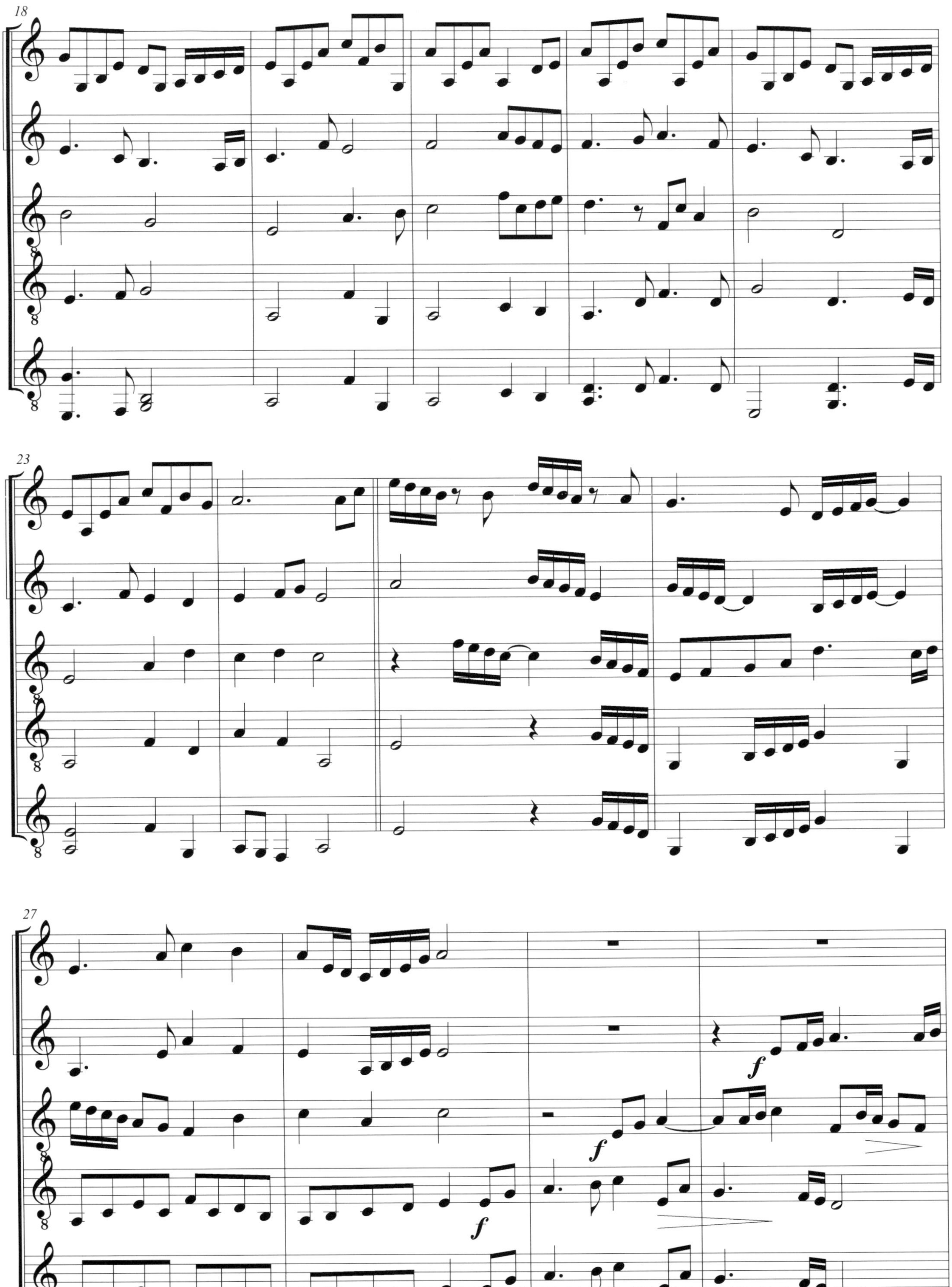
18
23
27
f
f
f
f

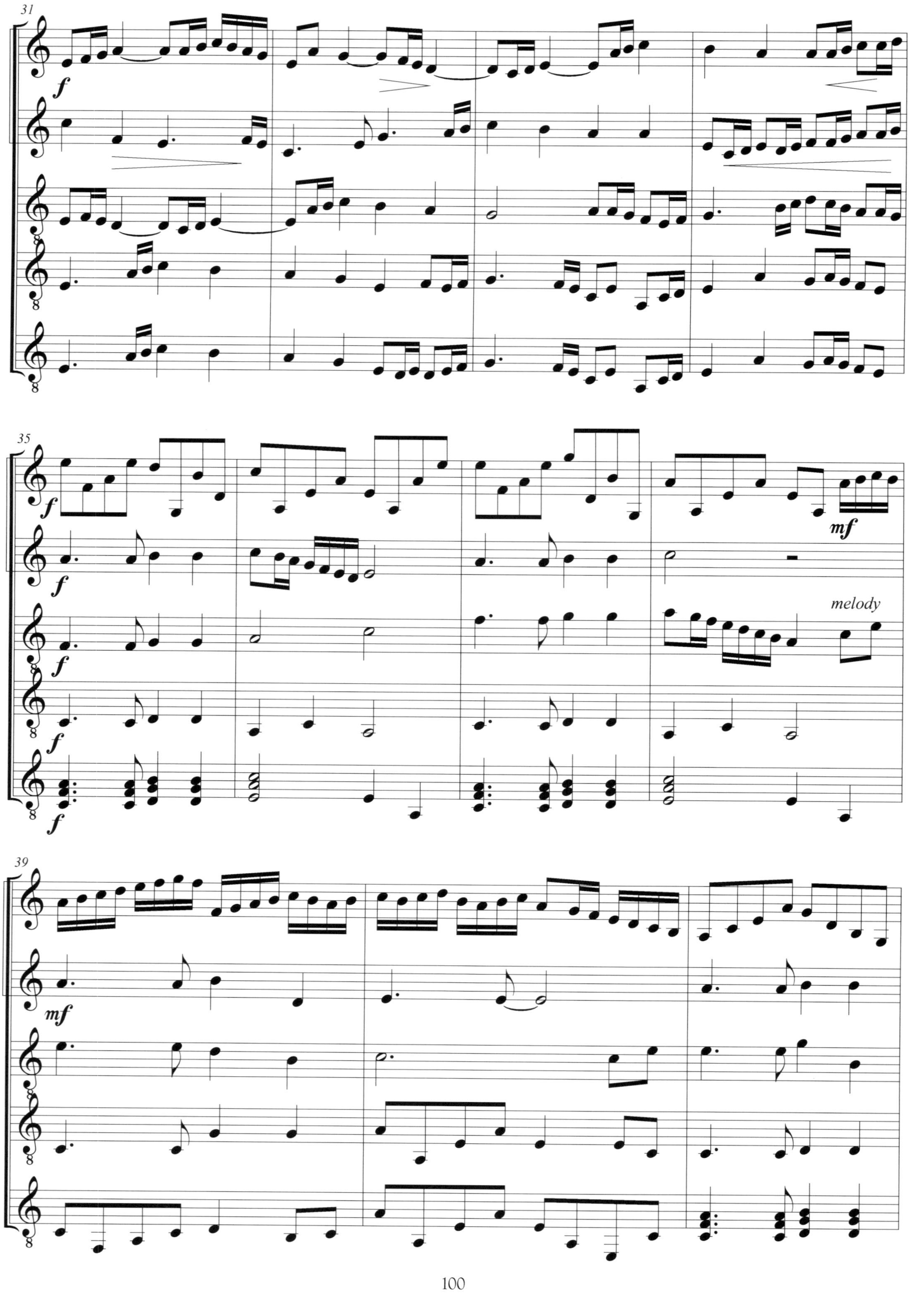
31
35
melody
39

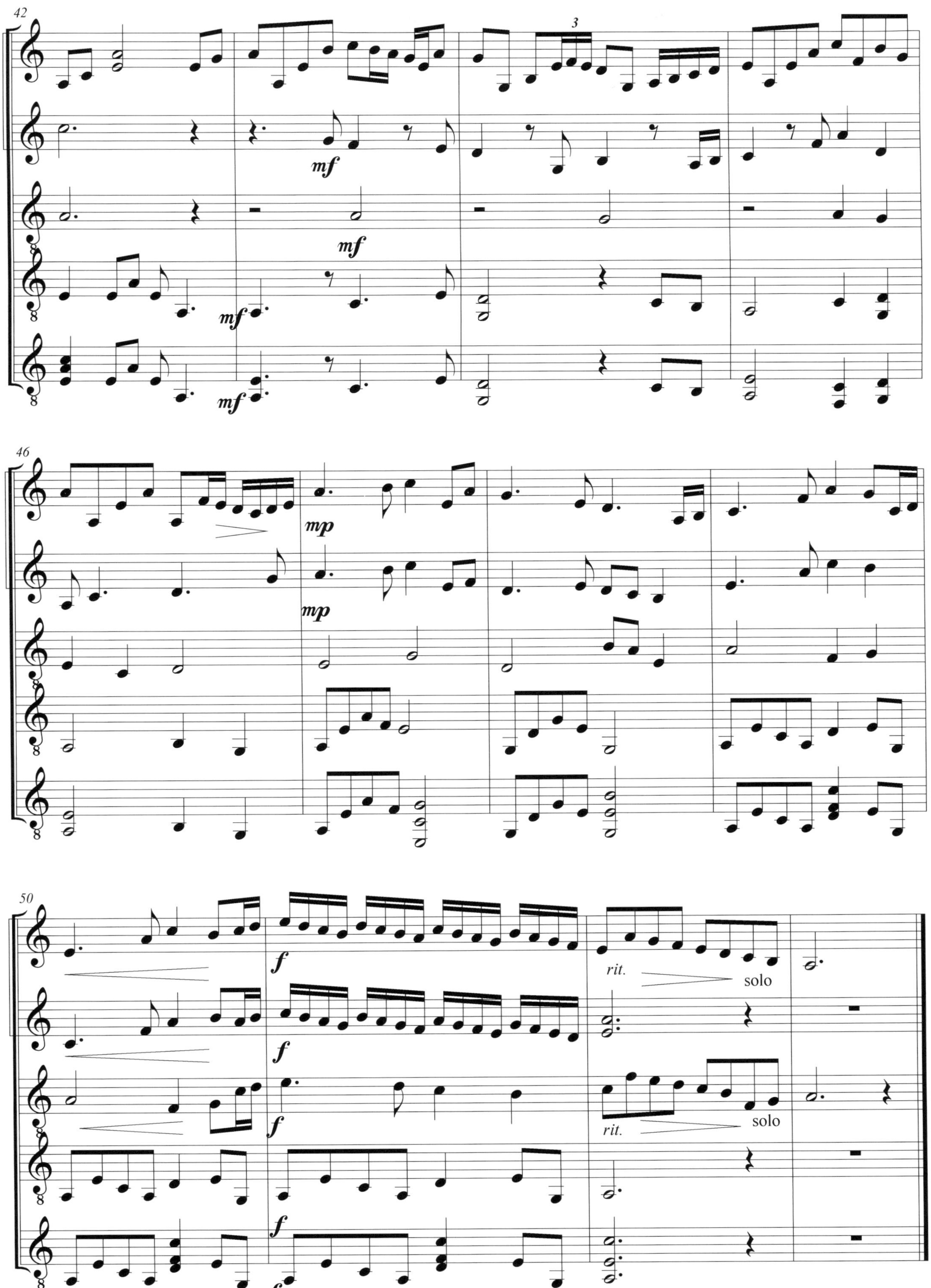
42
3
mf
mf
mf
mf
46
mp
mp
50
f
f
f
f
f
rit.
solo
rit.
solo

Ayton's Farewell

Fantasia on a theme by Will Ayton

Mandolin 1

Marilynn Mair

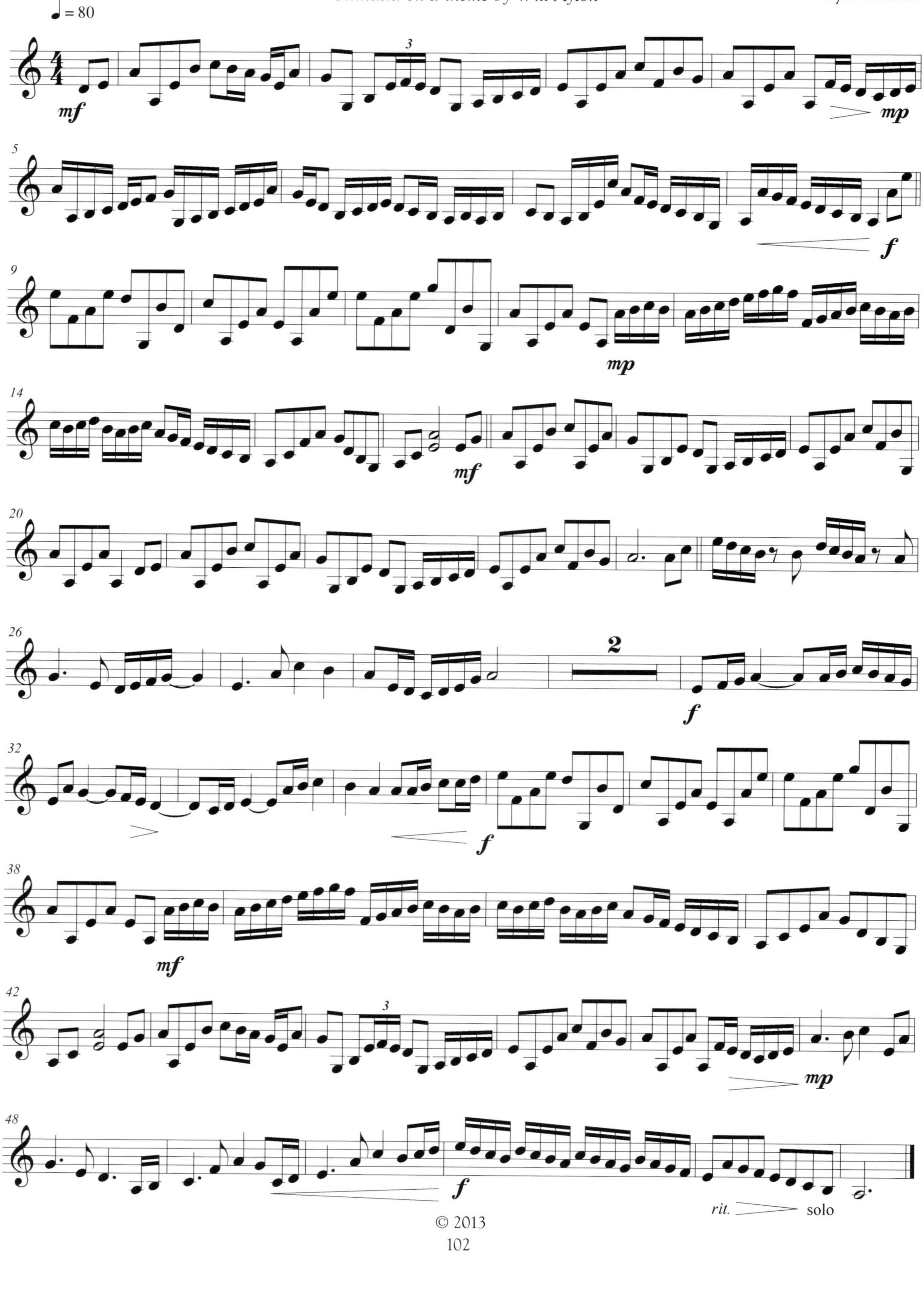

Ayton's Farewell

Fantasia on a theme by Will Ayton

Mandolin 2

Marilynn Mair

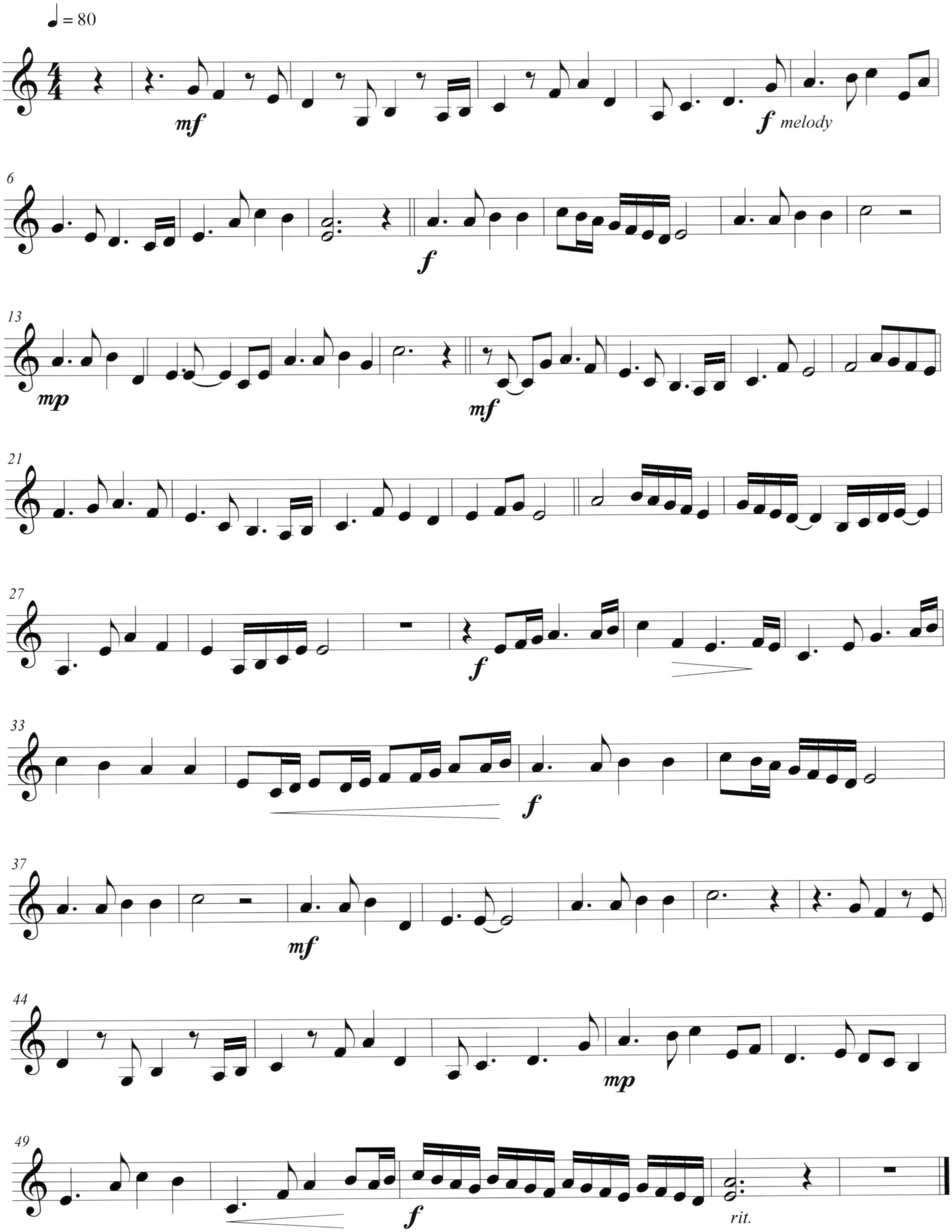

Ayton's Farewell

Mandola - transposed treble

Fantasia on a theme by Will Ayton

Marilynn Mair

♩ = 80

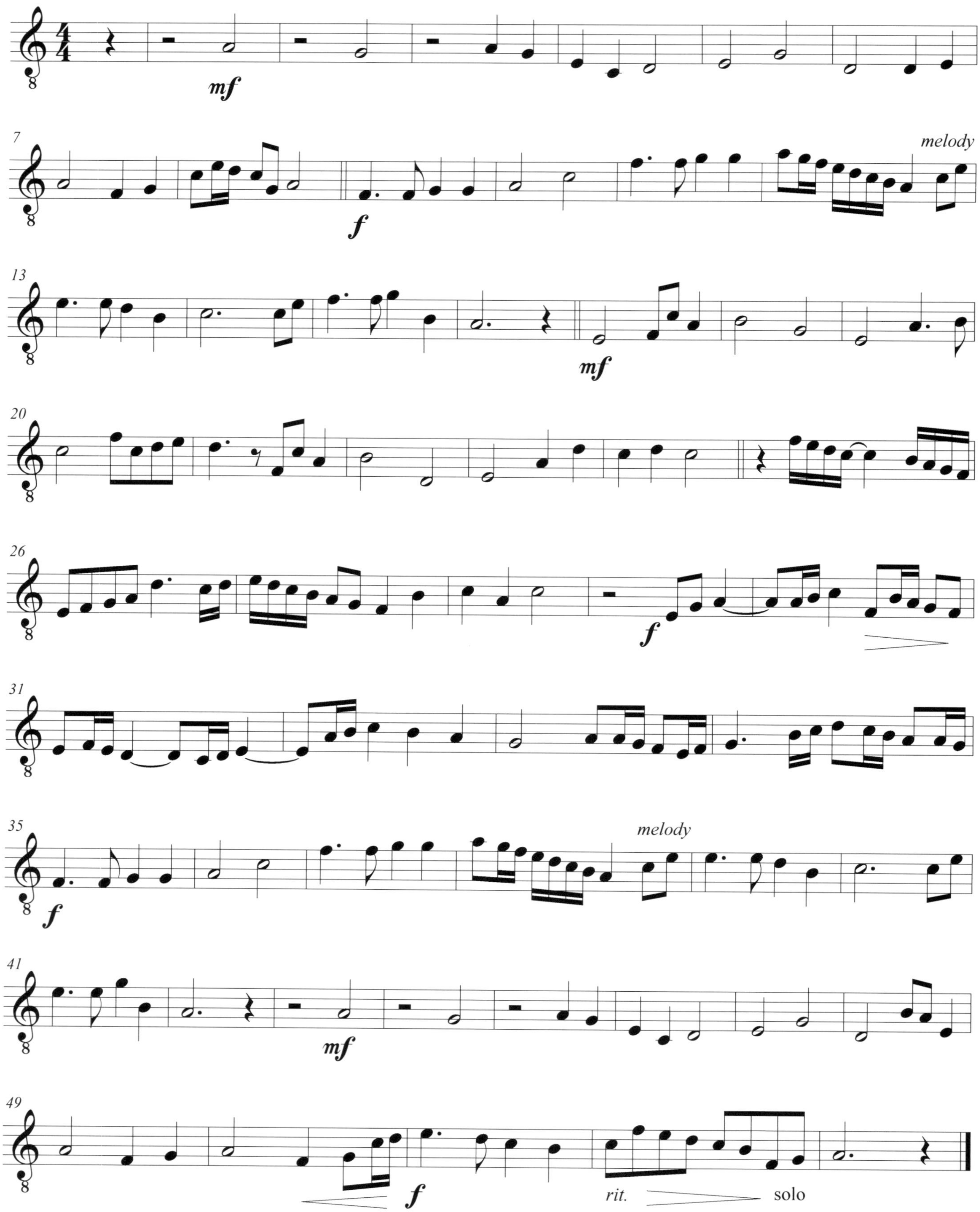

Ayton's Farewell

Fantasia on a theme by Will Ayton

Mandola - alto clef

Marilynn Mair

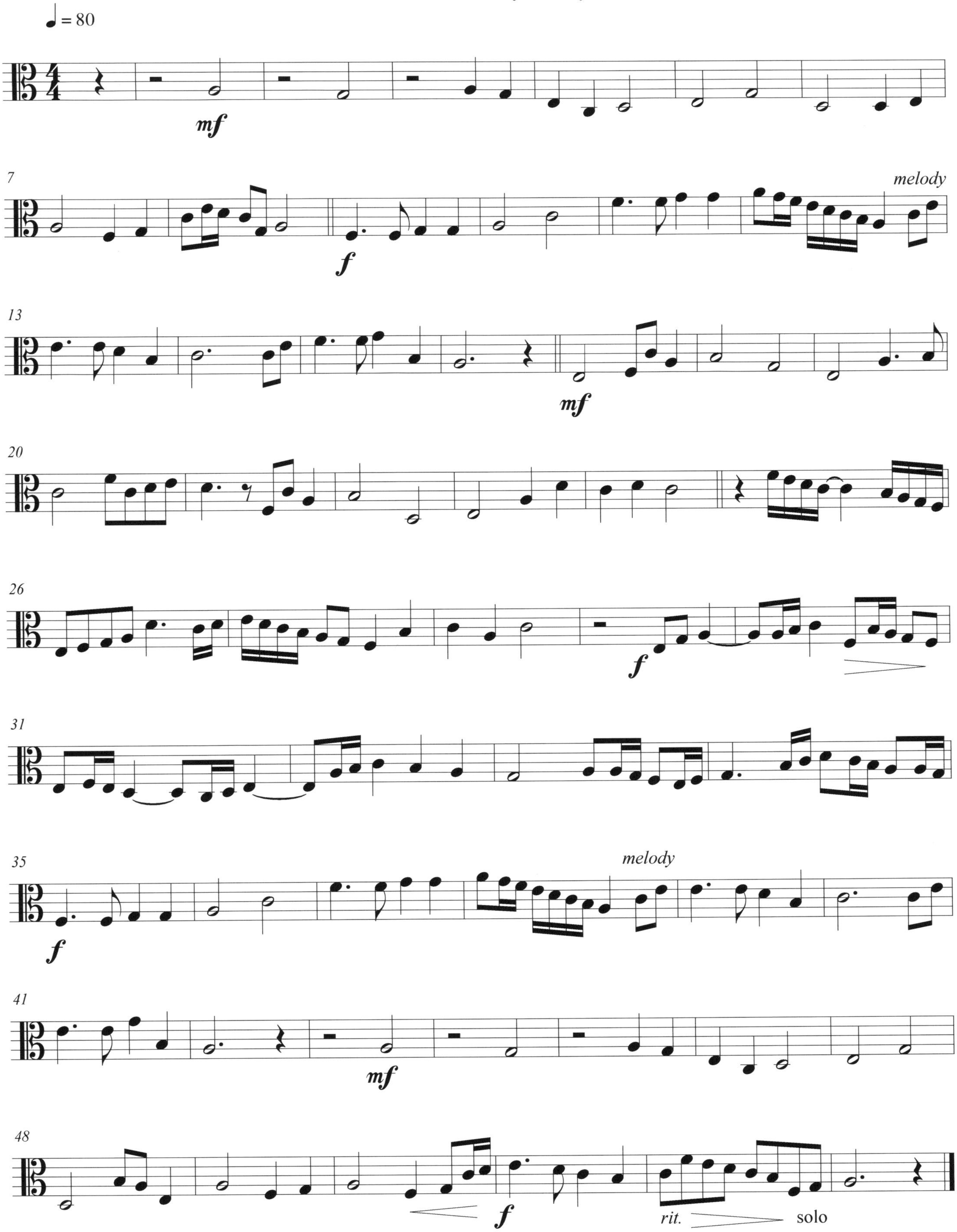

Ayton's Farewell

Octave Mandolin

Fantasia on a theme by Will Ayton

Marilynn Mair

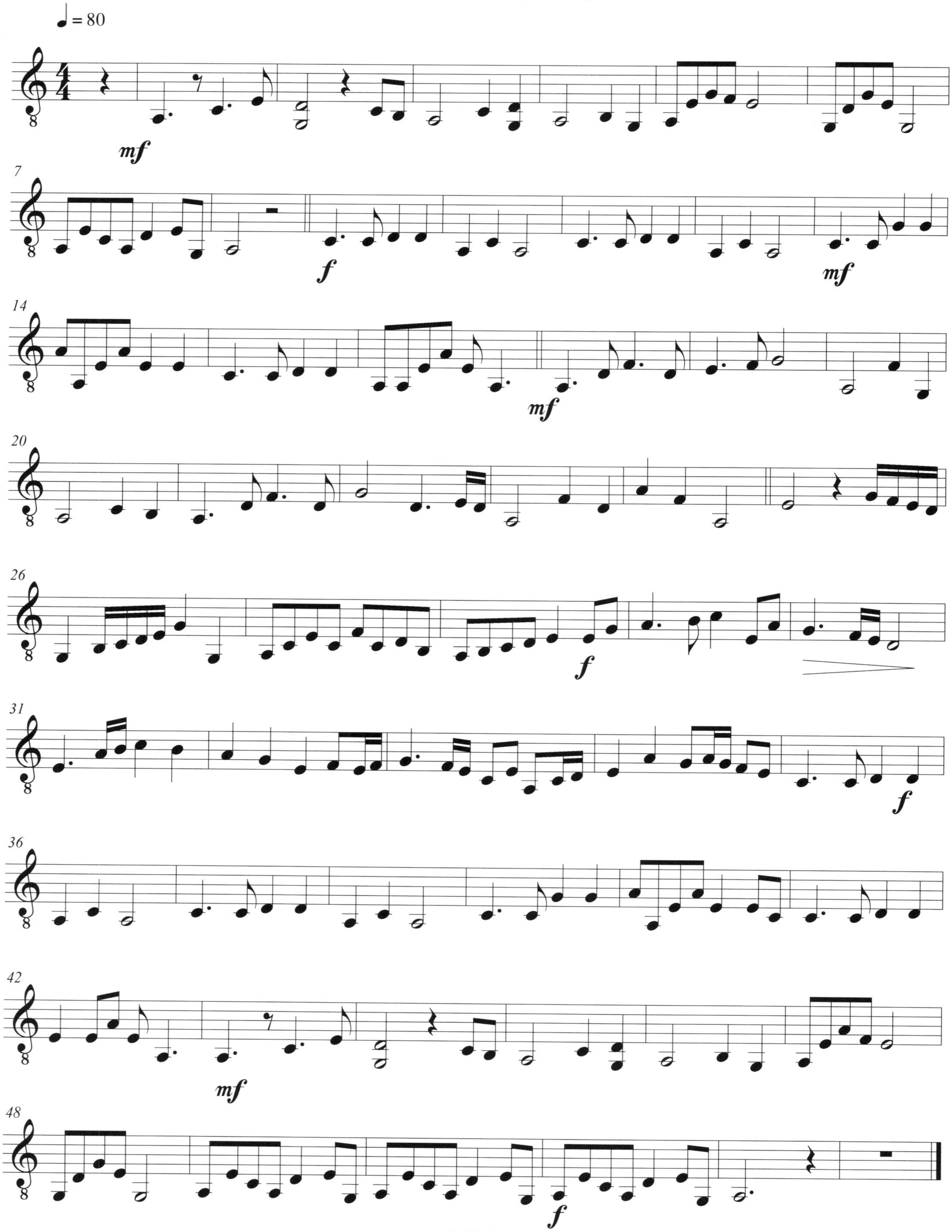

Ayton's Farewell

Fantasia on a theme by Will Ayton

Marilynn Mair

Guitar

♩ = 80

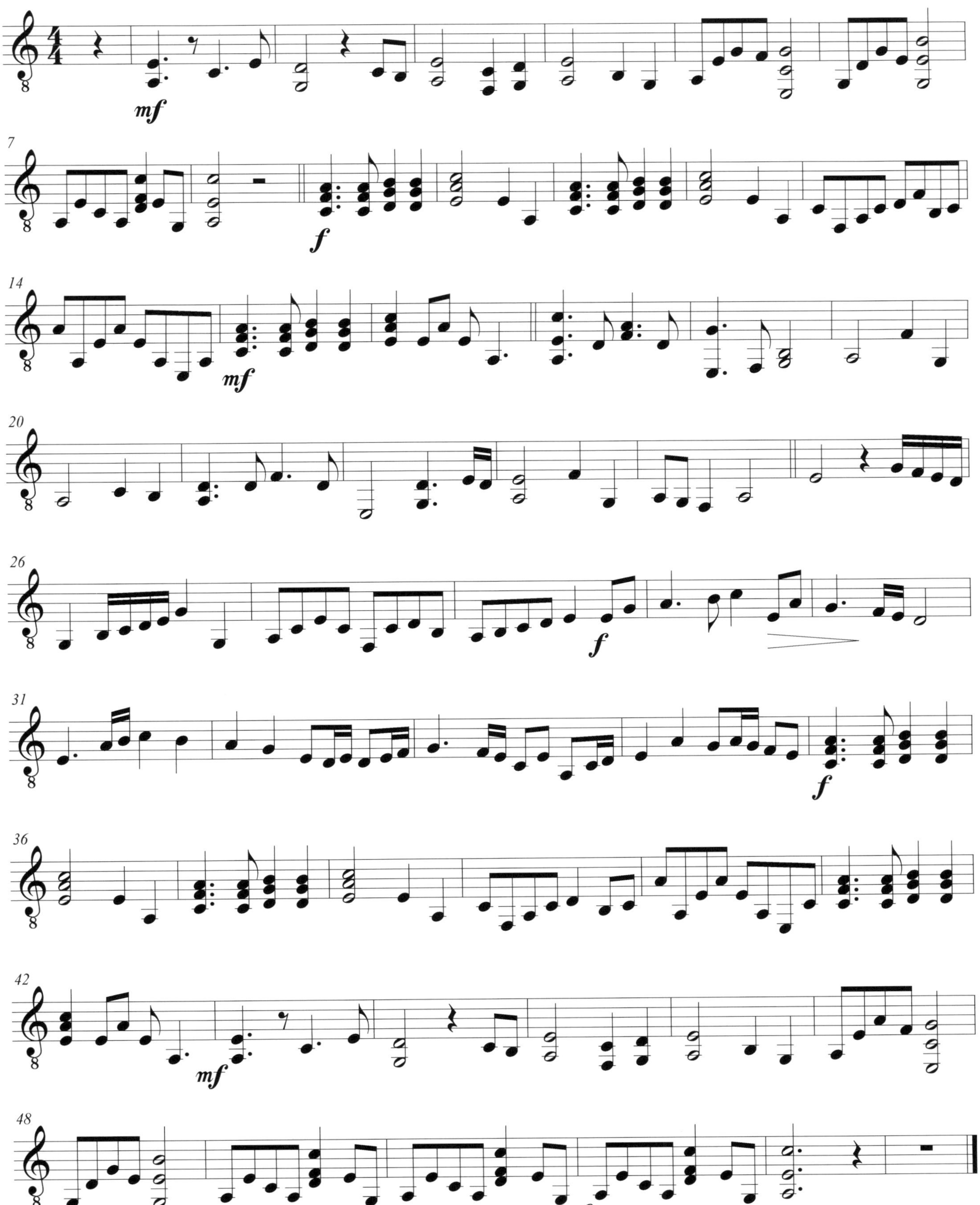

Badi no Rio

Badi in Rio
after Bach's Badinerie

Marilynn Mair

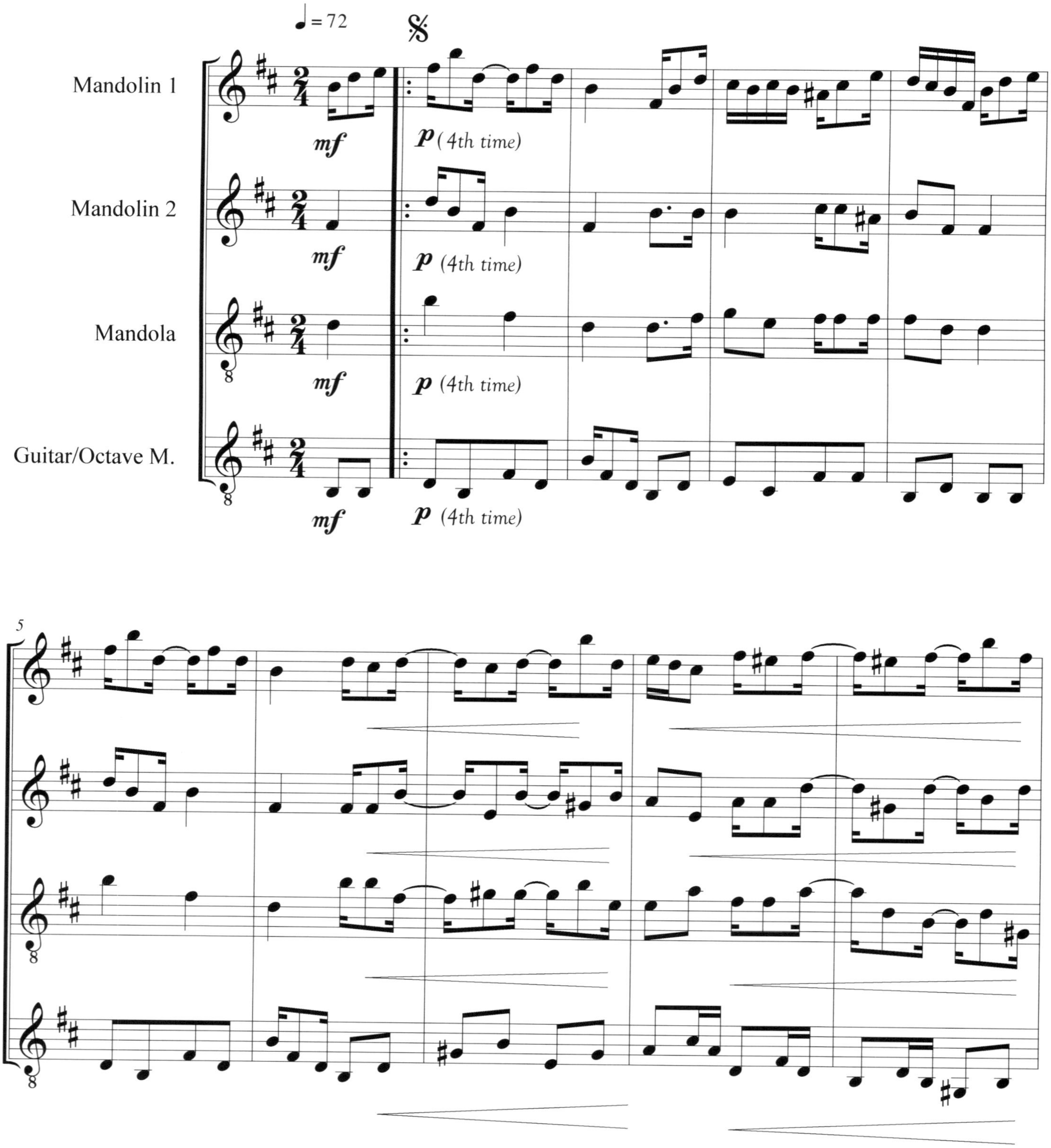

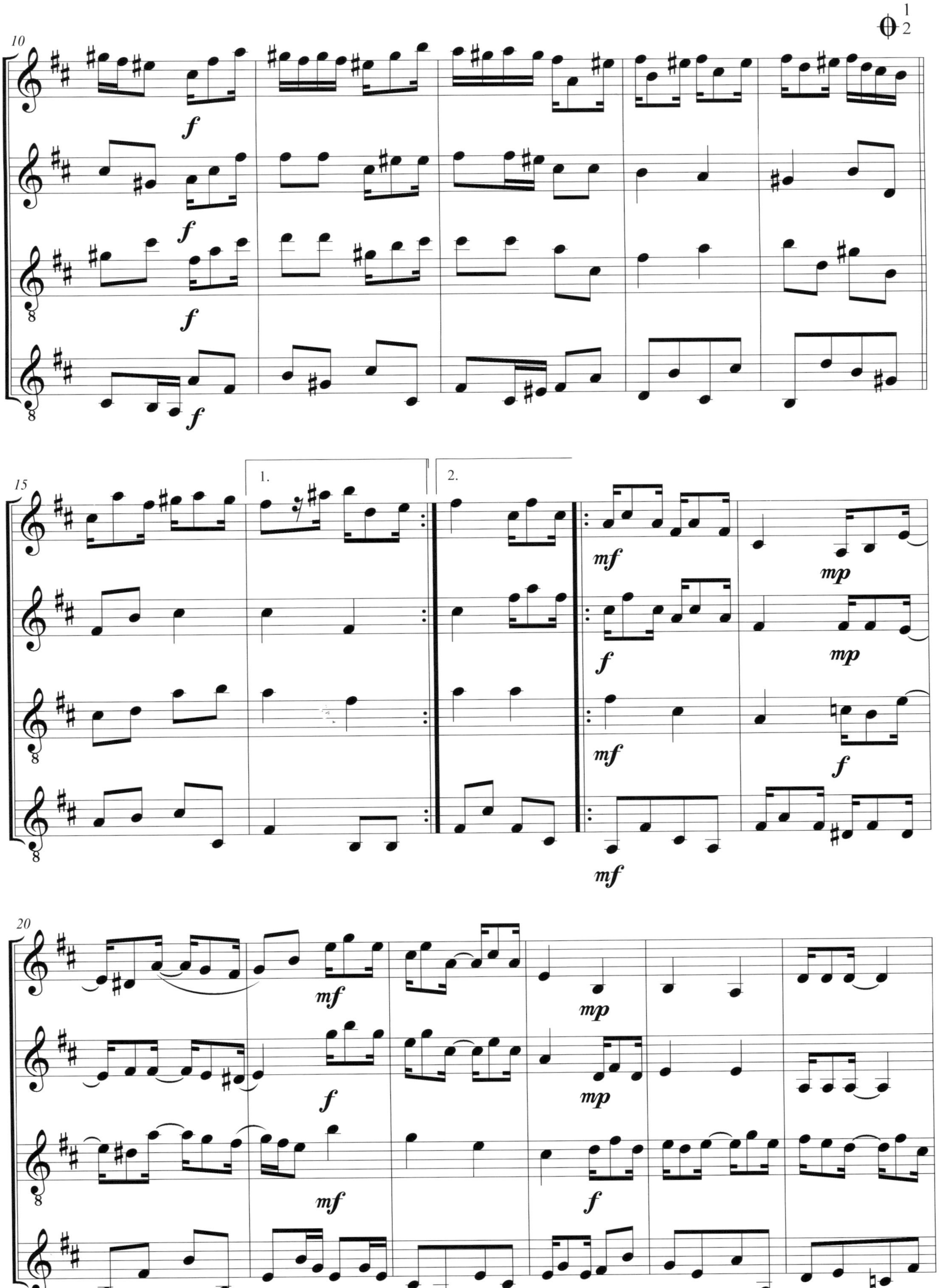
10
15
1.
2.
20

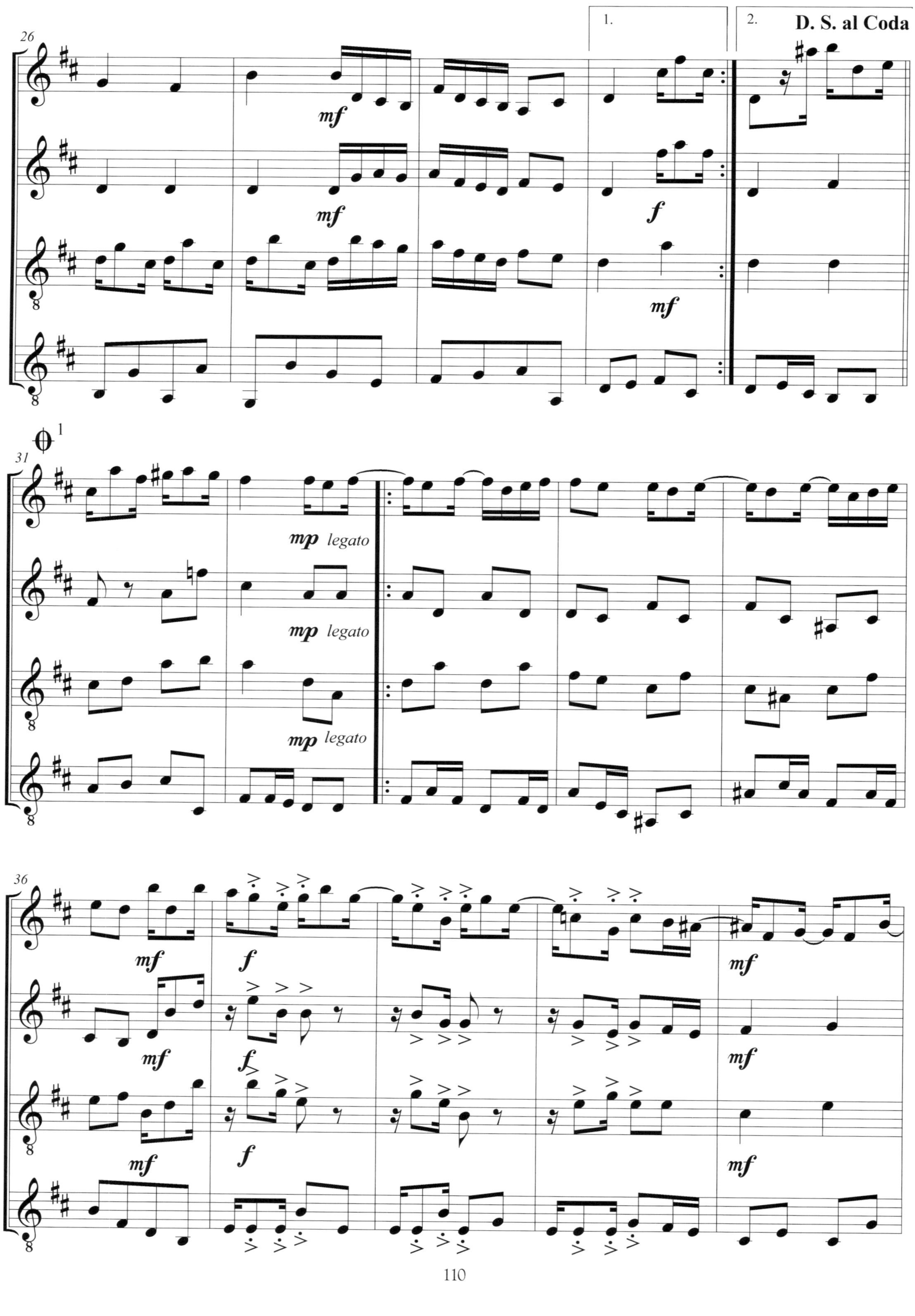
1.
2.
D. S. al Coda
mf
f
mp legato

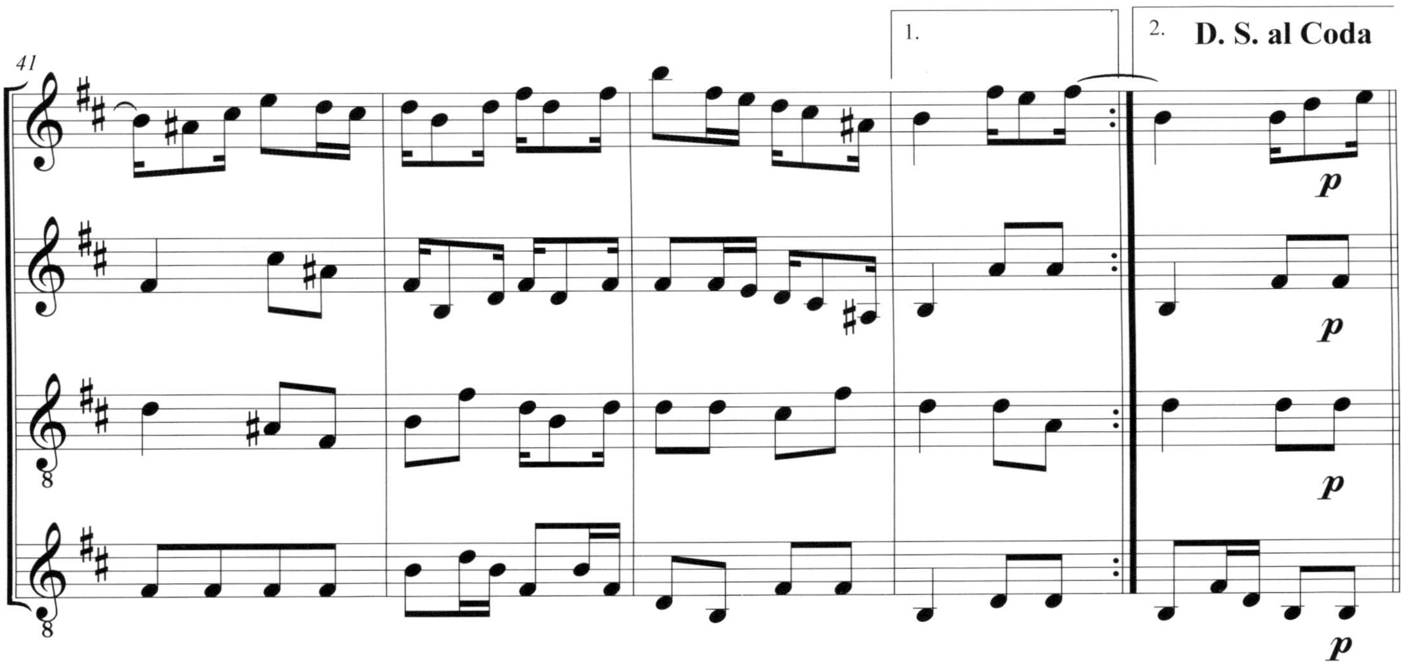

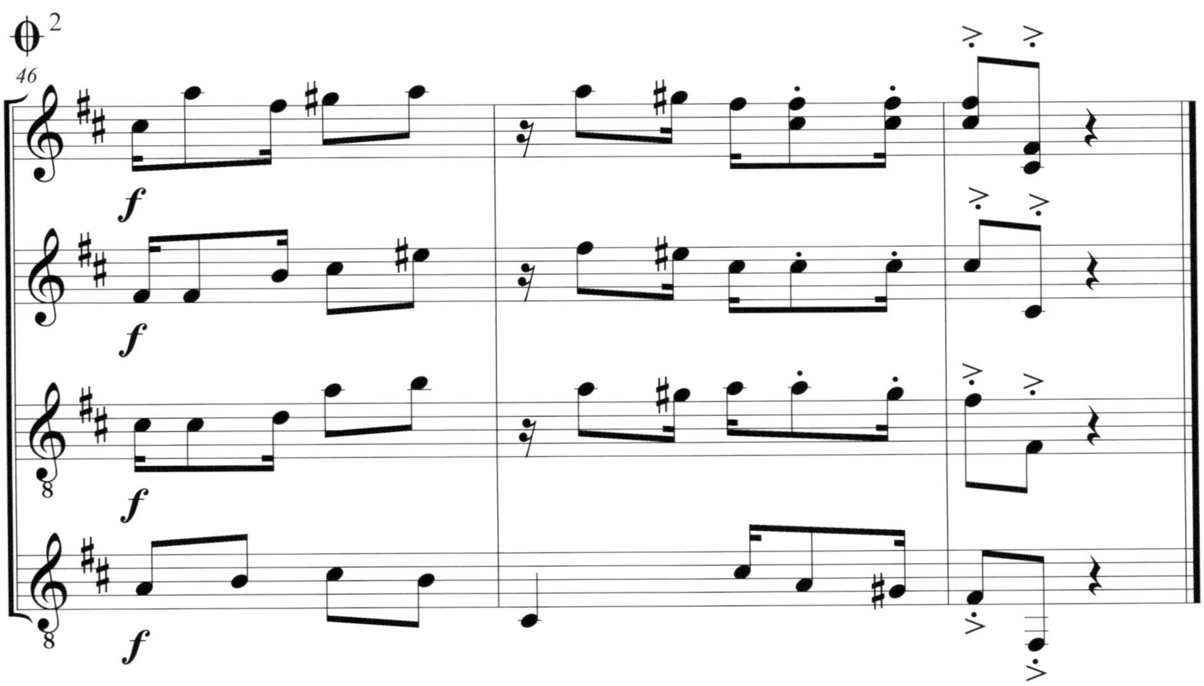

This piece explores my fantasy of how the music world would have evolved differently had Bach been born in Rio de Janeiro in the late 19th century. Badi follows the typical Choro roadmap: AA-BB-A-CC-A-Coda.

Badi no Rio

Badi in Rio
after Bach's Badinerie

Mandolin 1

Marilynn Mair

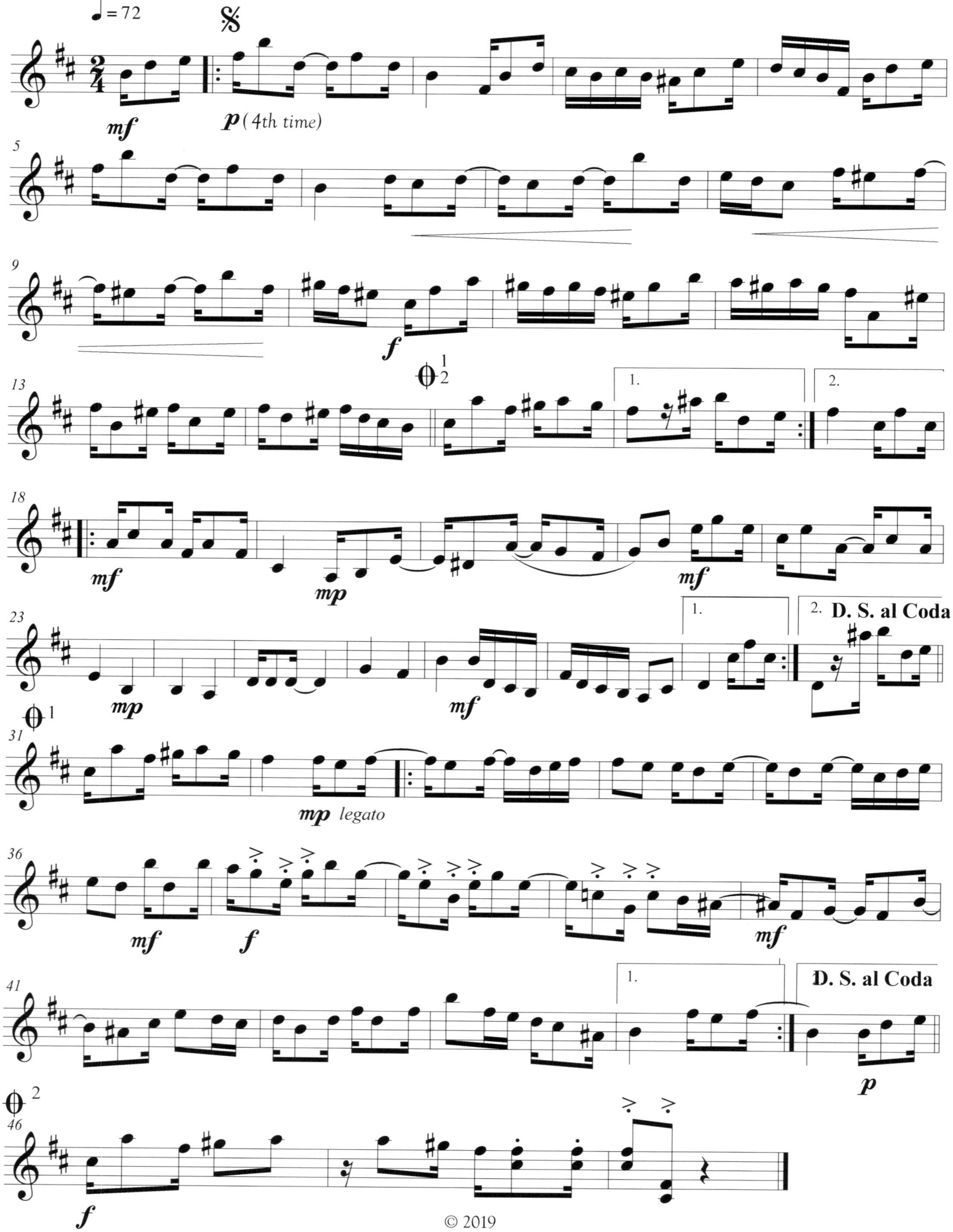

Mandolin 2

Badi no Rio

Badi in Rio

after Bach's Badinerie

Marilynn Mair

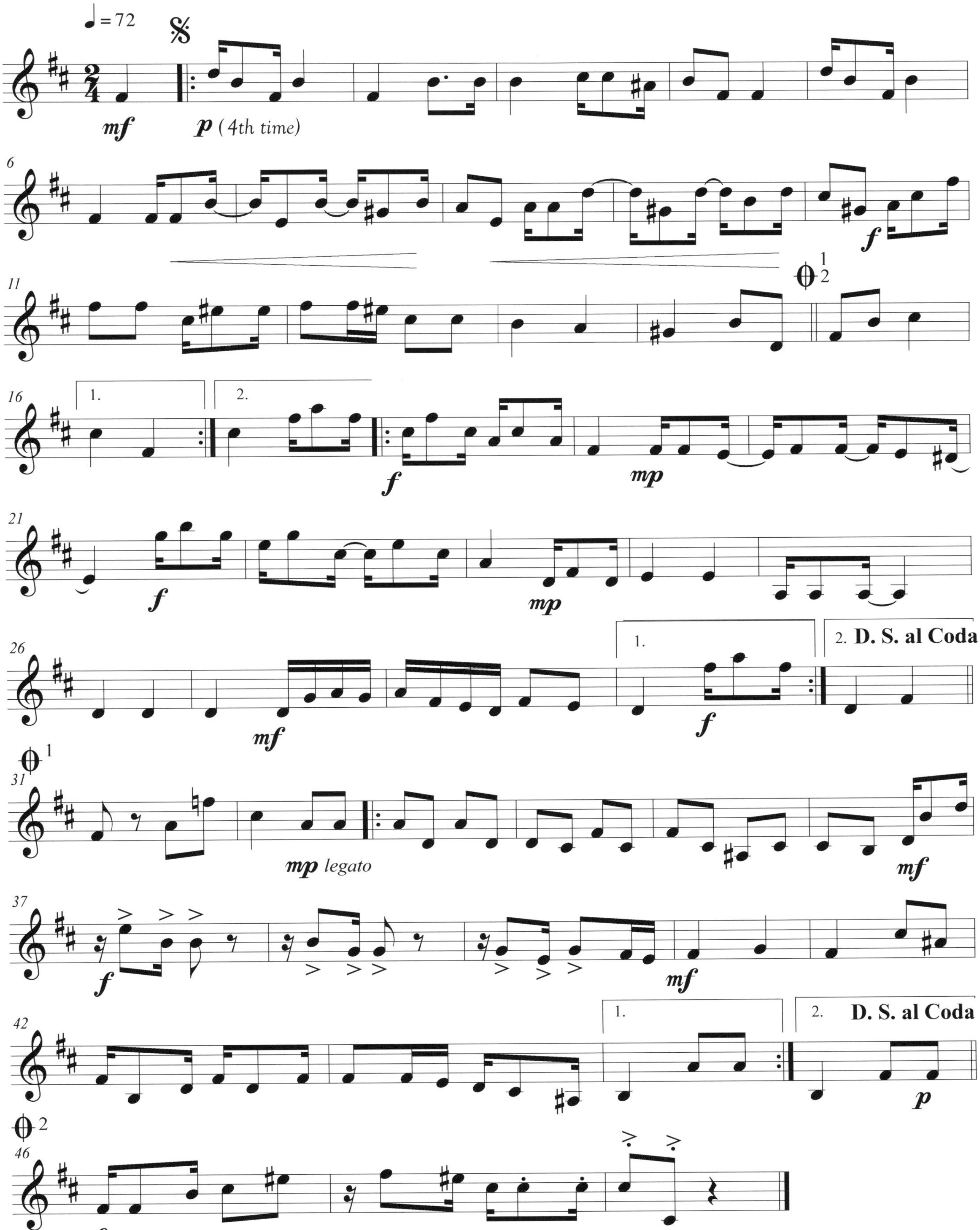

Badi no Rio

Badi in Rio

after Bach's Badinerie

Mandola- transposed treble

Marilynn Mair

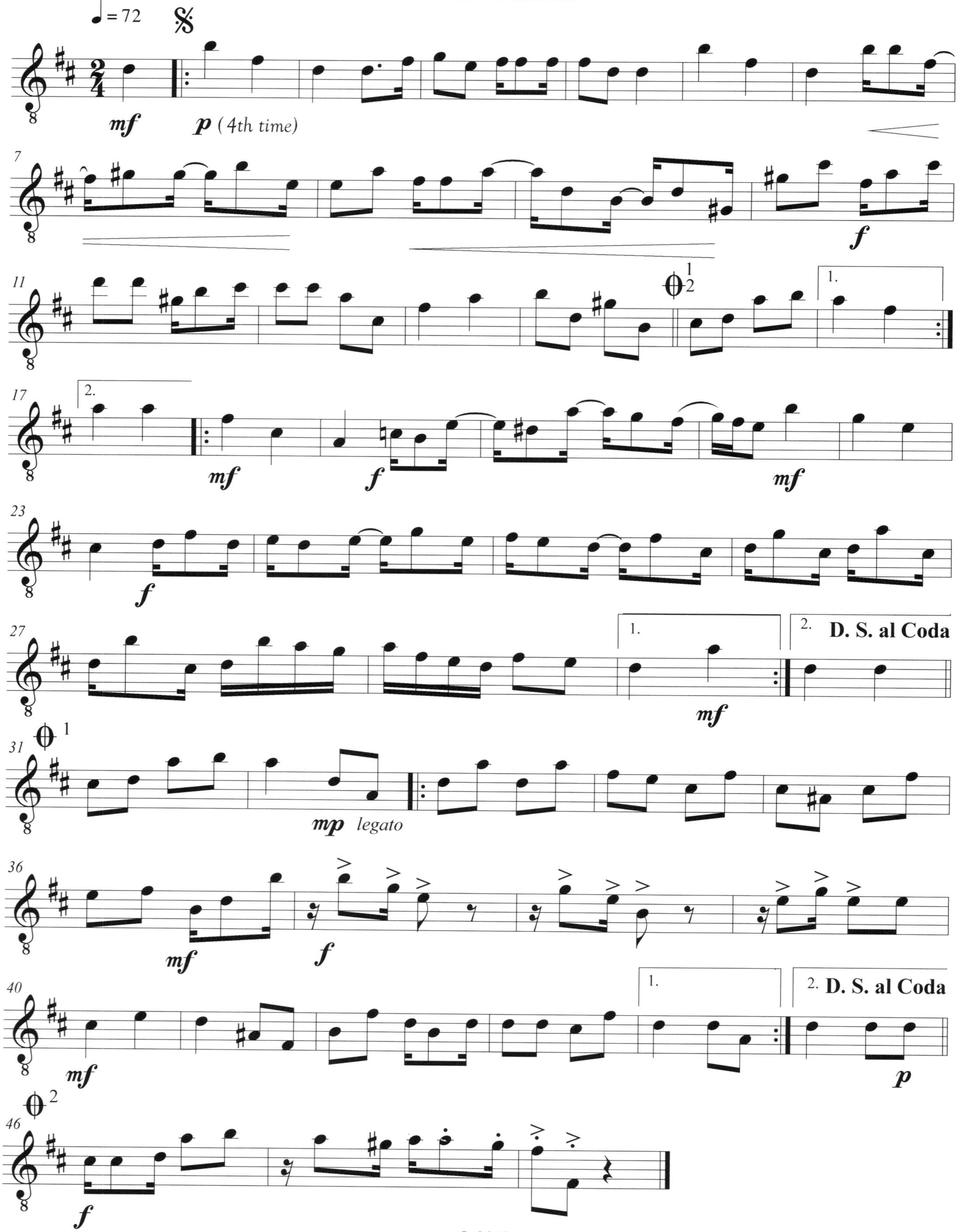

Badi no Rio

Mandola- alto clef

Badi in Rio

after Bach's Badinerie

Marilynn Mair

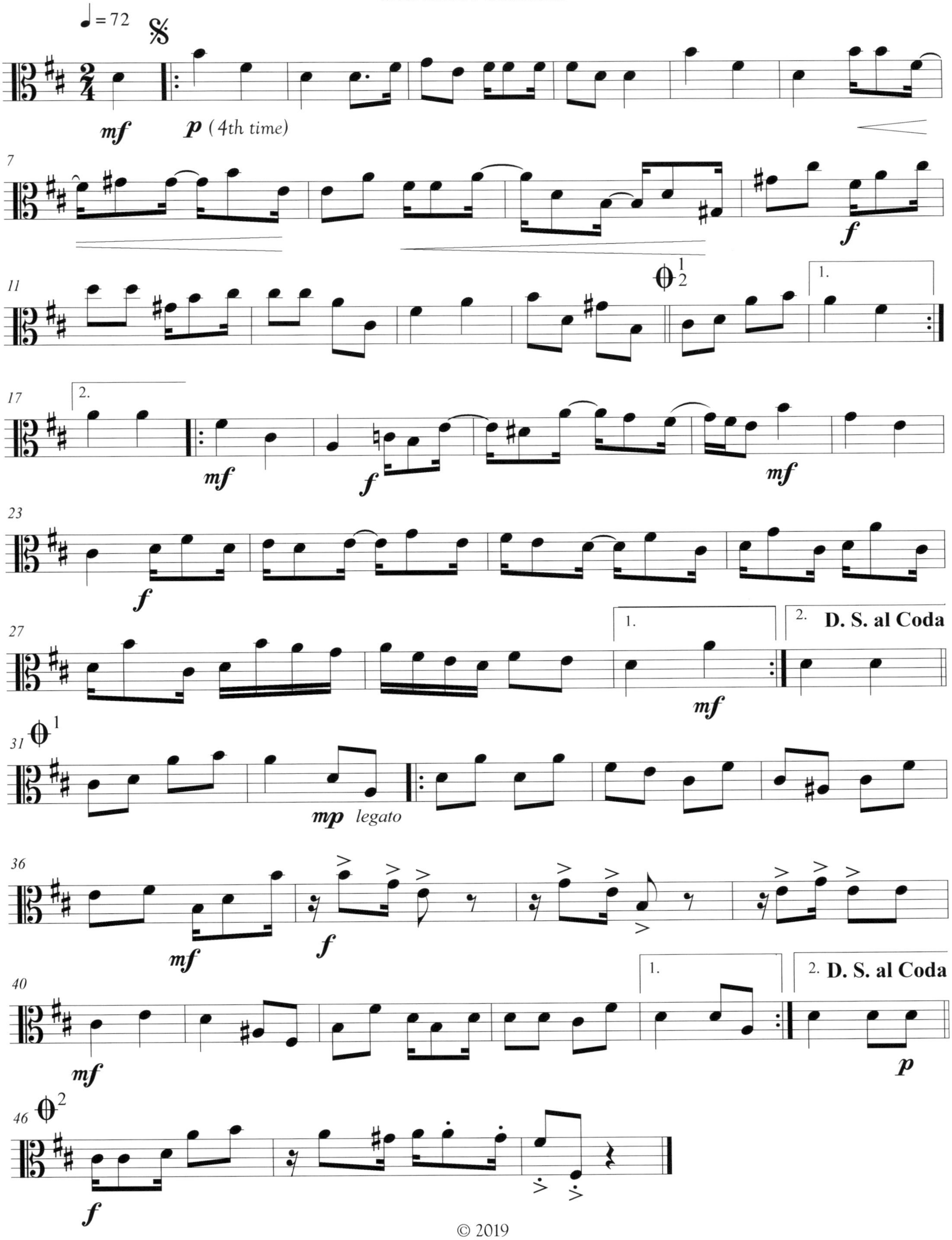

Badi no Rio

Guitar/Octave Mandolin

Badi in Rio
after Bach's Badinerie

Marilynn Mair

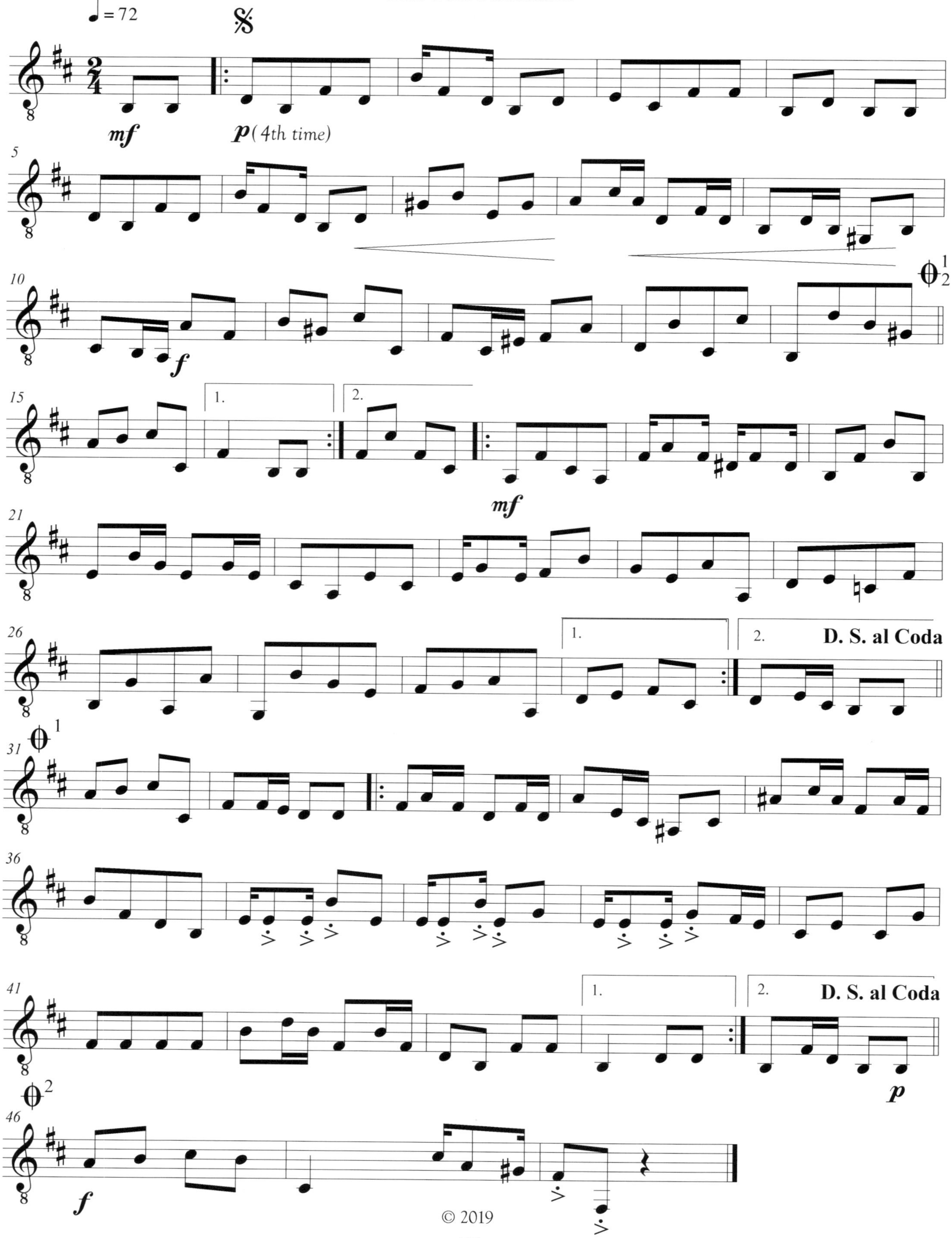

Badi no Rio

Mandocello

Badi in Rio
after Bach's Badinerie

Marilynn Mair

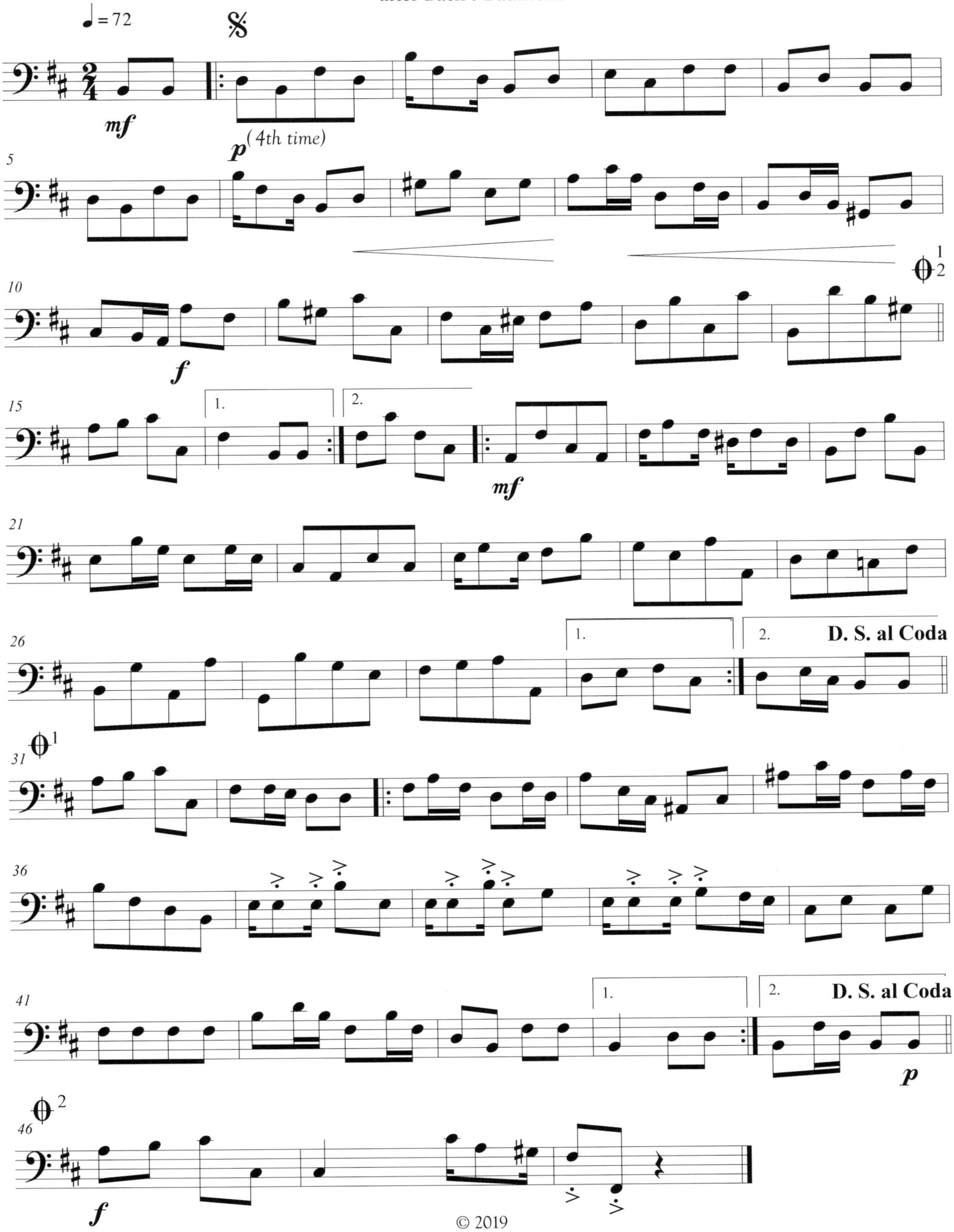

36

Enrolado

Spaceshot

for Enigmatica

Marilynn Mair

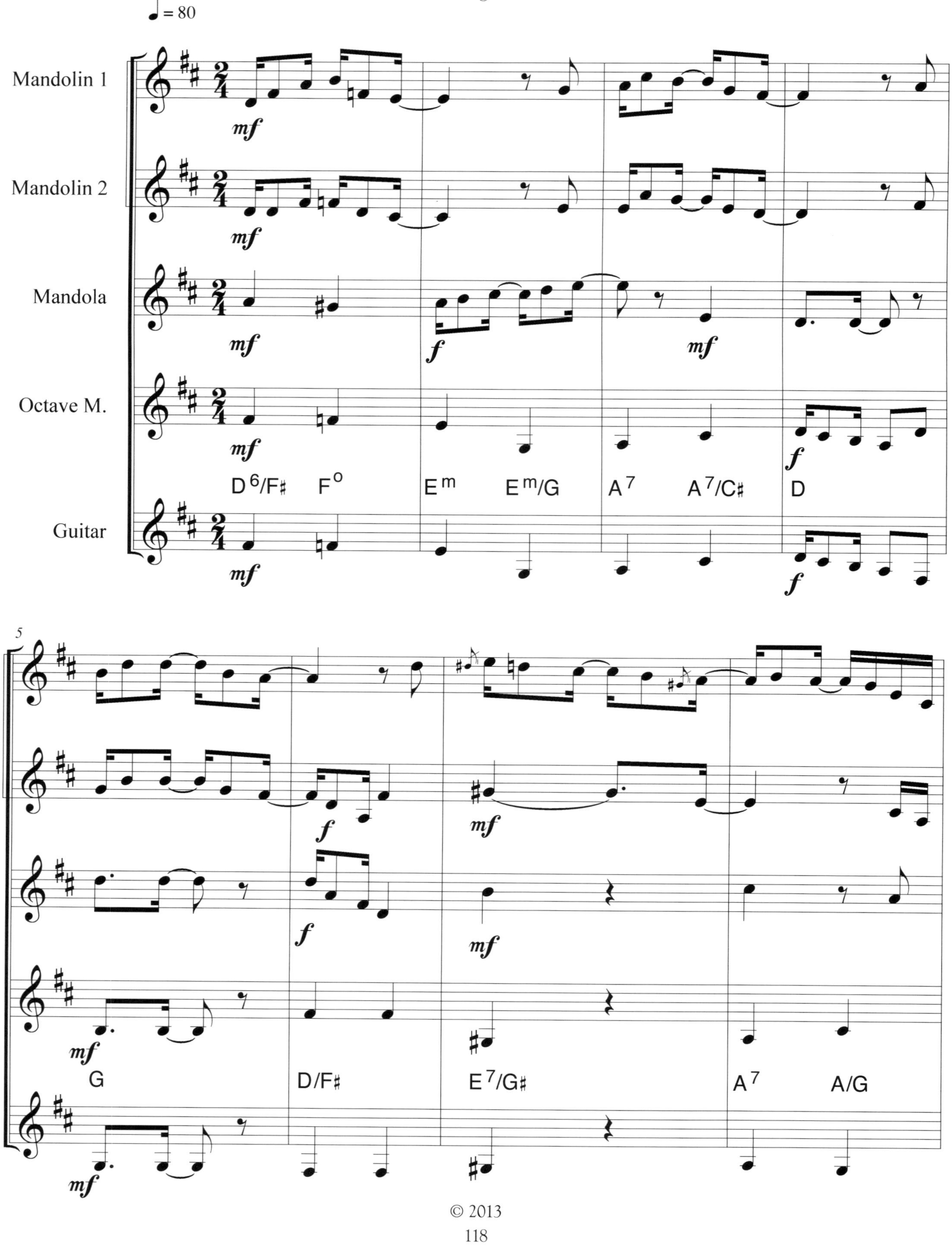

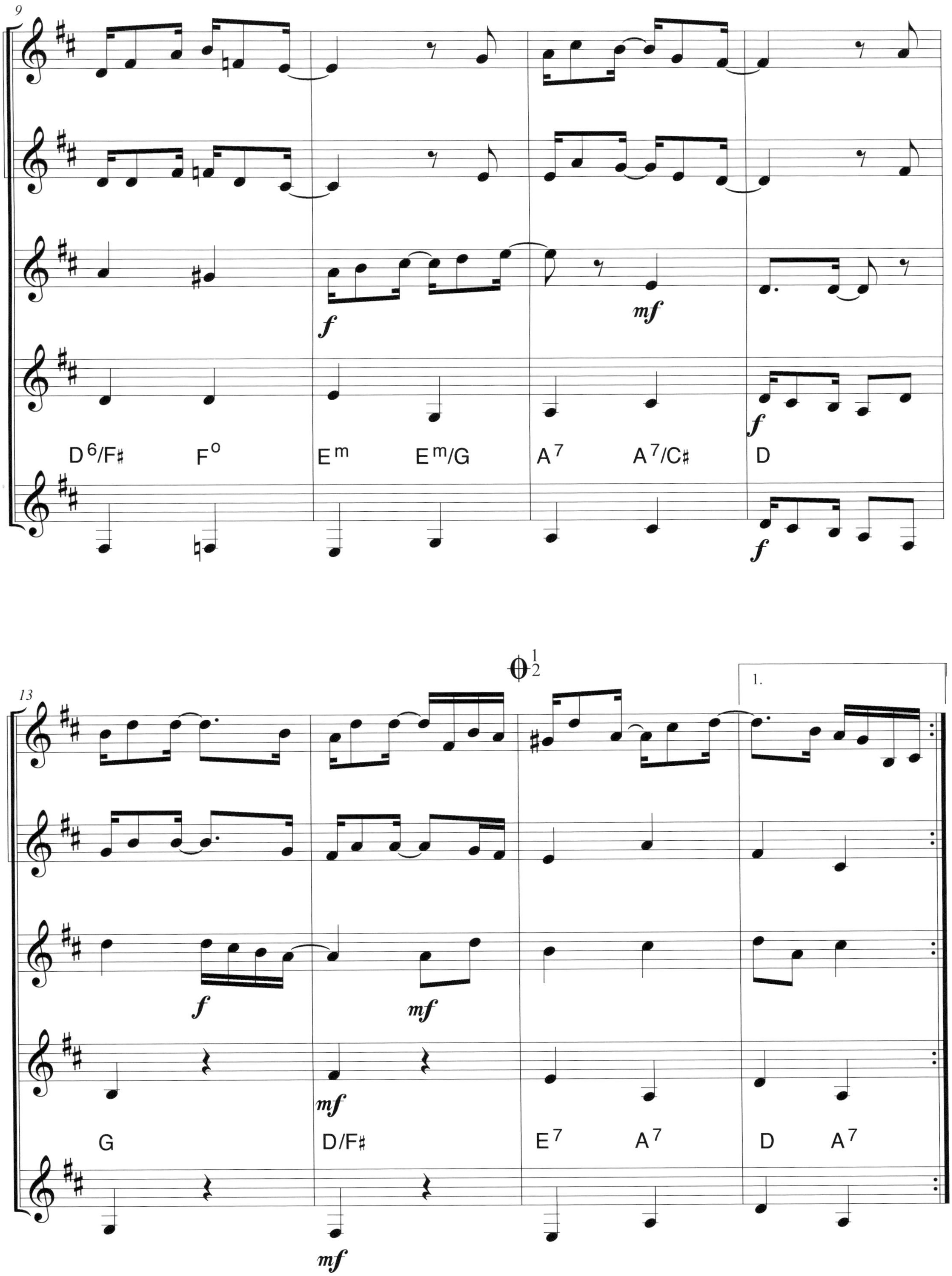
9
D6/F♯ F° Em Em/G A7 A7/C♯ D
13
1.
G D/F♯ E7 A7 D A7

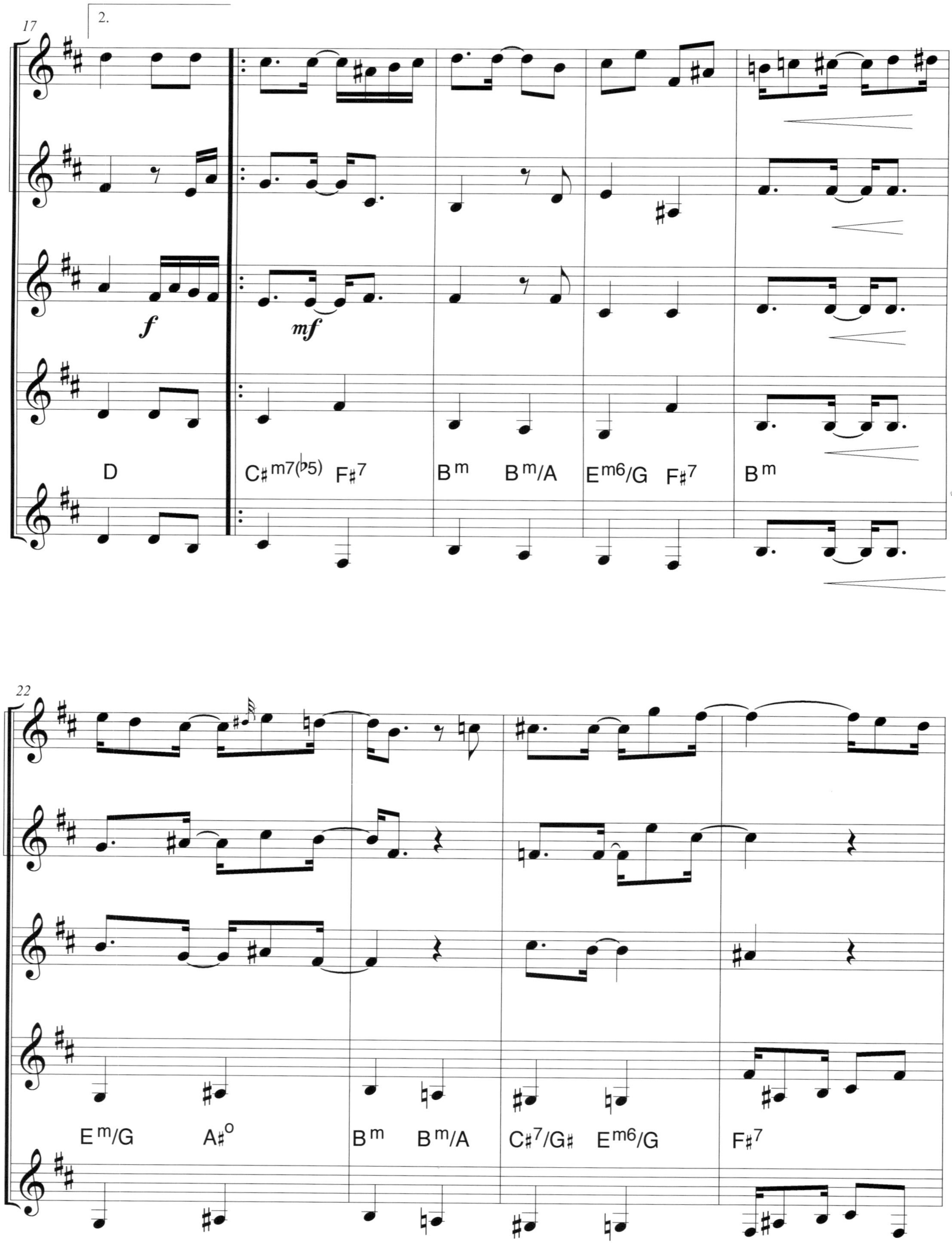
17
2.
f
mf
D
C♯m7(♭5) F♯7
Bm Bm/A
Em6/G F♯7
Bm
22
Em/G A♯o
Bm Bm/A
C♯7/G♯ Em6/G
F♯7

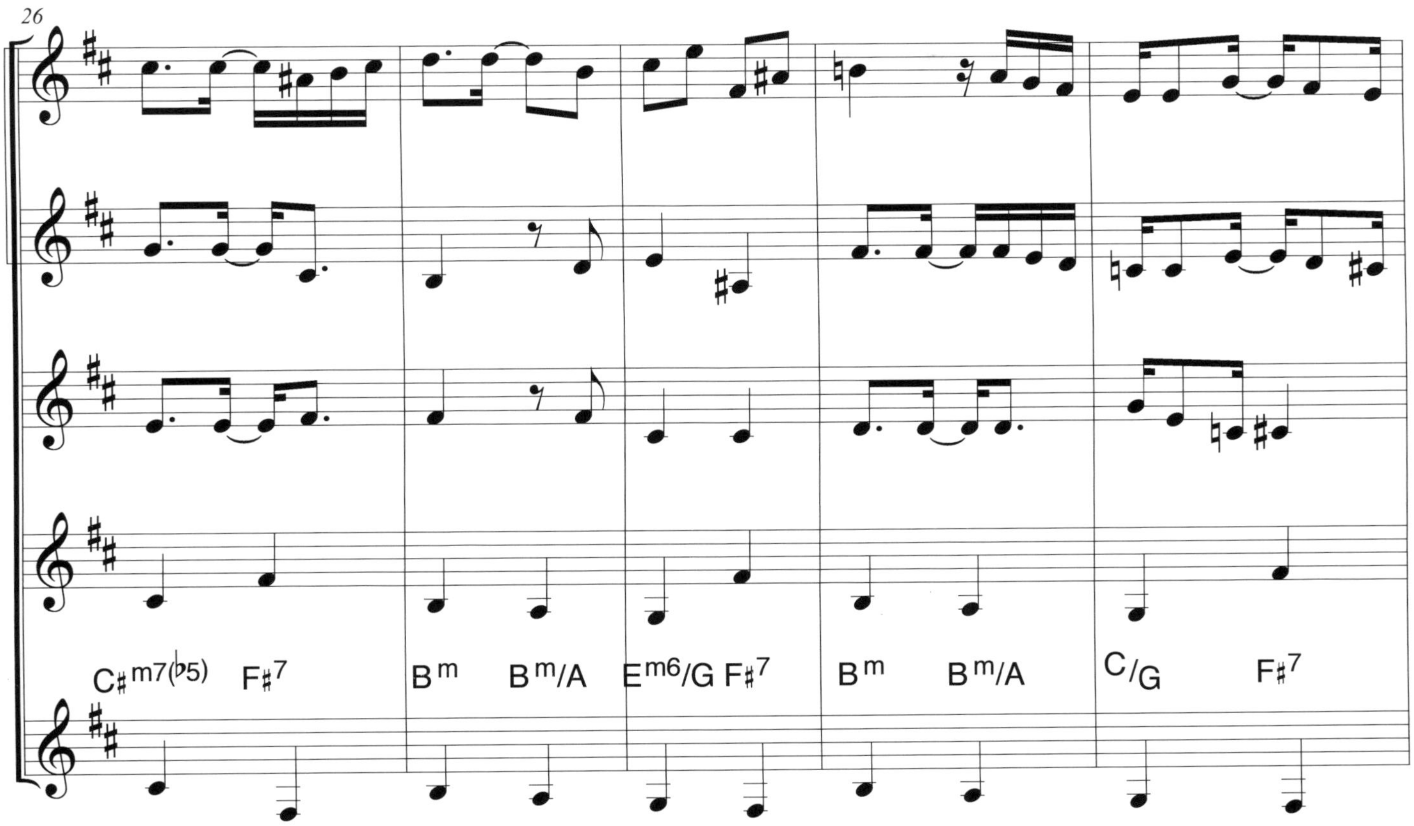
26
C♯m7(♭5) F♯7
Bm Bm/A
Em6/G F♯7
Bm Bm/A
C/G F♯7

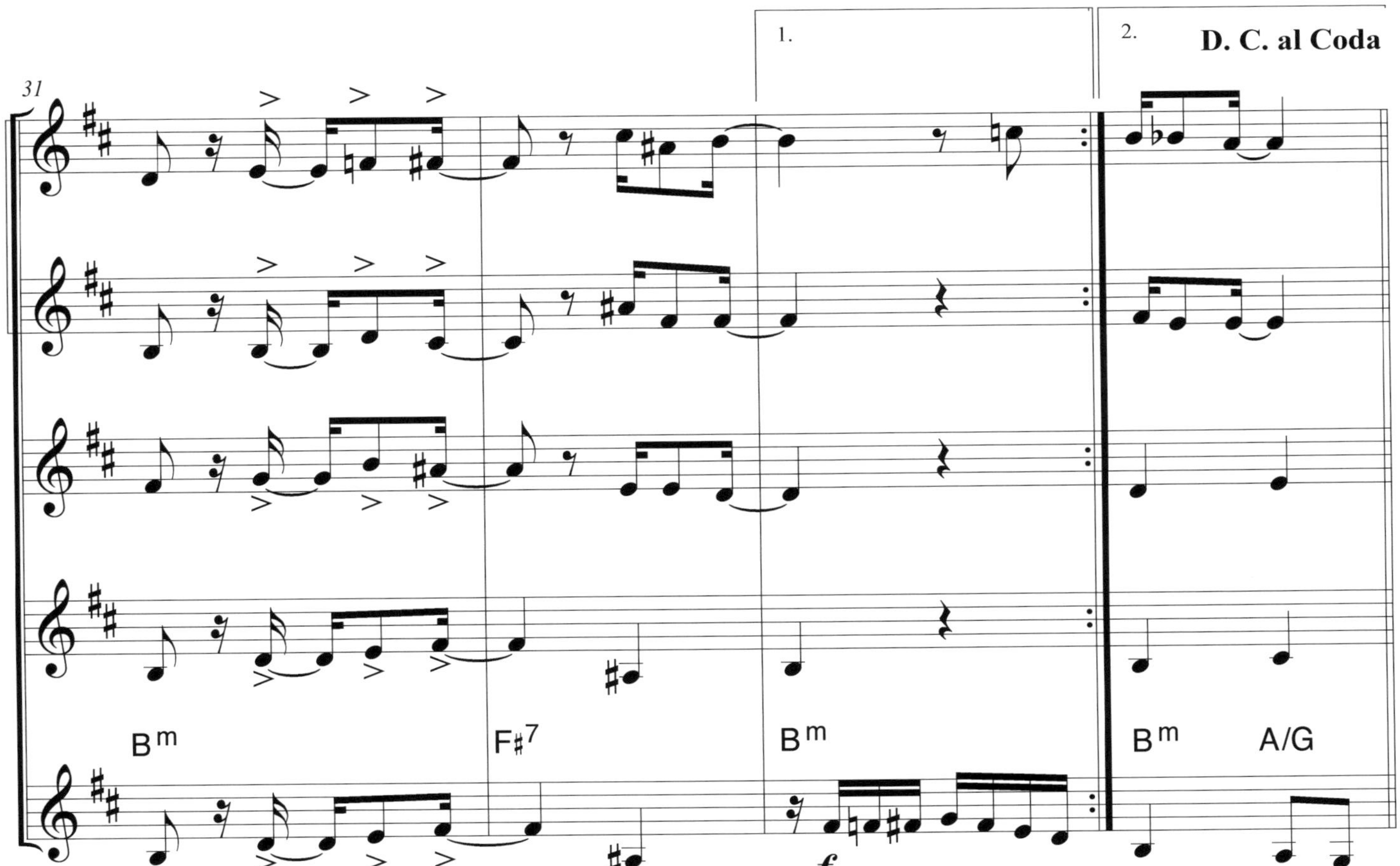
31
1.
2.
D. C. al Coda
Bm
F♯7
Bm
Bm A/G
f

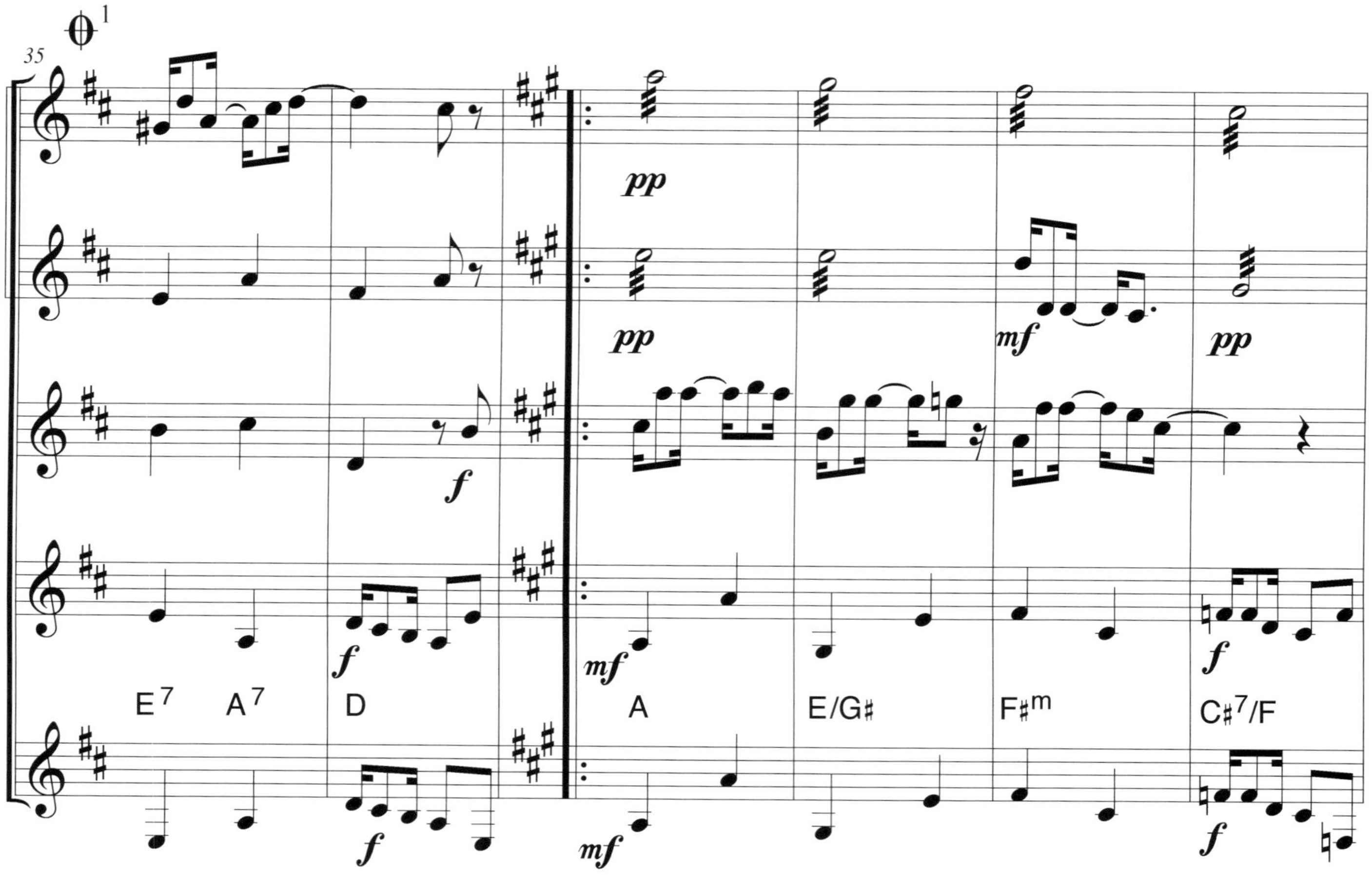
35
pp
mf
f
E7 A7 D A E/G♯ F♯m C♯7/F

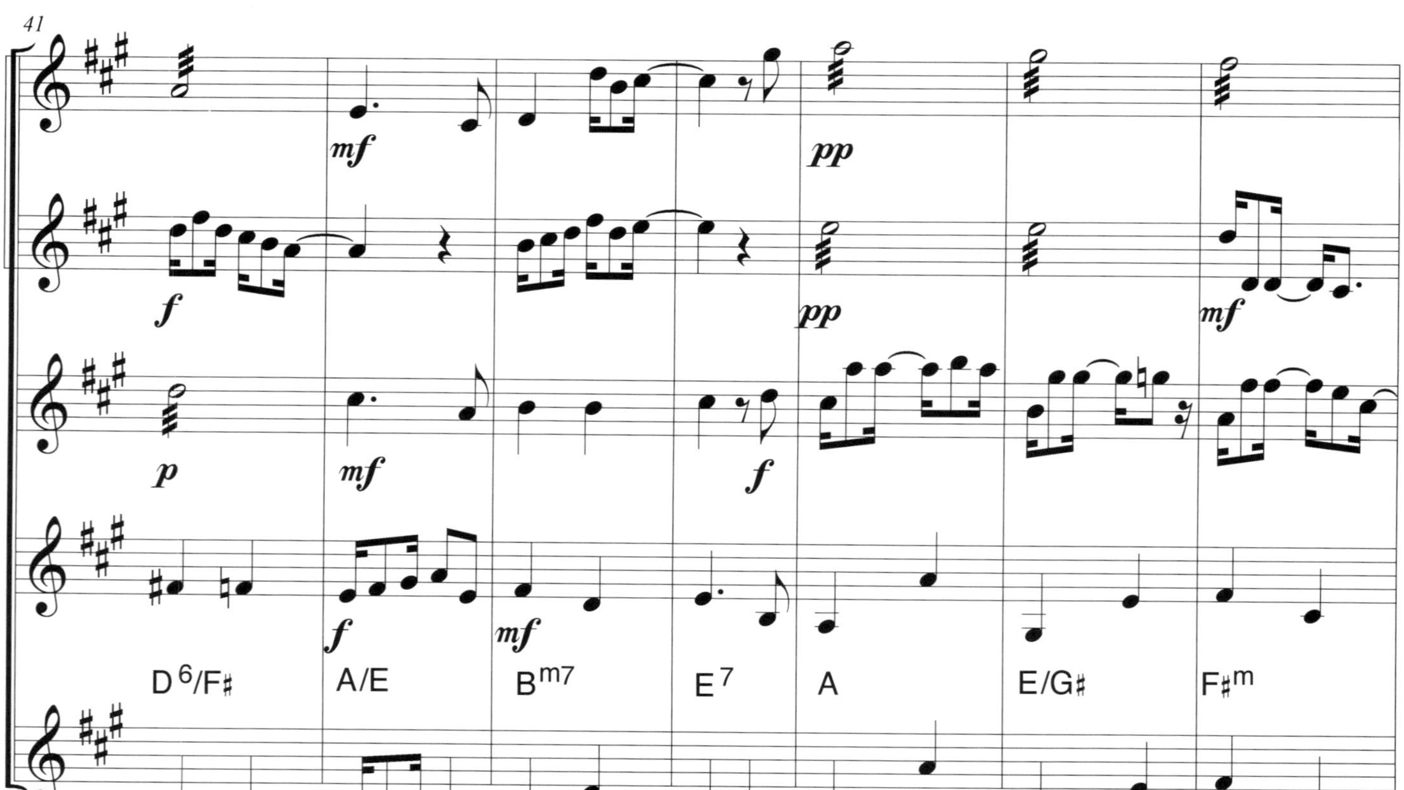
41
f
mf
pp
p
D6/F♯ A/E Bm7 E7 A E/G♯ F♯m

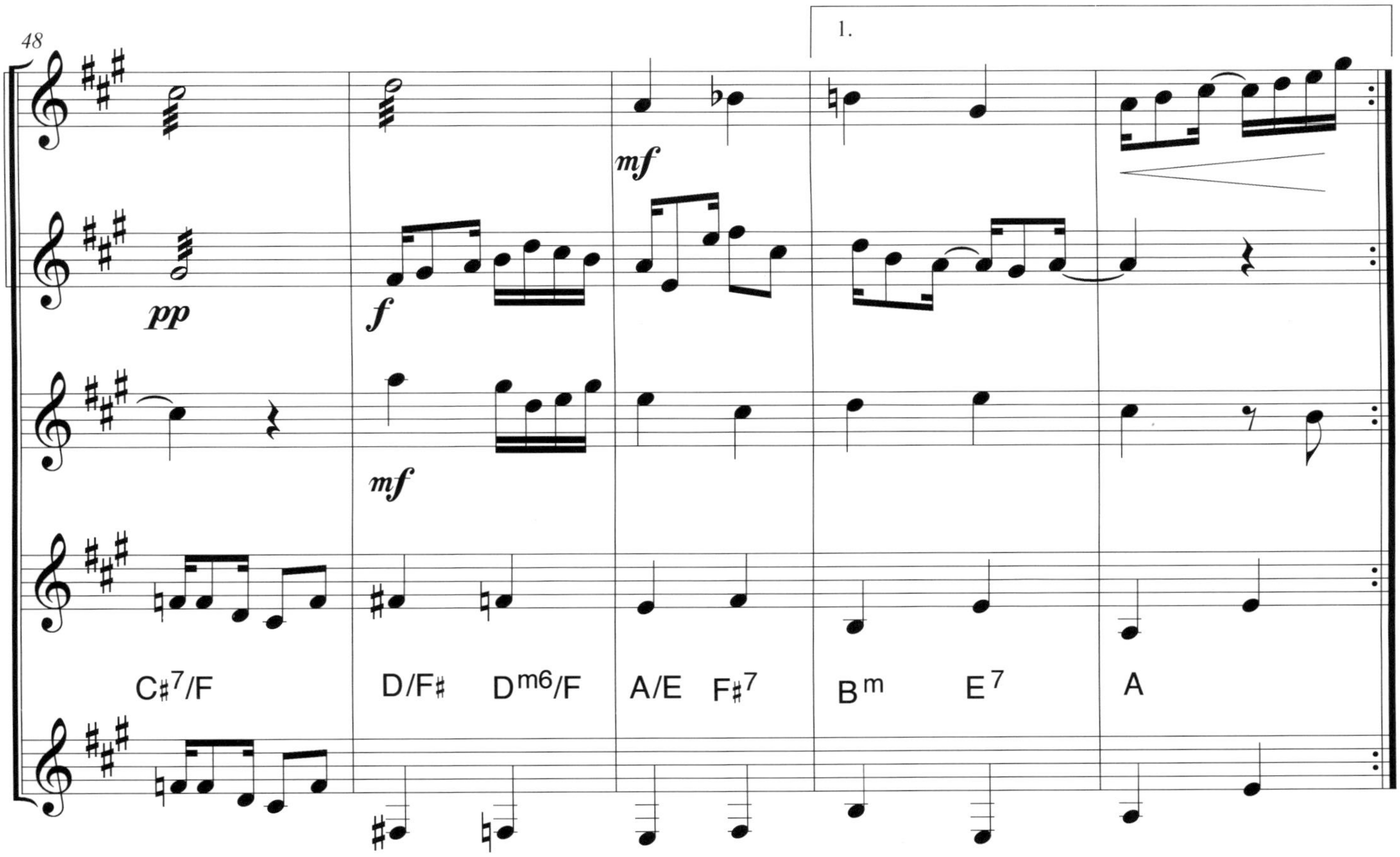

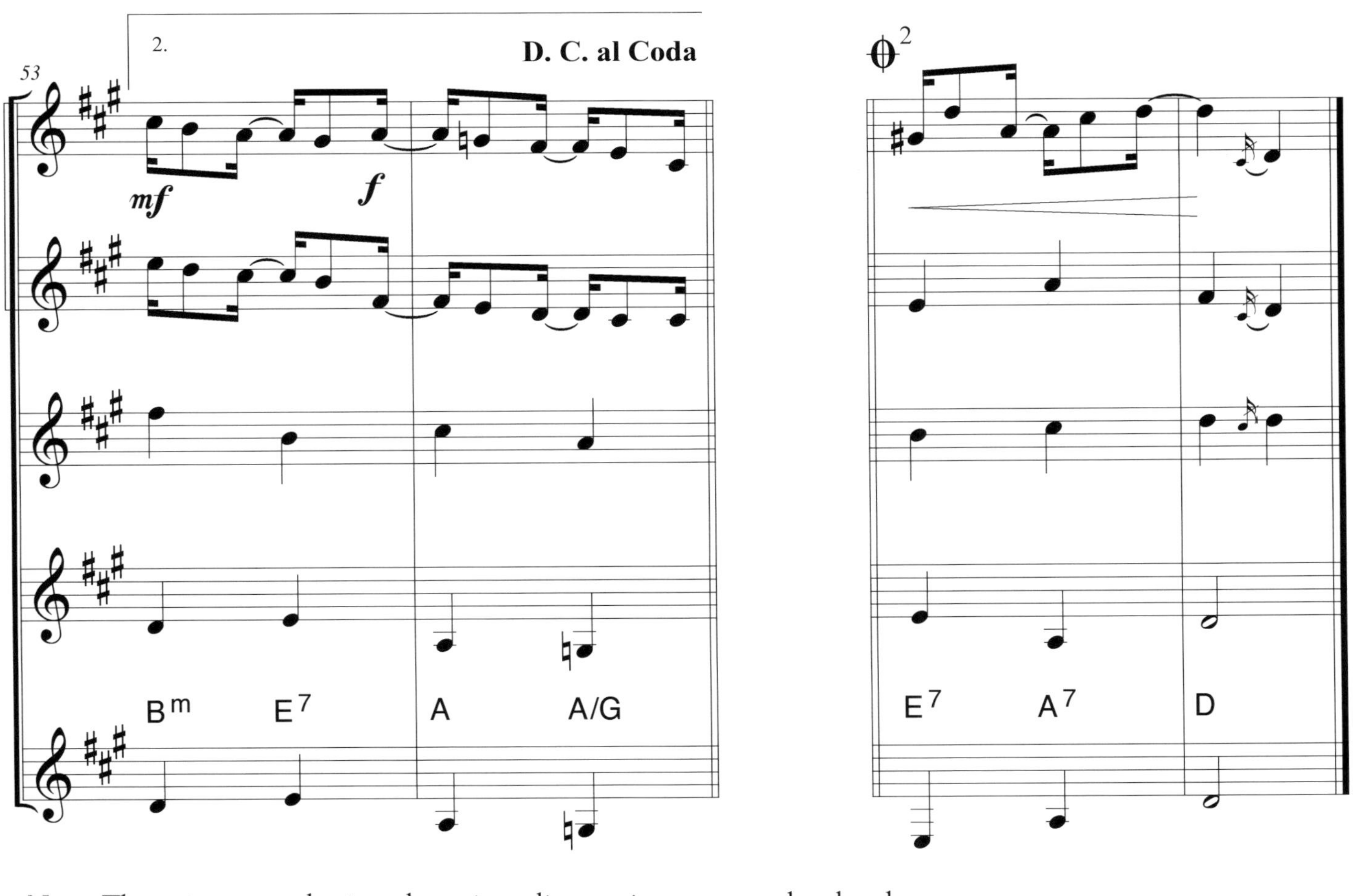

Note: The guitar may play just the written line, or incorporate the chords.

Mandolin 1

Enrolado

Spaceshot

for Enigmatica

Marilynn Mair

♩ = 80

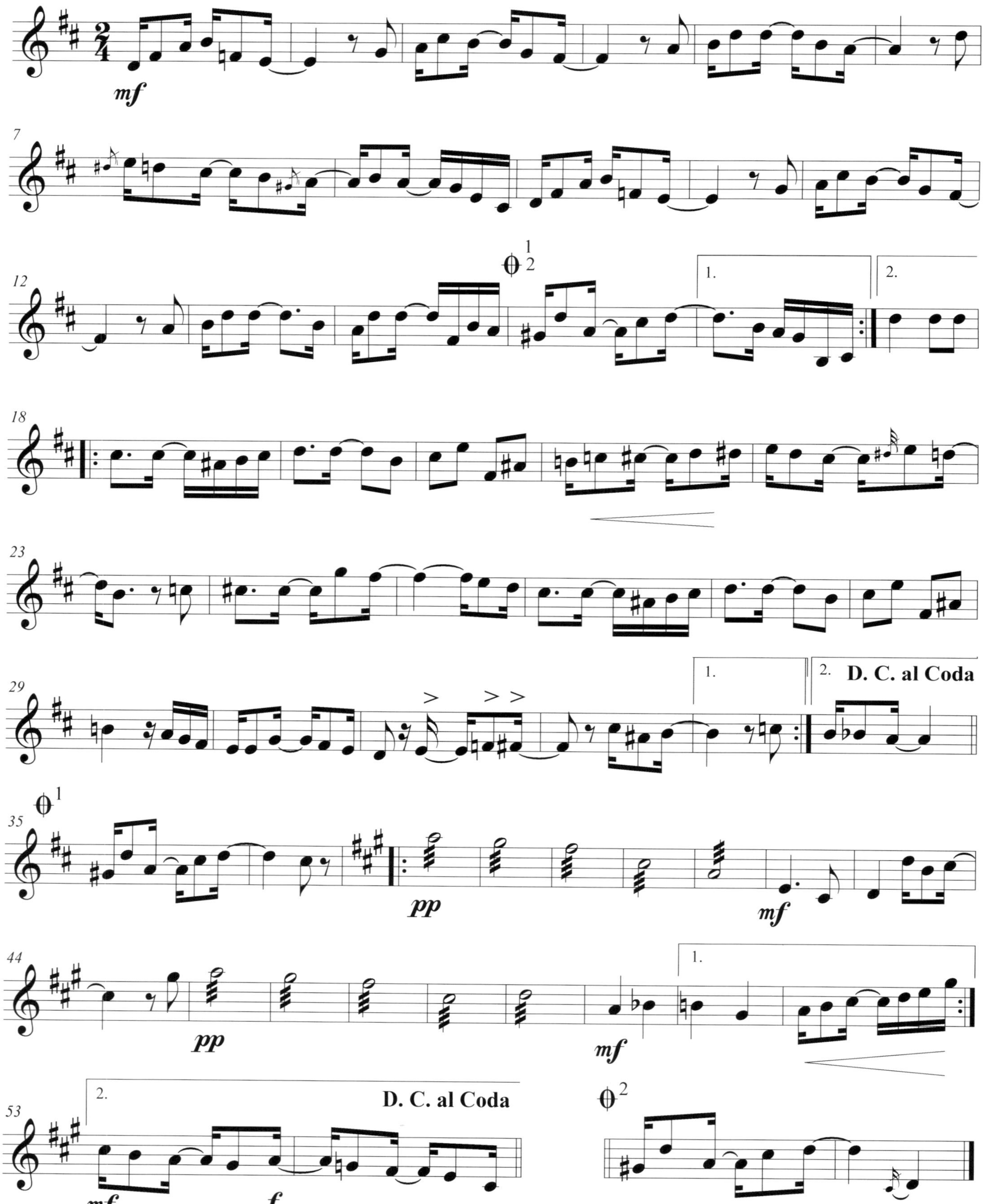

Enrolado

Spaceshot

for Enigmatica

Mandolin 2

Marilynn Mair

♩ = 80

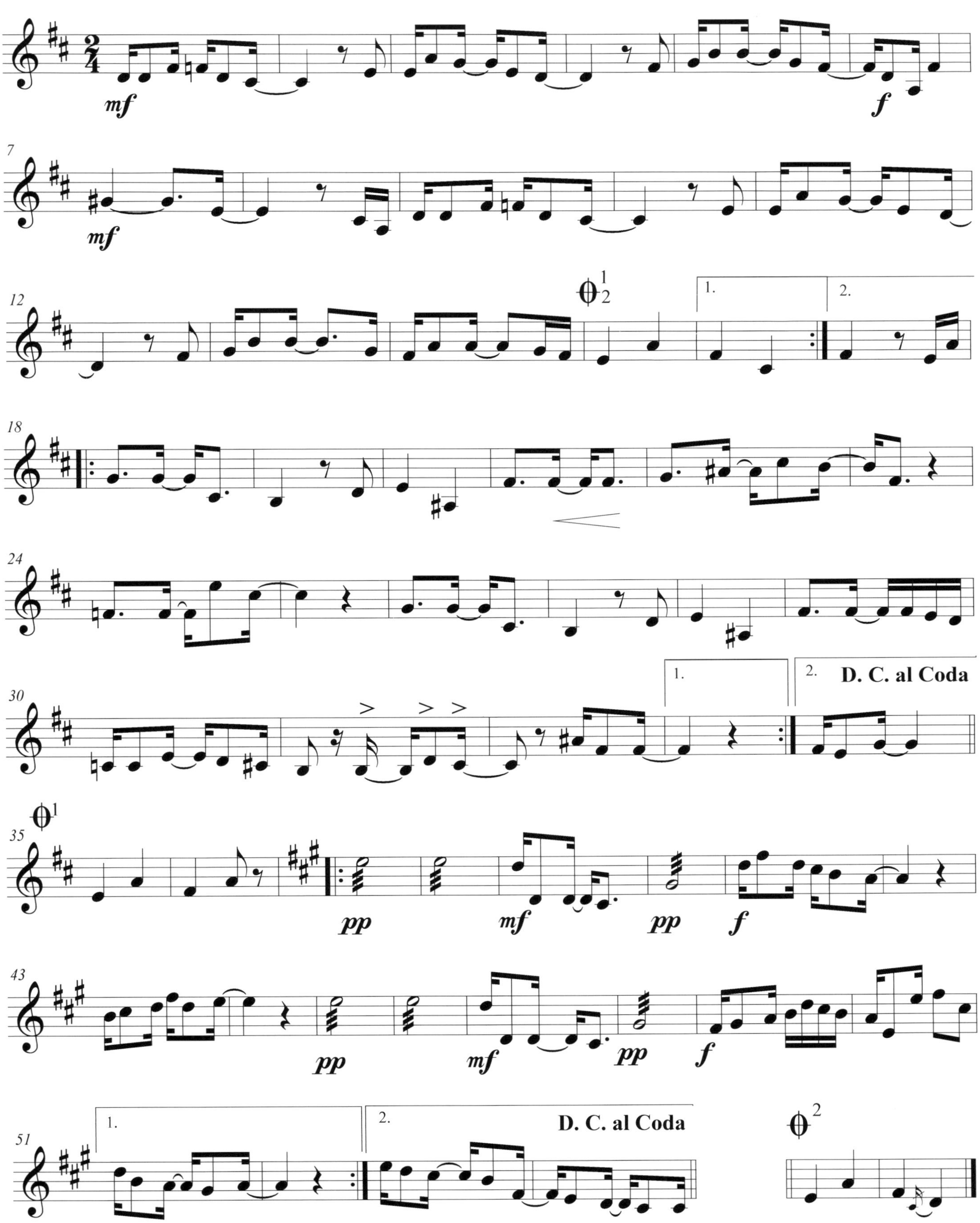

Enrolado

Spaceshot

for Enigmatica

Mandola- transposed treble

Marilynn Mair

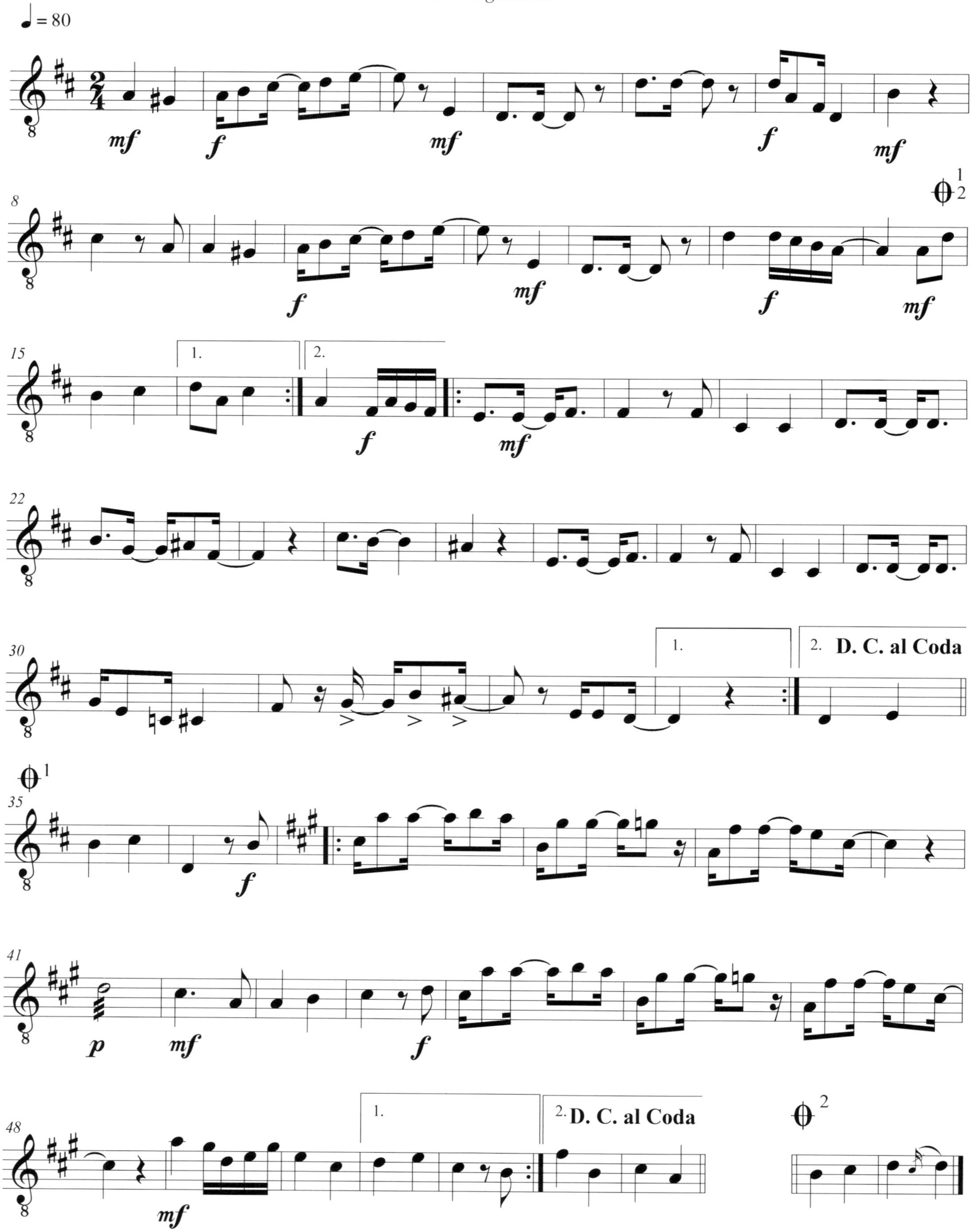

Enrolado

Spaceshot

for Enigmatica

Marilynn Mair

Mandola- alto clef

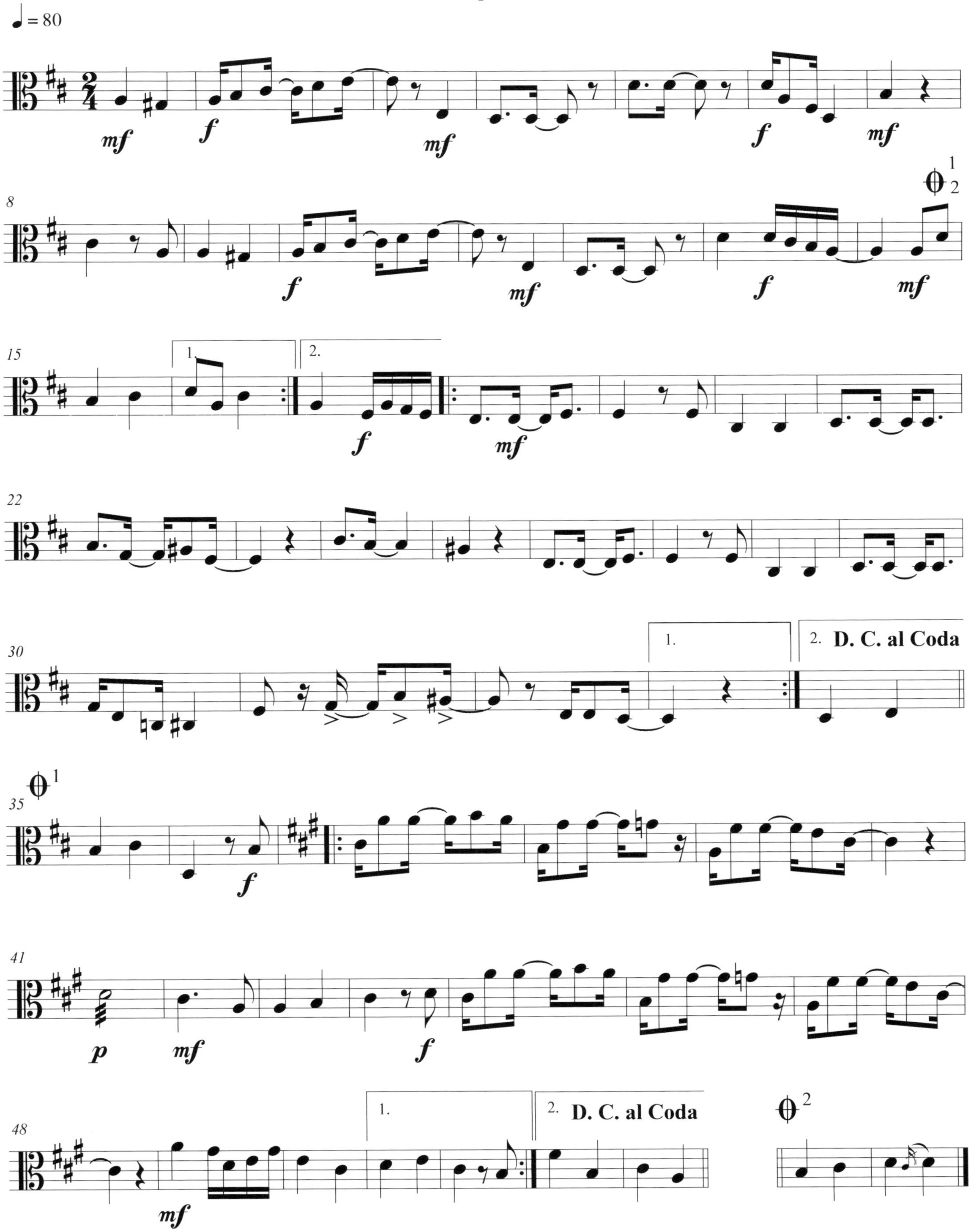

Enrolado

Spaceshot

for Enigmatica

Octave Mandolin

Marilynn Mair

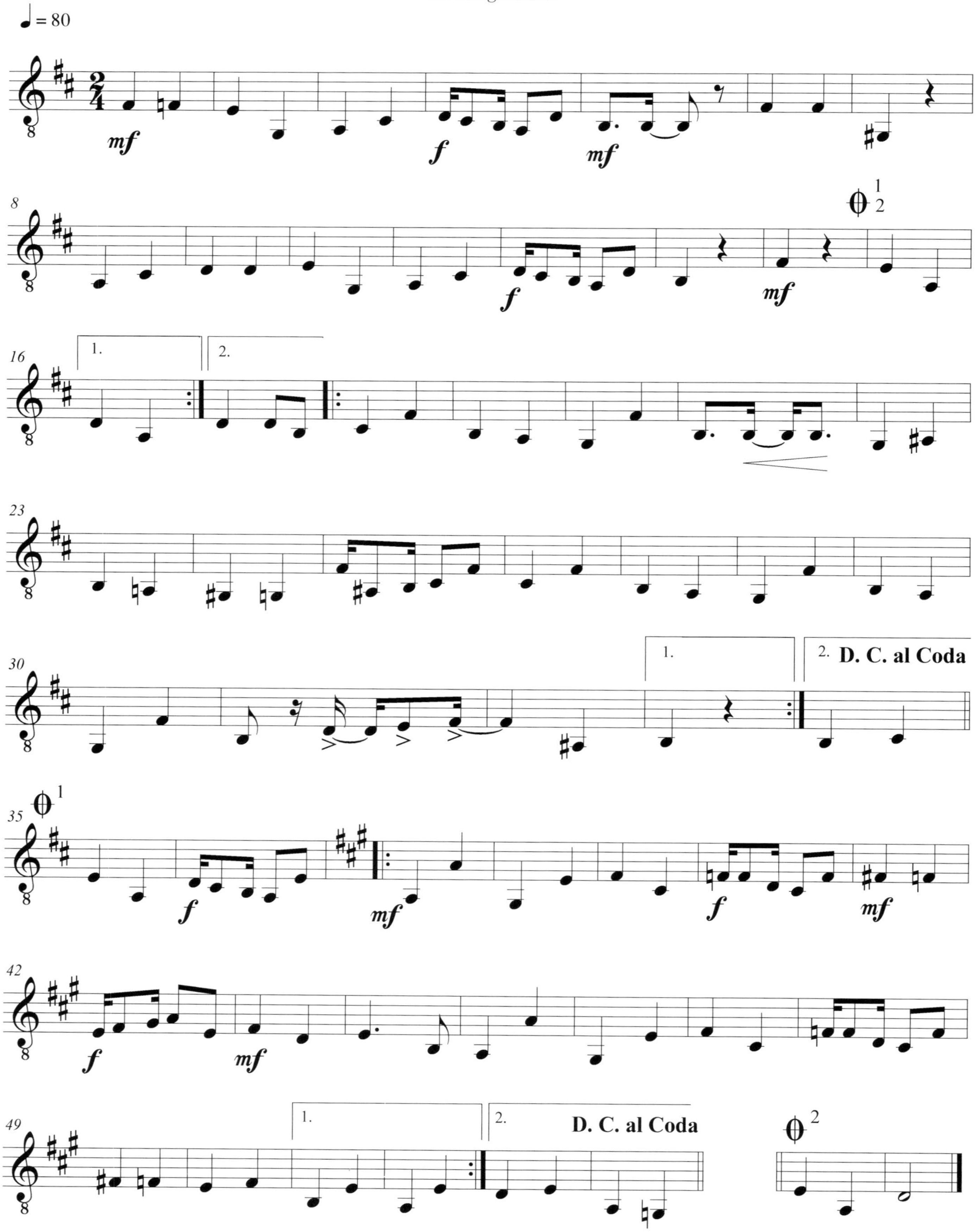

Guitar

(can play bass line or chords or both)

Enrolado

Spaceshot

for Enigmatica

Marilynn Mair

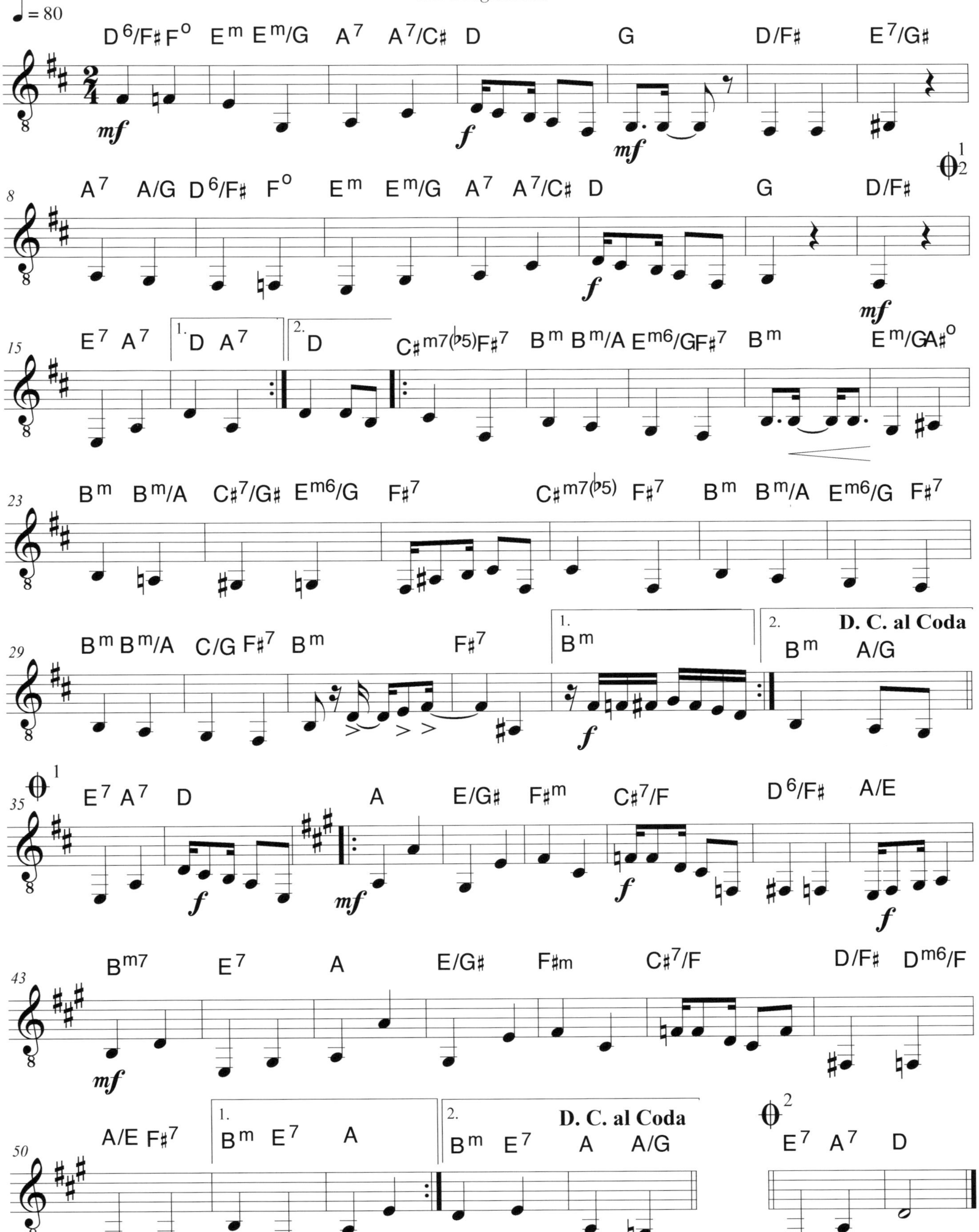

Mandocello

Enrolado

Spaceshot

for Enigmatica

Marilynn Mair

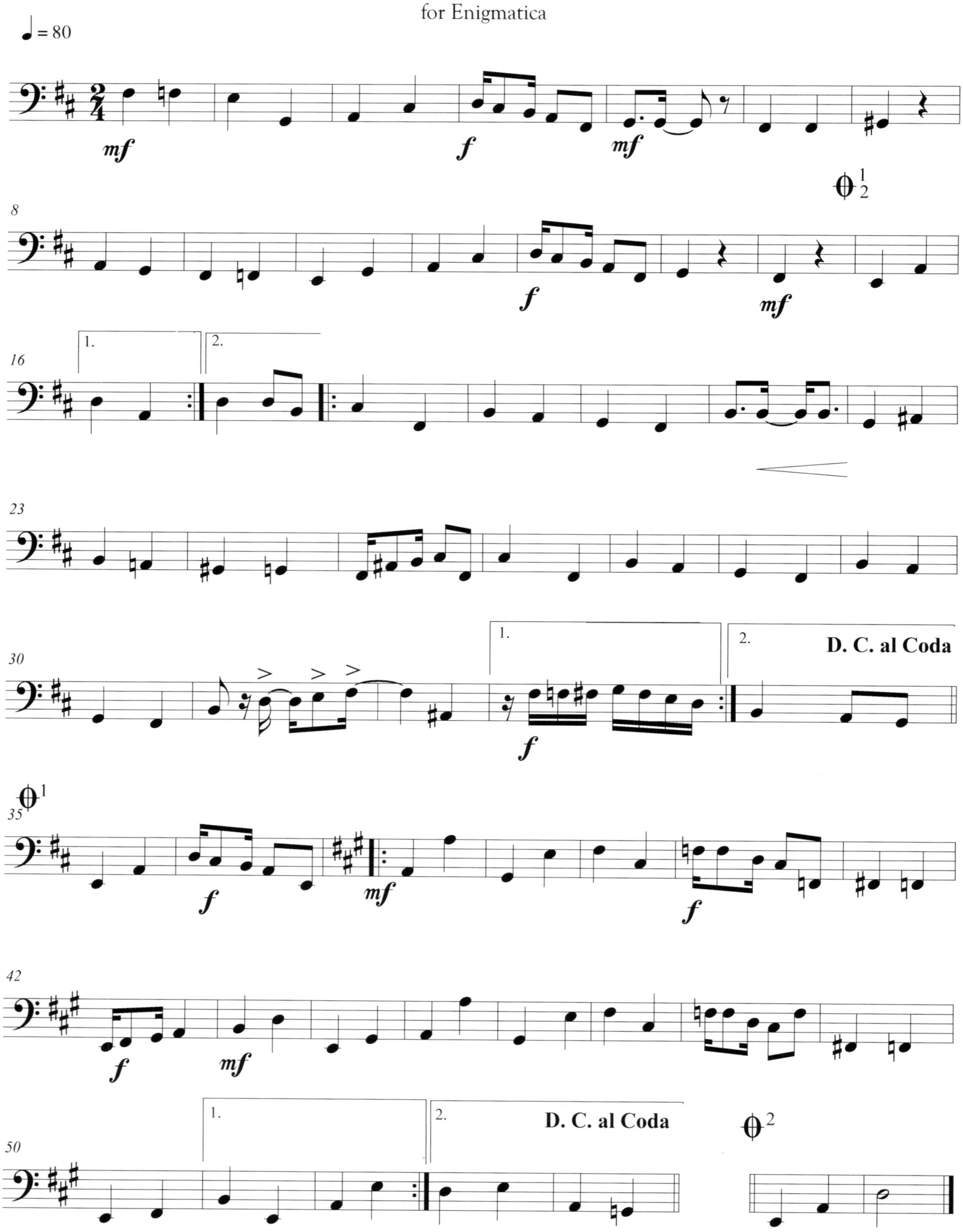

Nadando em Luz

Swimming in Light

Marilynn Mair

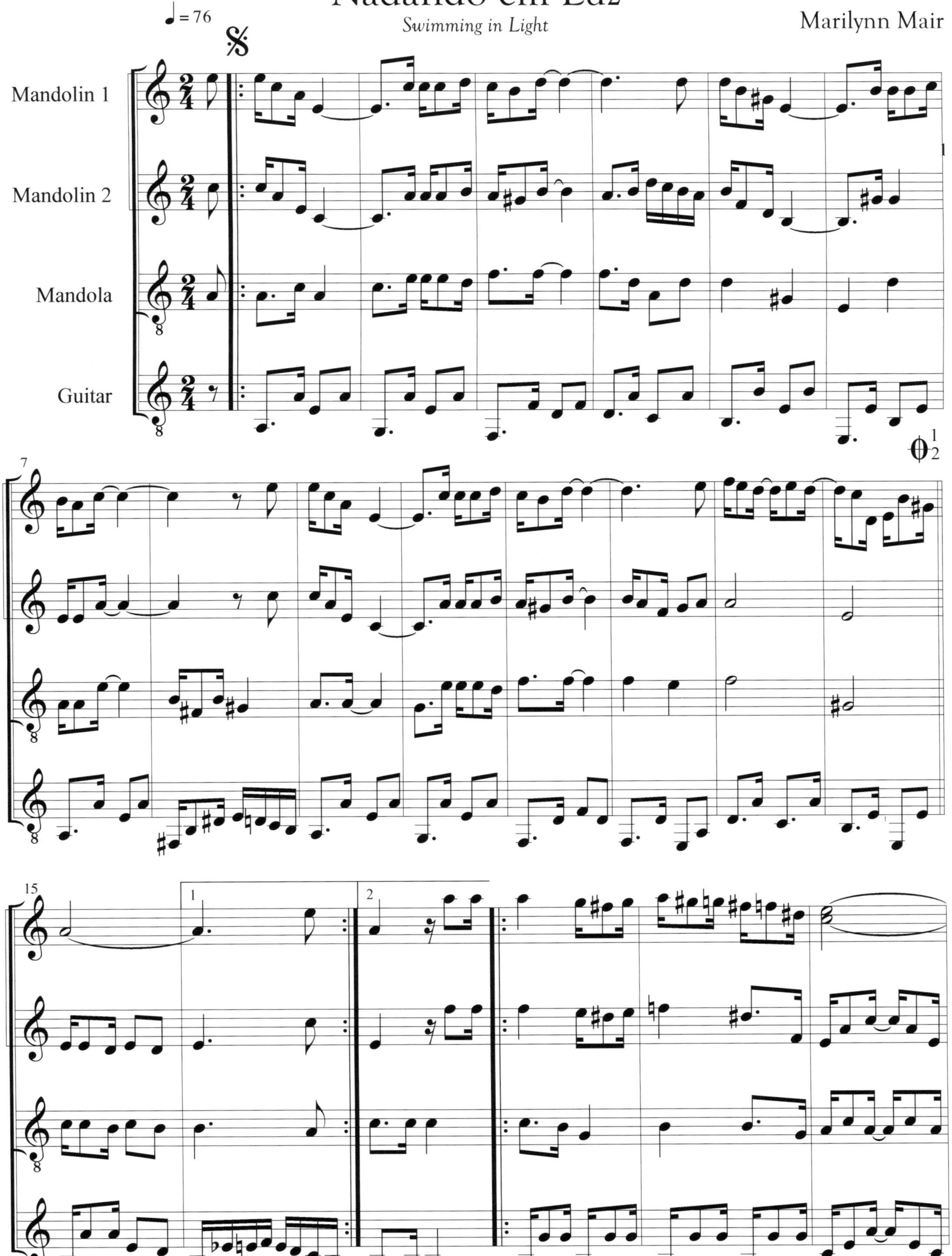

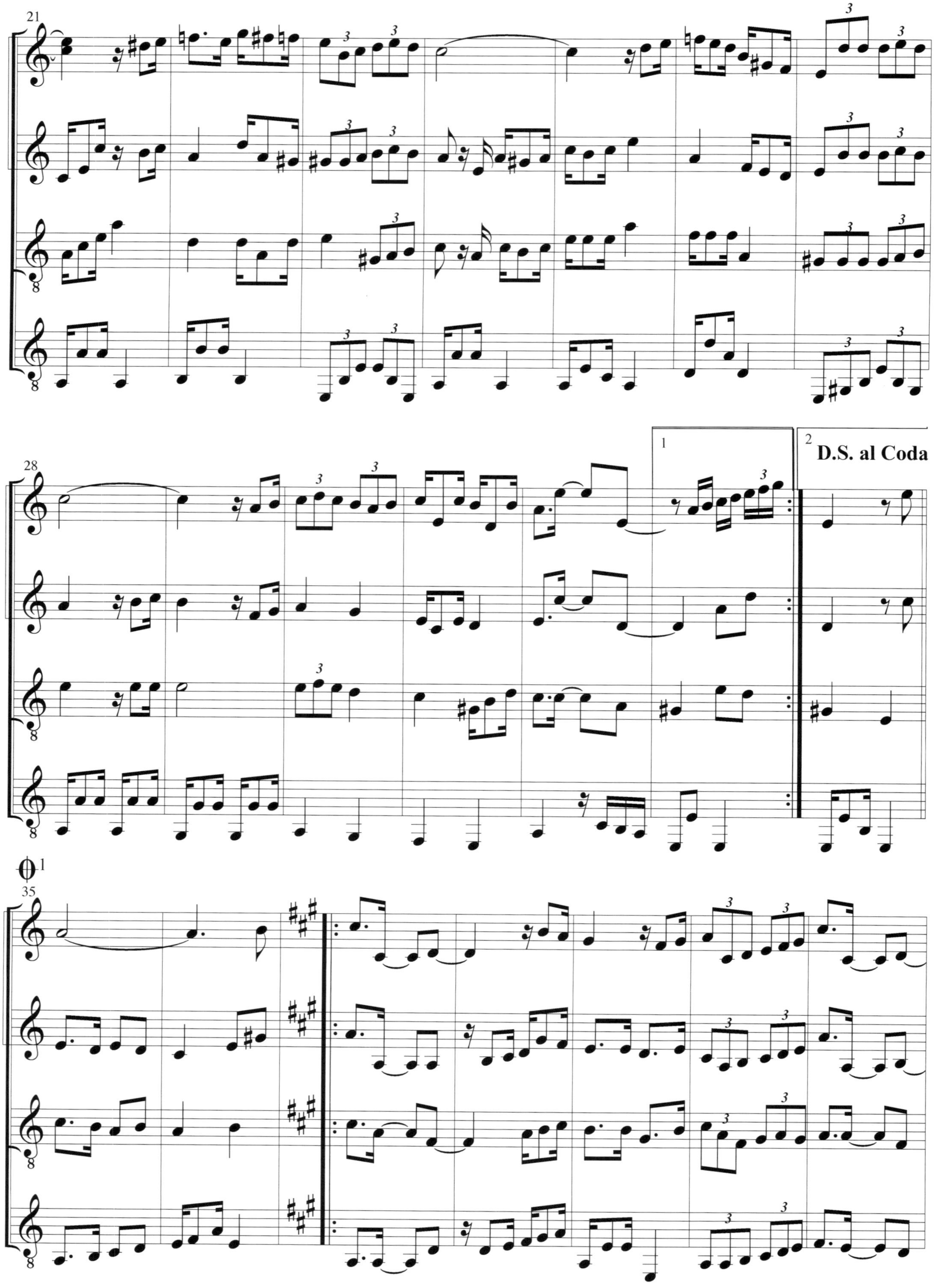
21
28
1
2
D.S. al Coda
35

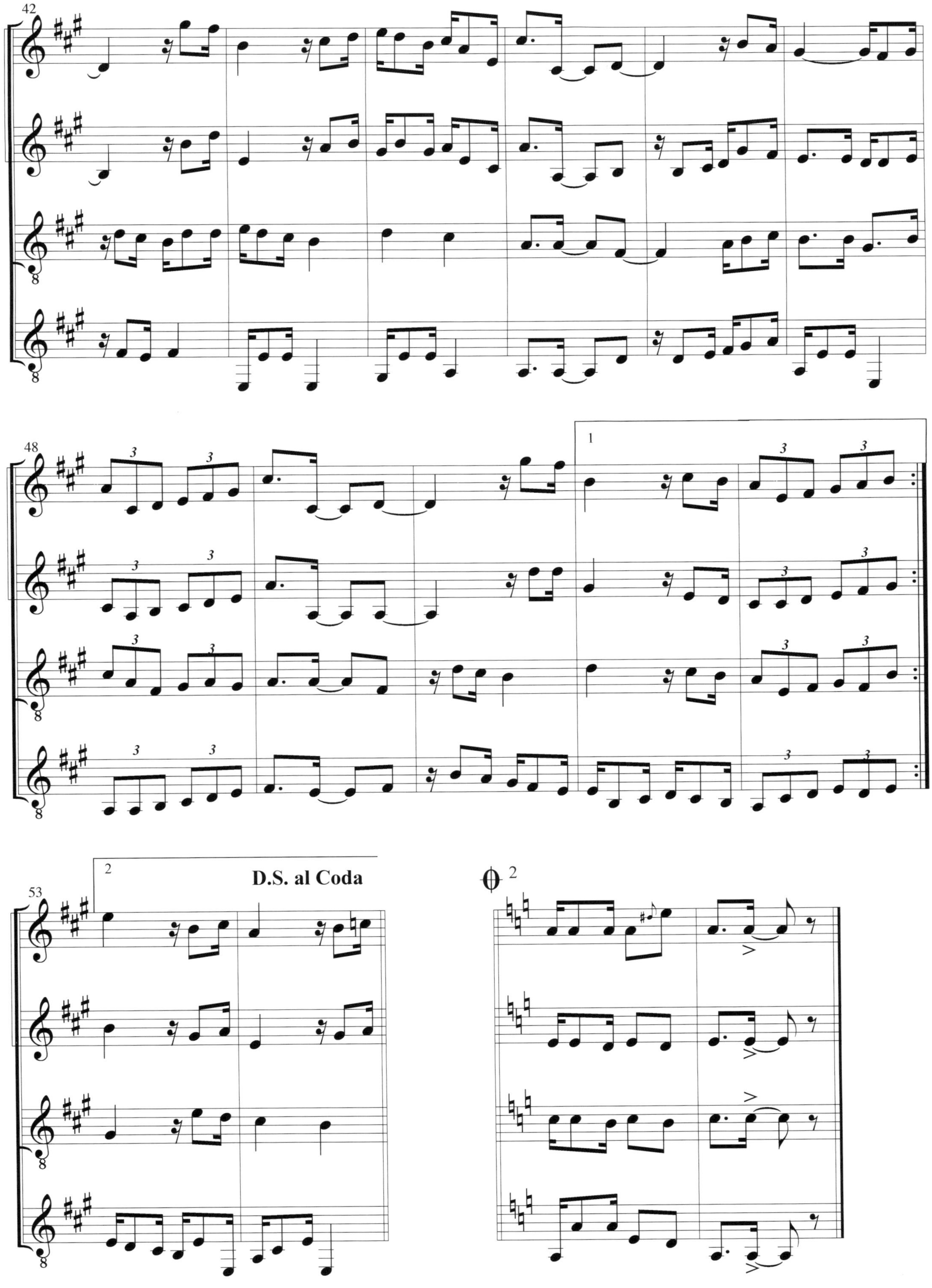
D.S. al Coda

Nadando em Luz

Mandolin 1

Swimming in Light

Marilynn Mair

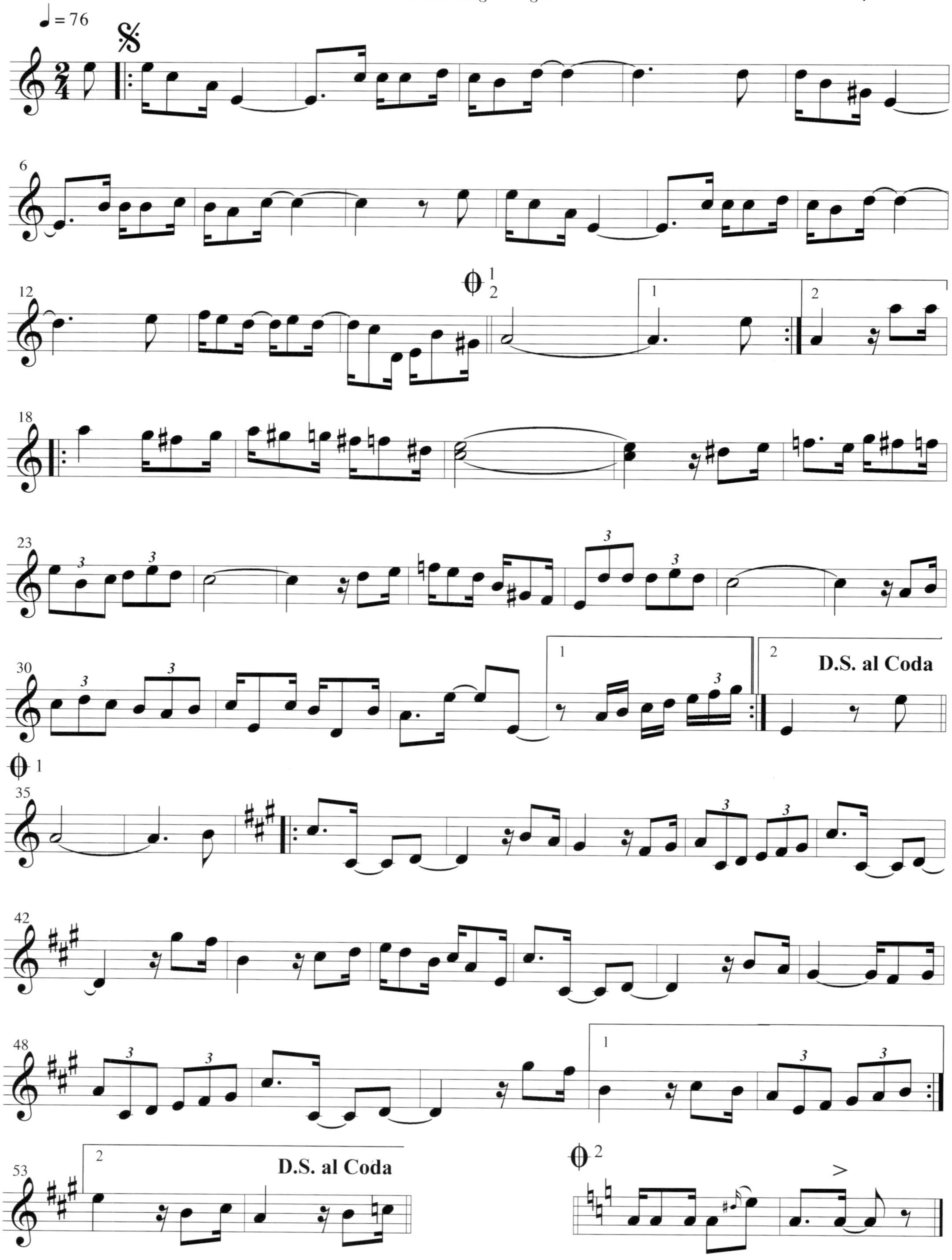

Mandolin 2

Nadando em Luz

Swimming in Light

Marilynn Mair

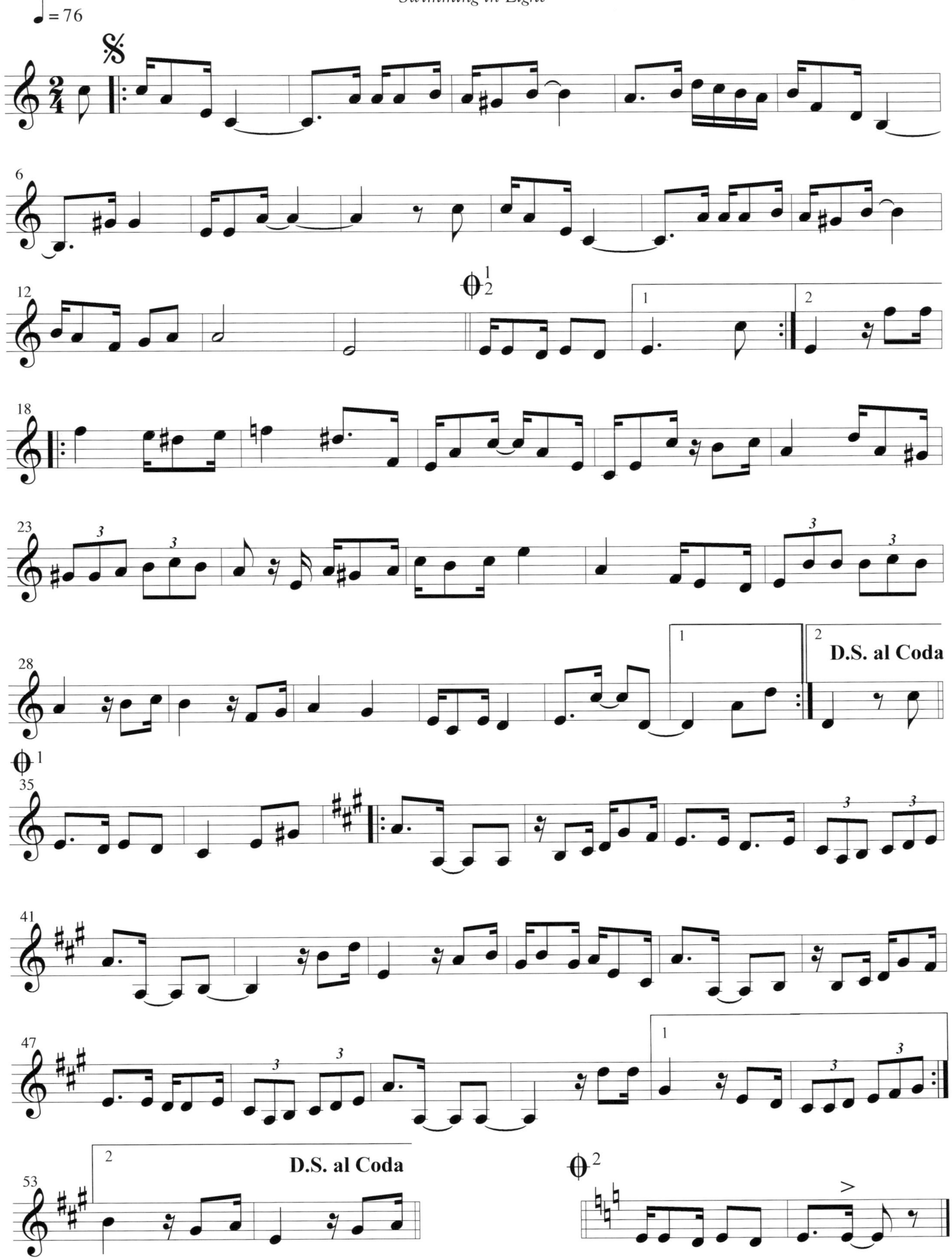

Mandola transposed treble

Nadando em Luz

Swimming in Light

Marilynn Mair

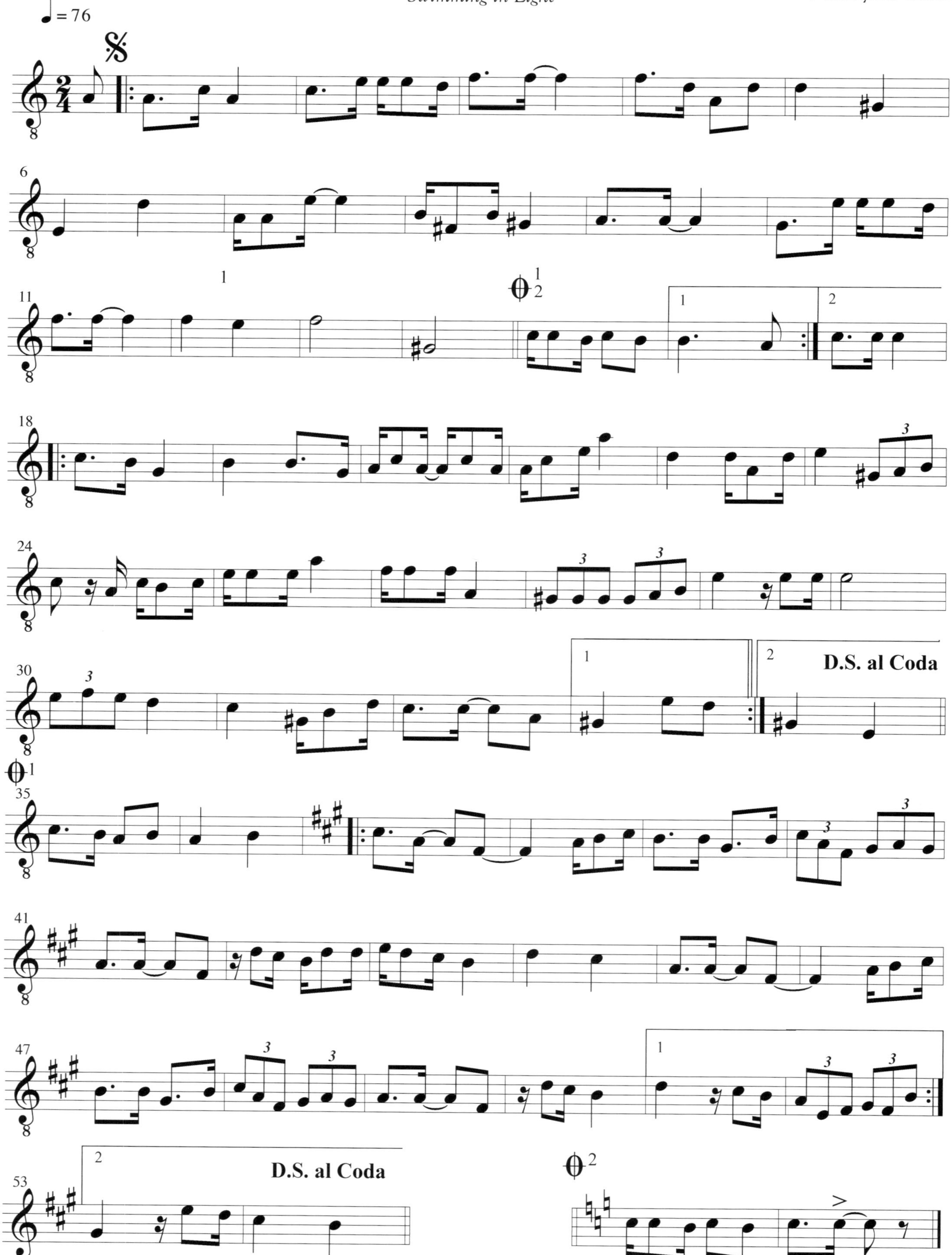

Mandola alto clef

Nadando em Luz

Swimming in Light

Marilynn Mair

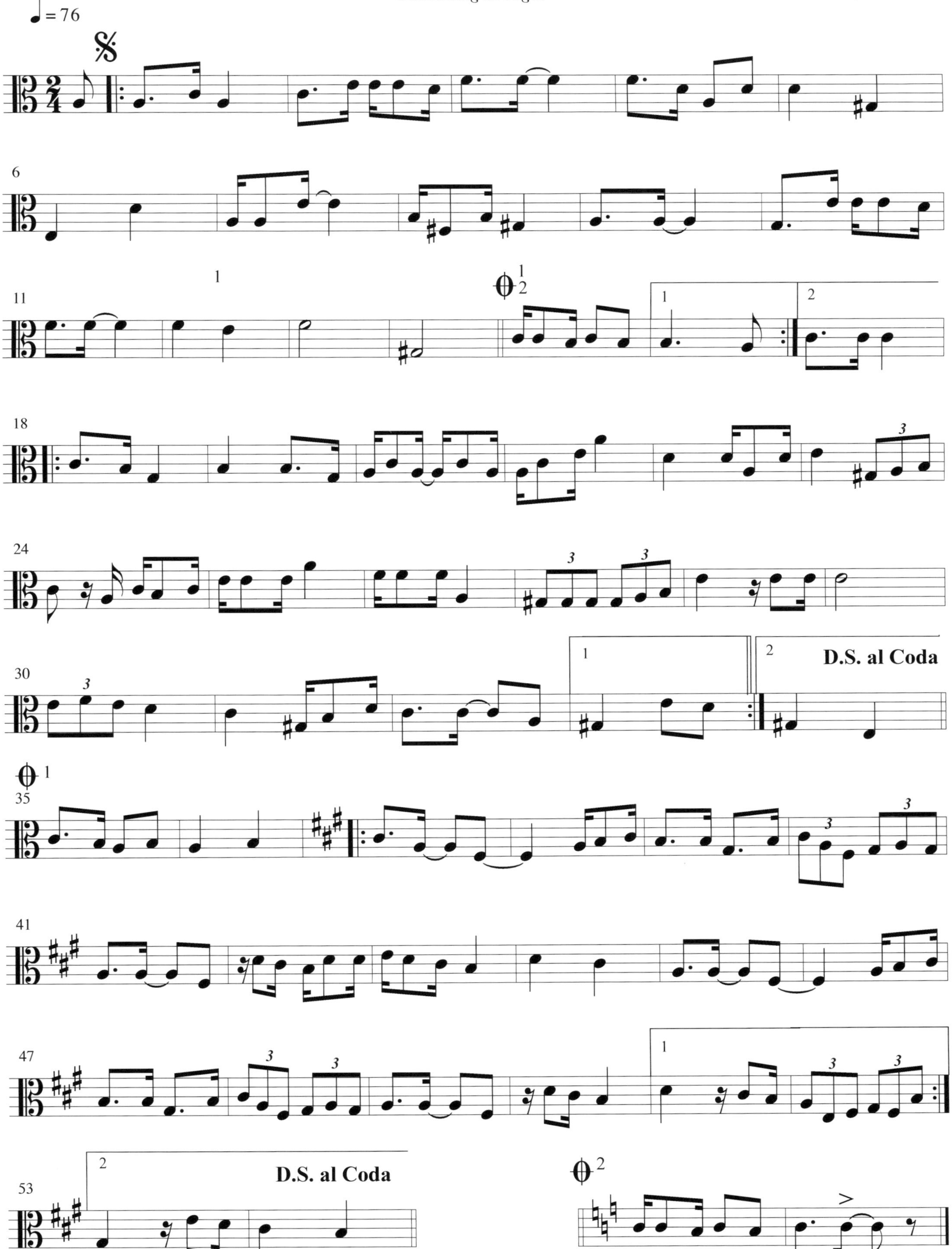

Nadando em Luz

Swimming in Light

Guitar

Marilynn Mair

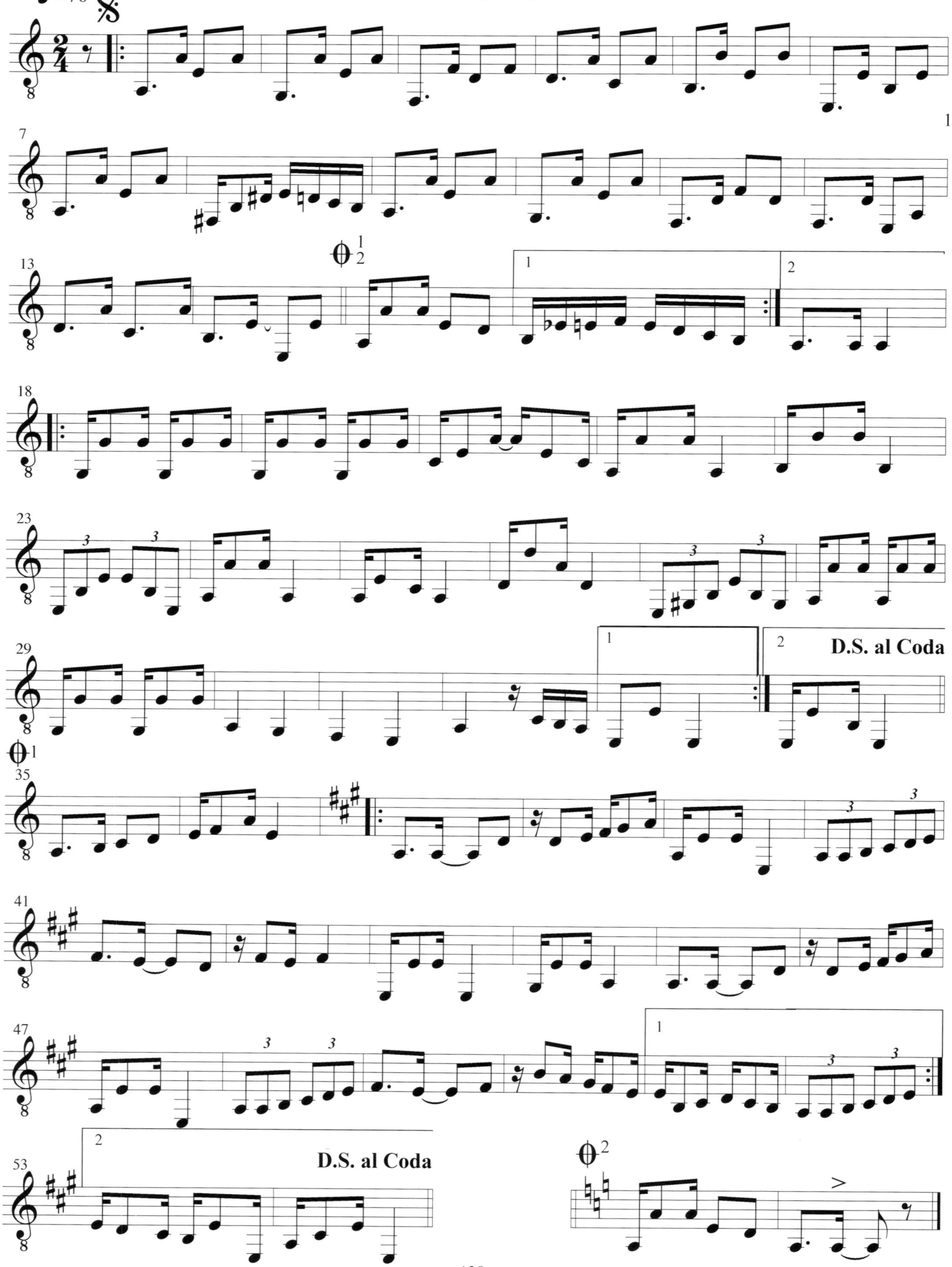

Mandocello

Nadando em Luz

Swimming in Light

Marilynn Mair

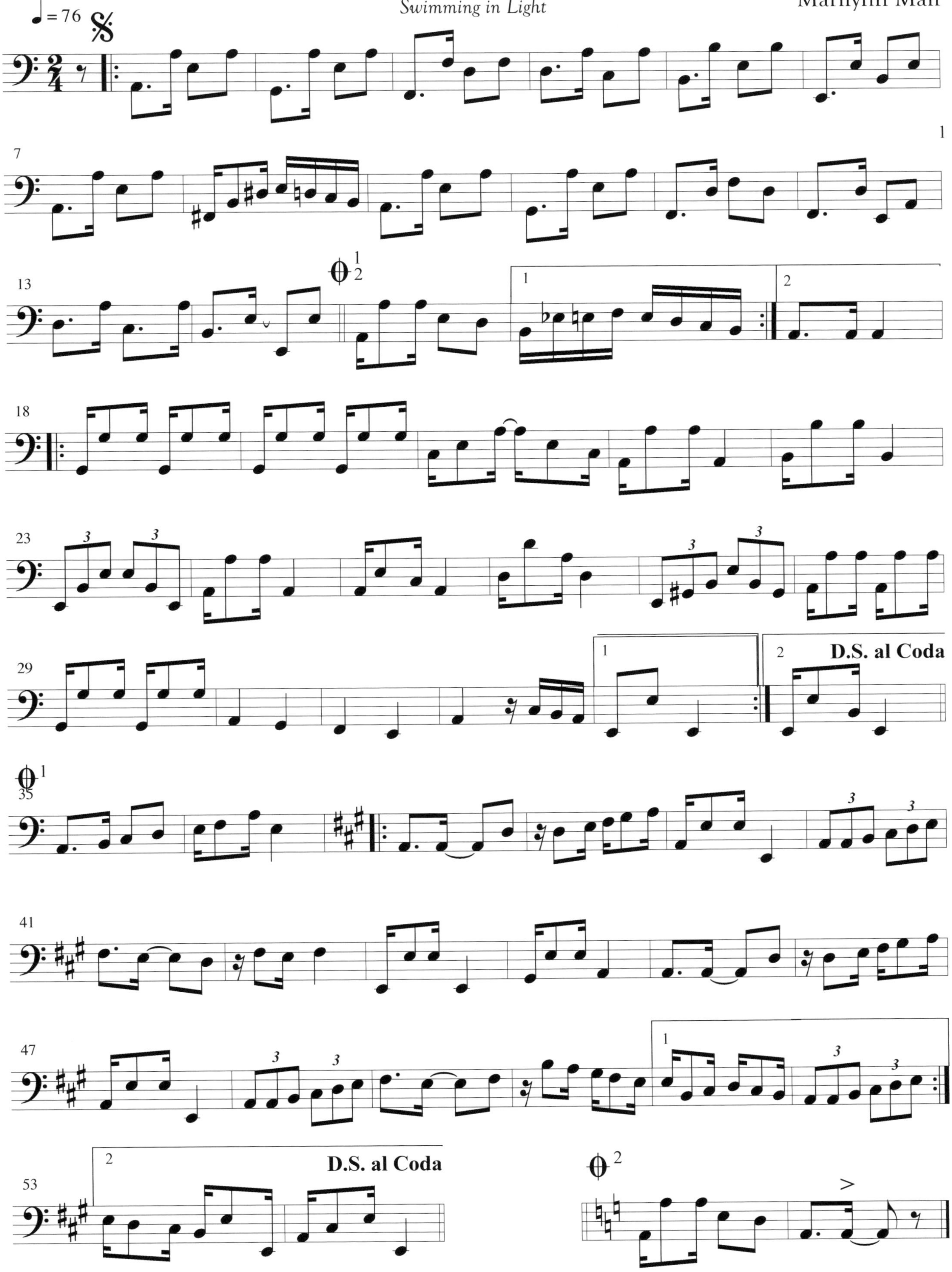

Goodin's Gigue

in memory of John

Marilynn Mair

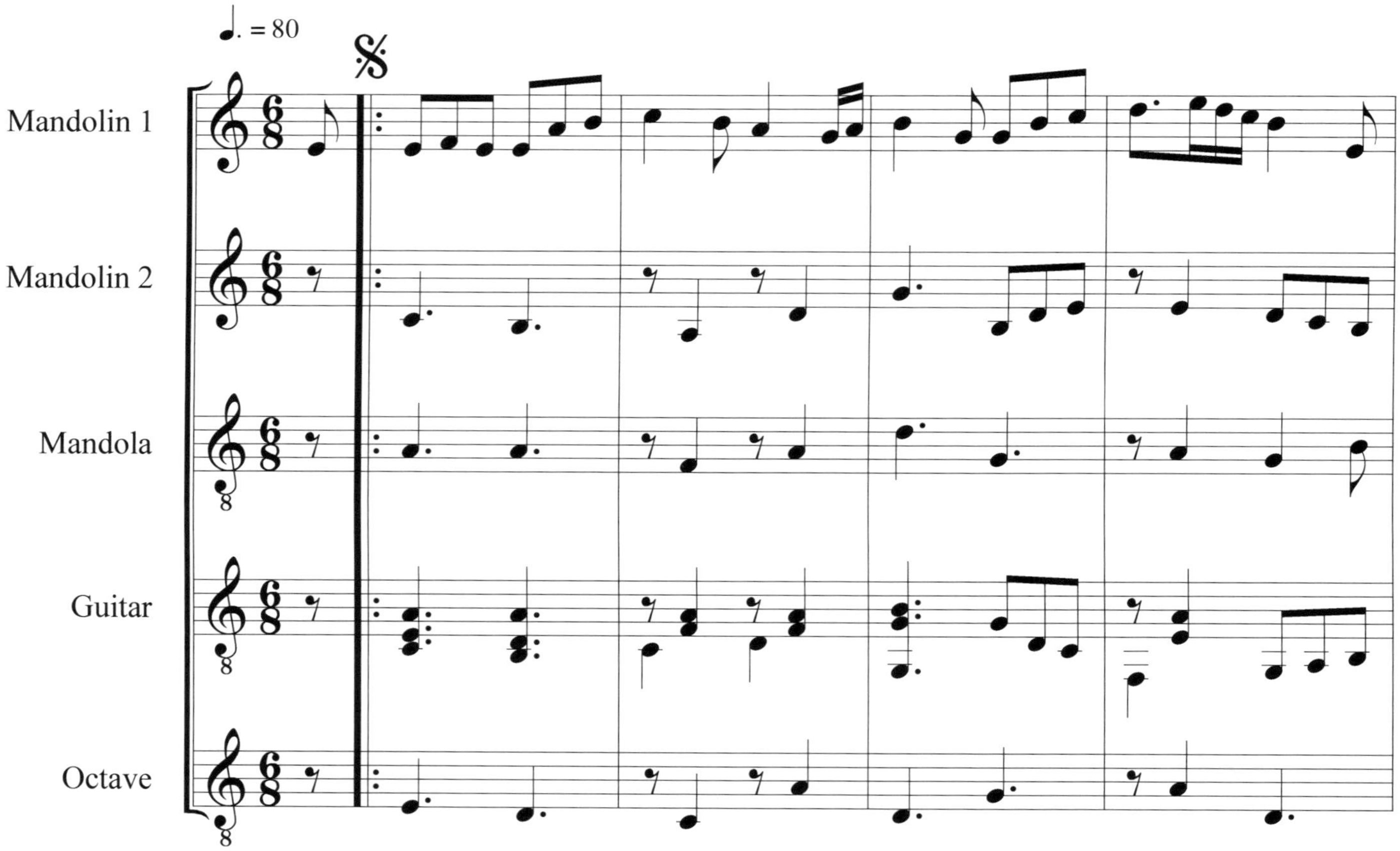

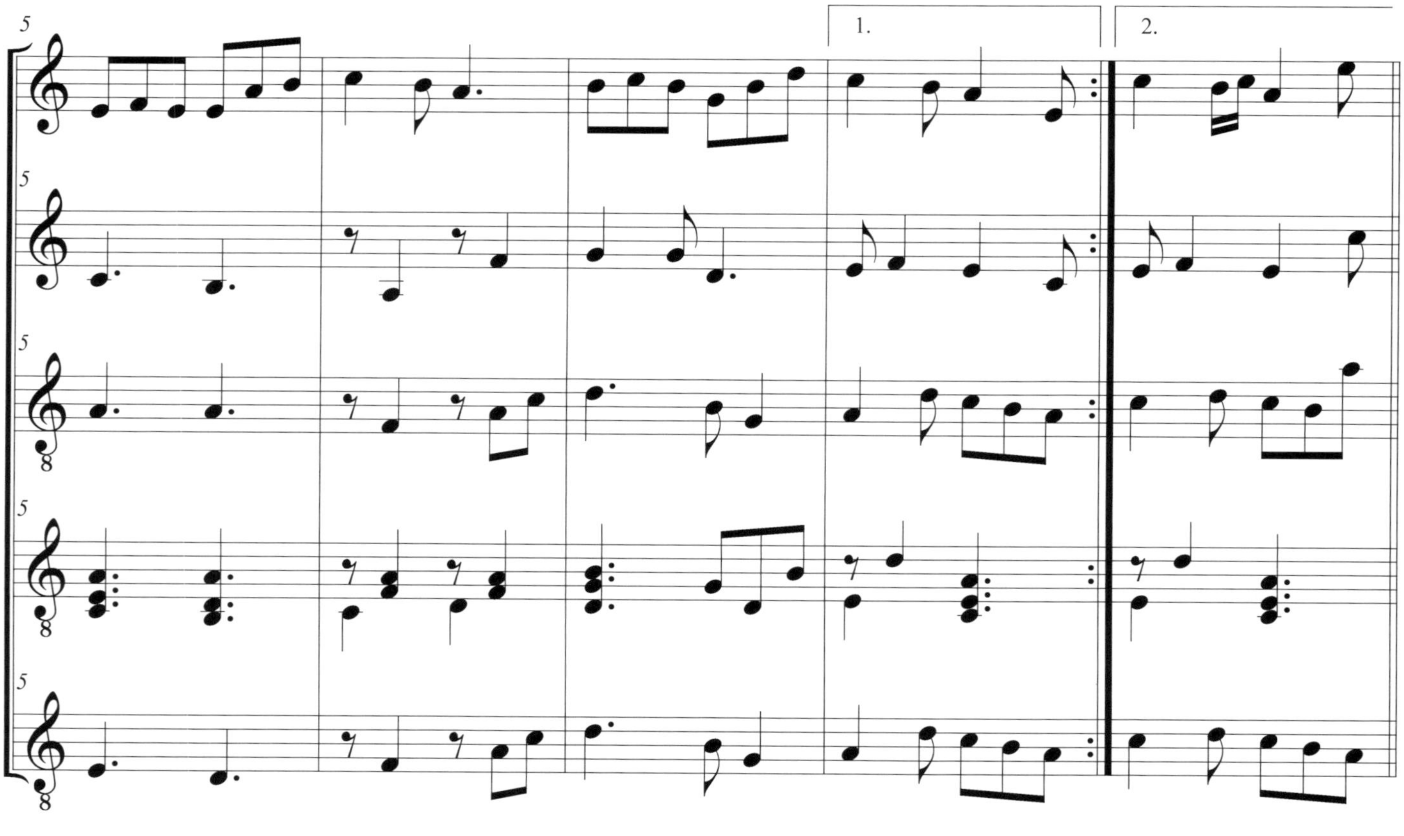

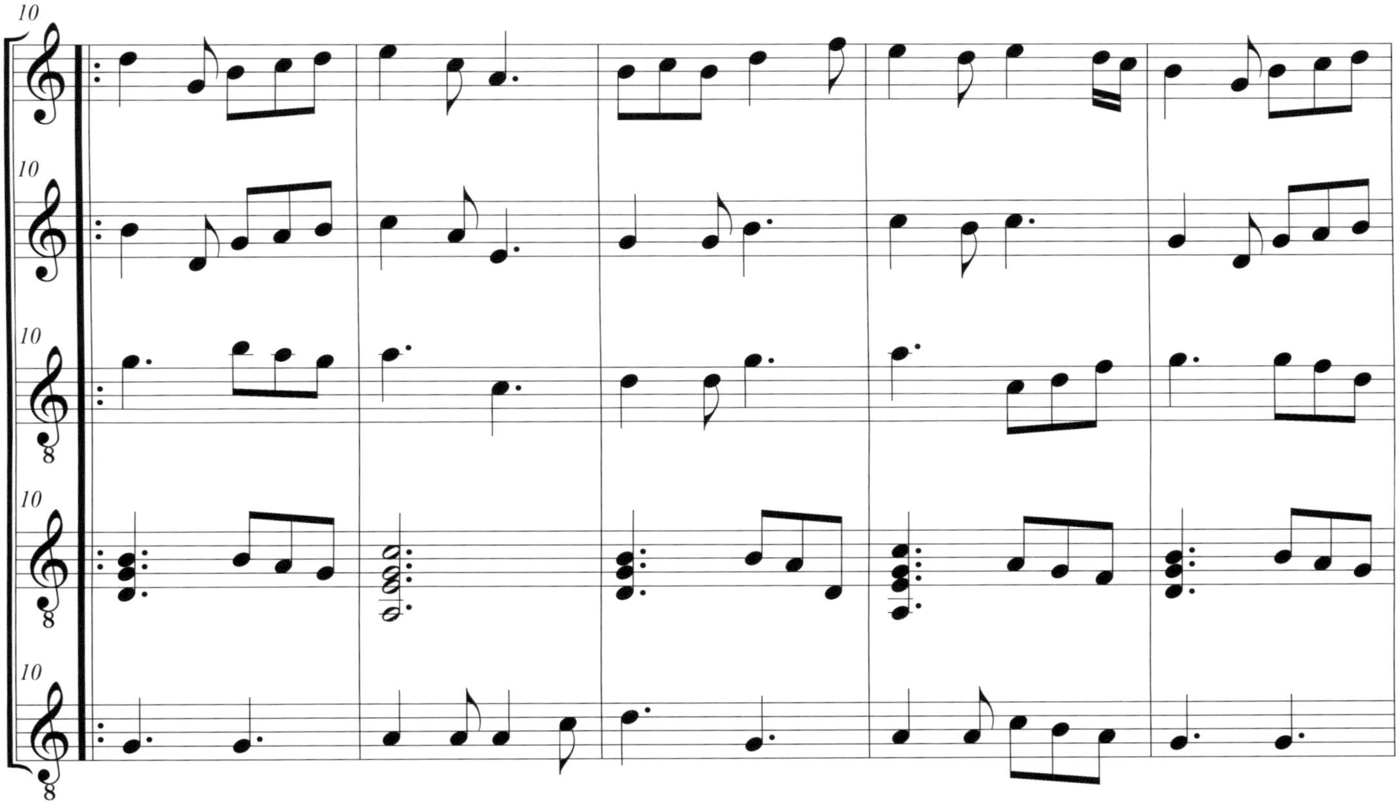

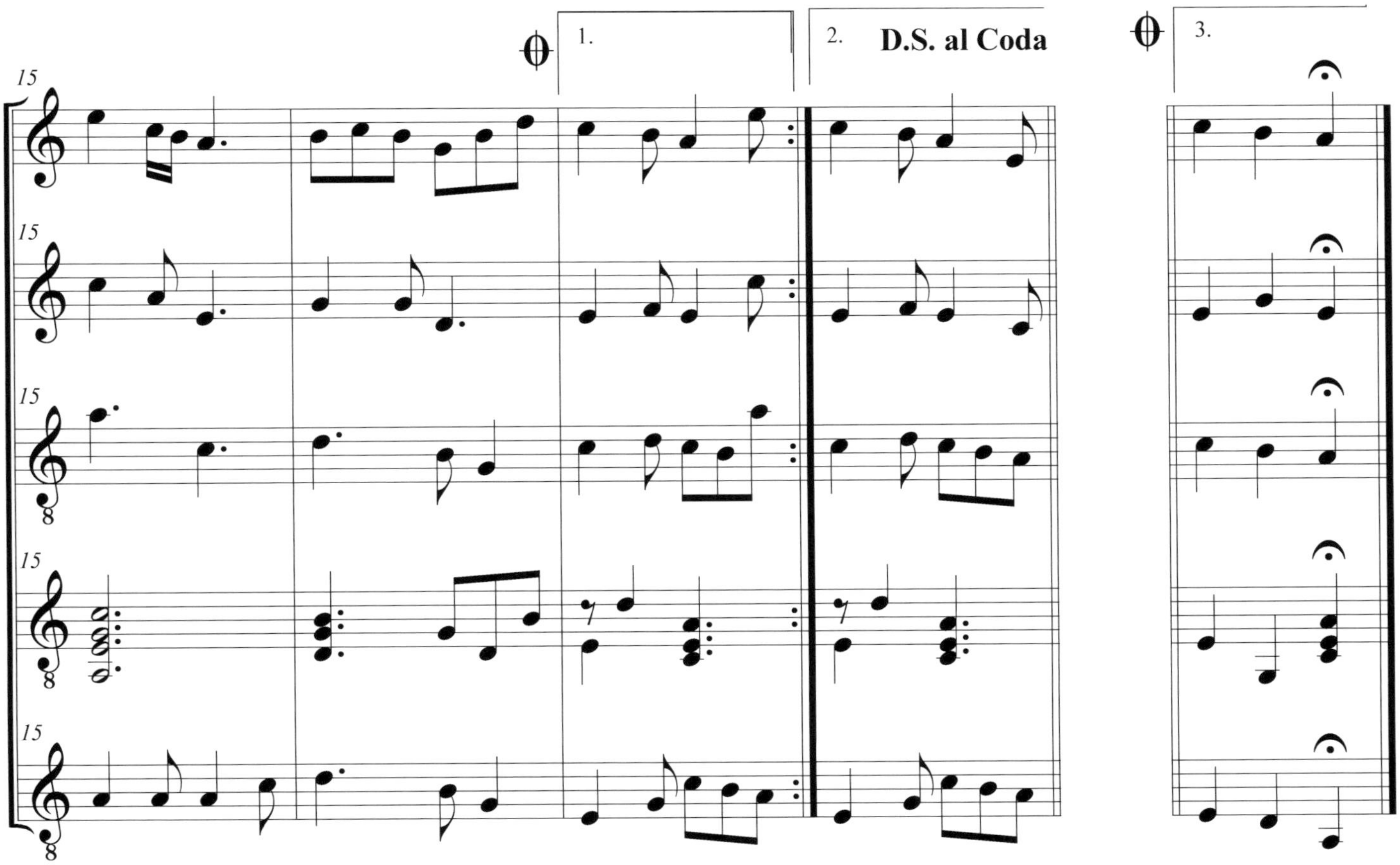

The melody for this tune came to me in a dream shortly after John Goodin, mandolinist, composer, and fabulous human being, died. I scribbled it down when I woke and arranged it for Enigmatica. We played it at our next gig, in a set with some of John's own music. It's short enough to play from the score, but I've added parts in other useful clefs on the next page.

Goodin's Gigue

in memory of John

Marilynn Mair

Mandola in Alto clef

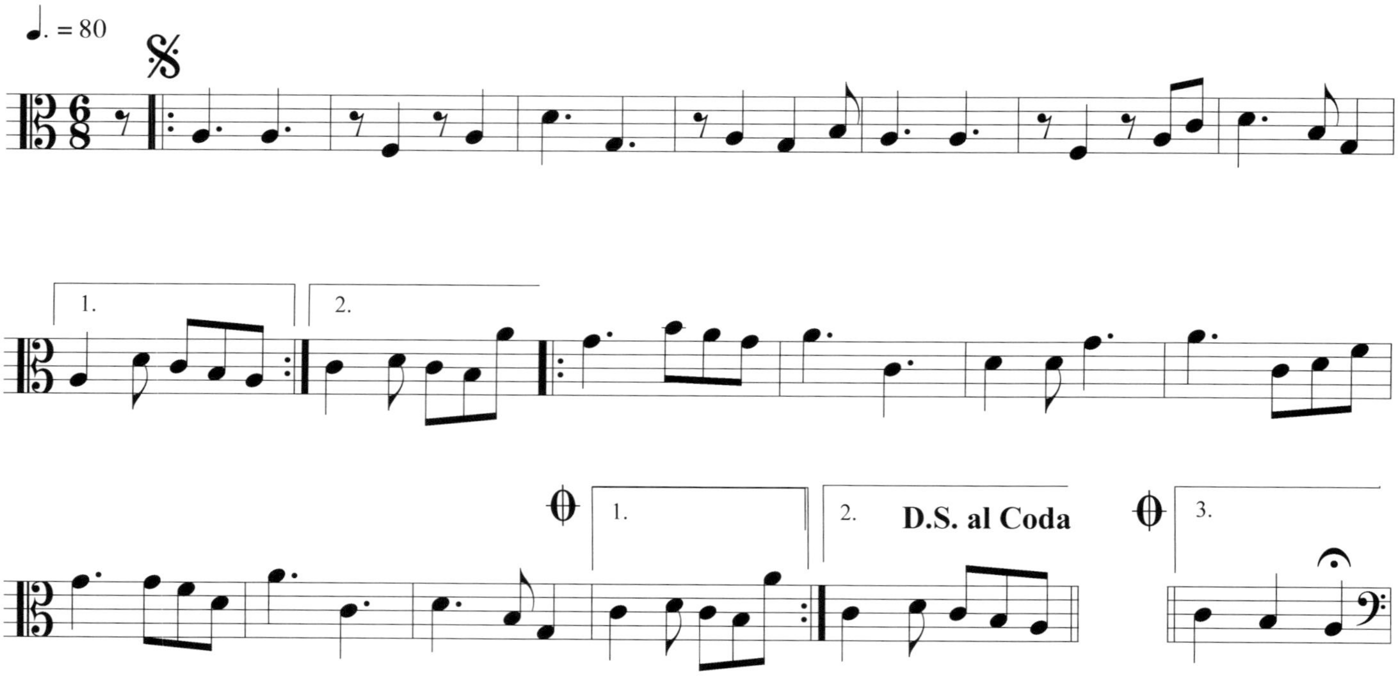

Mandocello

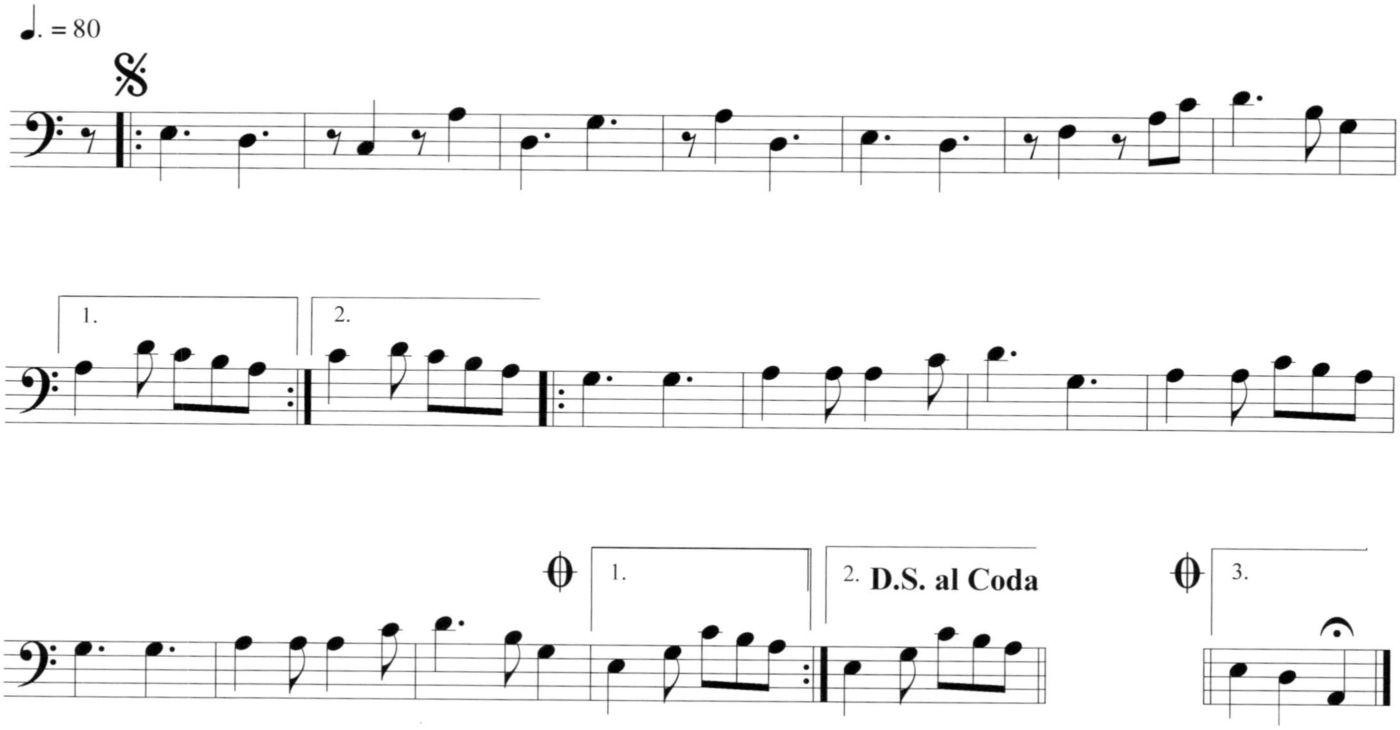

East of Here

Marilynn Mair

♩ = 60 *with a feeling of carefree optimism*

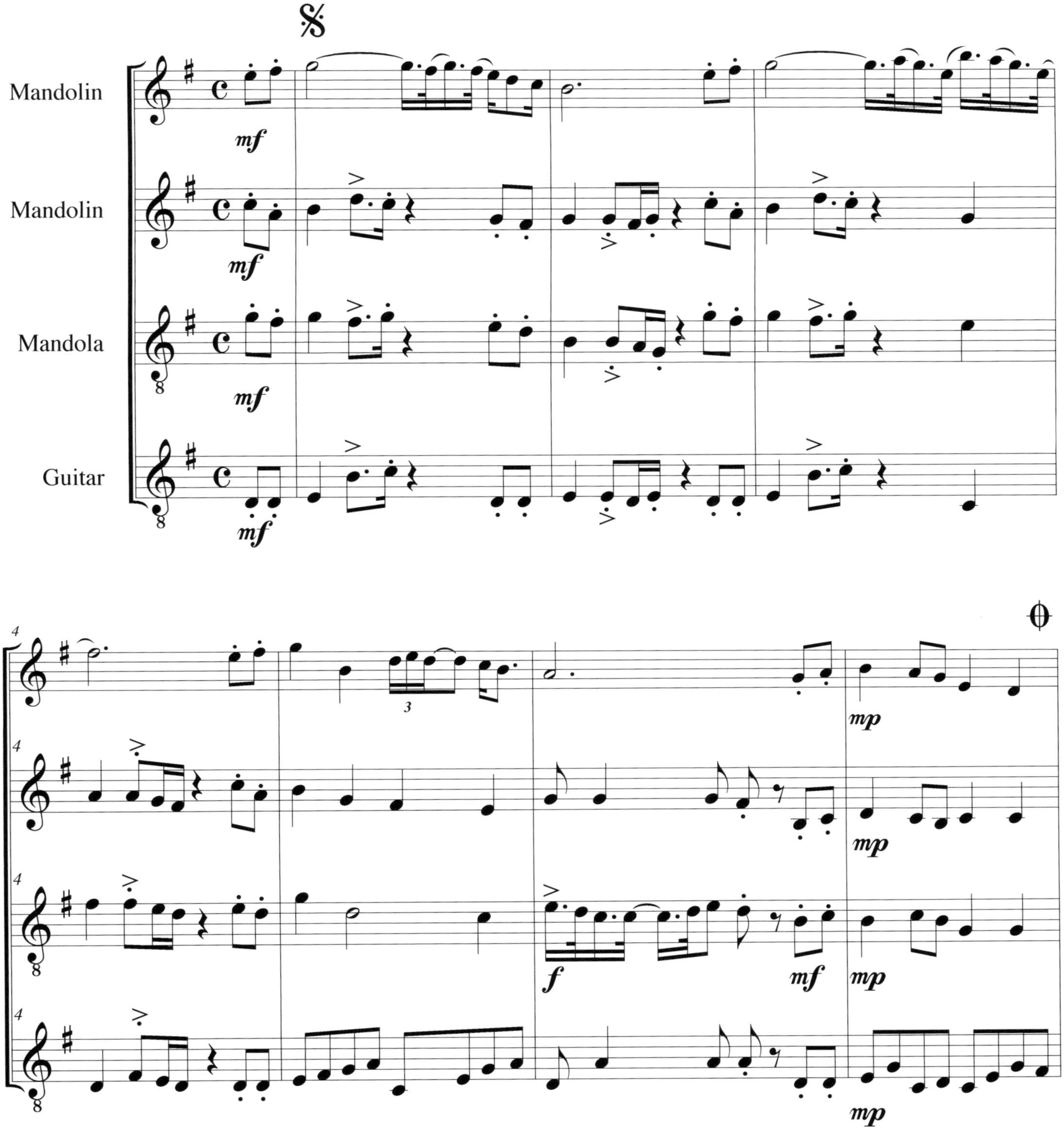

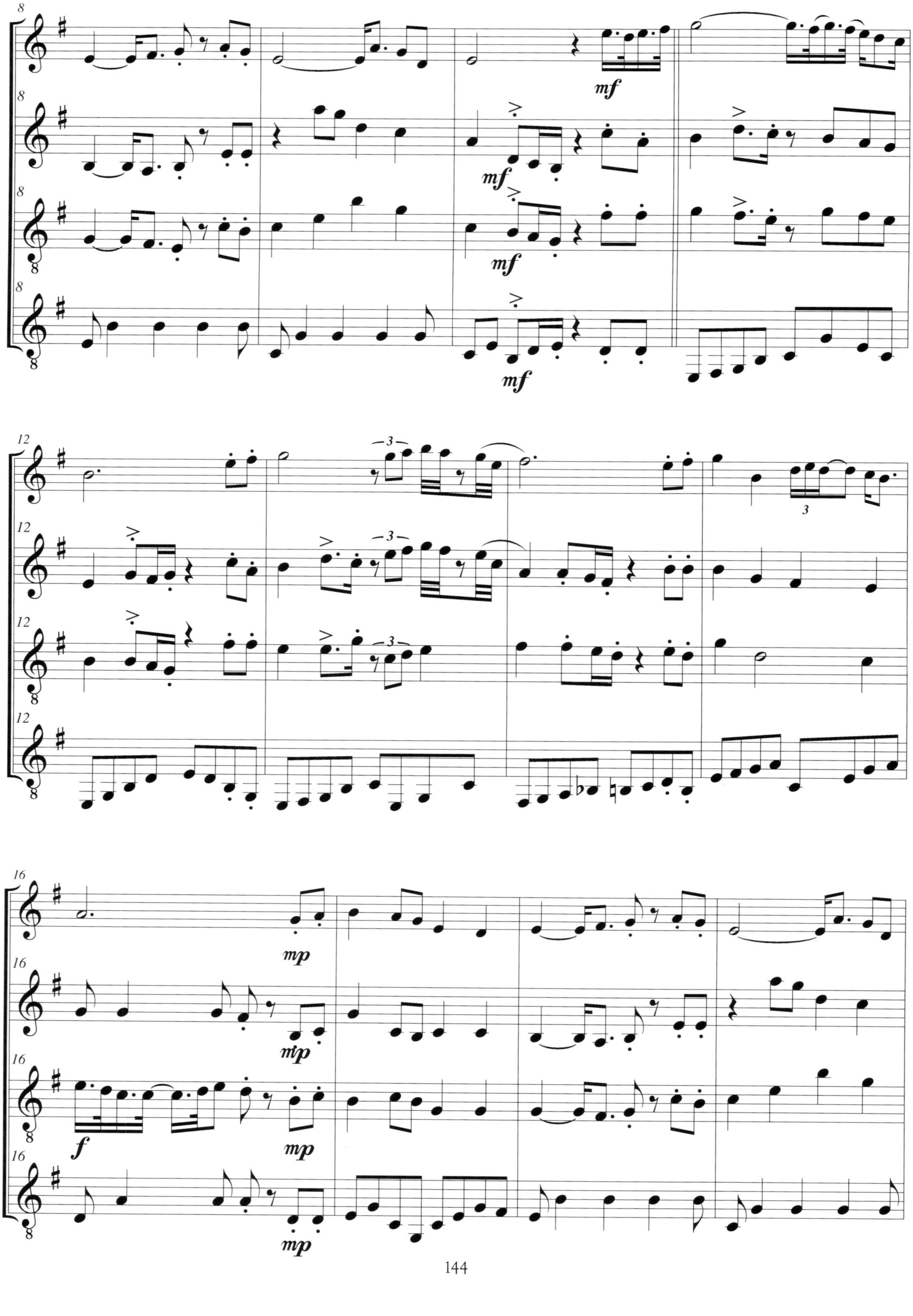
mf
mp
f

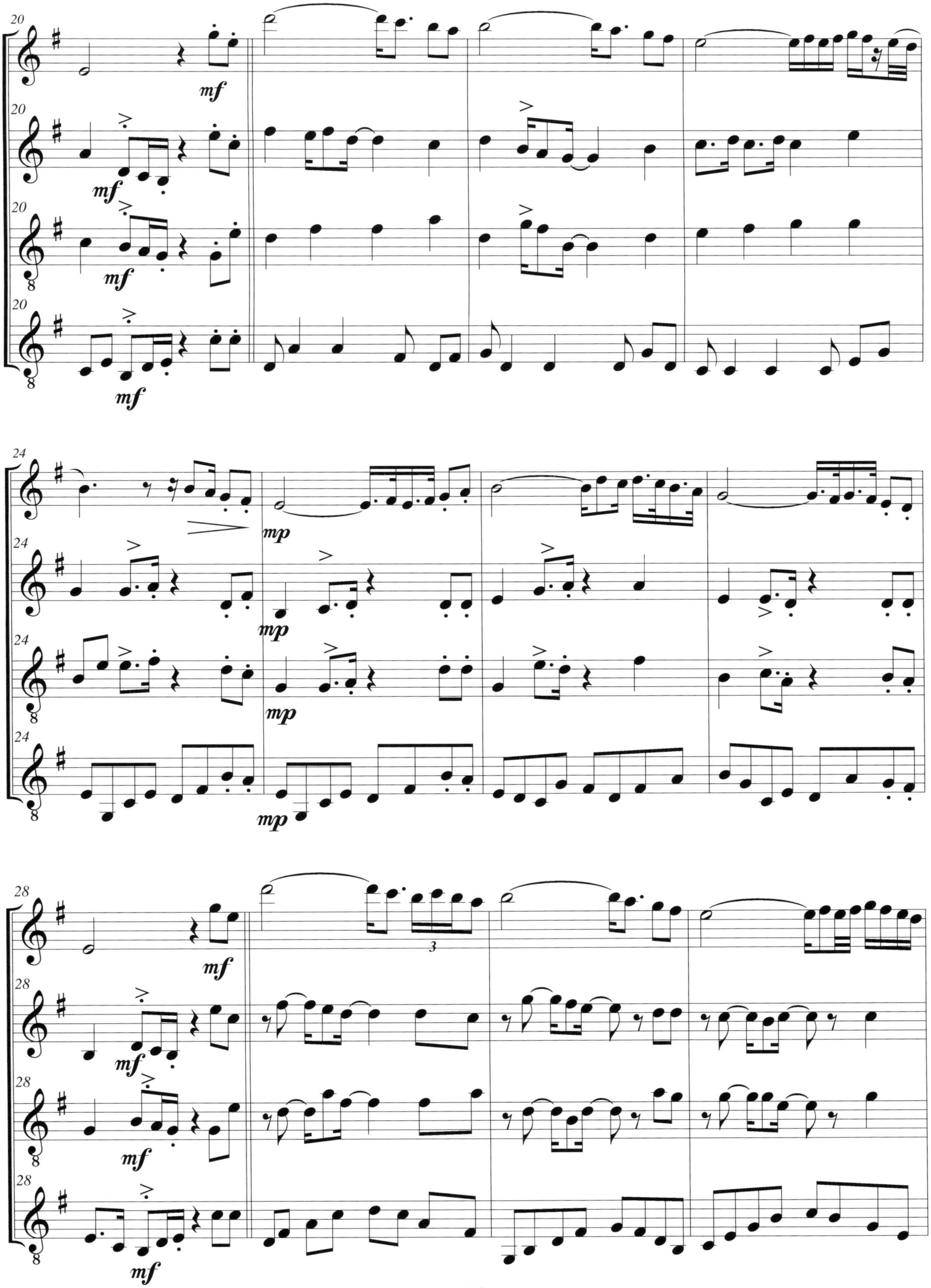
20
mf
24
mp
28
mf
3

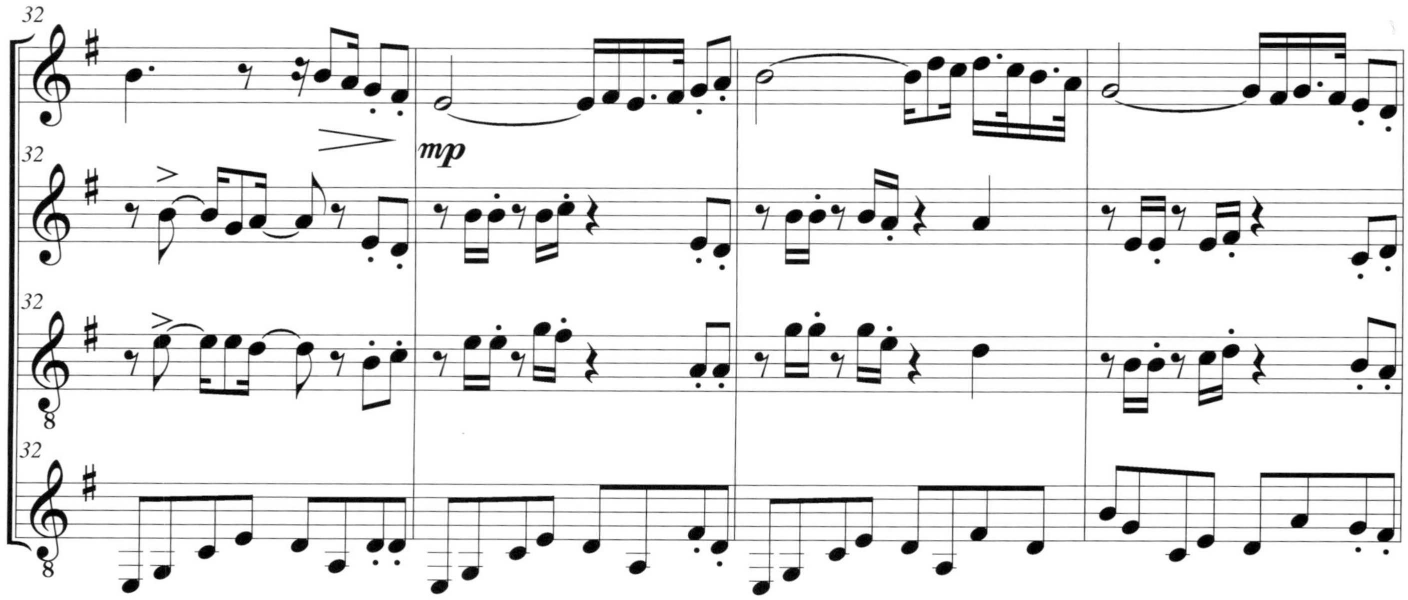

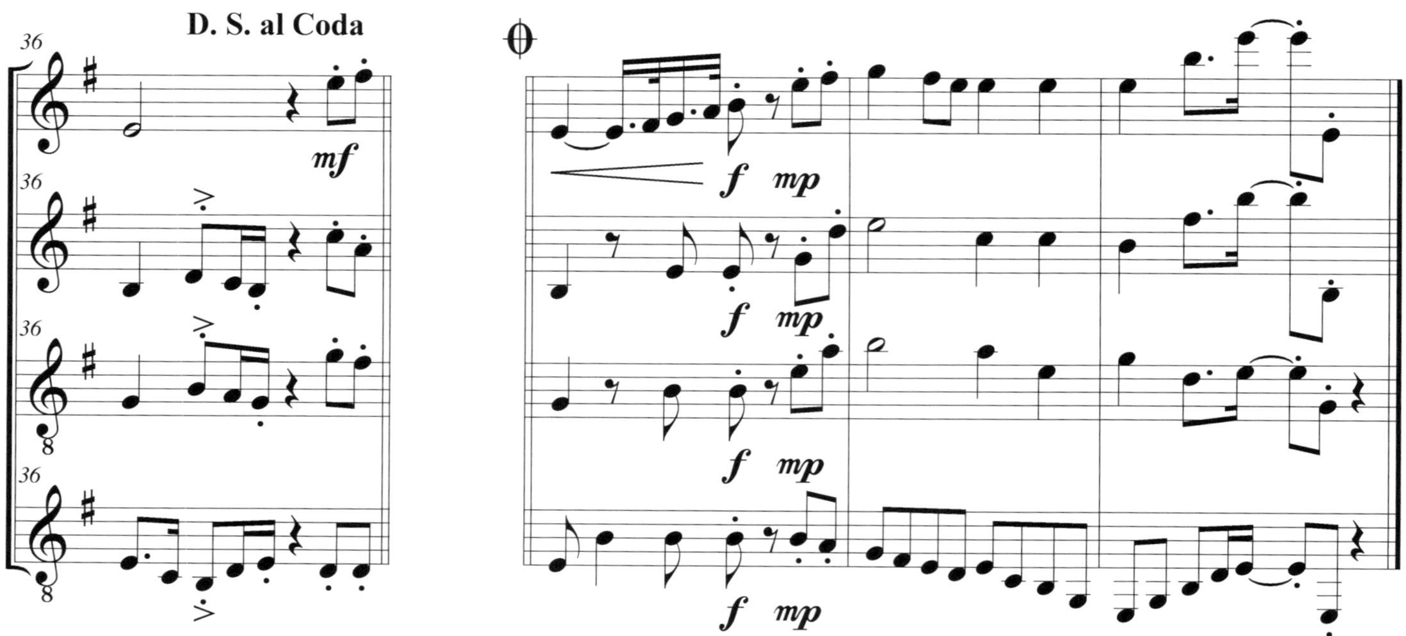

This piece began as a mandolin solo, but my friend Mitch Nelin requested to arrange it for our jazz mandolin quartet, the New England Mandolin Ensemble. It was such a success that I decided to follow his lead and make a version for a classical quartet with the same general feel, but more precise notation. This is the result, test driven by my mandolin octet, Enigmatica. The melody originally came to me walking on the beach early on a cloudy morning after a hurricane had blown through.

Mandolin 1

East of Here

Marilynn Mair

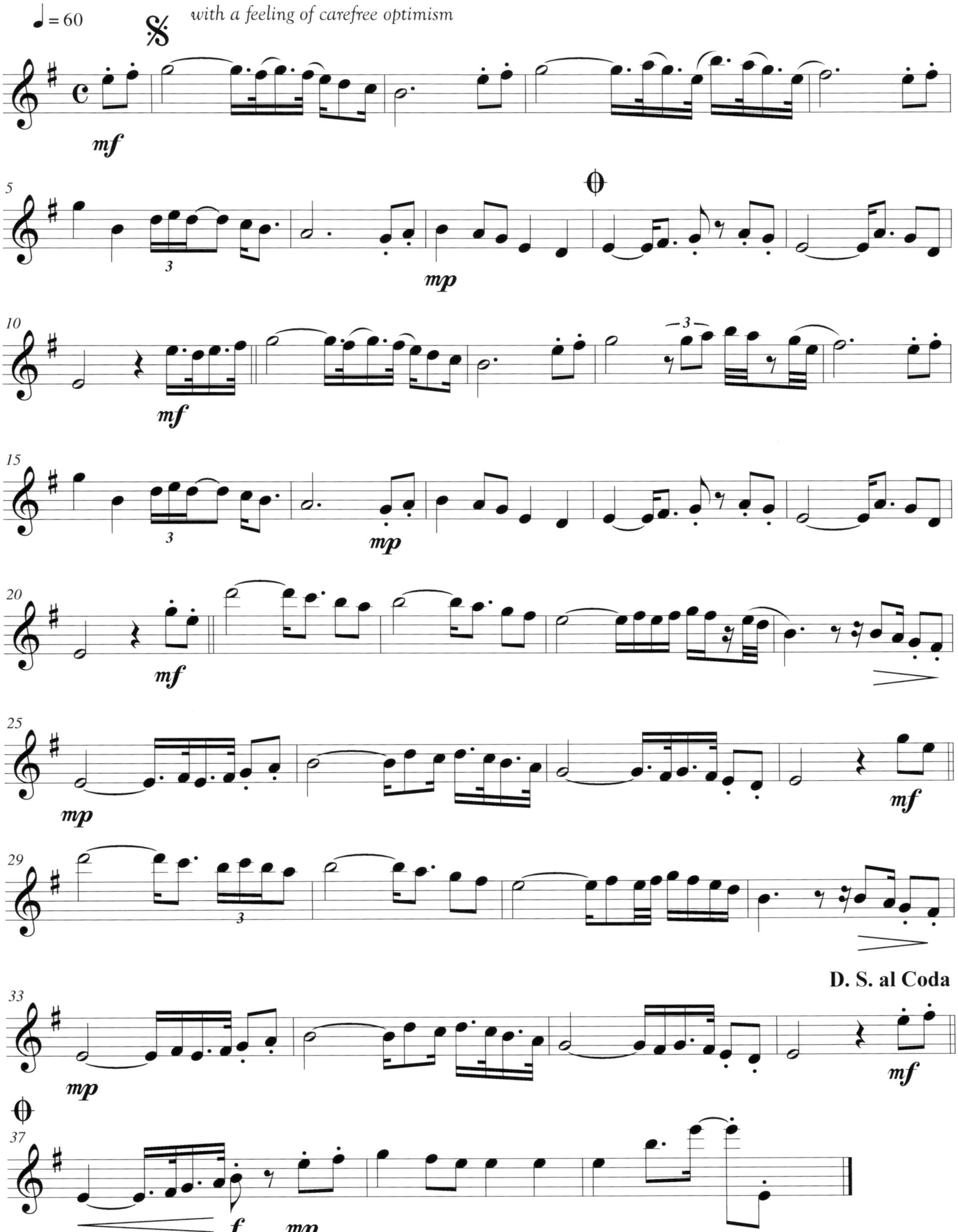

Mandolin 2

East of Here

Marilynn Mair

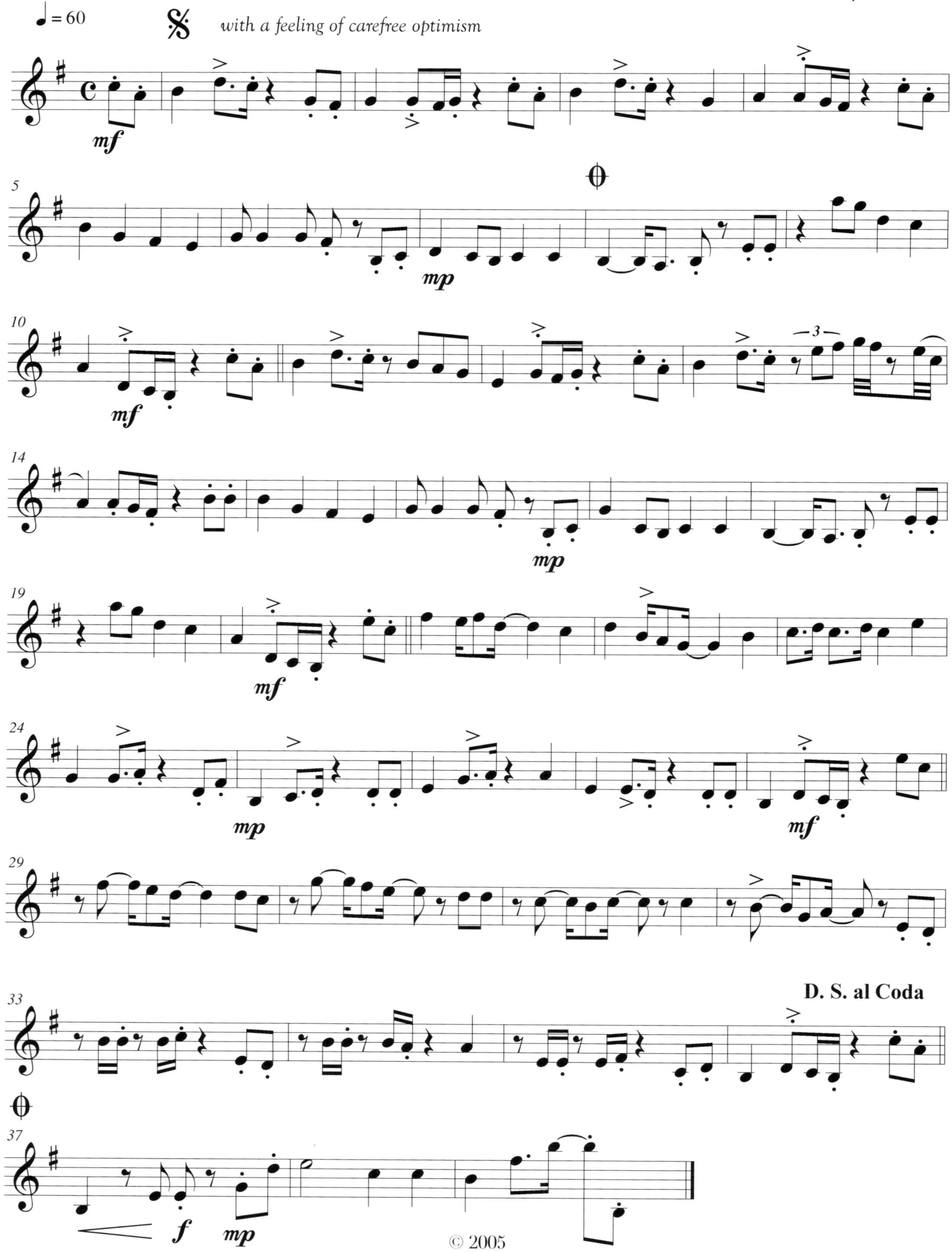

East of Here

Mandola - transposed treble

Marilynn Mair

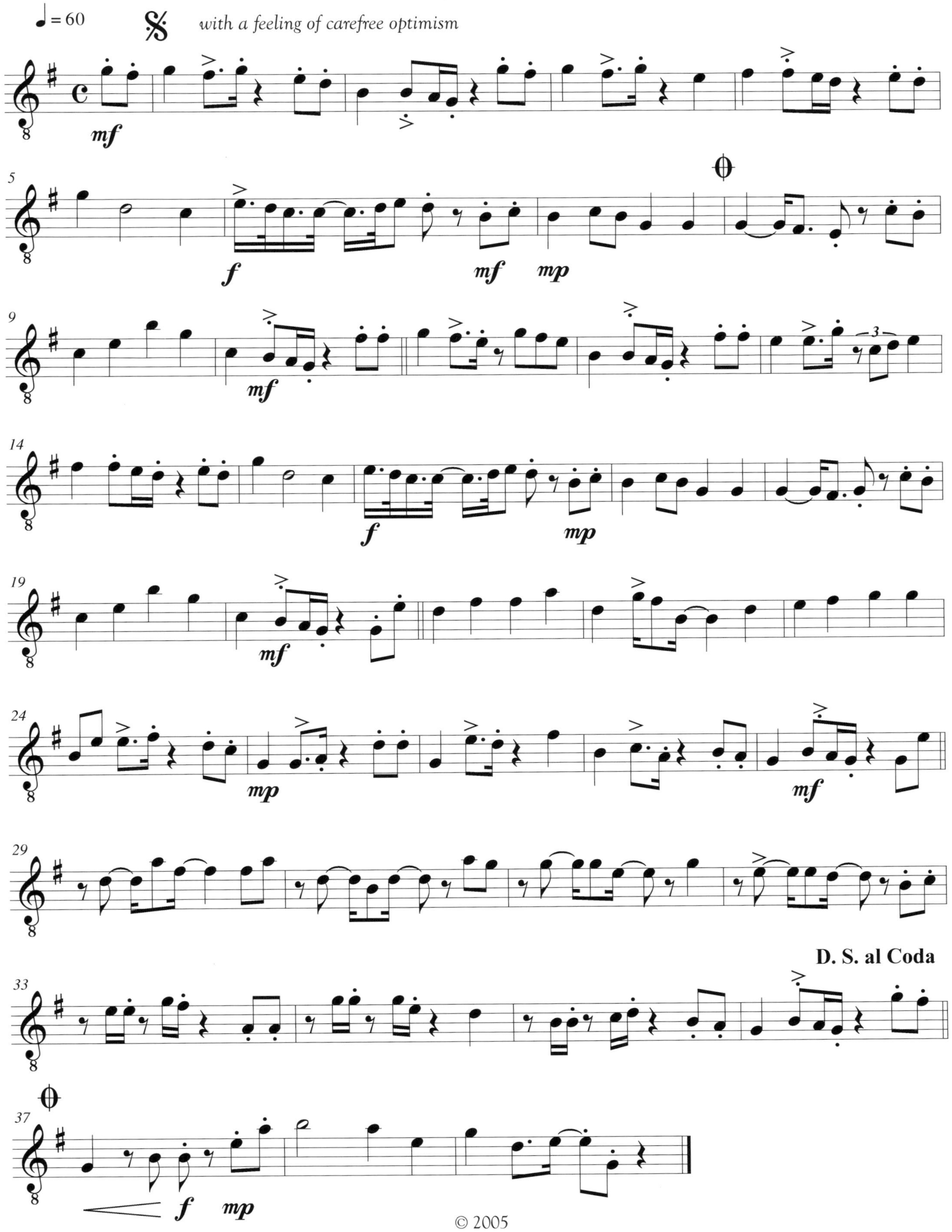

East of Here

Mandola - alto clef

Marilynn Mair

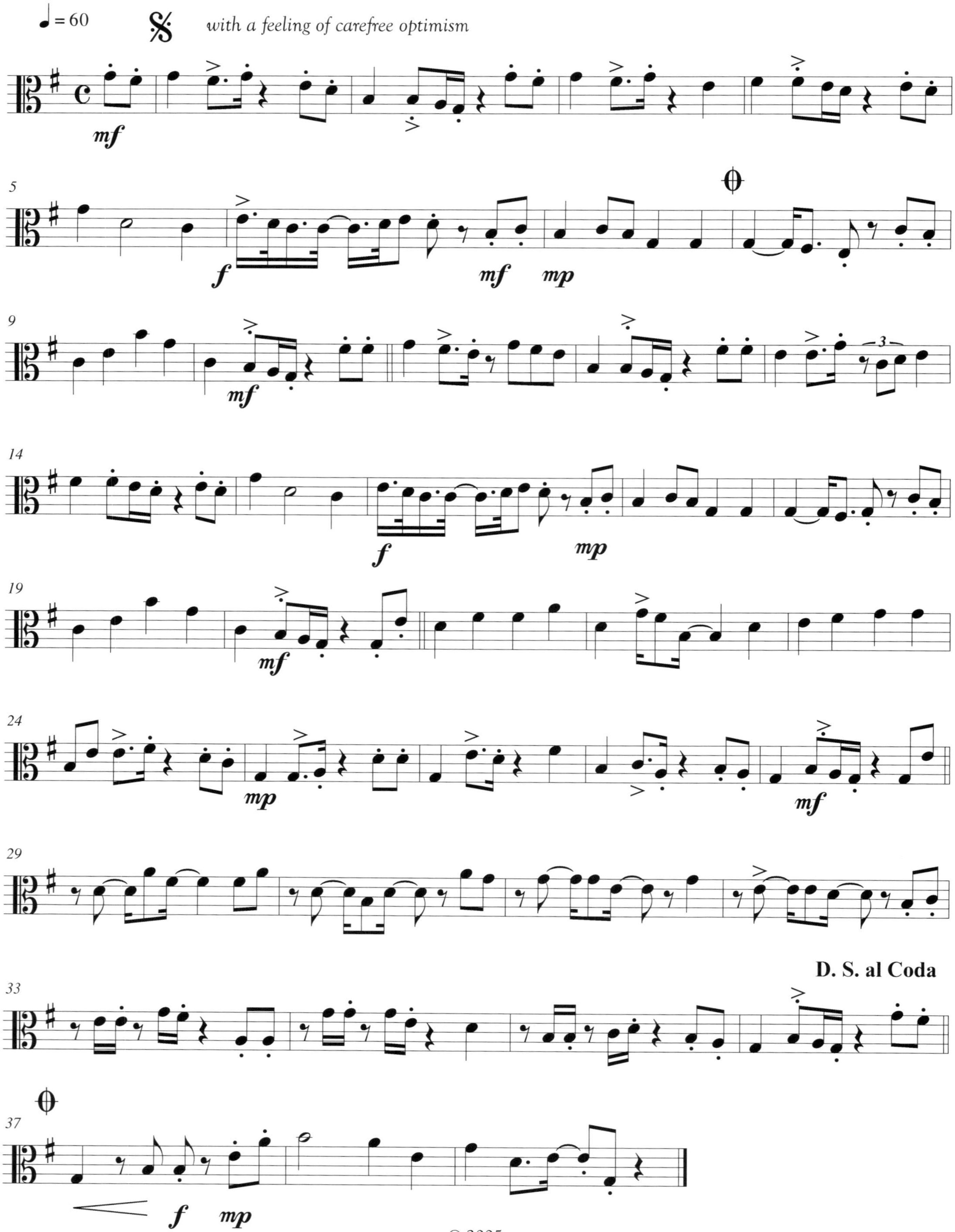

Guitar

East of Here

Marilynn Mair

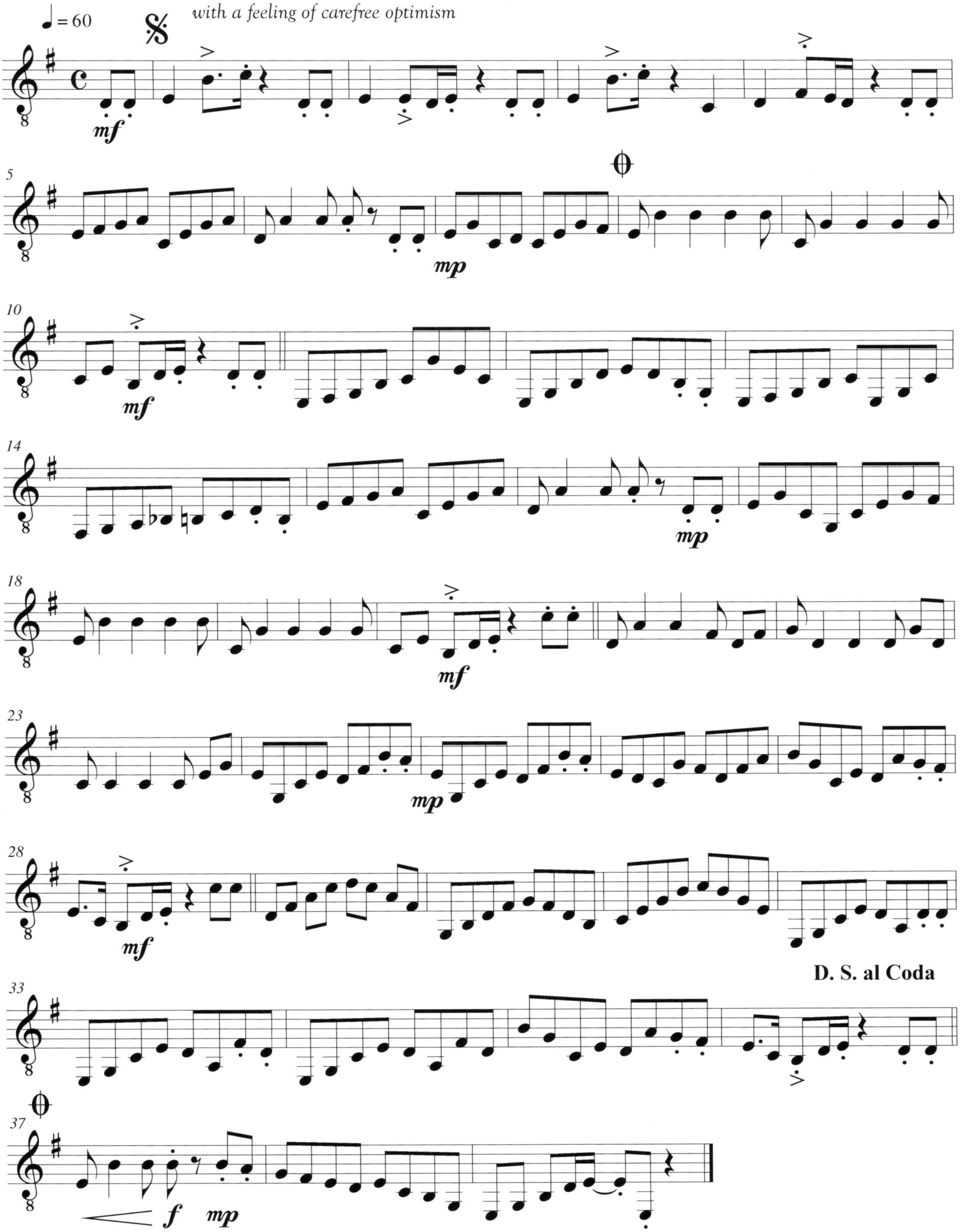

East of Here

Mandocello

Marilynn Mair

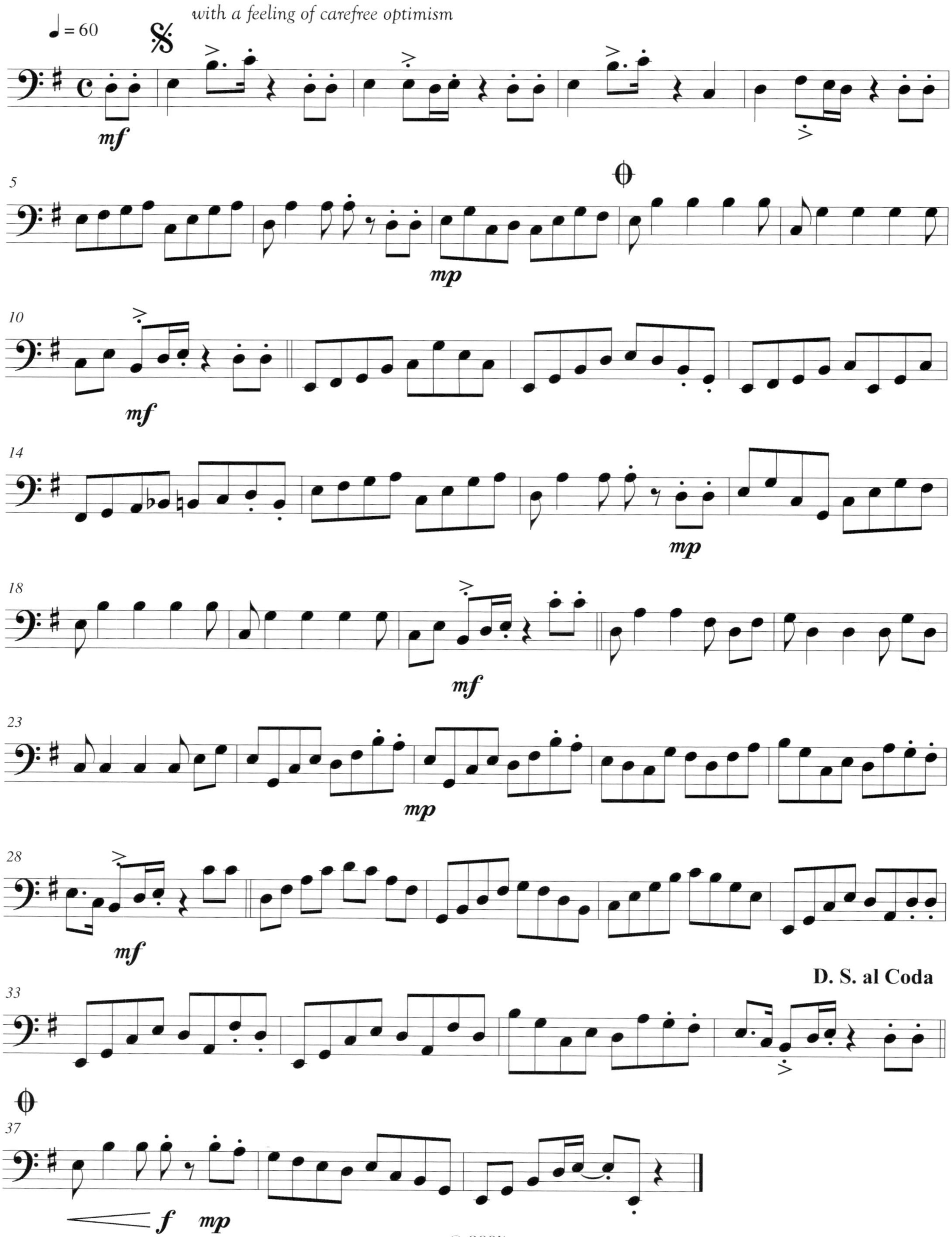

The Jabberwock

setting of a poem by Lewis Carroll

Marilynn Mair

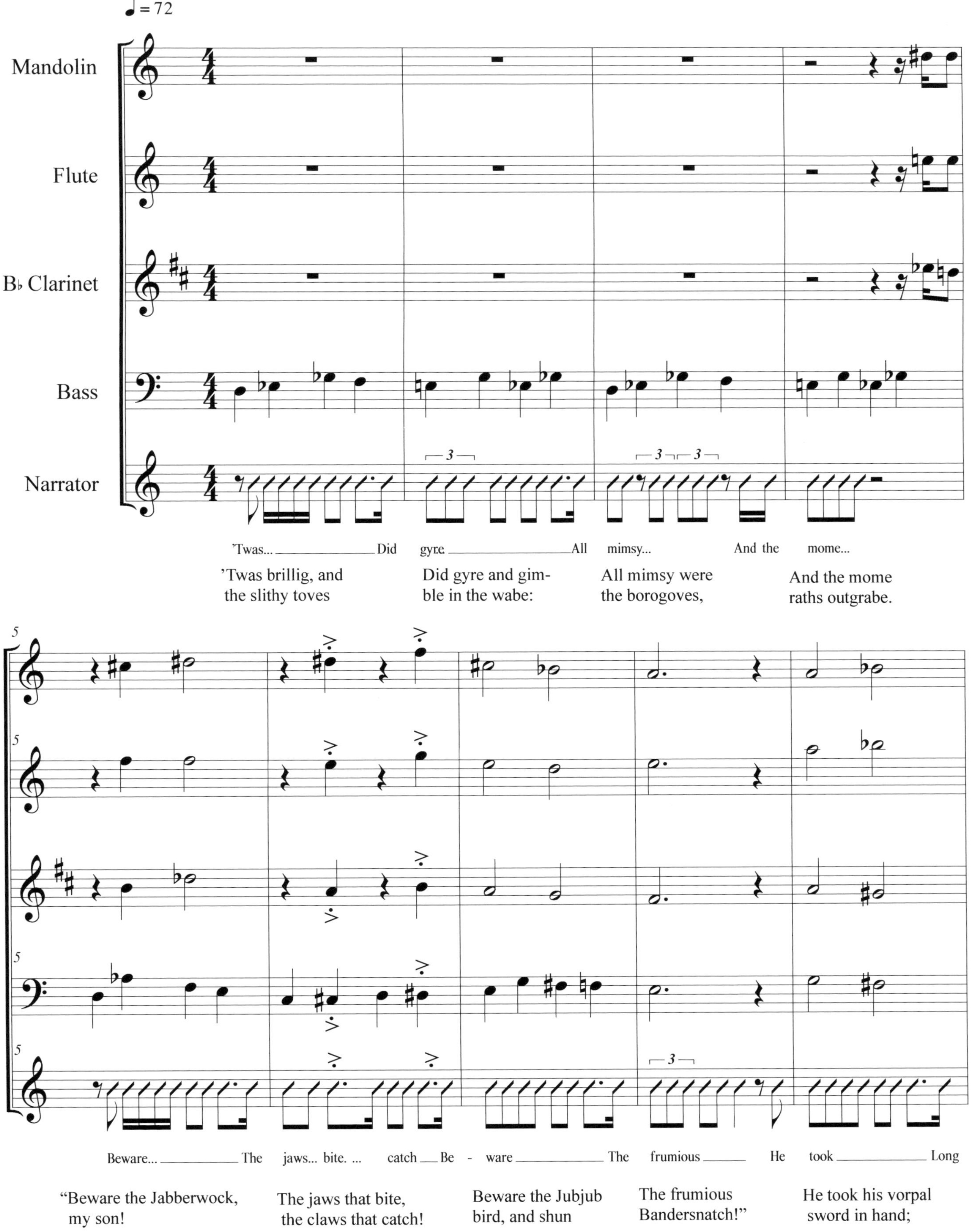

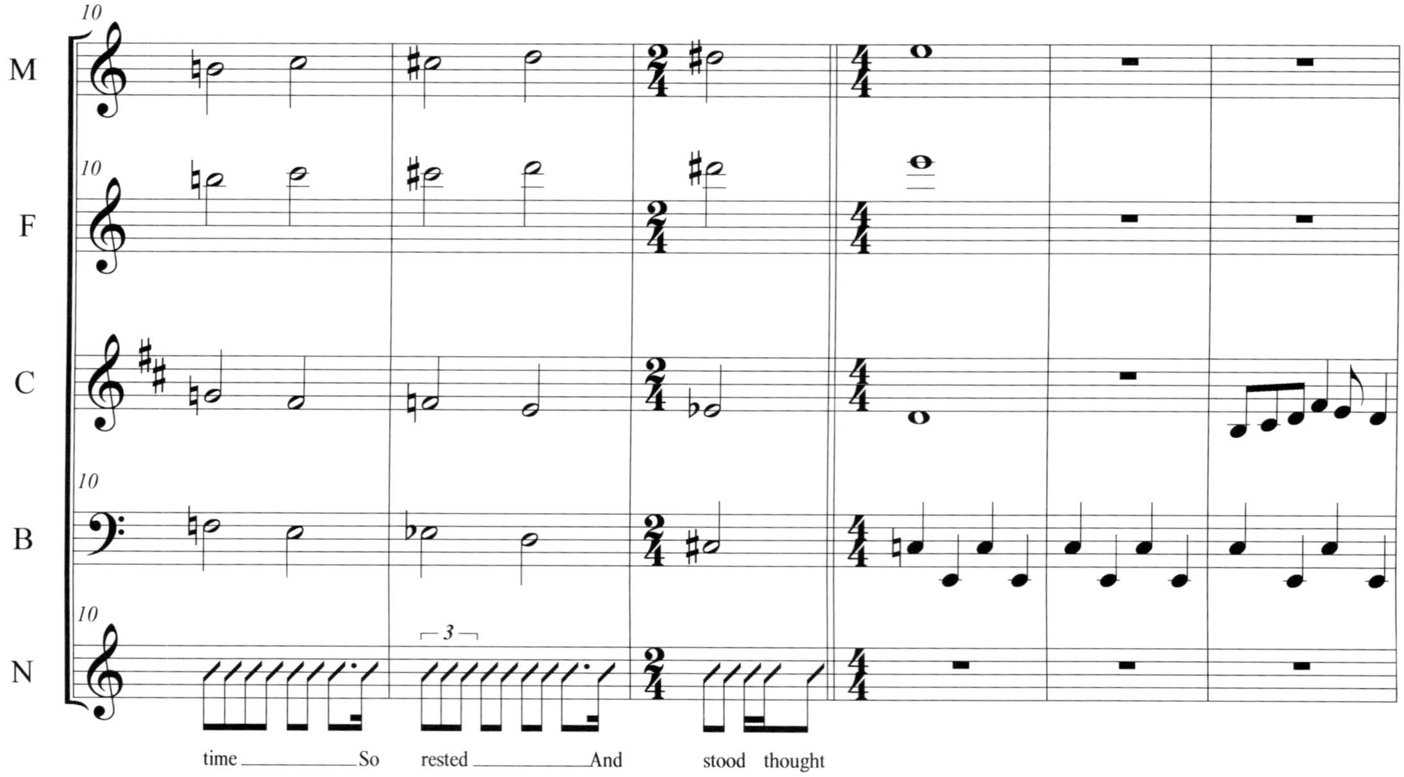

Long time the manxome foe he sought—

So rested he by the Tumtum tree

And stood awhile in thought.

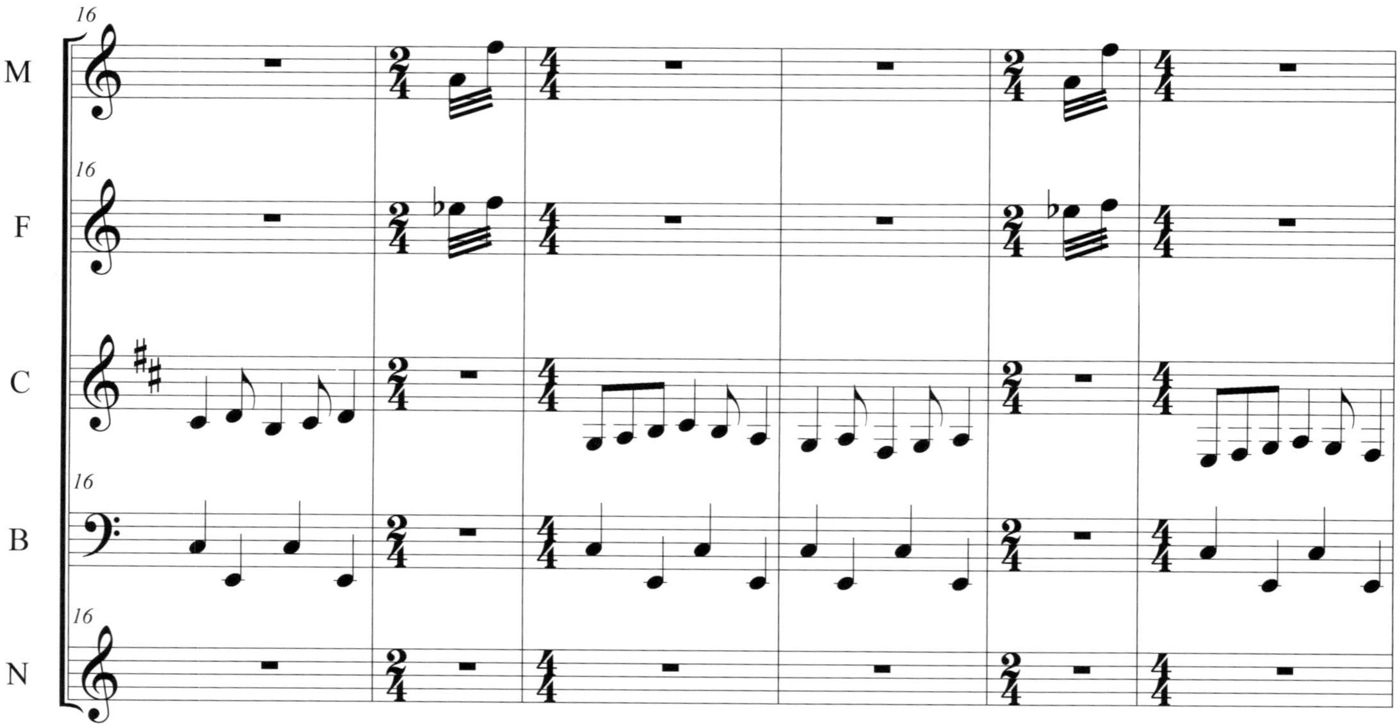

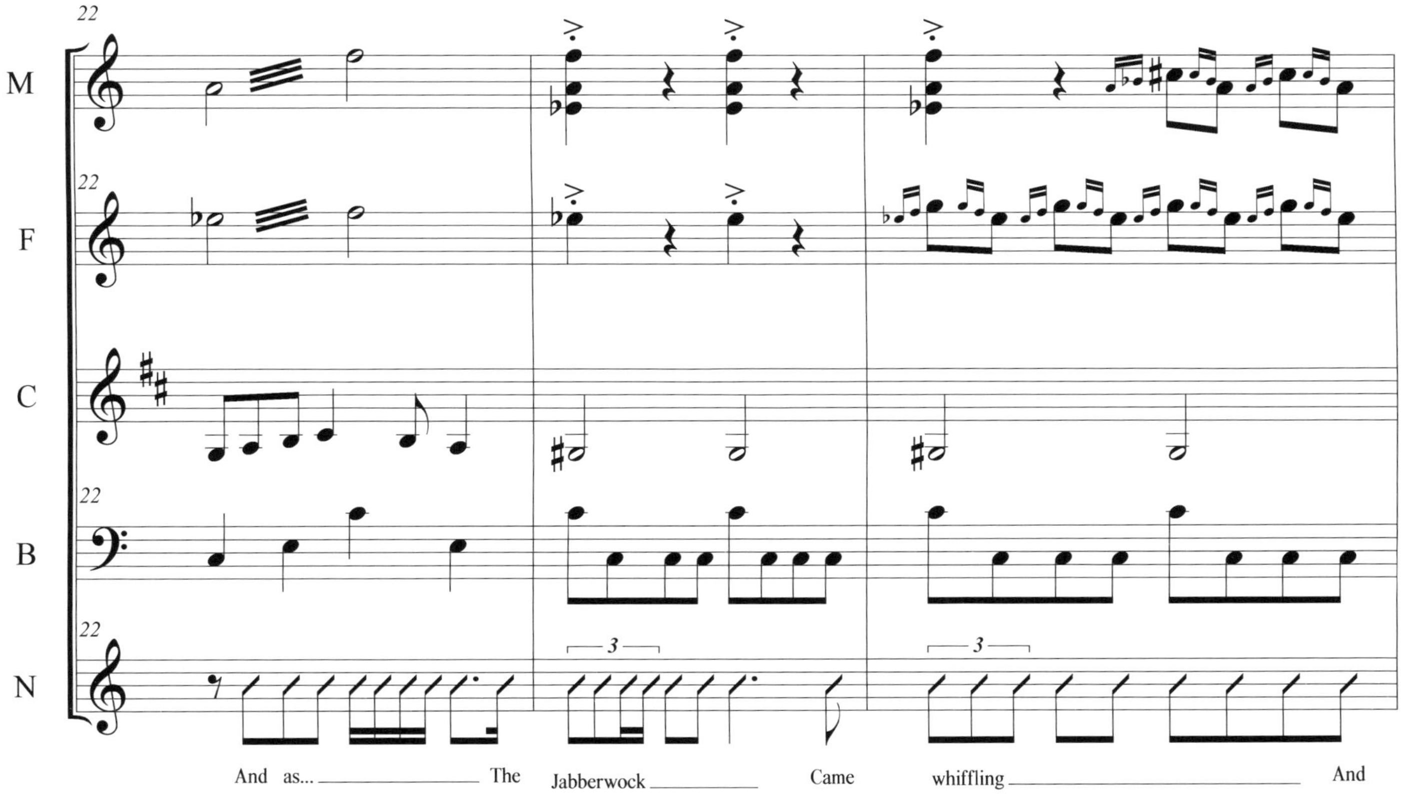

And, as in uffish thought he stood,

The Jabberwock, with eyes of flame,

Came whiffling through the tulgey wood,

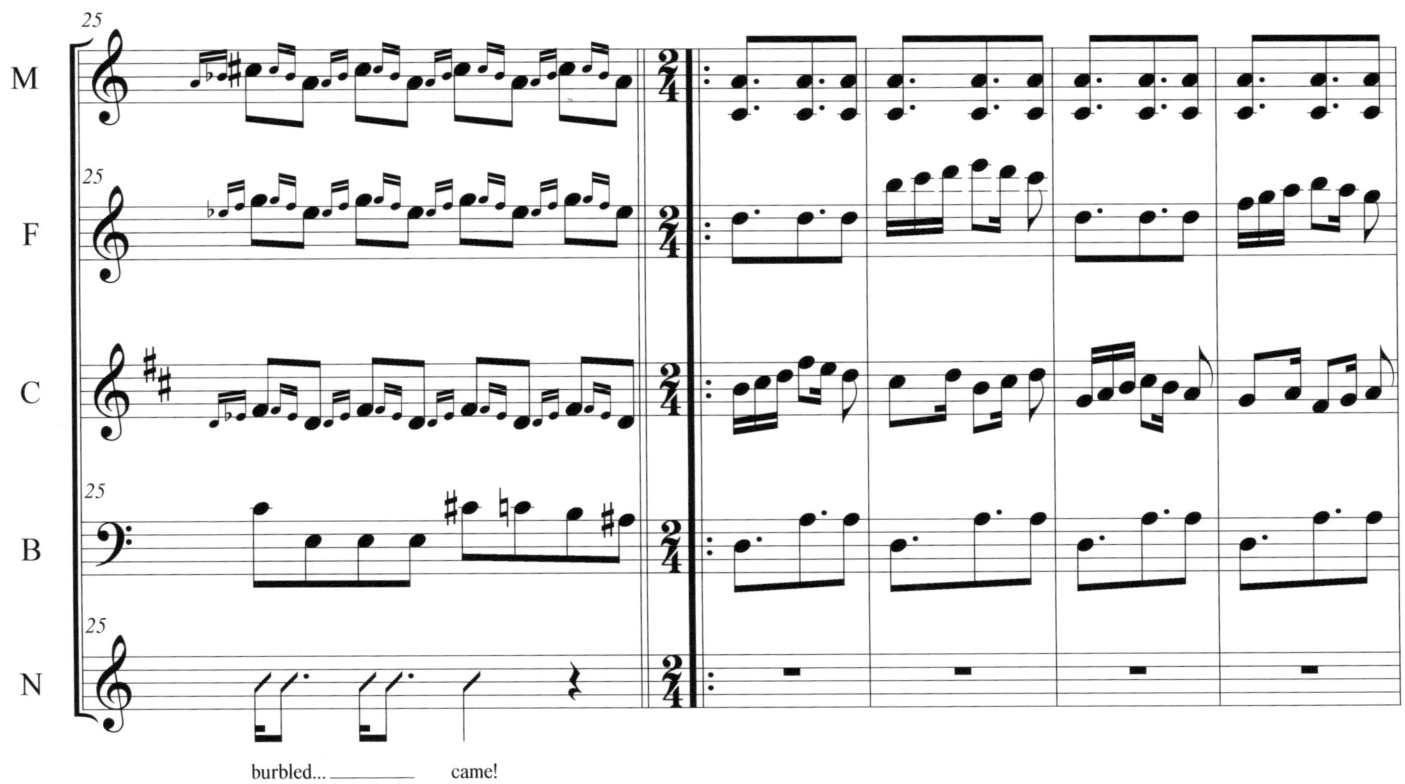

And burbled as it came!

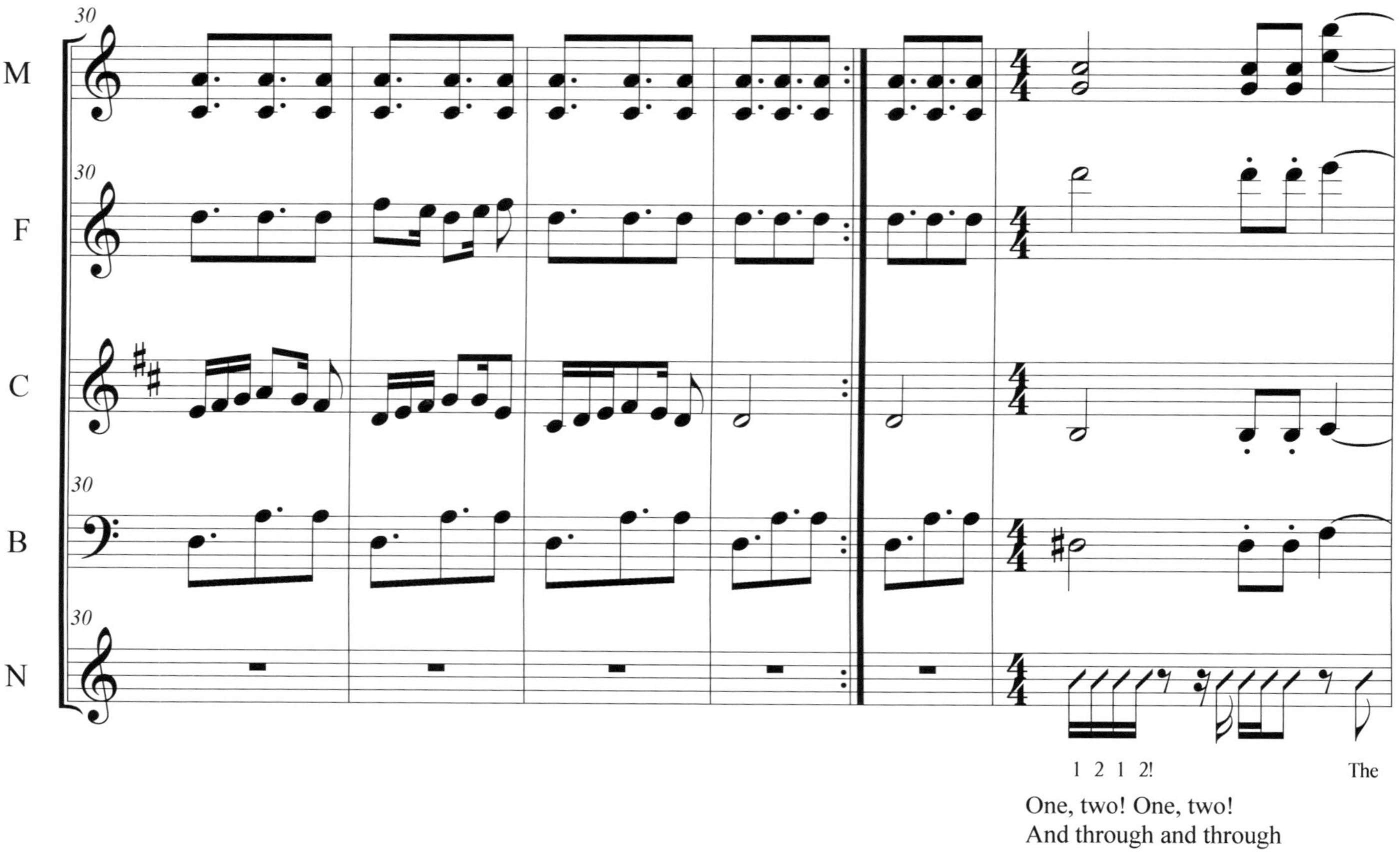
30
M
F
C
B
N
1 2 1 2!
The
One, two! One, two!
And through and through

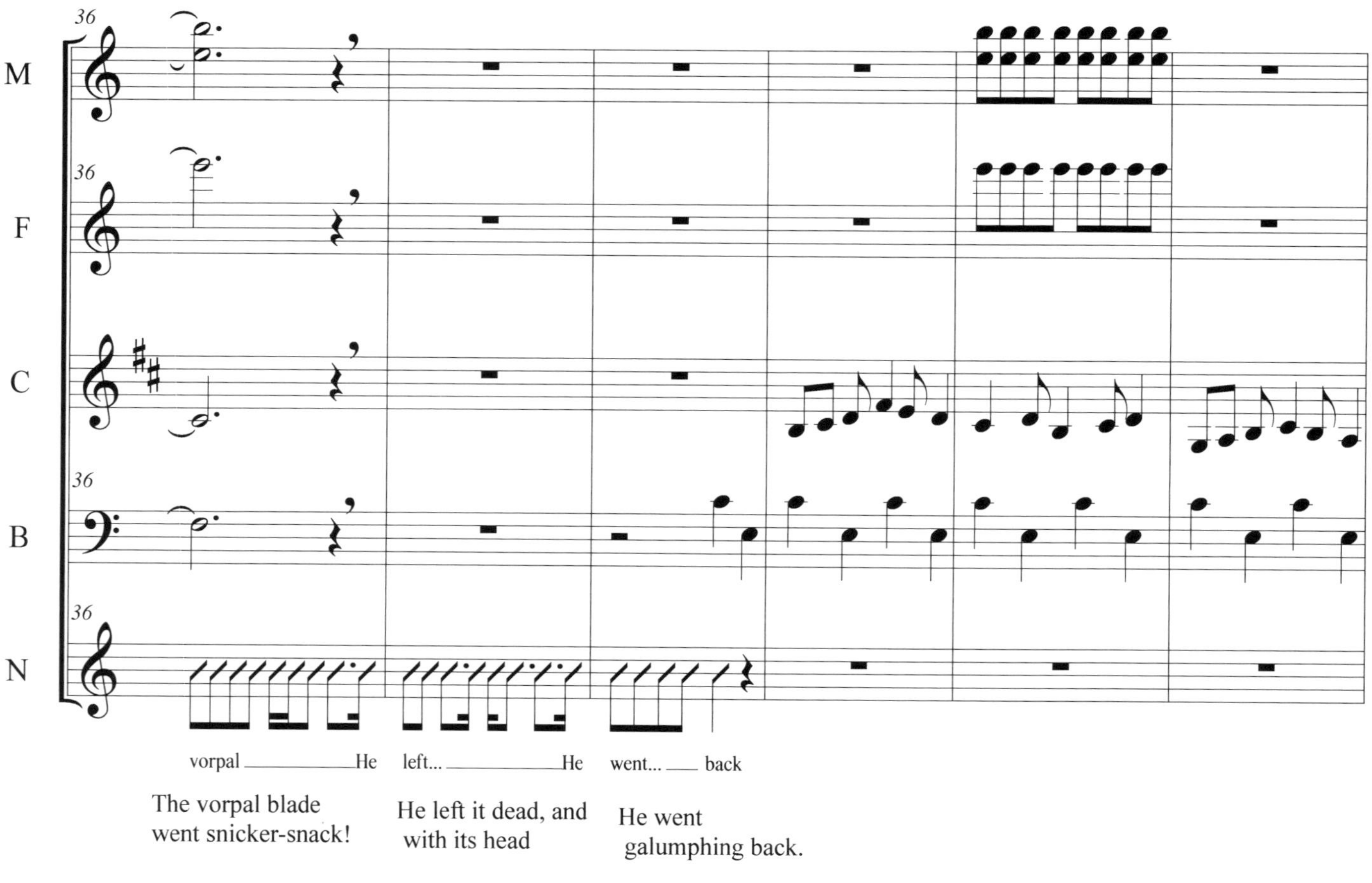
36
M
F
C
B
N
vorpal He
left... He
went... back
The vorpal blade
went snicker-snack!
He left it dead, and
with its head
He went
galumphing back.

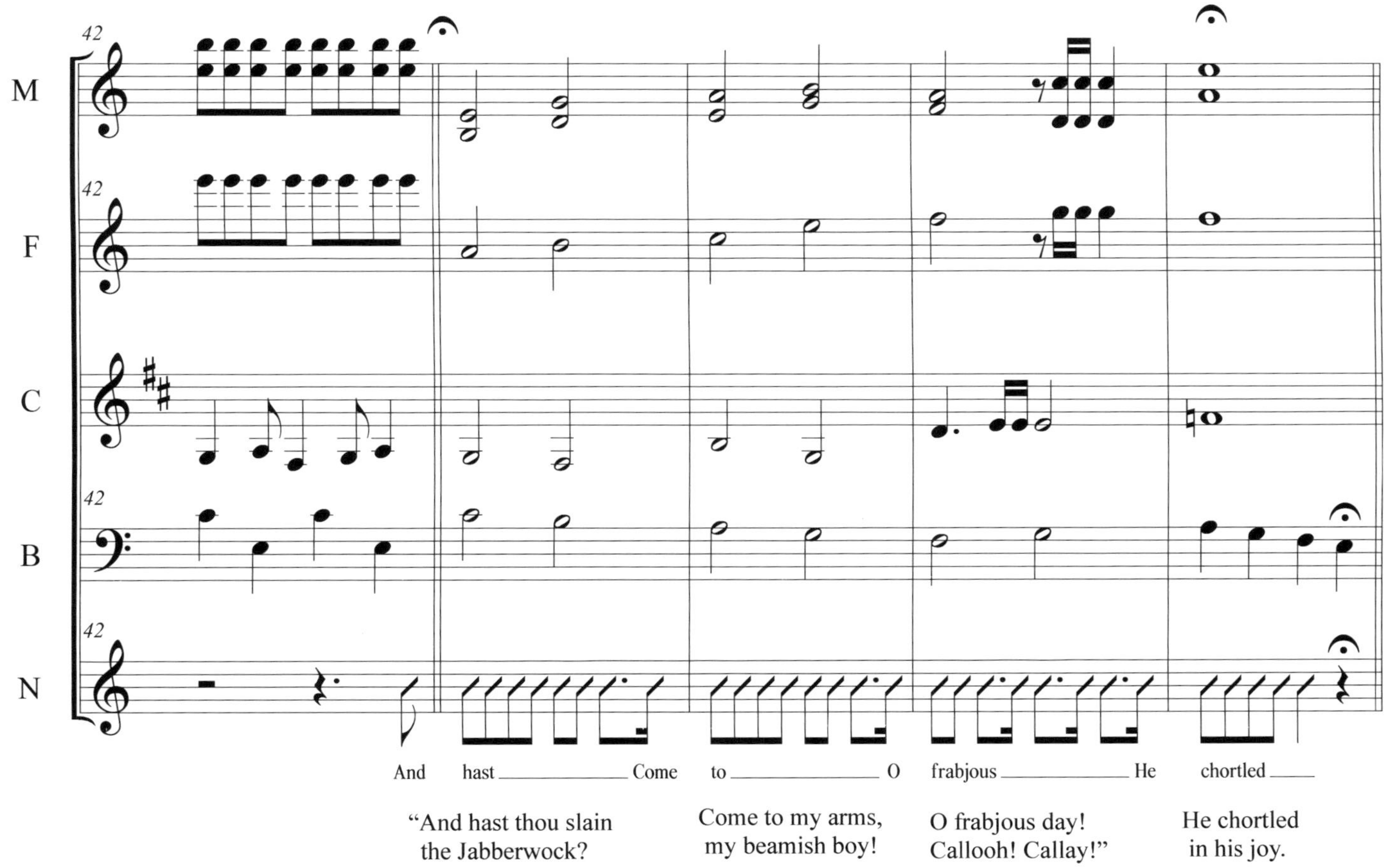

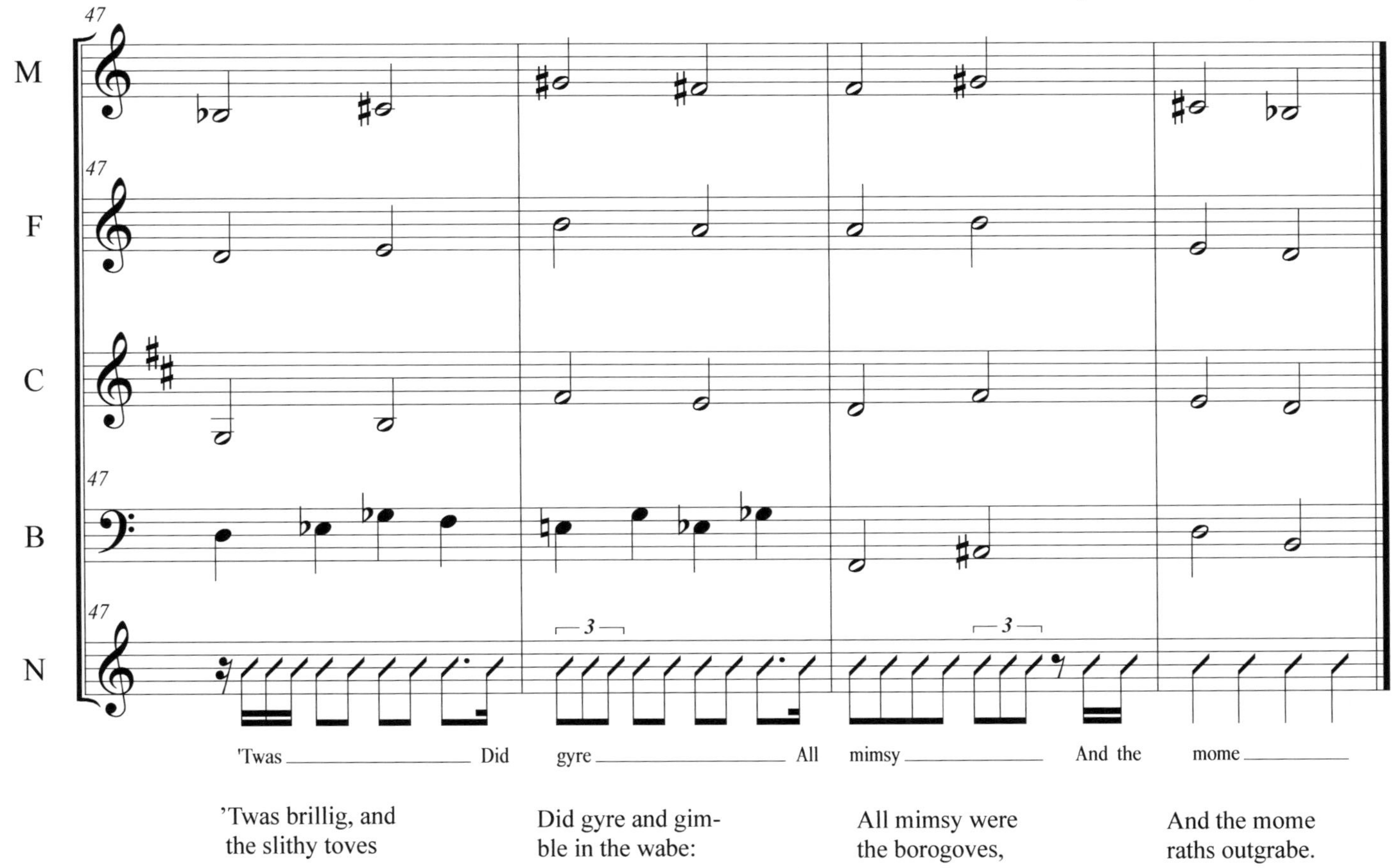

I wrote this early in my performing career for one iteration of the Contemporary Social Orchestra, a fluid group of musical friends. I've also performed it with other instrumentation, and I've included parts for plucked strings as well as the original. The rhythm for the narrator is approximate, included to set parameters. Add tremolo for theatrical effect, but keep the rhythm precise.

The Jabberwock

Mandolin

setting of a poem by Lewis Carroll

Marilynn Mair

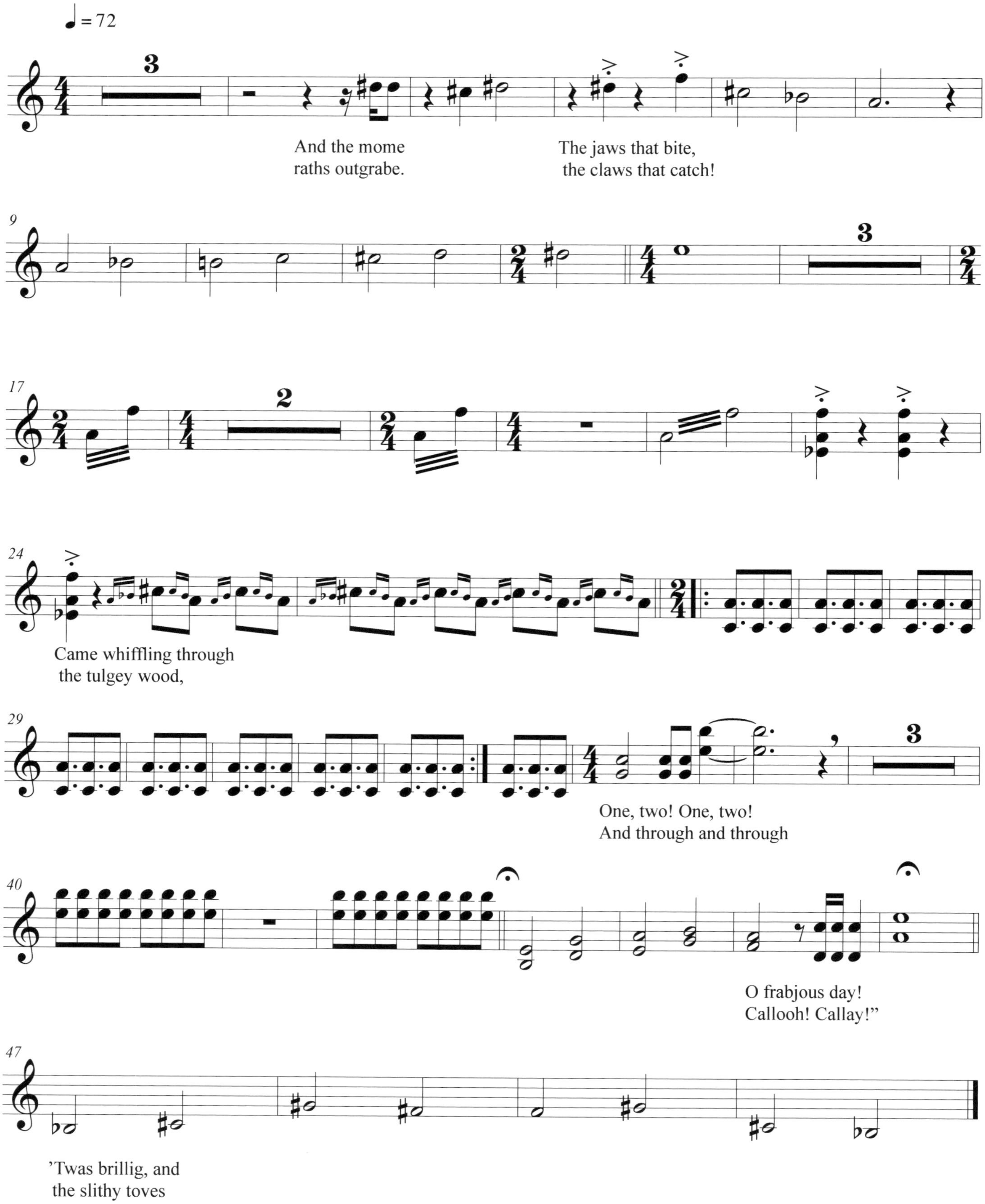

The Jabberwock

setting of a poem by Lewis Carroll

Marilynn Mair

Flute/Mandolin

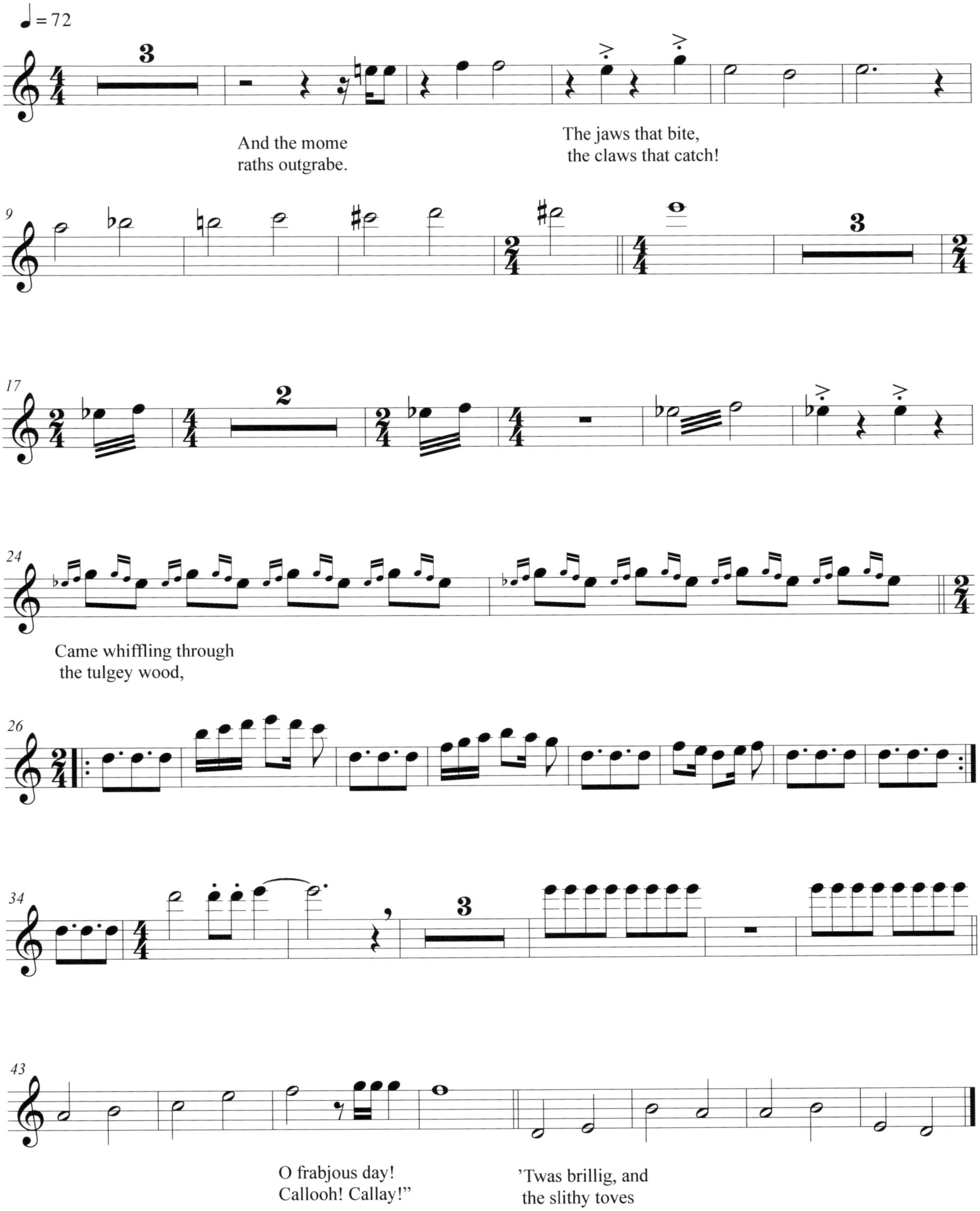

B♭ Clarinet

The Jabberwock

setting of a poem by Lewis Carroll

Marilynn Mair

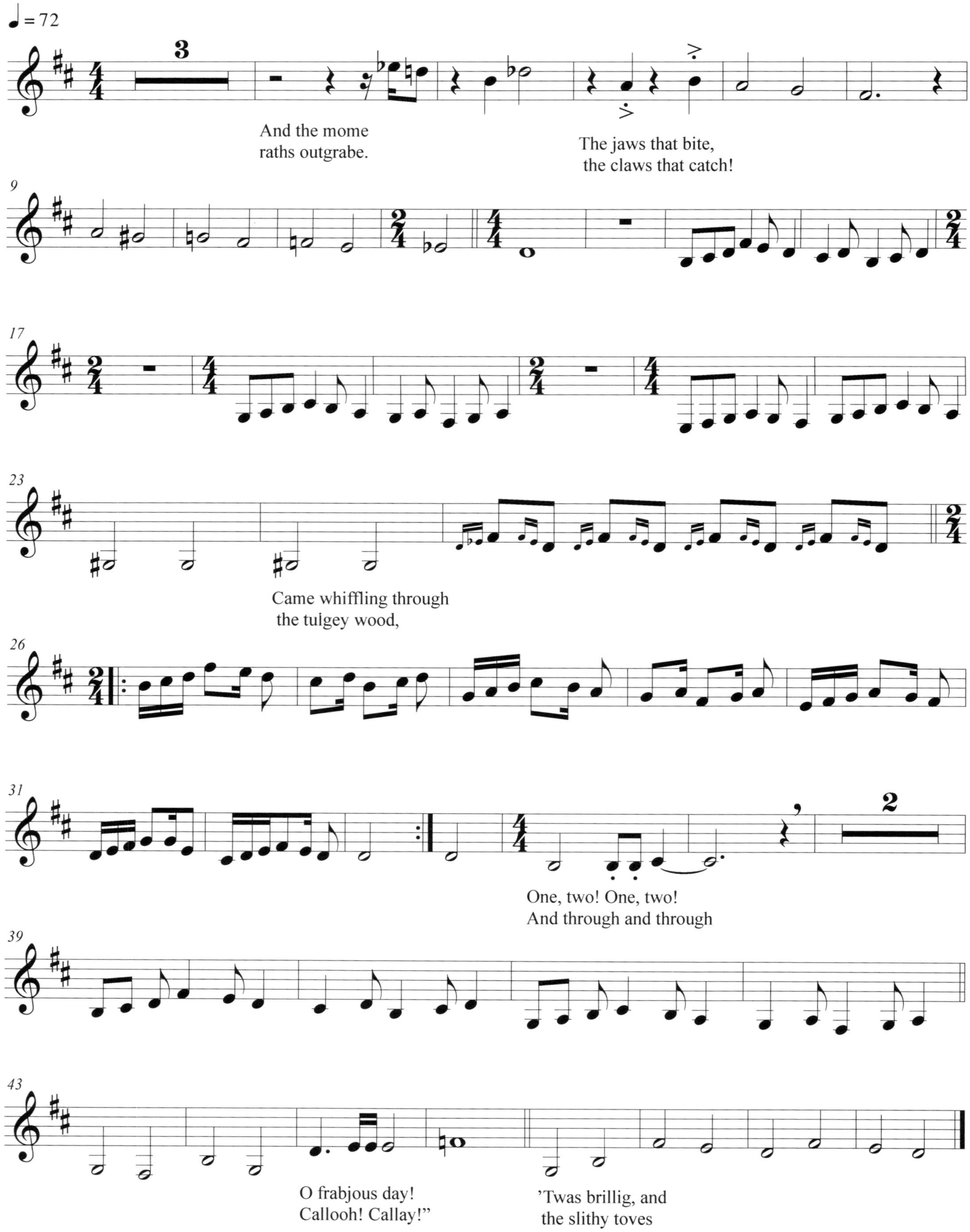

The Jabberwock

Clarinet part for Mandola/G

setting of a poem by Lewis Carroll

Marilynn Mair

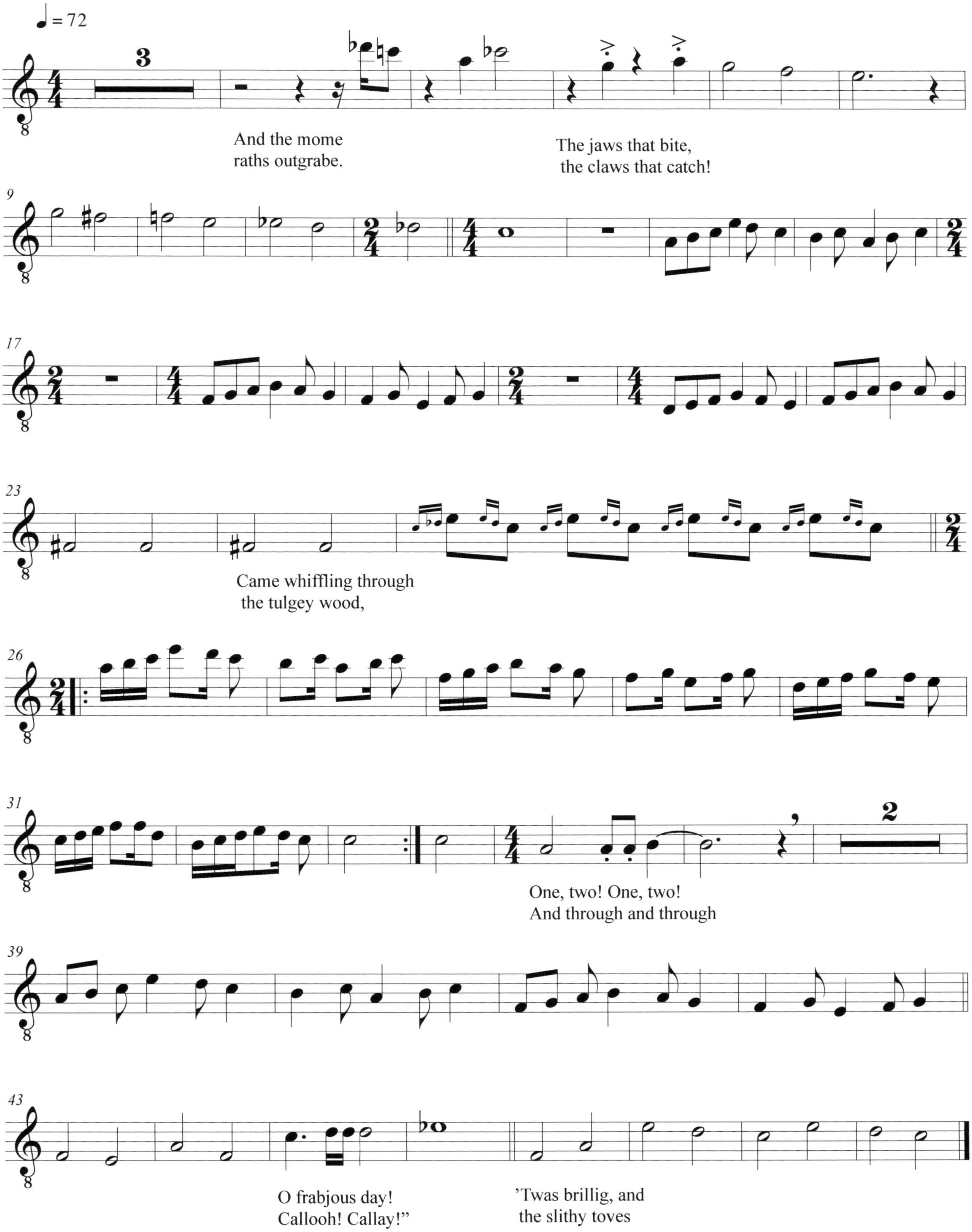

Clarinet part for Mandola/C

The Jabberwock

setting of a poem by Lewis Carroll

Marilynn Mair

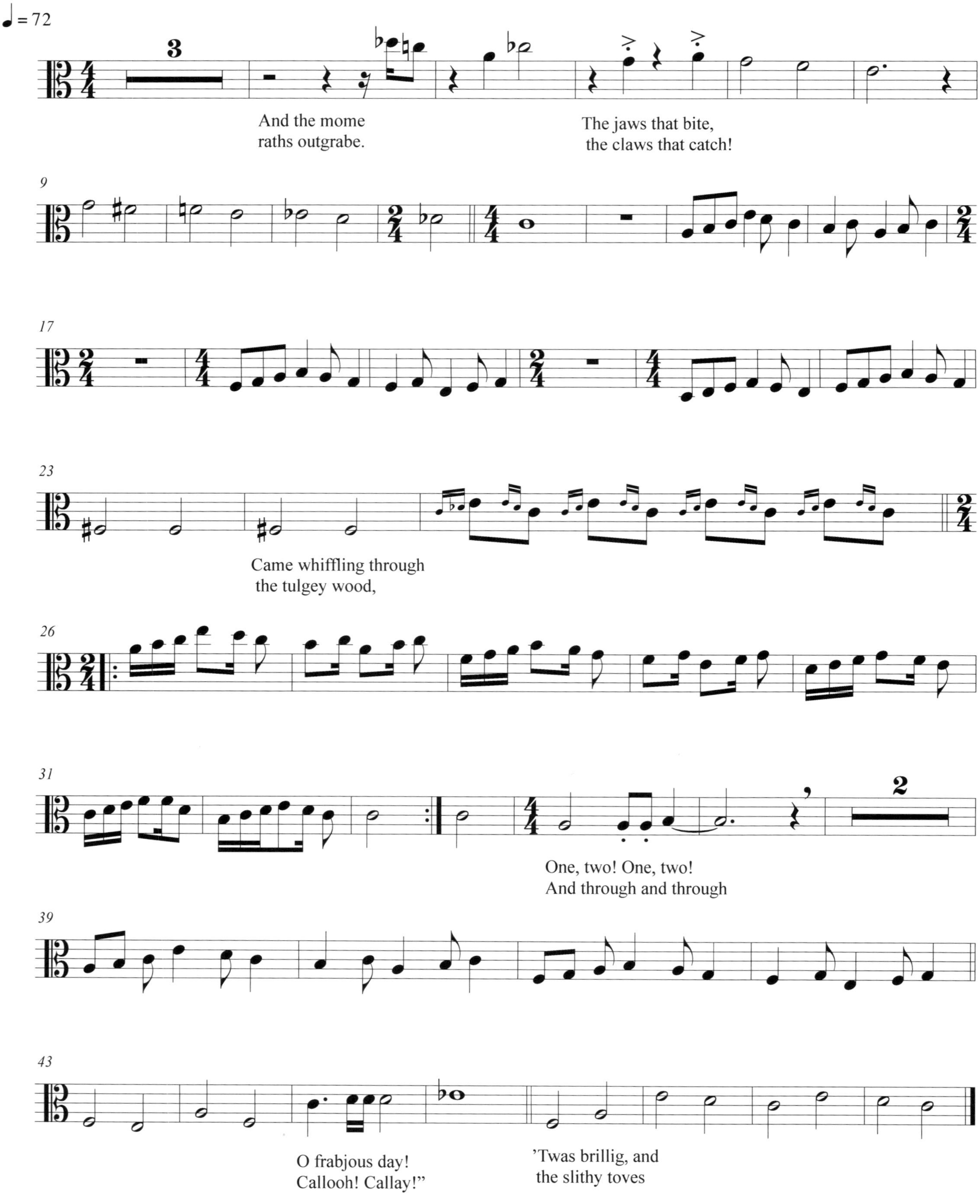

The Jabberwock

setting of a poem by Lewis Carroll

Marilynn Mair

Bass

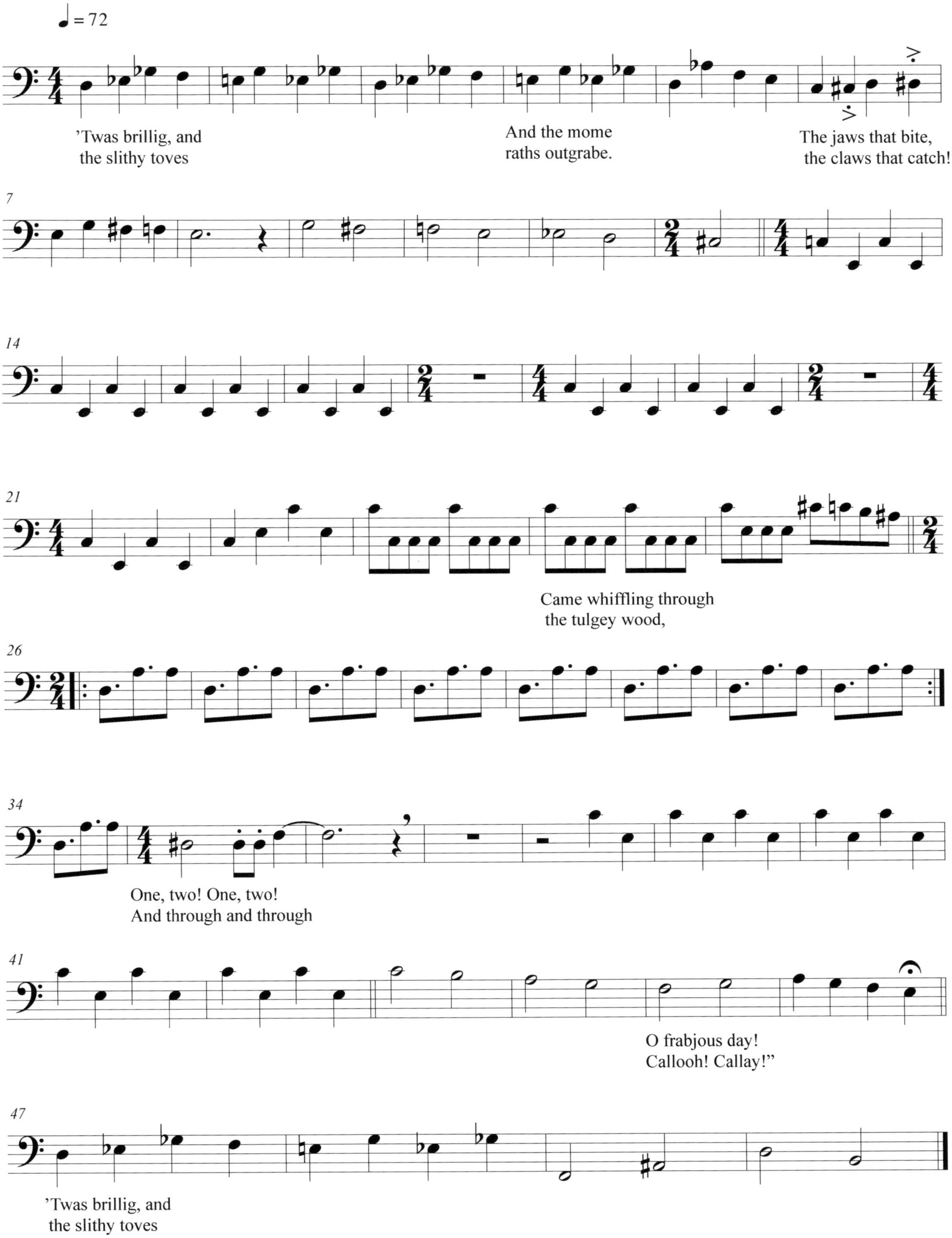

The Jabberwock

Bass for Guitar

setting of a poem by Lewis Carroll

Marilynn Mair

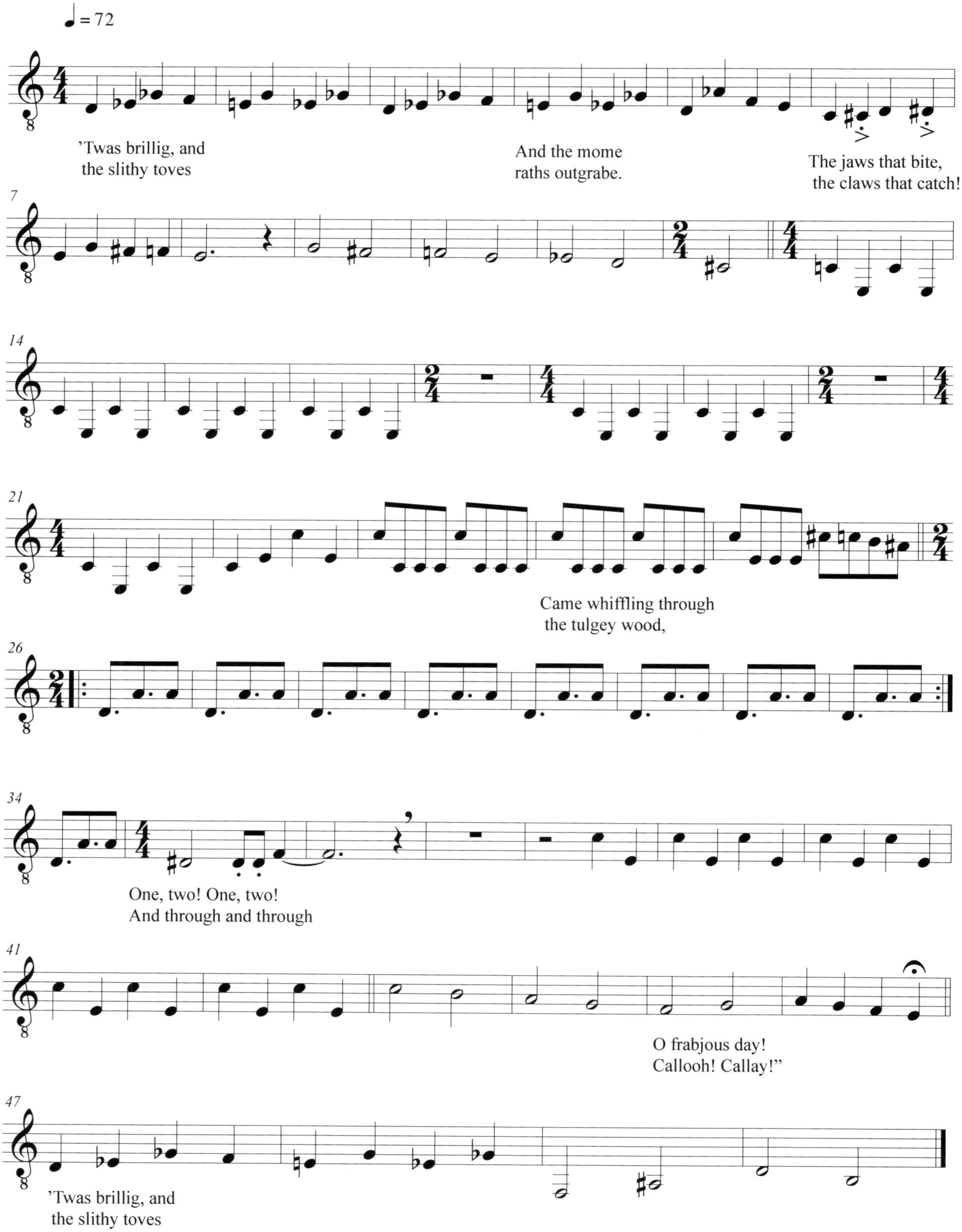

The Jabberwock

setting of a poem by Lewis Carroll

Narrator

Marilynn Mair

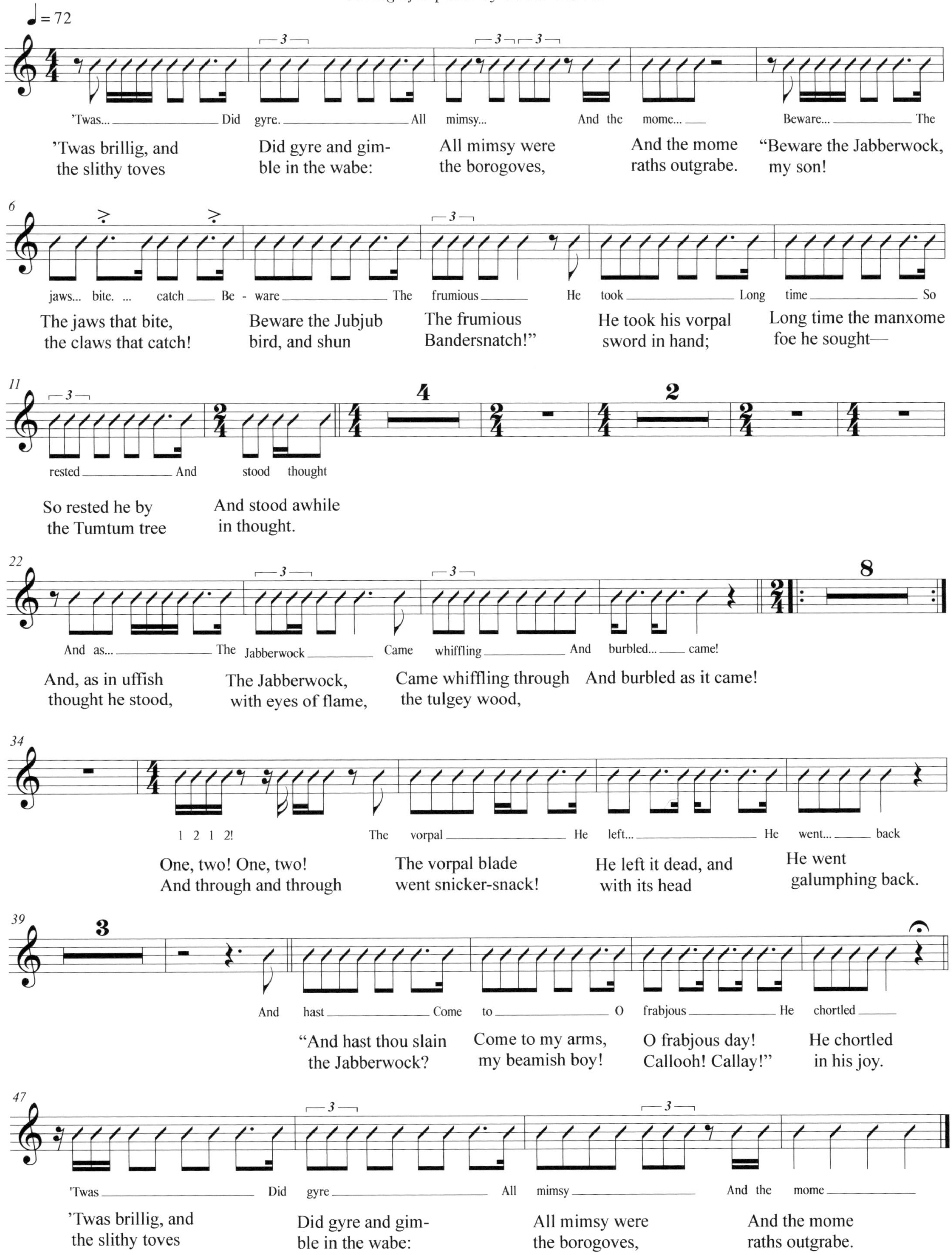

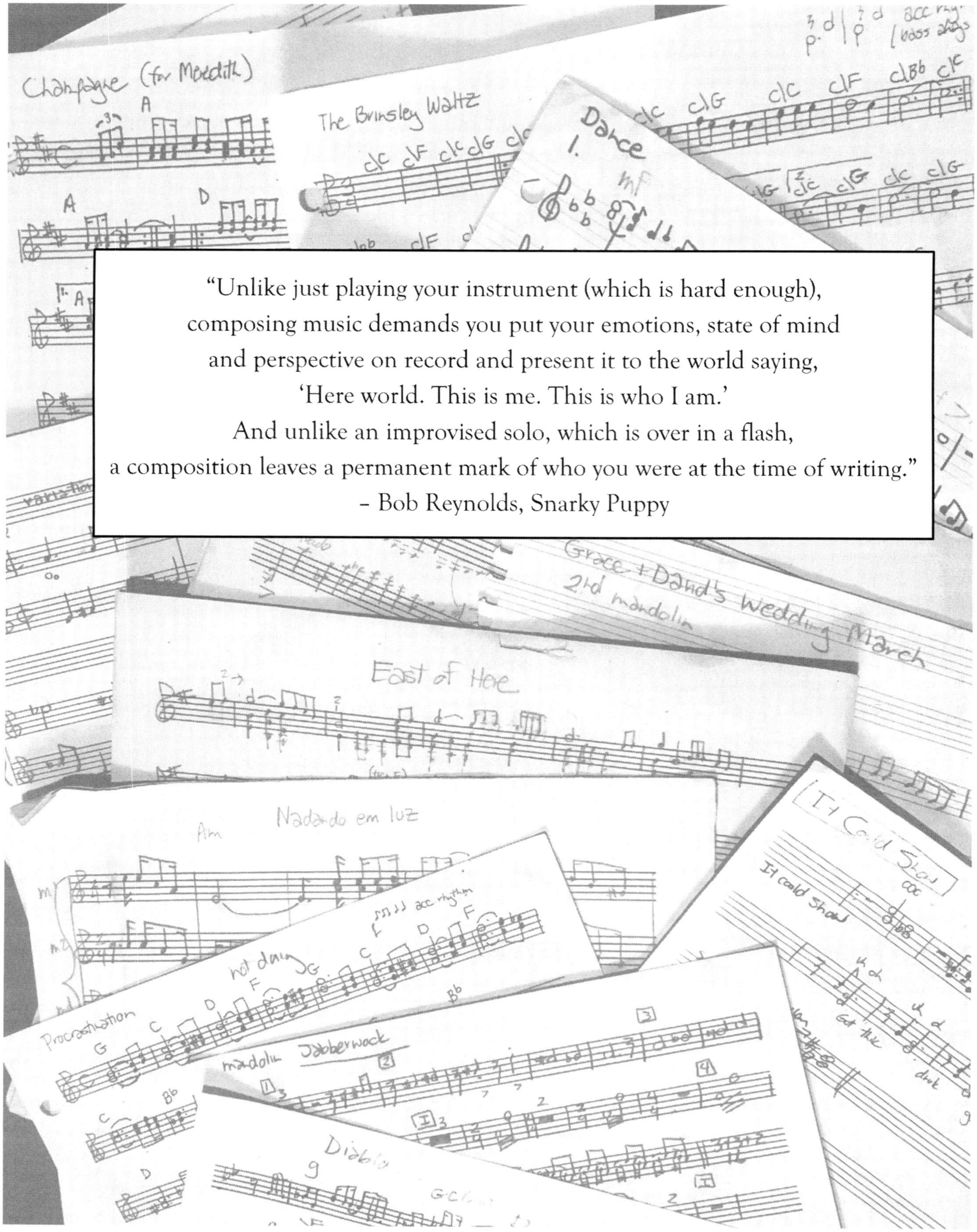

"Unlike just playing your instrument (which is hard enough),
composing music demands you put your emotions, state of mind
and perspective on record and present it to the world saying,
'Here world. This is me. This is who I am.'
And unlike an improvised solo, which is over in a flash,
a composition leaves a permanent mark of who you were at the time of writing."
– Bob Reynolds, Snarky Puppy

Selected Early Works

East of Here

3-4-3 (4/3)

And She Has Flown

Margery

Champagne

Diablo

The Brinsley Waltz

Valse Isabel

3 Directions

When Everything's Been Done

written from 1980 - 2005

Selected Early Works

East of Here began as a tune hummed while walking on a Cape Cod beach in 2005, the morning after Hurricane Ophelia had passed. I first wrote the mandolin solo, and then the leadsheet. In the previous "Ensembles" section I included my newly created quartet.

3–4–3 (4/3) is a mandolin- electric bass duet, written and performed for the third anniversary celebration of the Minneapolis modern dance troupe, Three Dances, on March 4, 2004. The 3 movements are dedicated to the dancers who founded the company, Brinsley Davis, Jamie Garner, and Suzanne Wiltgen. I first performed it with Alex Wohlhueter on bass, and later with Will Ayton on viola da gamba.

And She Has Flown was written for my dear friend Carleigh Hoff, at her kitchen table in Tucson, Arizona, when I arrived a day too late to say goodbye. I performed it the next day at her memorial service.

Margery, the earliest piece I've included in this book, is a sprightly 12-tone oboe-mandolin duet containing hints of Frank Zappa, that I wrote for a college composition class. It also works well as a mandolin duet.

Champagne began as an accordion tune, one of many I wrote while exploring an instrument different in every aspect from the mandolin. I include it here as a leadsheet and also in its later mandolin duet version.

Diablo springs from the same source as "Champagne," and its rhythm is so specific I've written the leadsheet rhythms out. I also include its later mandolin duet version.

The Brinsley Waltz, dedicated to my lovely daughter, was also written on the accordion, and is included here in a version for mandolin and guitar.

Valse Isabel, written on accordion, is dedicated to Isabel Eccles, a mandolin-accordion playing friend. I've turned it into a mandolin solo/leadsheet.

3 Directions is an early piece I revised while compiling this manuscript. It had a good start, as I found it, but seemed to want renewal and renaming.

When Everything's Been Done is a piece I found in a hand-written manuscript while looking for tunes to include here. It seemed a fitting title for the last piece in this book.

"There is a vitality, a life force, an energy, a quickening that is translated through you into action, and because there is only one of you in all time, this expression is unique. And if you block it, it will never exist through any other medium and will be lost."
– Martha Graham, choreographer

East of Here

Marilynn Mair

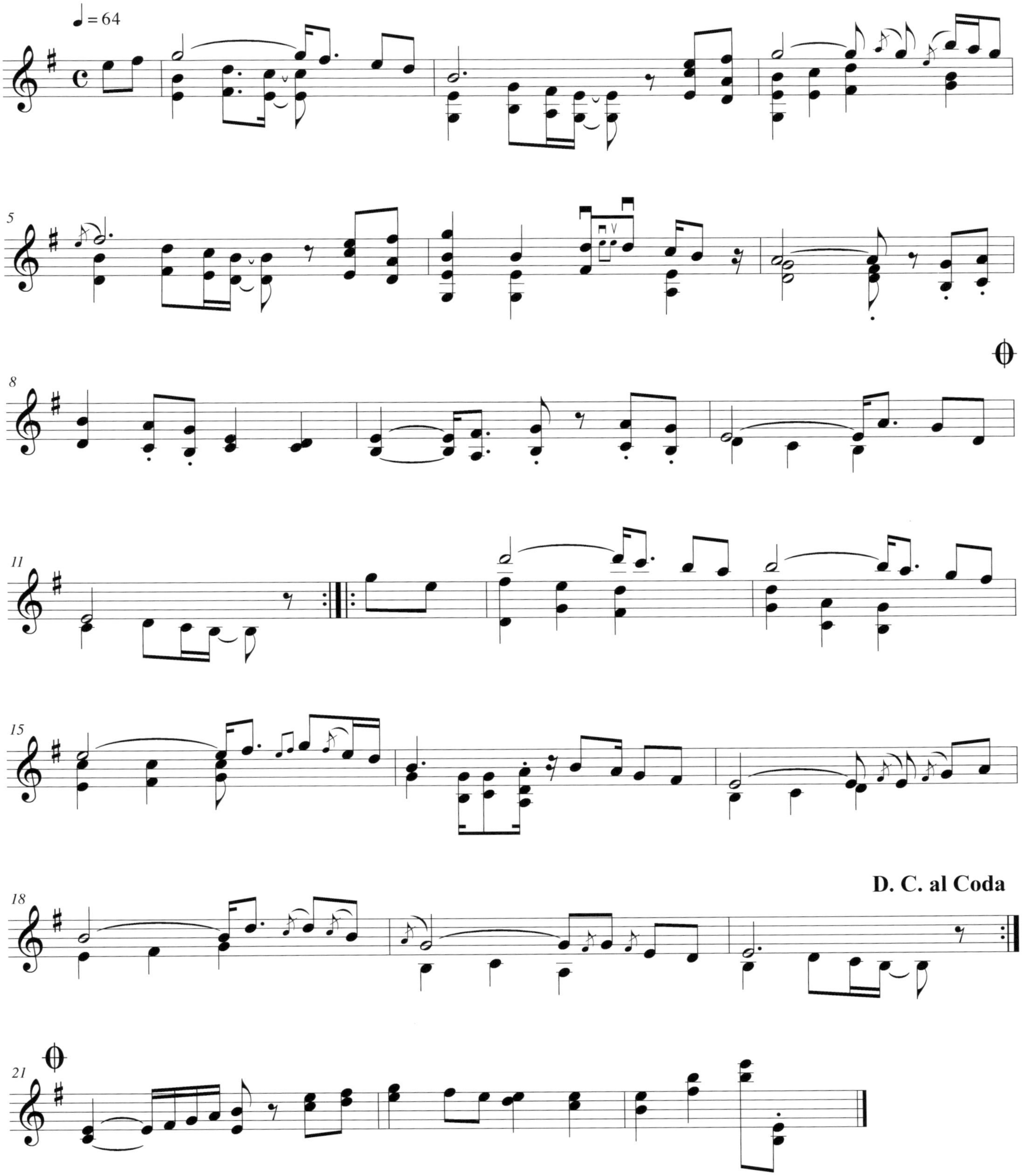

This is the first version of "East of Here" that I wrote down. There's now a leadsheet version and a couple of different quartets, and it appears on a couple of CDs. You'll find the leadsheet on the next page.

East of Here

Marilynn Mair

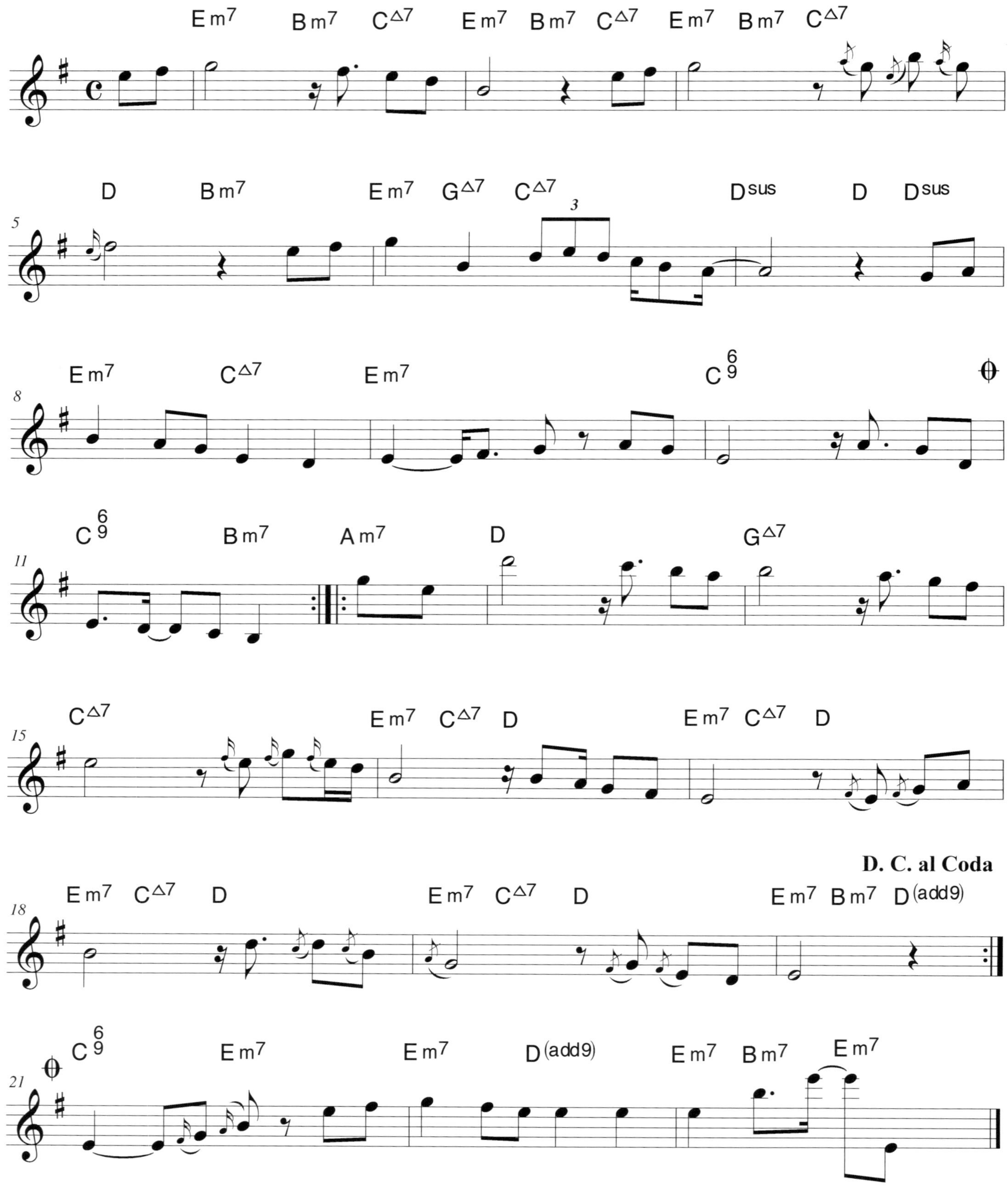

Play the grace notes quickly before the beat, making sure the main note is always played right on the beat.

3-4-3 (3/4)

Dedicated to Three Dances on their Third Birthday Celebration
March 4, 2004, Patrick's Cabaret, Minneapolis, Minnesota

Marilynn Mair

37

1. maruque *(for Brinsley)*

♩ = 80

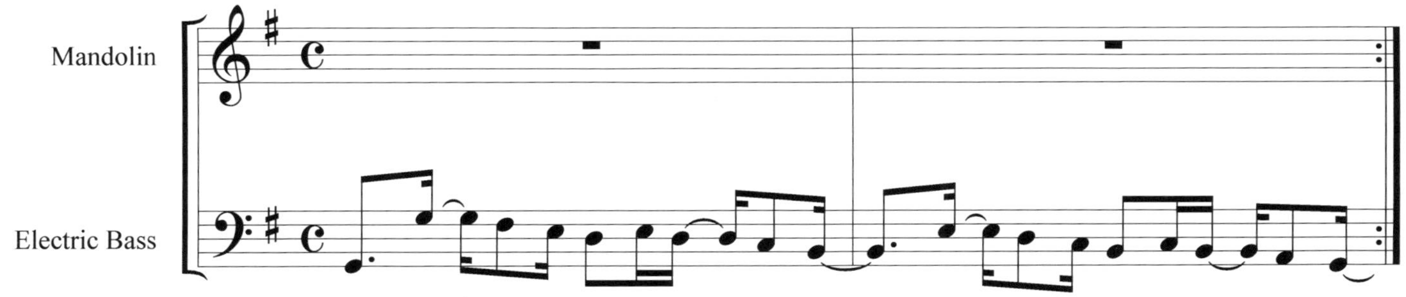

Note: the bass repeats this ostinato 22 times.
The mandolin may double the 2nd time.

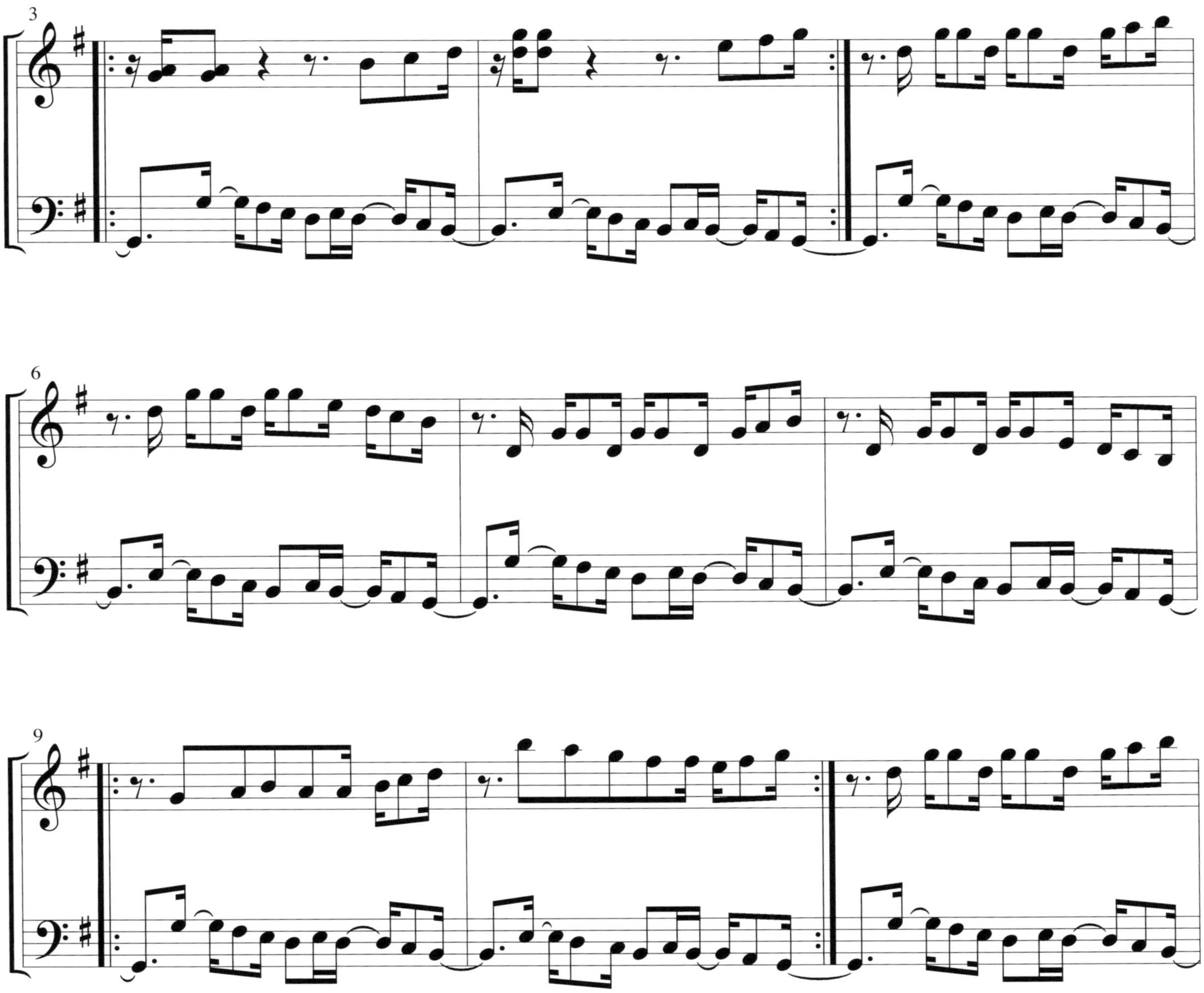

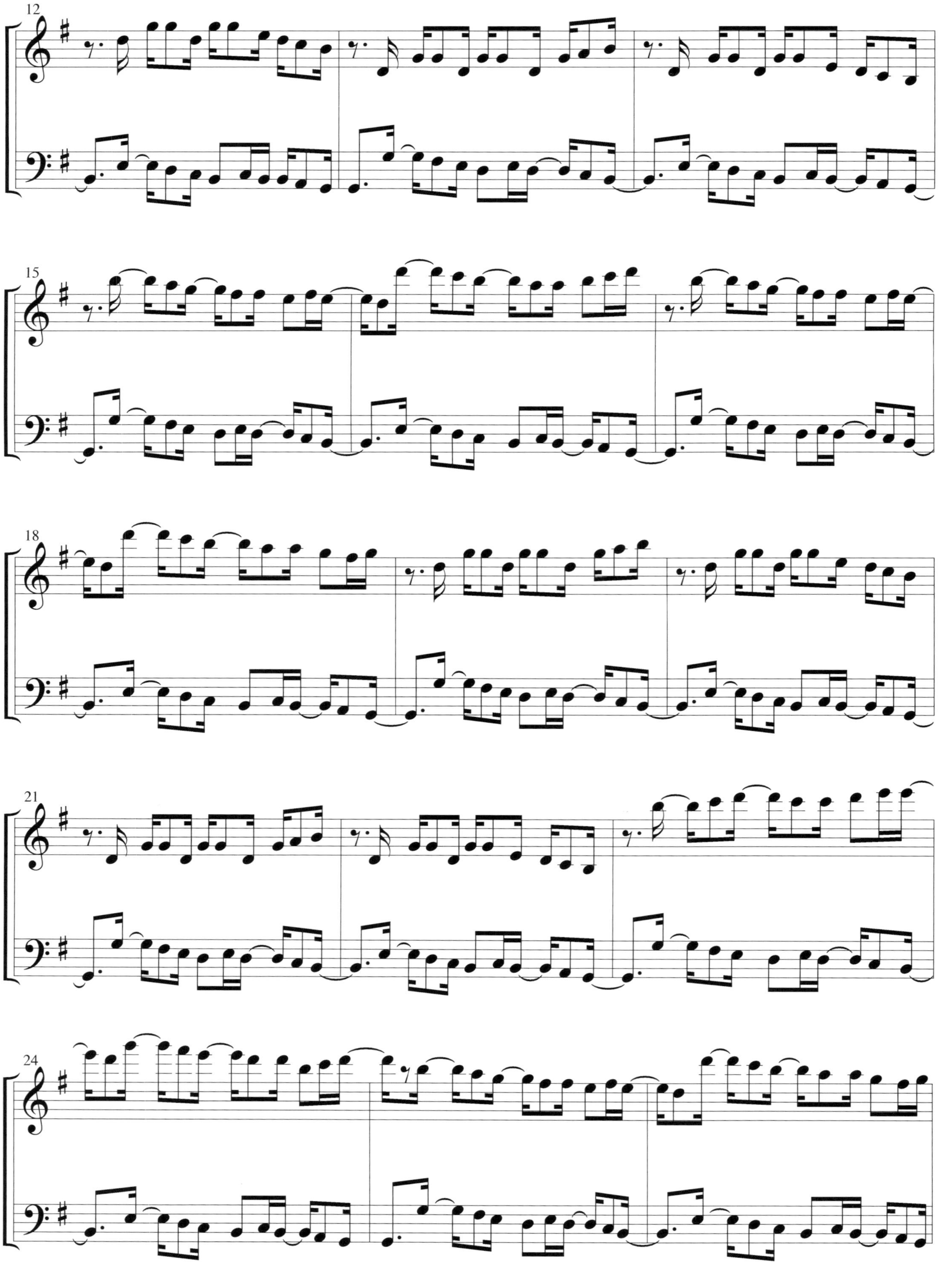
12
15
18
21
24

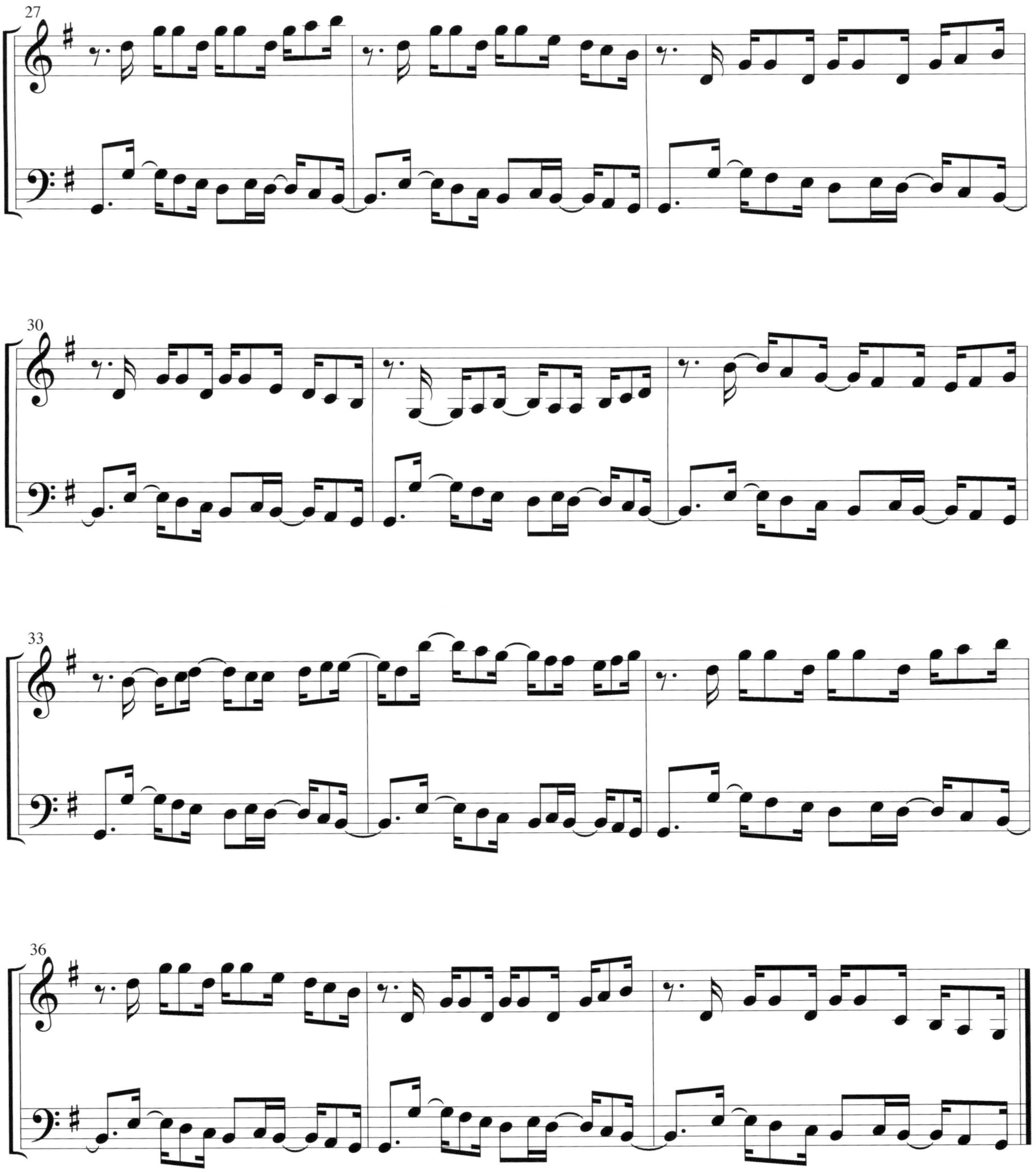
27
30
33
36

38

2. birthday waltz *(for Jamey)*

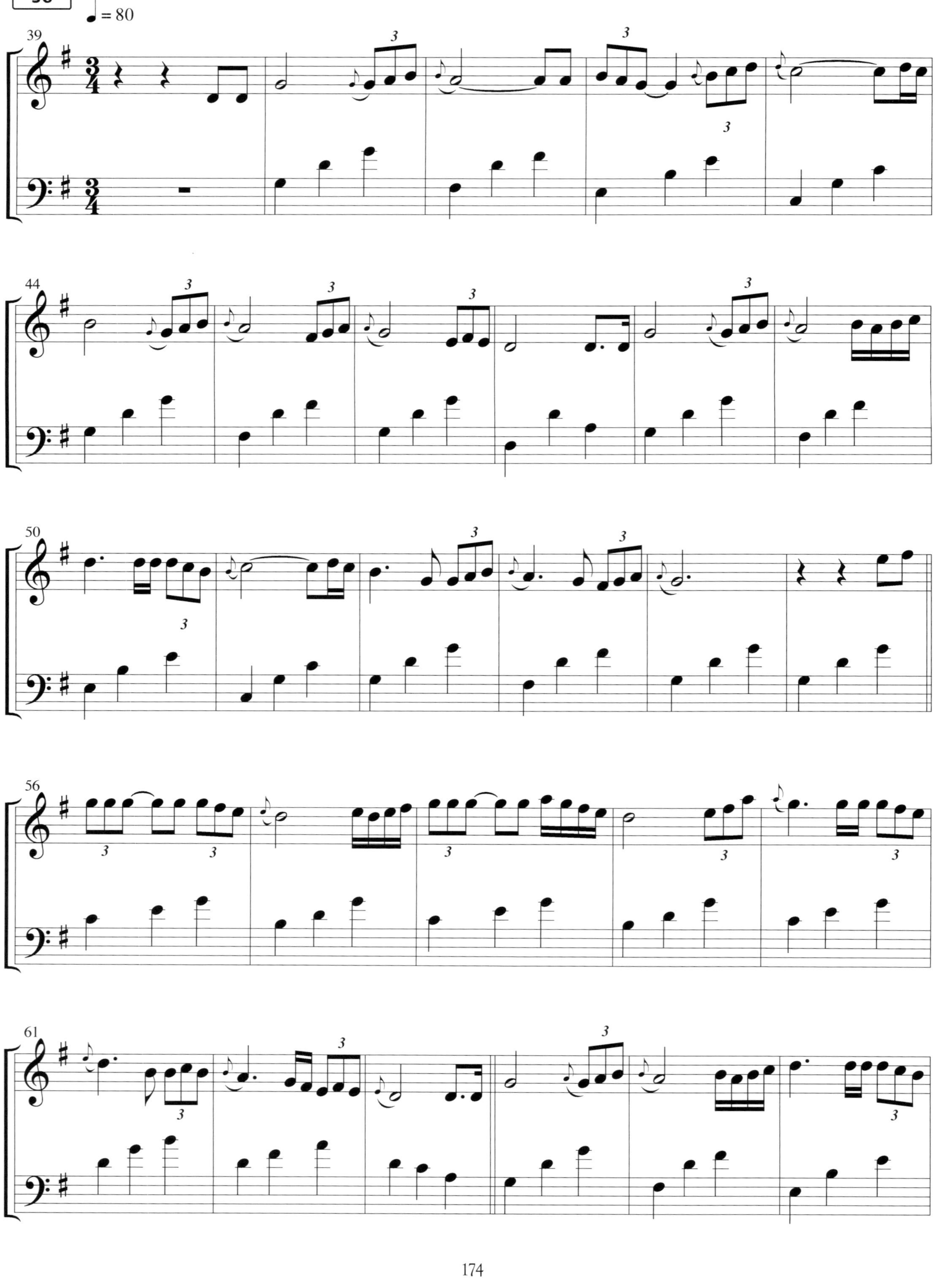

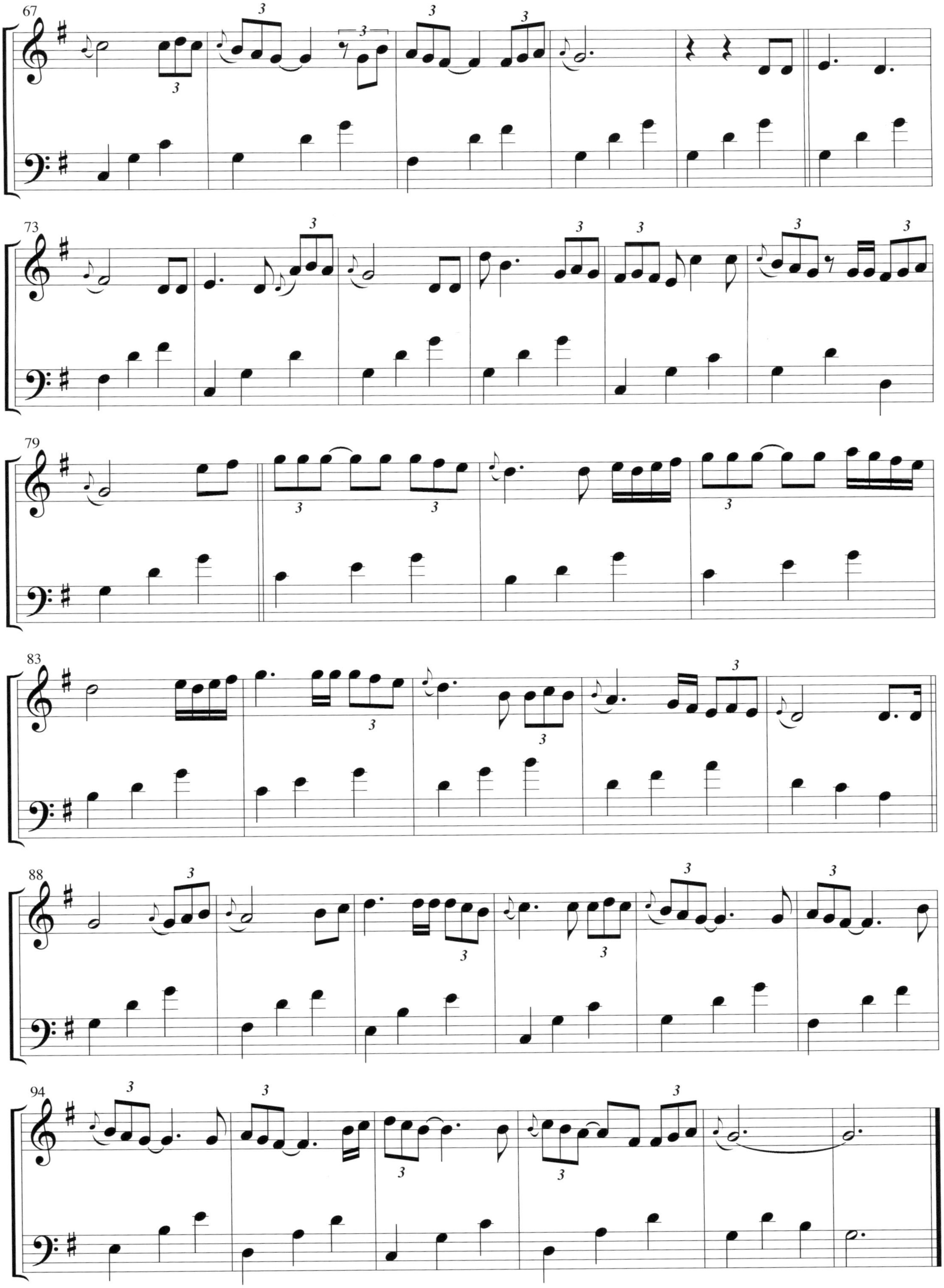
67
73
79
83
88
94

39

3. wedding hoedown *(for Suzanne)*

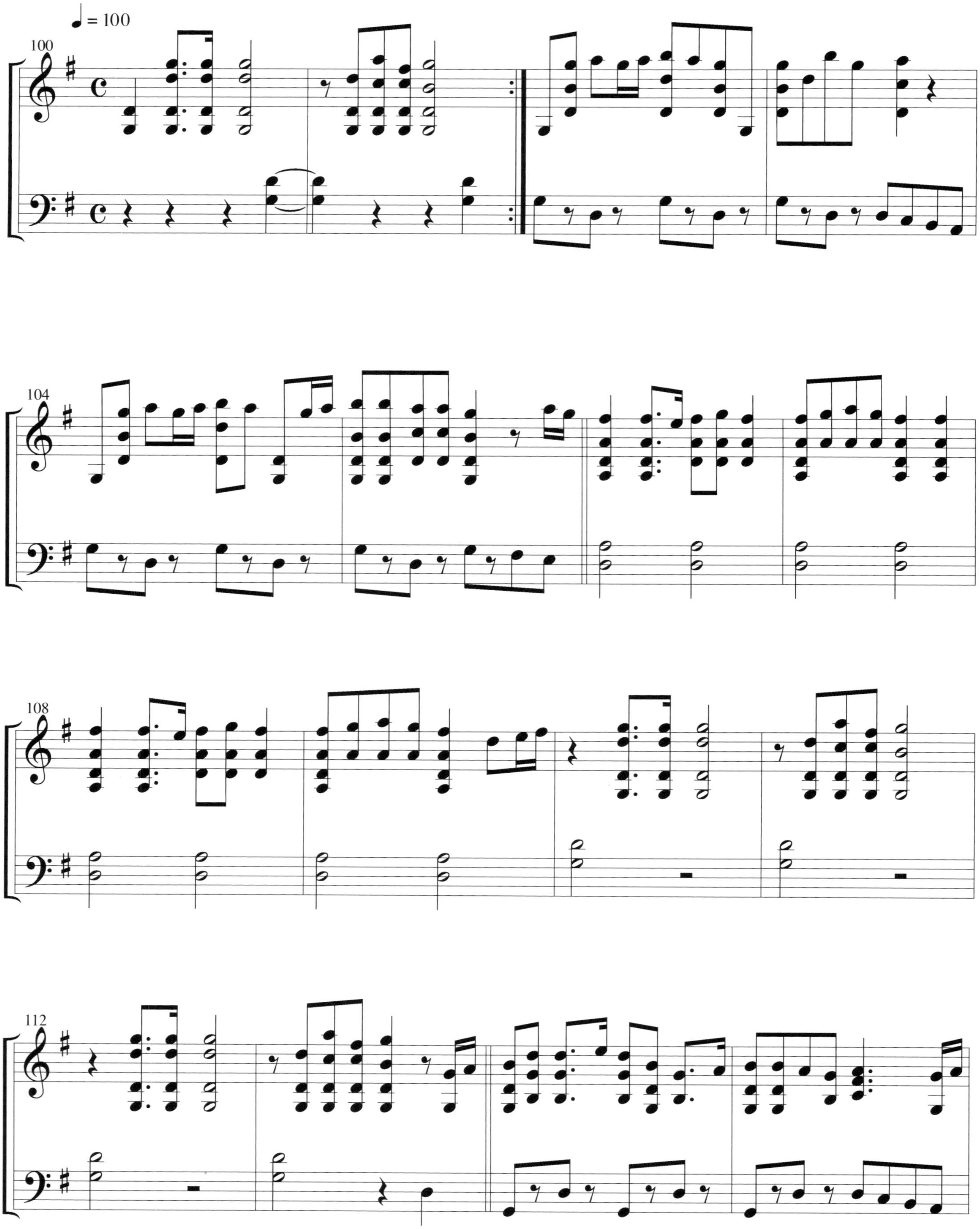

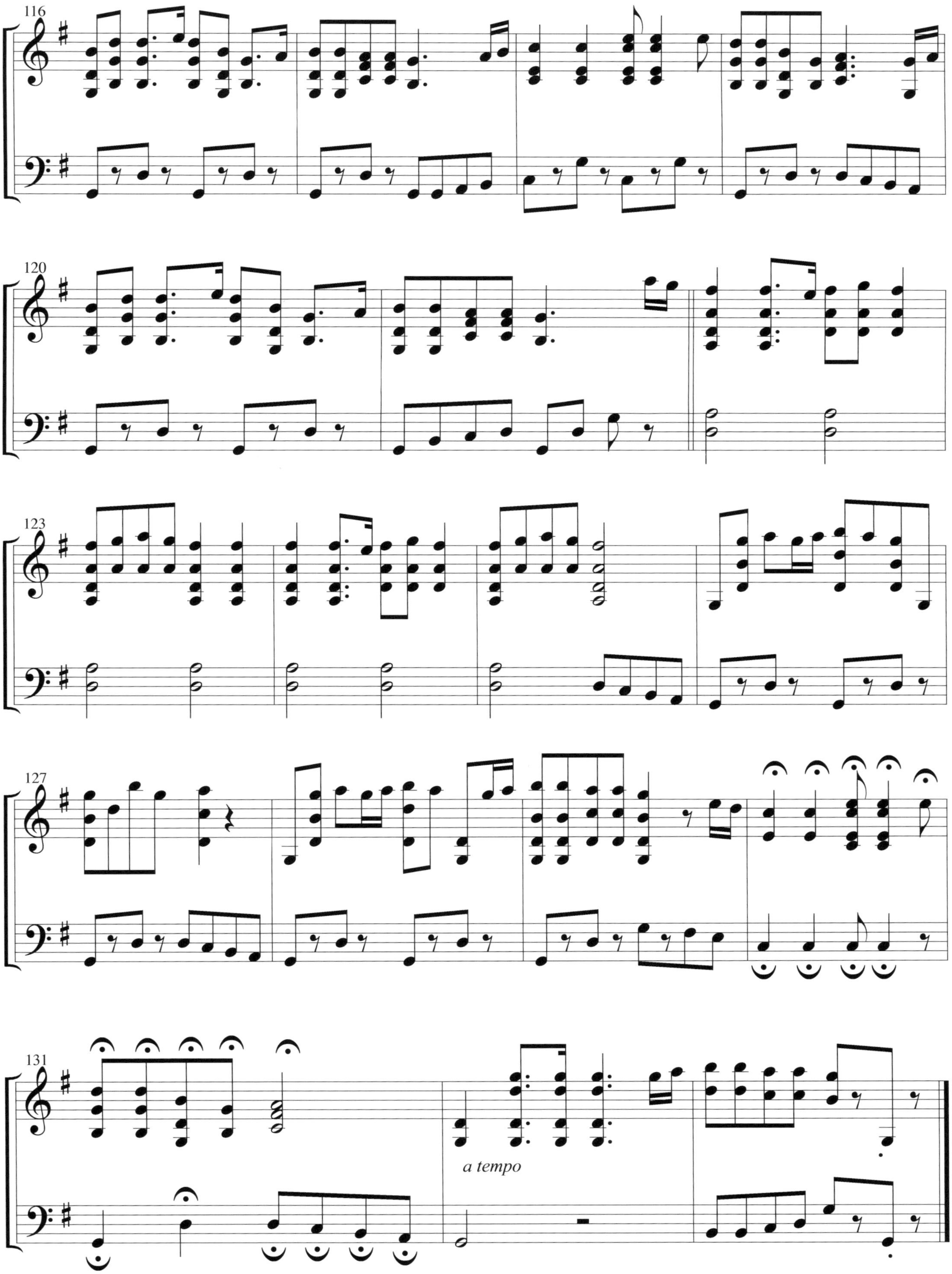
116
120
123
127
131
a tempo

And She Has Flown

for Carleigh

Marilynn Mair

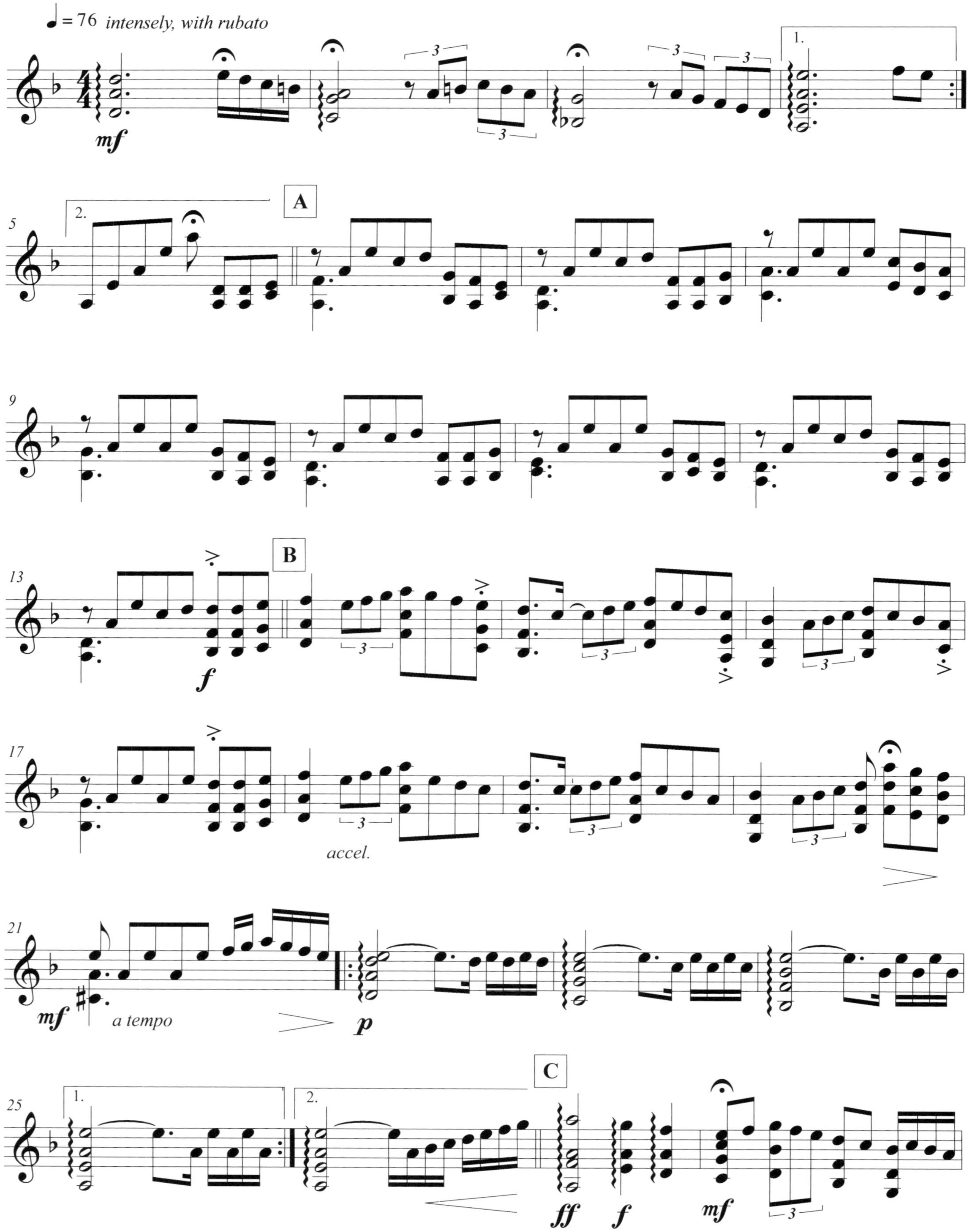

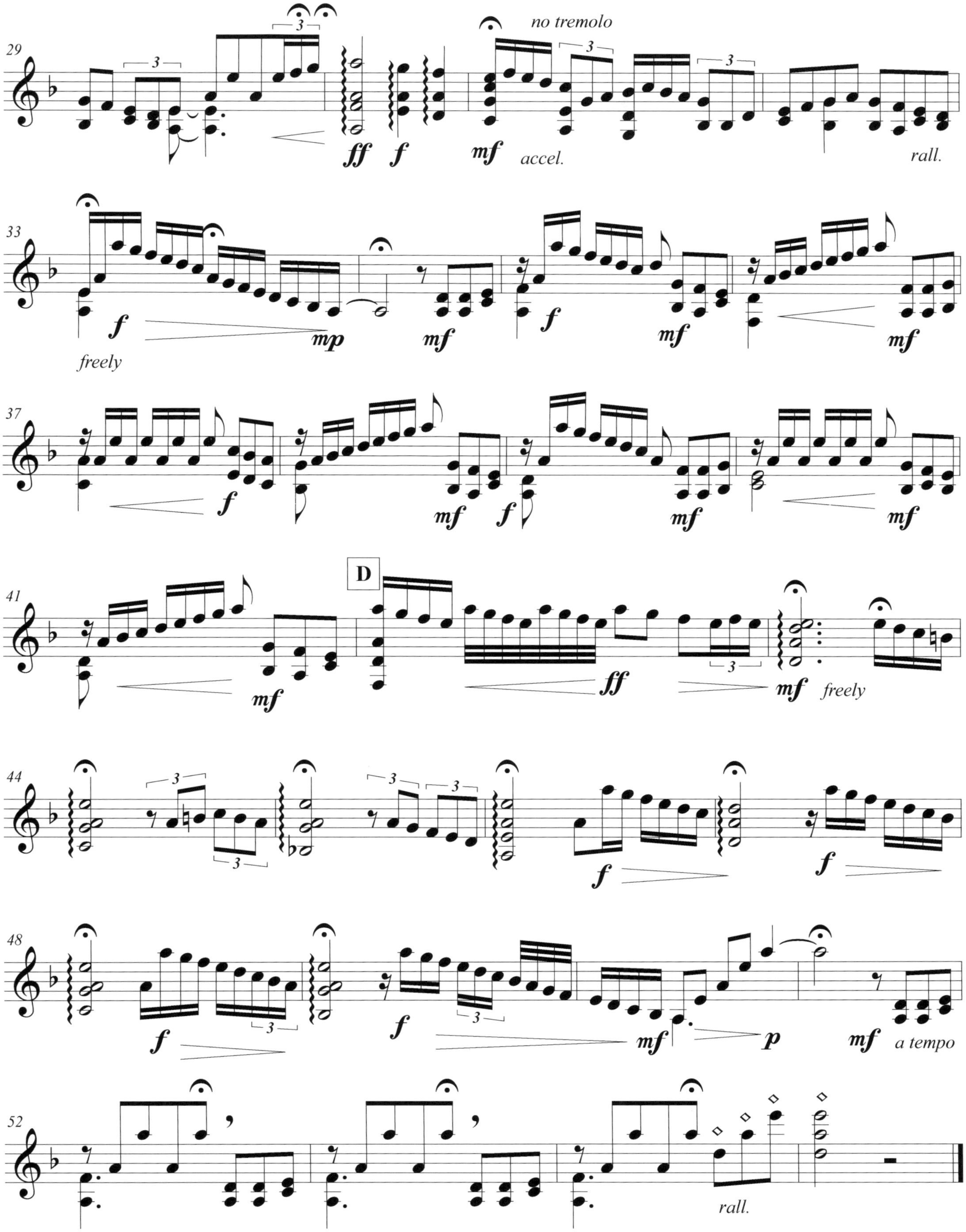

My plane arrived a day too late to see my longtime friend Carleigh Hoff before she died. So I sat at her kitchen table with my mandolin and wrote this solo to play at her service. I've used letters to designate four sections of the piece as each describes a different feeling. I leave the use of tremolo mostly up to you.

Margery

variations on an English round

Marilynn Mair

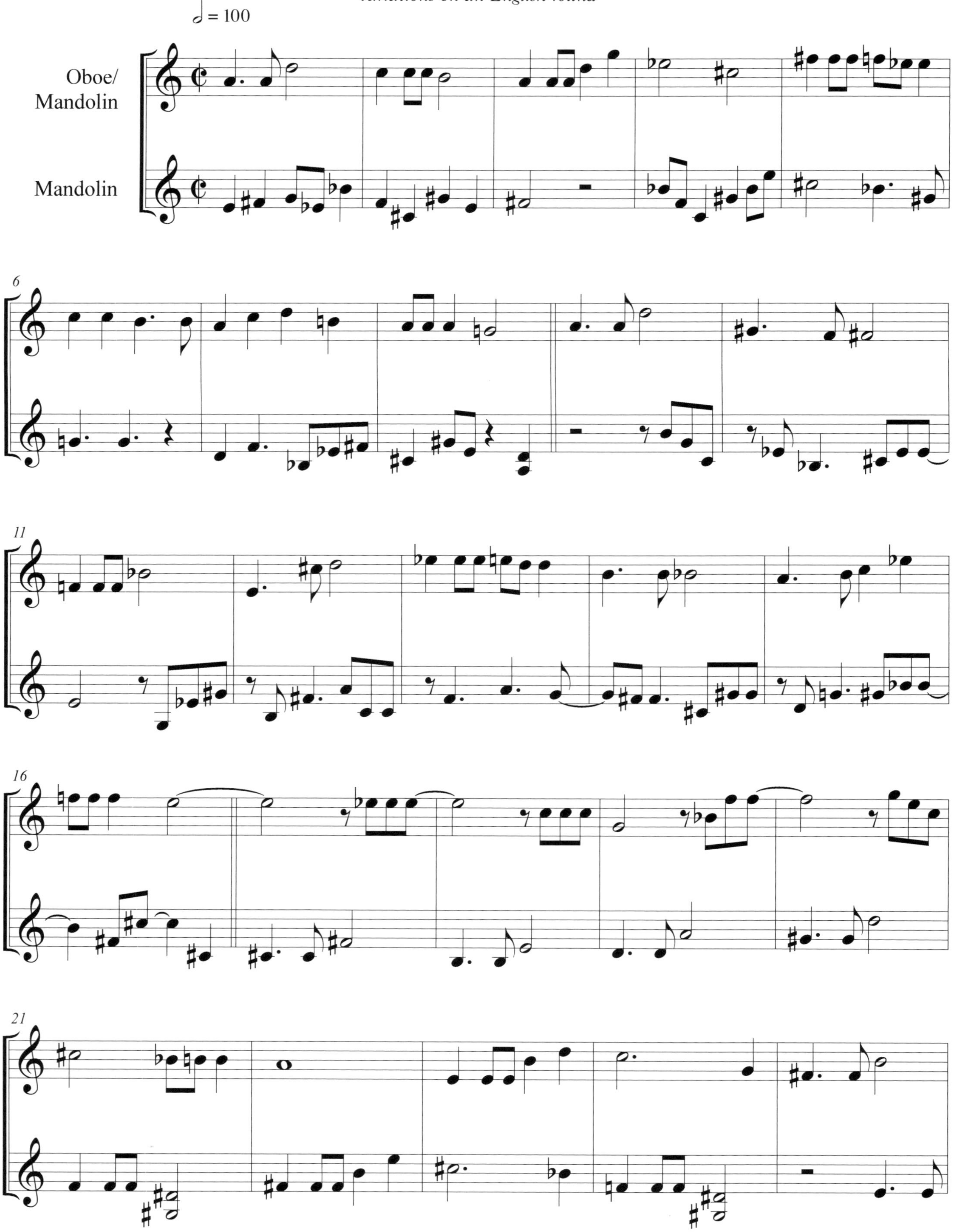

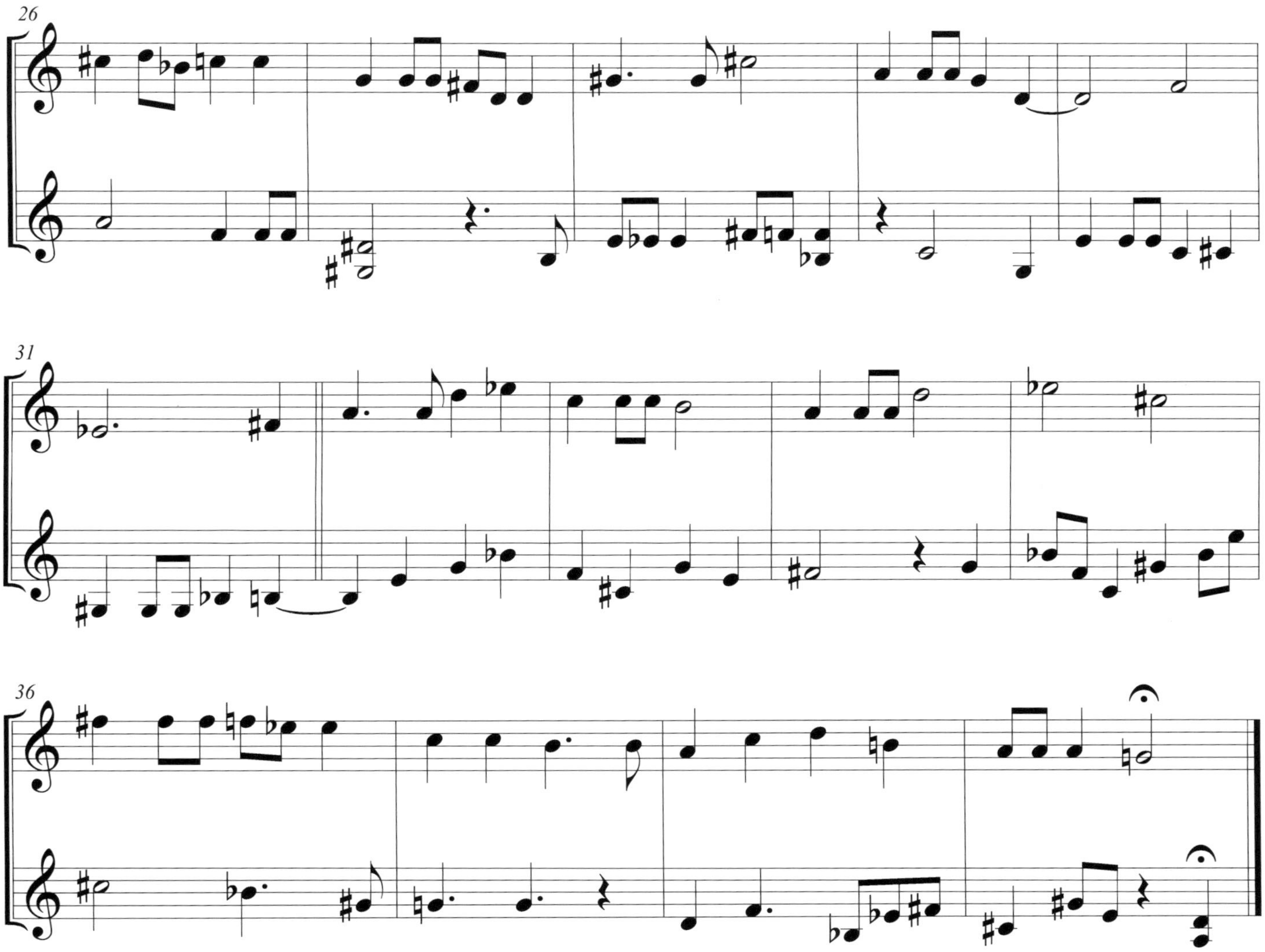

And now for something different. I wrote this as an assignment for a composition class. Originally it was scored for oboe and mandolin, the instruments available in my class, but I think it also works for two mandolins. And I still like it. The assignment was to write a 12-tone composition for two instruments, and I based mine on a quirky old English round I am fond of. I was pushing back against the idea that 12-tone pieces are, by their nature, amelodic. For those who are interested, or in doubt, this is the row I created and used to write the piece: E-A-F♯-D-G-E♭-B♭-F-C-C♯-G♯-B. It's a fun little duet that has been described as Zappa-esque.

Champagne

for Meredith

Marilynn Mair

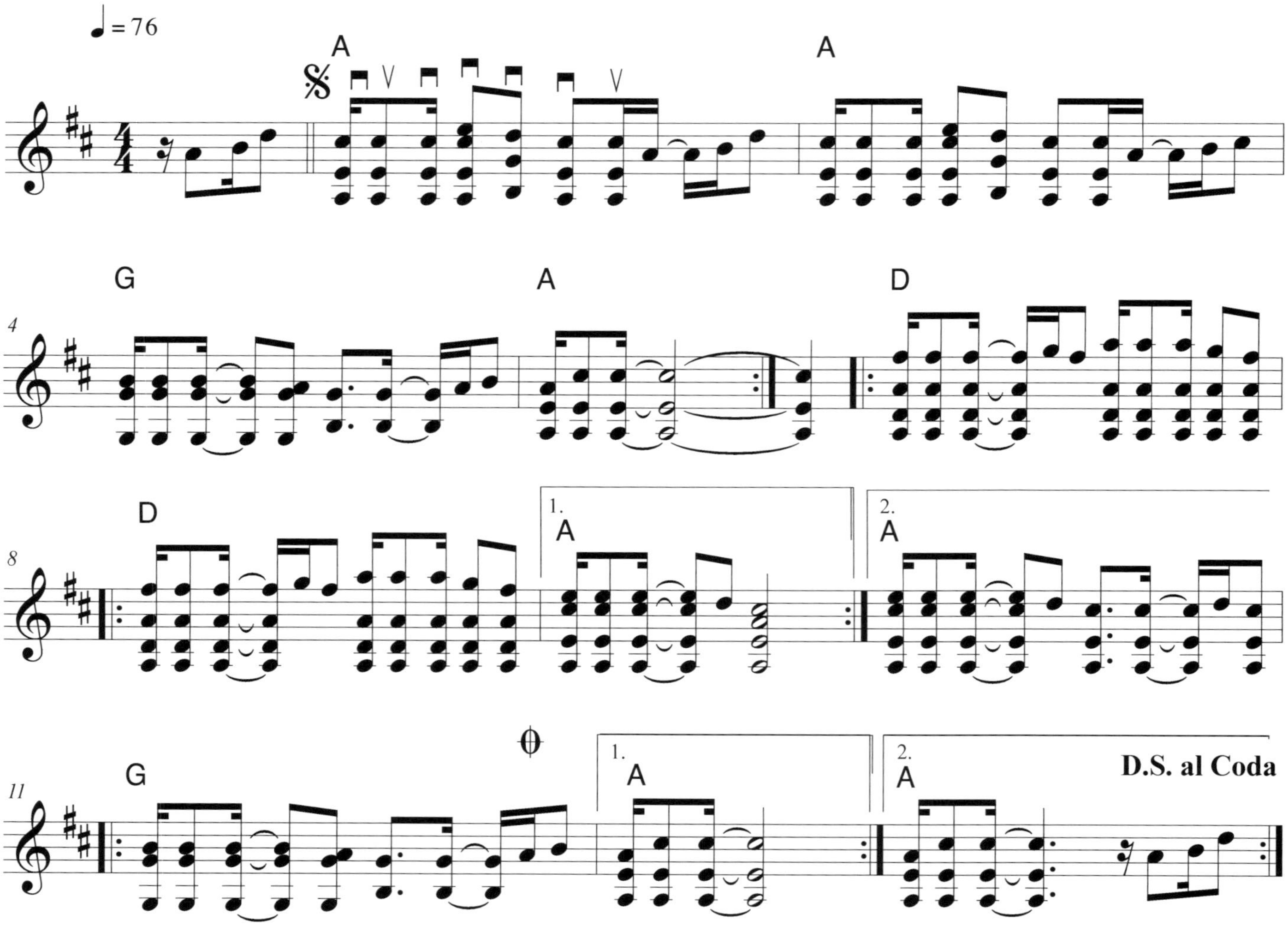

Play as often as you like, observing all repeats, and on the last time through jump to the Coda.

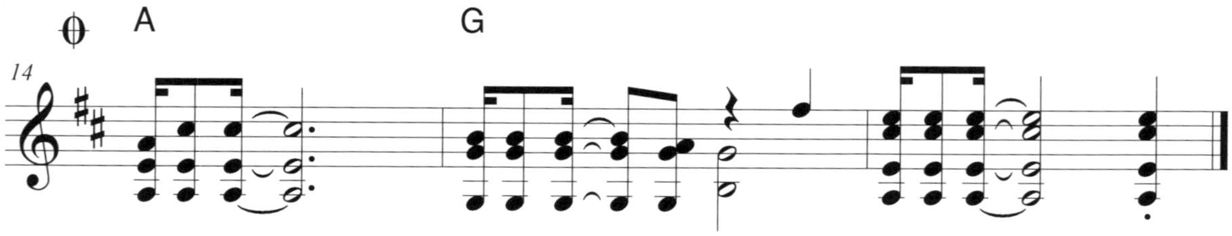

I wrote this piece for my neighbor, Meredith Steinbach, with whom I drank many glasses of champagne, to commemorate the evening we both leapt onto my back porch swing, glasses in hand, only to have the fraying rope break and tumble us onto the floor, laughing. It is a great cheerful processional that has often been played at events with friends. It also works nicely paired with "Diablo." Don't be put off by the triple- and quadruple-stops they are merely simple folk chords. I recorded this with the World Café Quartet on the CD *Metro*.

Diablo

for my son, Nate

Marilynn Mair

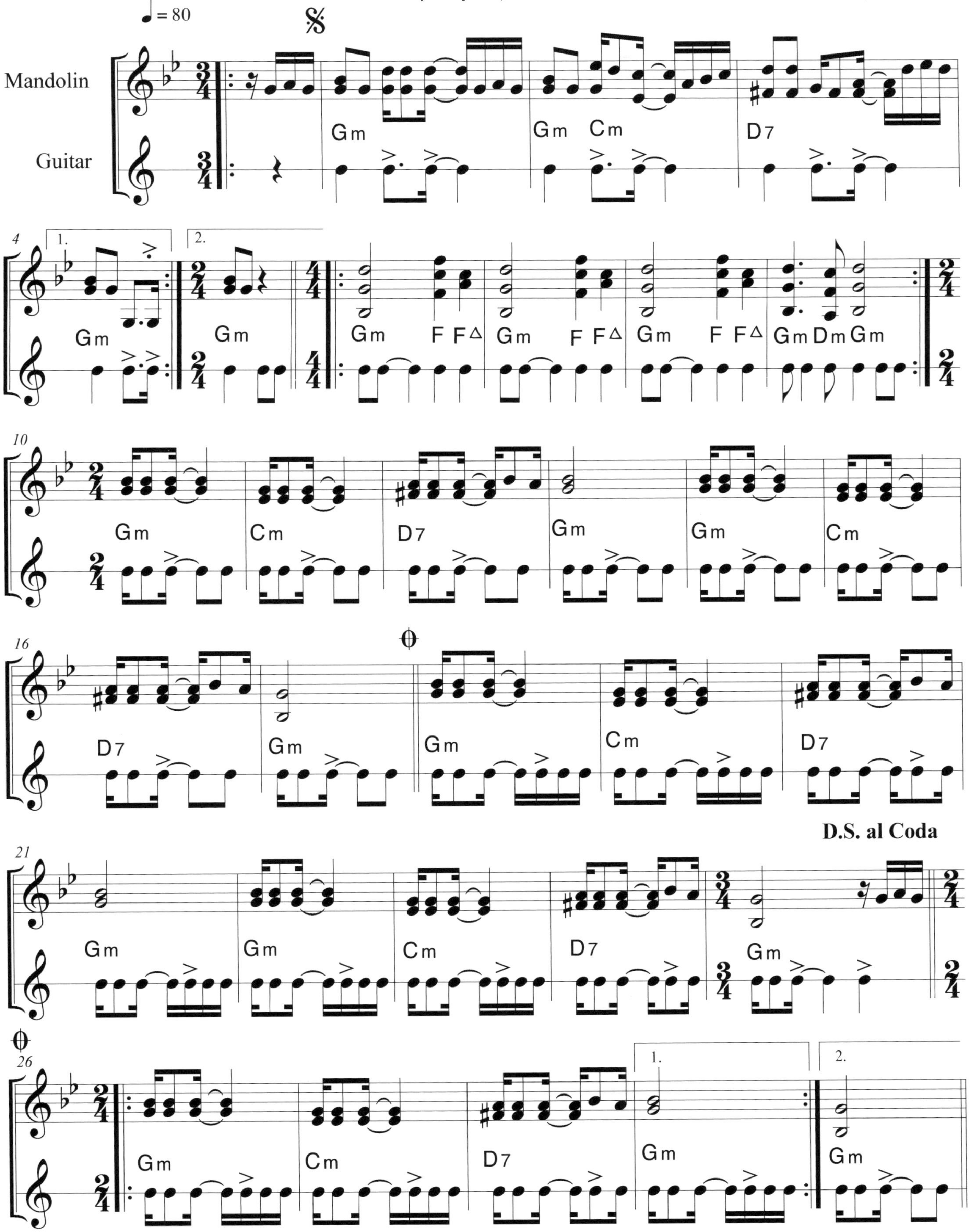

Repeat the whole Coda a couple of times, fading out. Rhythms can be varied; the written line is a suggestion.

Champagne

for Meredith

Marilynn Mair

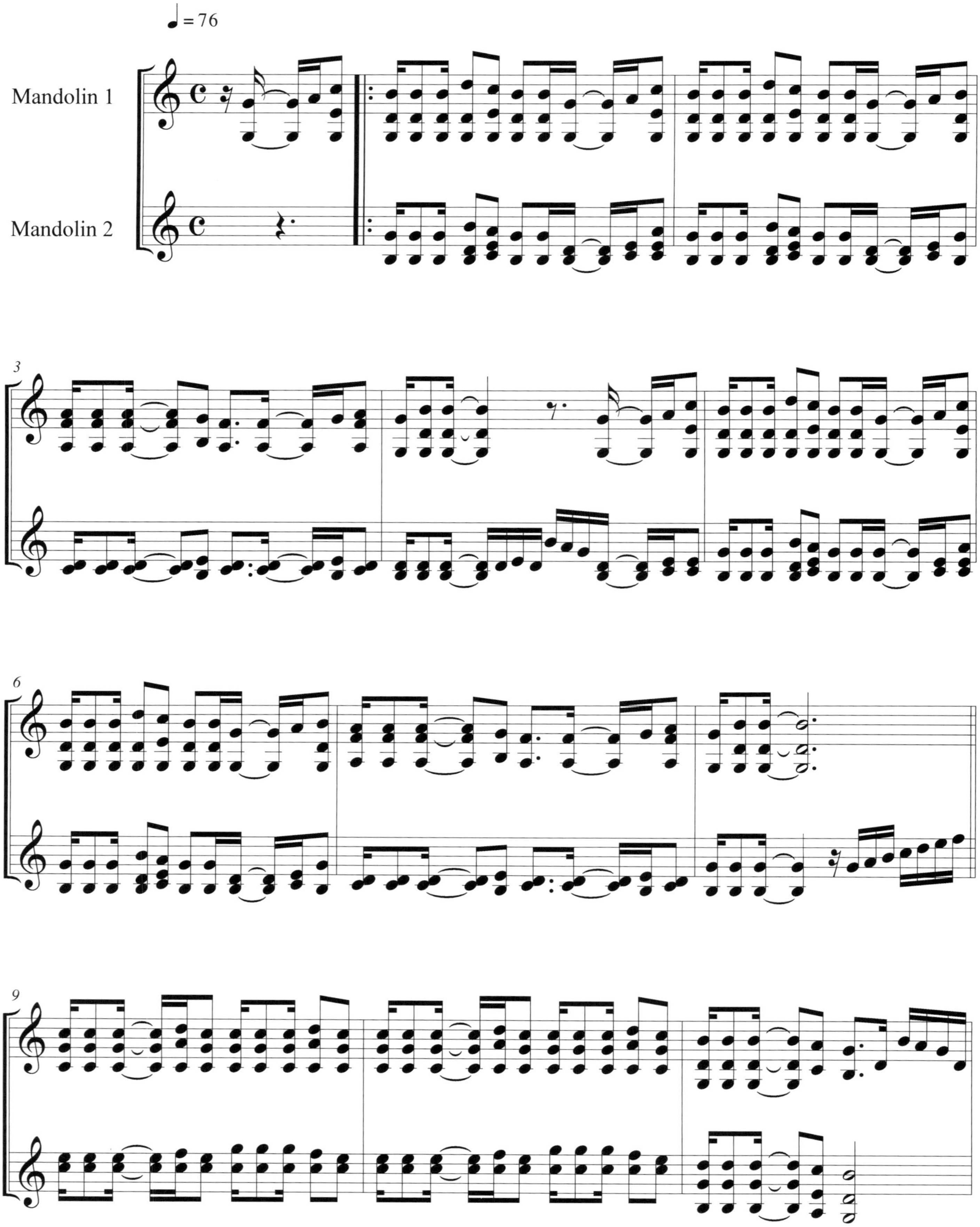

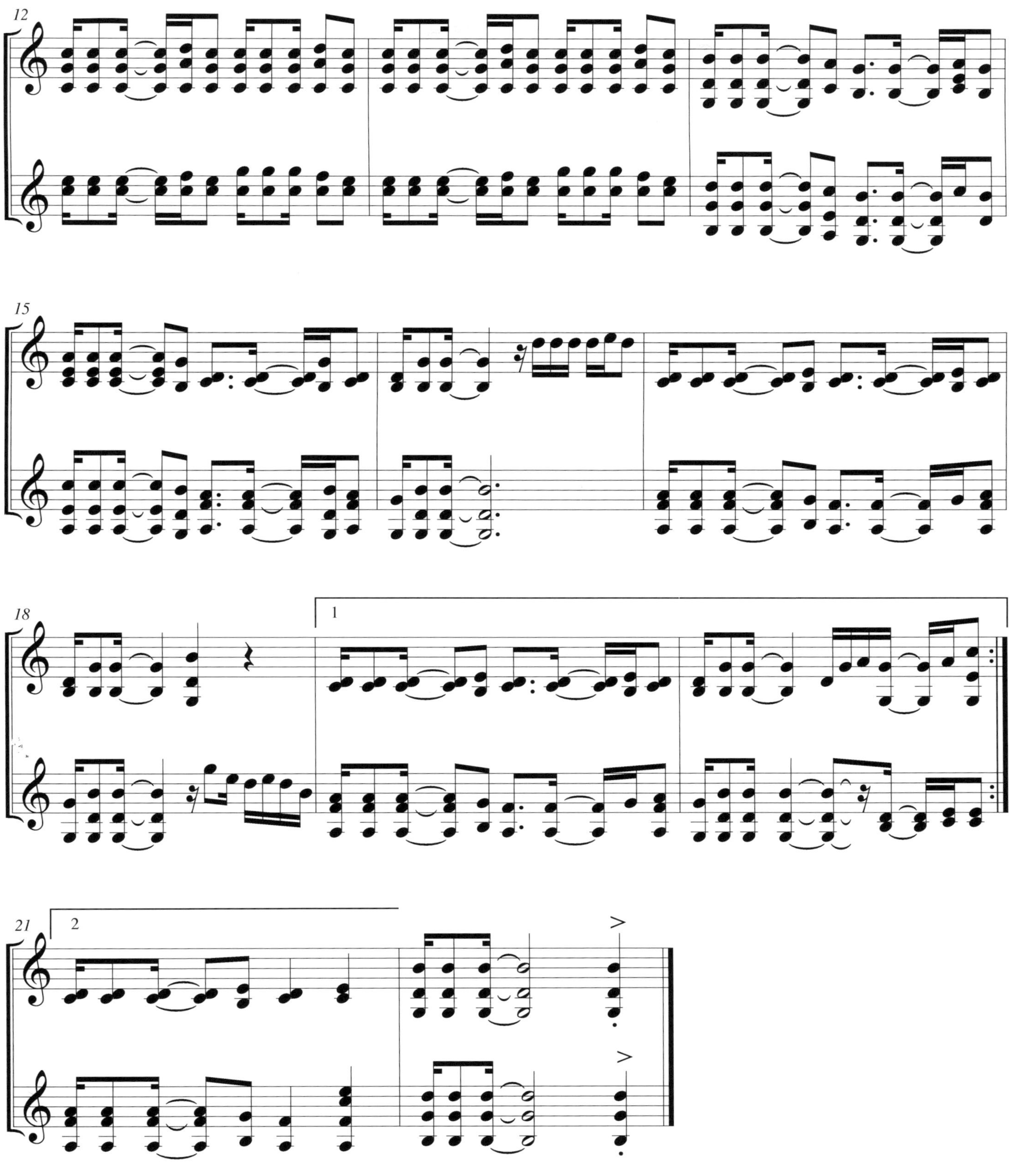

I created this duet version of the original in 2006, to play with Radim Zenkl in our Mandolin World Summit. We recorded it for my CD, *Leave Something Unexplained.*

Diablo

for my son, Nate

Marilynn Mair

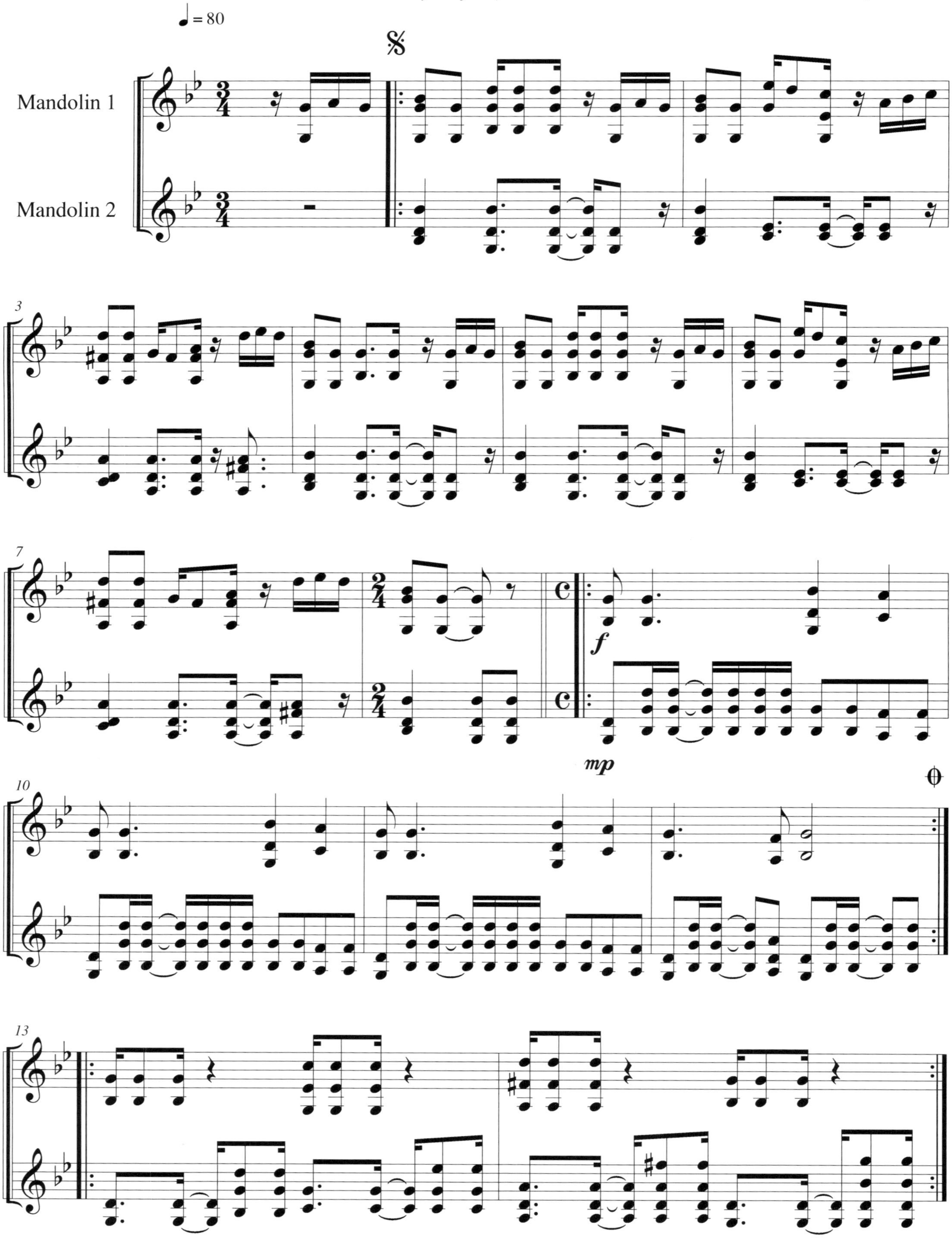

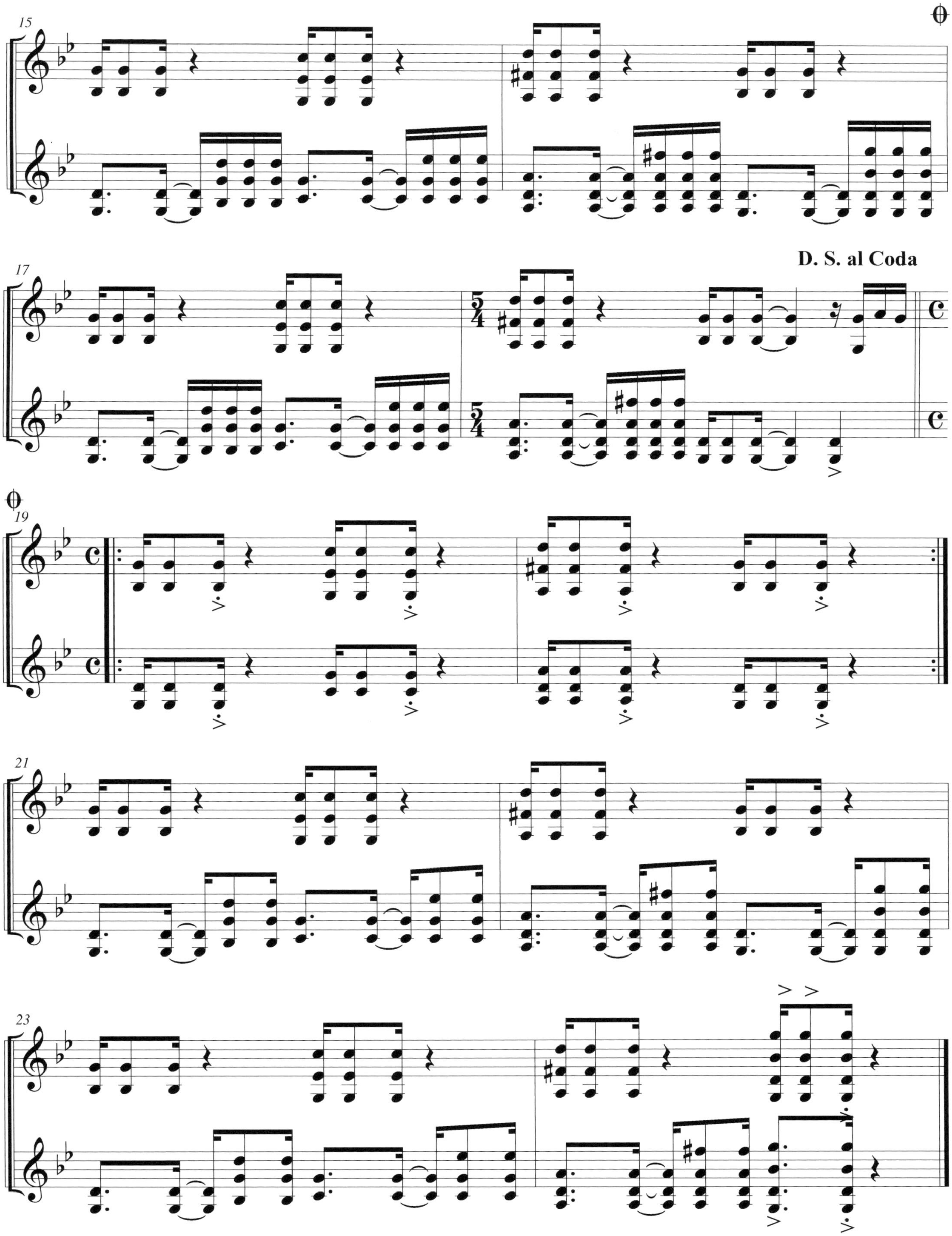

A duet version of the original, from 2006, written for Mandolin World Summit, with Paulo Sá and Radim Zenkl, and recorded on my CD, *Leave Something Unexplained.*

The Brinsley Waltz

for my daughter

Marilynn Mair

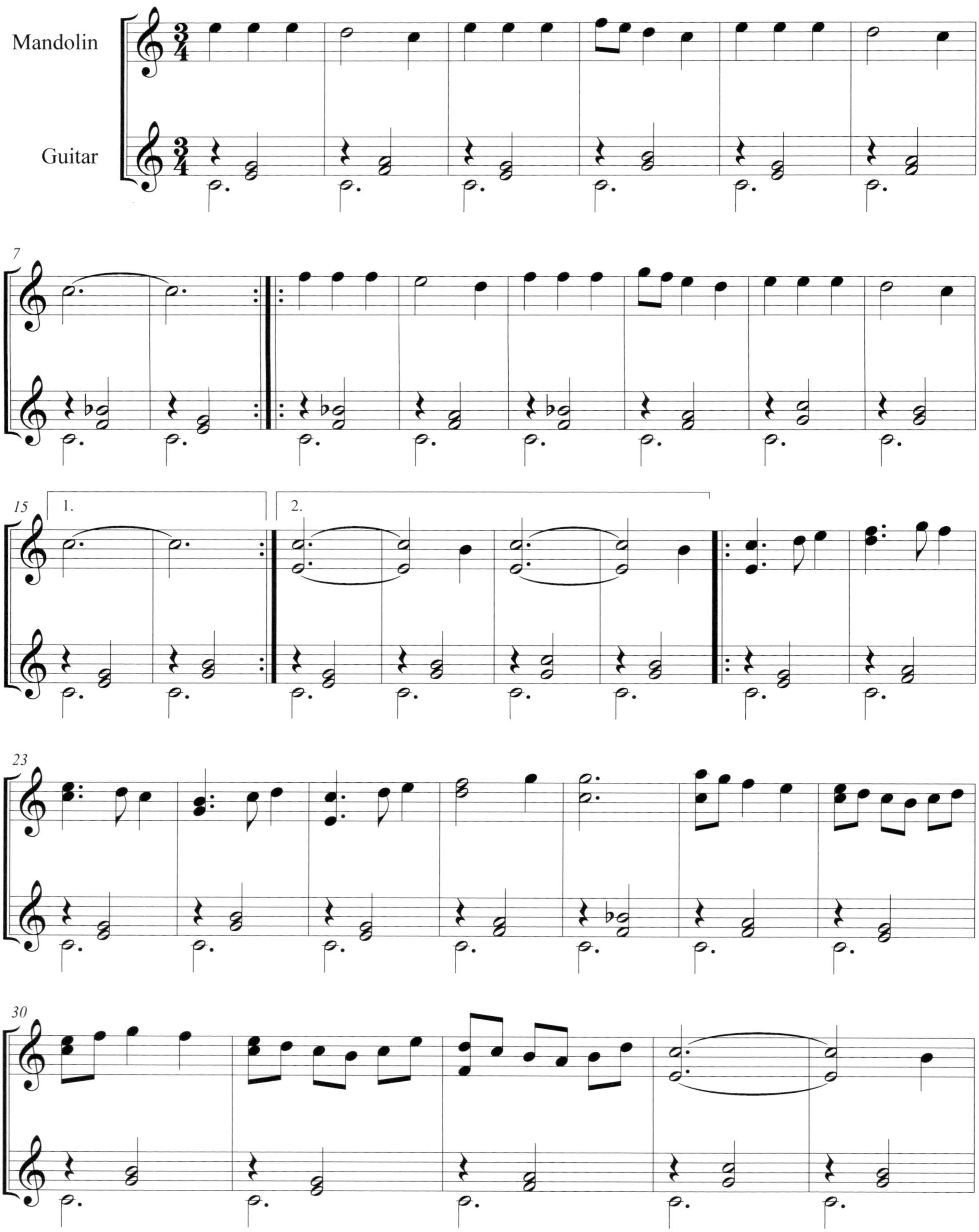

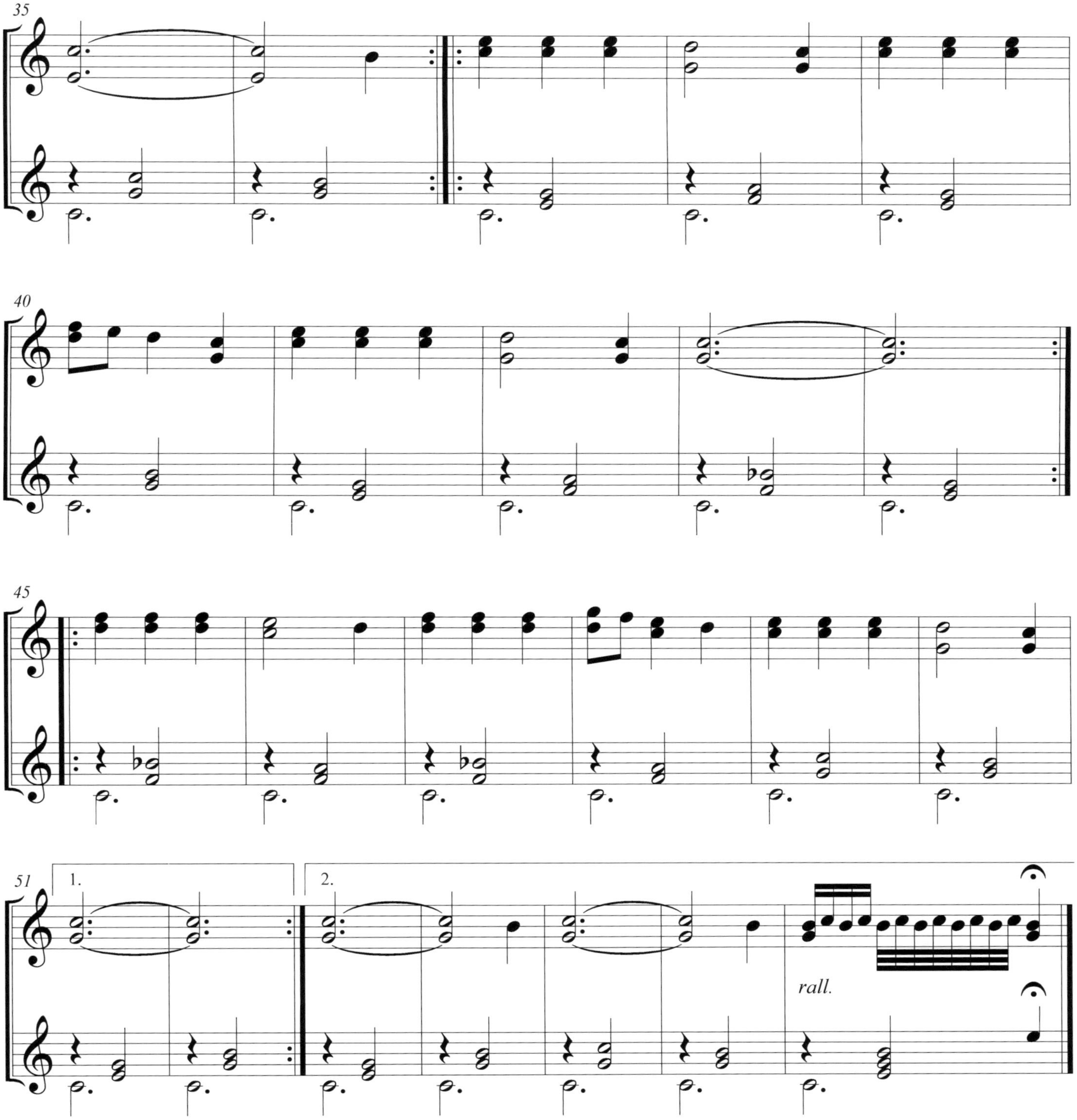

I wrote this for the instrumentation of the World Cafe Quartet, a family band, and we recorded it with melodica, mandolin, accordion, guitar, and bass, for our CD, *Metro*.

Valse Isabel

Marilynn Mair

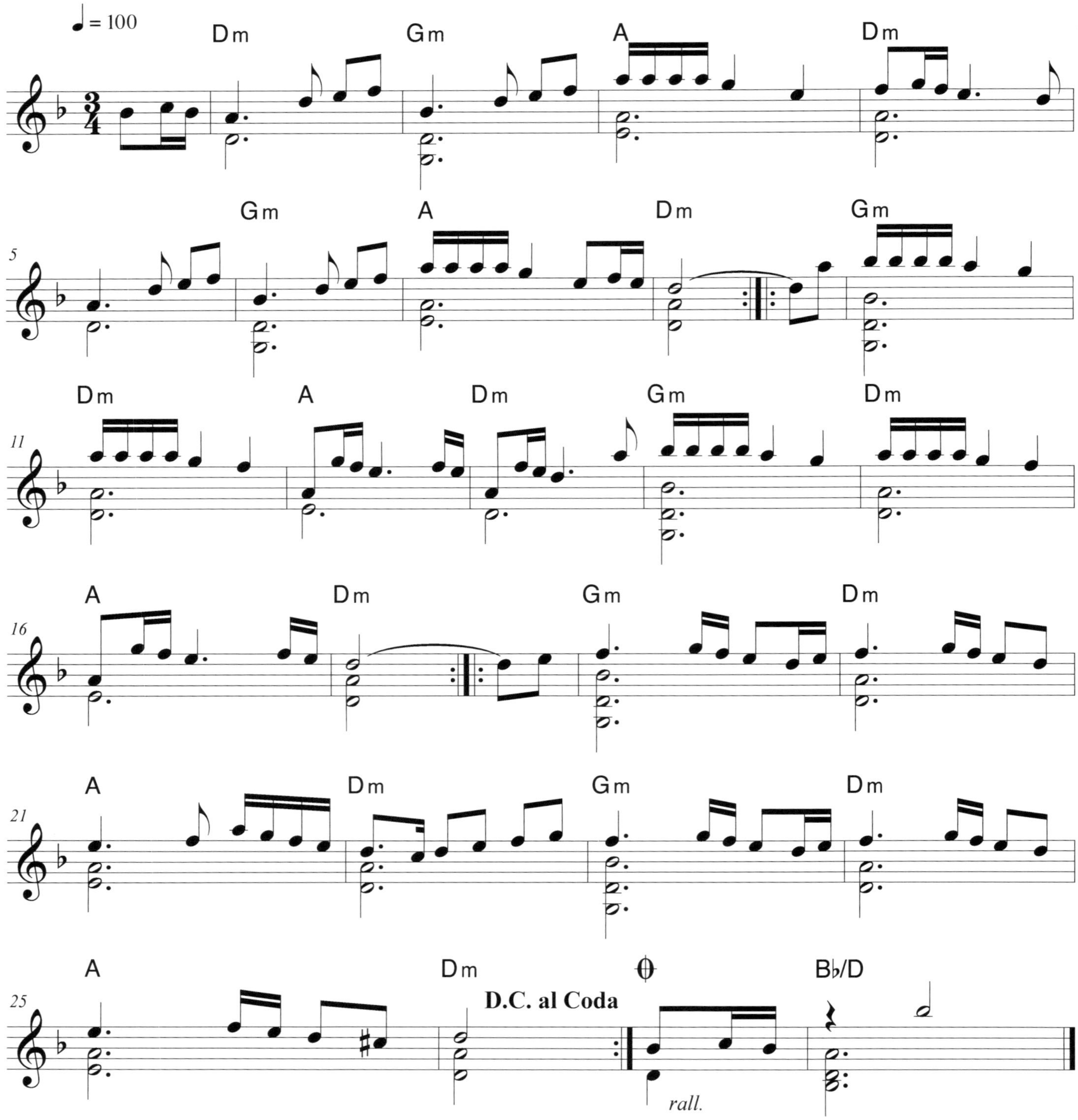

I wrote this piece for my mandolin/accordion playing friend, Isabel Eccles. Because the melody lies almost entirely on the E-string, this piece can make an effective solo by adding a simple drone accompaniment on the lower strings, so I have added that here. If you are playing with an accompanist you may find it best to leave the lower notes out. The D. C. indicates you should play the whole piece again, without repeats, before playing the final 2 measures.

3 Directions

Marilynn Mair

1. Looking Back

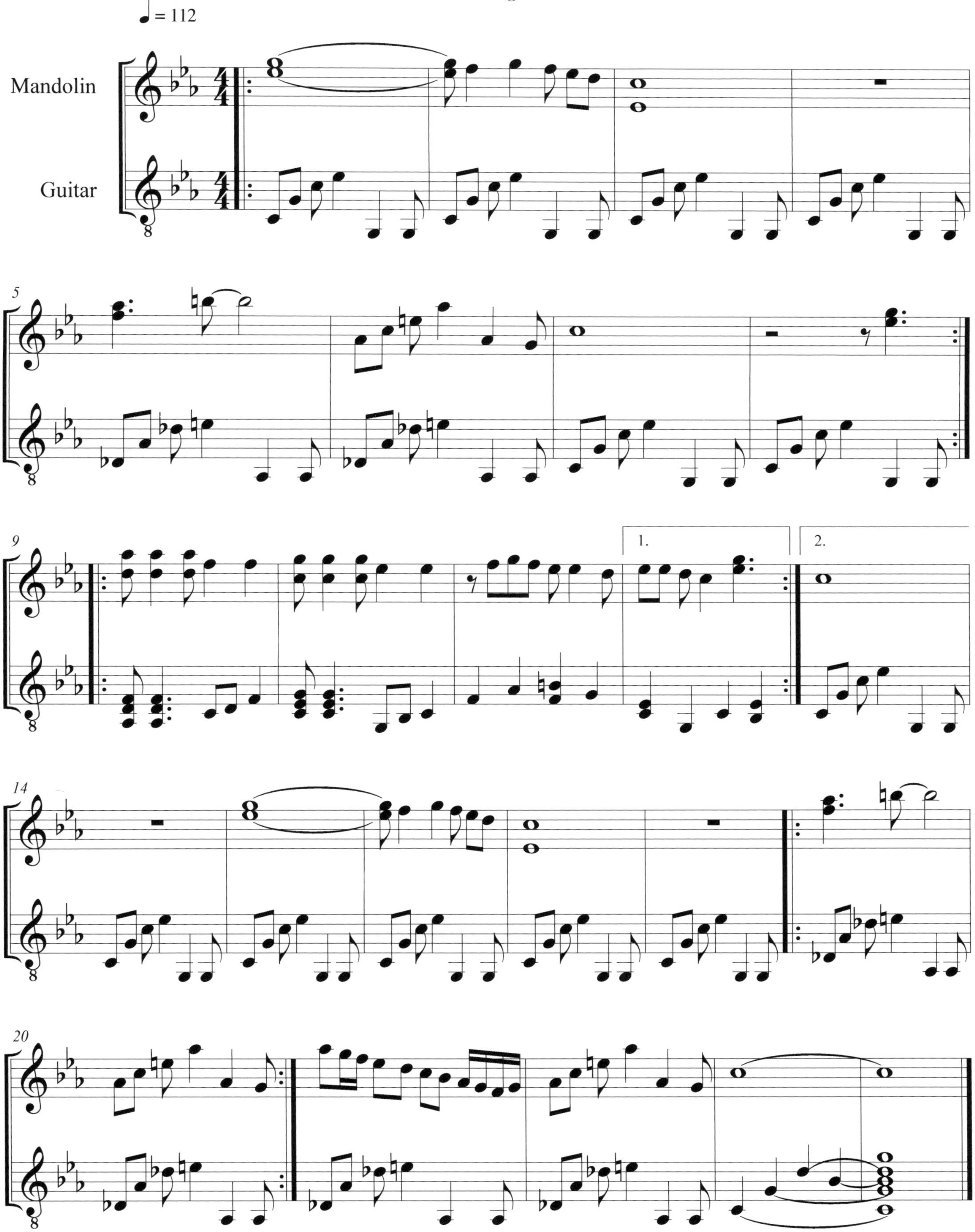

3 Directions

Marilynn Mair

♩ = 84

2. Hesitation

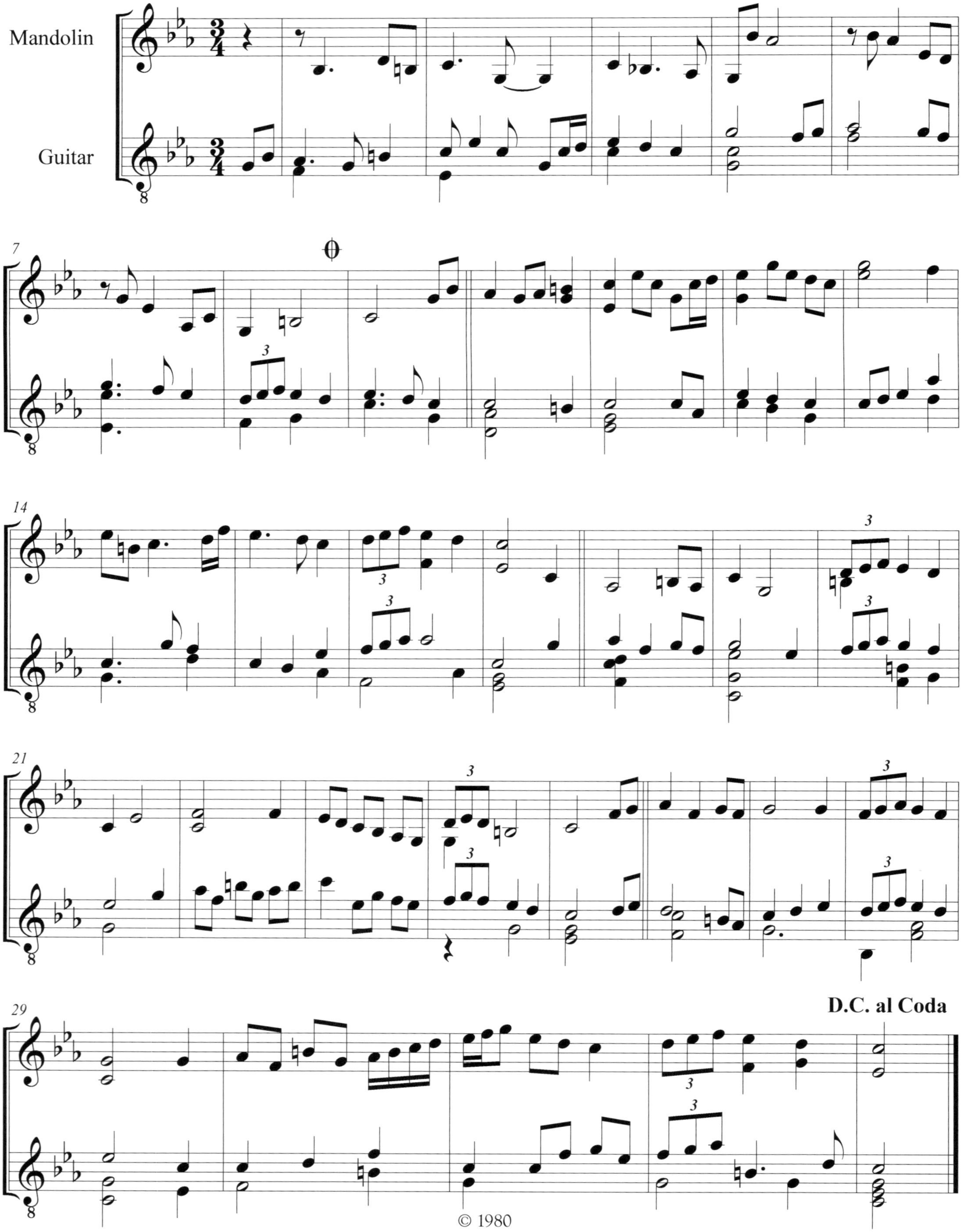

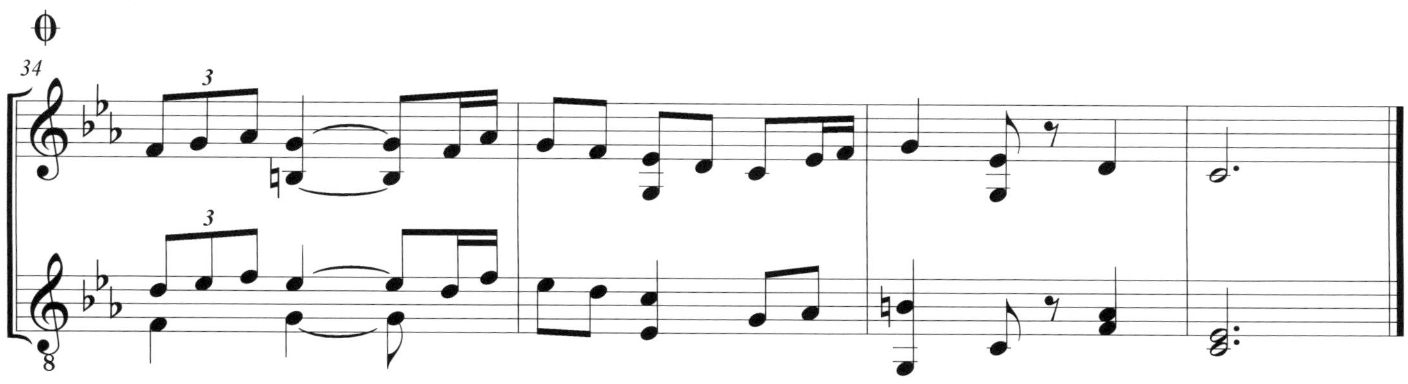

3. Moving On

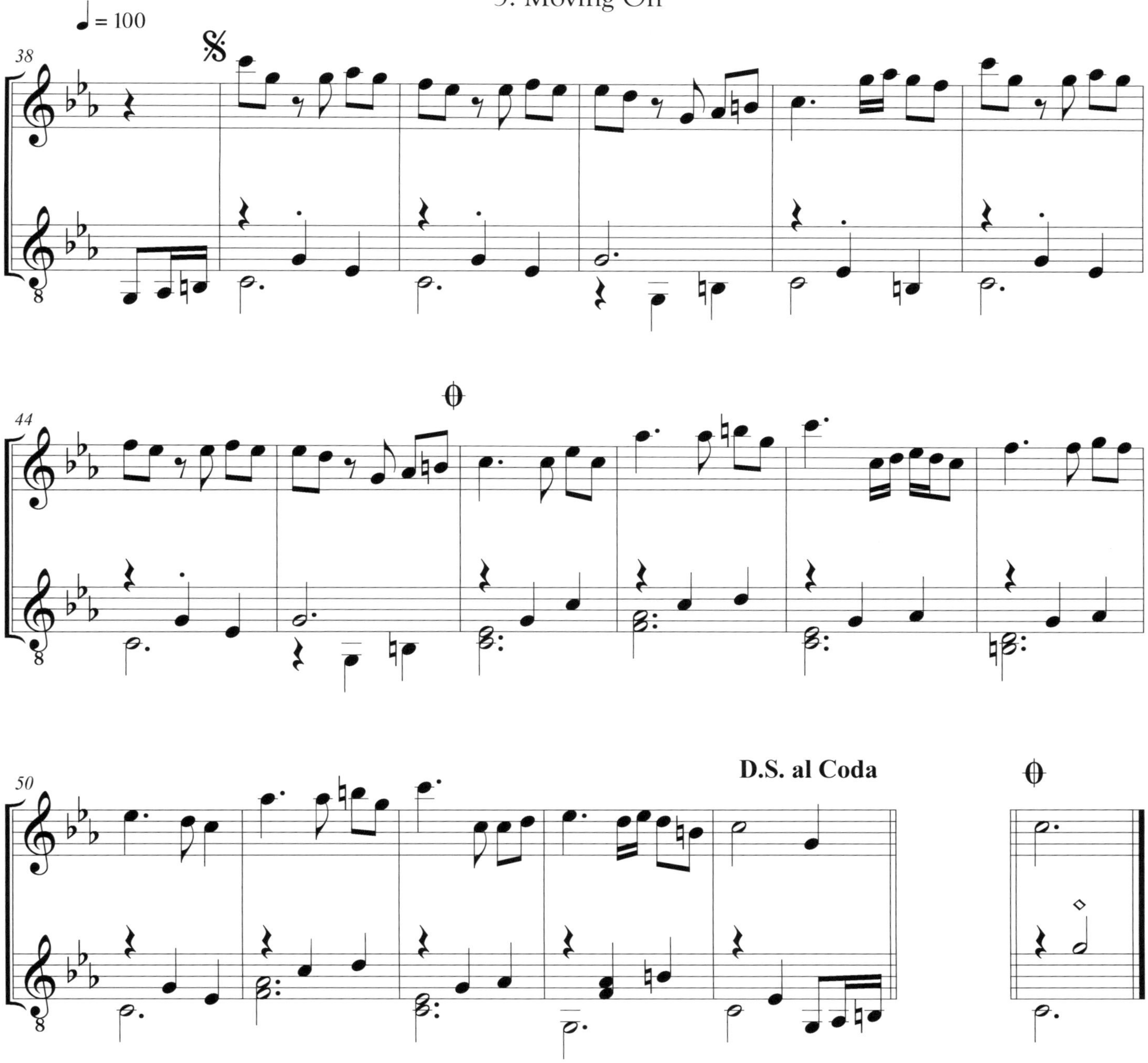

A new setting for an early effort. The bones of this are from the first original instrumental piece I can remember playing in a concert, near the start of my career. Well received by the audience, it propelled me ahead, and so I tip my cap to the younger me and add a measure of wisdom.

When Everything's Been Done

for Ralph

Marilynn Mair

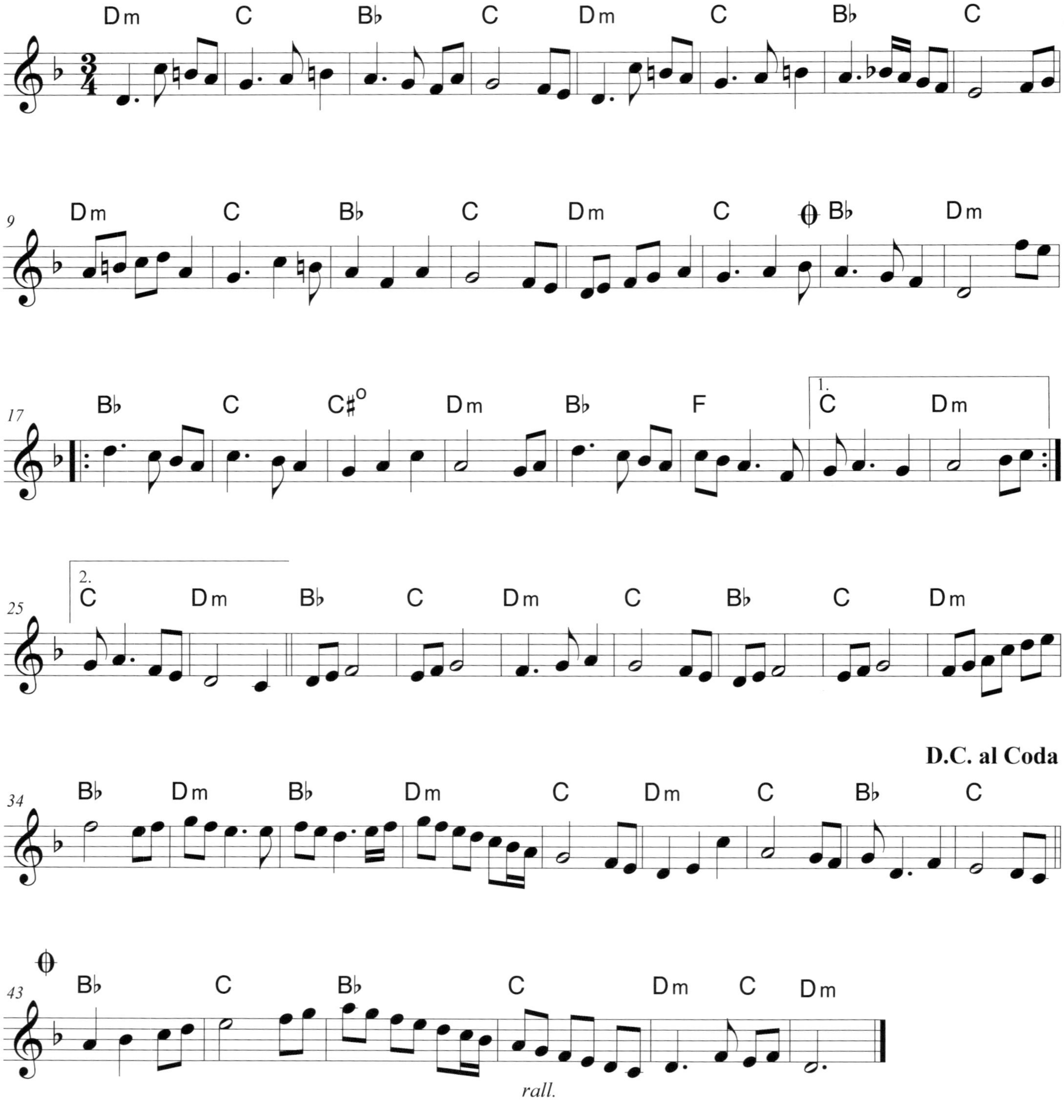

This sweet little waltz was a surprise waiting for me when I went looking for old scores to include. Scribbled in pencil, I had never played it, so the copyright date is approximate. It brings to mind sitting on my back porch with Ralph Costanza after a sucessful week of our American Mandolin & Guitar Summer School, exhausted, happy, and proud to have pulled it off one more time. Appropriately, Ralph and I played the premiere in the faculty recital of AMGuSS 2022, about two decades after it was written.

Final Thoughts

"I've written so many verses and keep on writing so many more
that I became afraid that if I didn't write them into one big book,
I might forget some of them." – Edna St. Vincent Millay, poet

I have now collected, in this book, the majority of my favorite instrumental pieces. The original impetus was to gather together the newest, the 28 pieces written in the past two years, while we were all in isolation, when playing music together was impossible. These pieces represent a period when, for the first time, I completely immersed myself in the compositional process, writing daily. The pandemic had shut down the touchstones of my musical world and composing filled the empty musical space.

"While we were sequestered here due to Covid 19 cancellations...
I exploded into creativity. This is how it goes. One never knows what/how/when.
Life gives the topics." – Stephanie Cole, artist, on her work *Corona*

While I was at it, I began to gather my Choro together, finishing up three that had languished, to bring the Brazilian total to 20. These pieces are full of the spirit of Rio, my second home, a city I was cut off from due to pandemic travel restrictions. Their sunny sounds warmed my heart, and reminded me that things would get better. So now my pile of pieces had reached 48.

Next, I looked at the ensemble pieces I had written for my octet, Enigmatica. And combing through my files I rediscovered some earlier ensembles, and one I had always meant to complete, so now the total was 55. And then I pulled out the box of hand-written manuscripts, traveling down memory lane, plucking up some and deciding to leave others behind. What did Charles Ives say? "Some of the songs...might prefer, if they had a say, to remain as they are; ... a song has a few rights, the same as other ordinary citizens." So some early works decided to remain in their scribbled form. When I considered my own songs, I thought about them carefully, enjoyed their quirky lyrics in my head once more, but decided it was time to draw the line. So the grand total of pieces for this book is 68.

As a performer and listener, I have always appreciated good musicianship above a show of virtuosity. Give me a musical artist over a musical athlete any day. I have written these pieces with the intention that many people will be able to play them, and some will be able to play them well. To succeed you'll need good technique, a healthy dose of expression, and an interest in playing outside the box. It will also help to have the heart of a poet and a ready spirit of adventure. I hope you will enjoy this look into my musical world, and perhaps it will inspire you to create some music of your own. For myself, I have opened this door and I am definitely going to keep walking through it.

"Don't think about making art, just get it done.
Let everyone else decide if it's good or bad, whether they love it or hate it.
While they are deciding, make even more art." – Andy Warhol, artist

Recordings

My Études, Fantasias, and Nocturnes are available in the digital download for this book, along with some earlier works. Many of the pieces I've written have been previously recorded on CDs listed here.

Silver Lining of a Quiet Year *(2022)* *Mair & Friends*

10 Fantasias in dialogue *for two mandolins*

- Floating
- Planting Gardens
- Peaches
- In the Dark
- Dragon Dream
- Trouble in Mind
- Holding Fast
- By the Sea
- Old Folks
- In the Groove

8 Nocturnes for Vincent *for mandolin & guitar*

- Sometimes when I am wearied suddenly
- Oh, oh, you will be sorry for that word!
- I shall go back again to the bleak shore
- Only until this cigarette is ended
- Mindful of you the sodden earth in spring
- The light comes back with Columbine
- Women have loved before as I love now
- Tranquility at length, when autumn comes

10 Études en couleurs *for solo mandolin*

- Grise
- Orange
- Verte
- D'ombre
- De crépuscule
- D'ambre
- Noire
- Blanche
- Bleue
- Violette

Saudades do Rio *for mandolin & guitar*

Madrugada *(2015)* *Marilynn Mair & Friends*

- Farrapinho
- Garoa
- Um Quinto do Ludwig
- Uma Coisa Feliz
- Balbuciando
- Enrolado
- Madrugada
- Outro Verão
- Sonatinha

Engimatica 3 *(2014)* *Enigmatica*

- Ayton's Farewell
- Enrolado *(ensemble version)*

Meu Bandolim *(2009)* *Marilynn Mair & Friends*

- Siga em Frente
- Por Que Não?
- Isso
- Terças no Trapiche

Sip a Little New *(2007)* *New England Mandolin Ensemble*

- East of Here *(ensemble version)*

Leave Something Unexplained *(2006)* *Mair & Friends*

- And She Has Flown
- Champagne *(duet version)*
- Diablo *(duet version)*
- East of Here

Nadando Em Luz *(2001)* *Marilynn Mair & Friends*

- Nadando em Luz

Metro *(1996)* *World Café Quartet*

- Champagne
- Diablo
- The Brinsley Waltz